The Confession

The Confession

JAMES E. McGREEVEY

WITH DAVID FRANCE

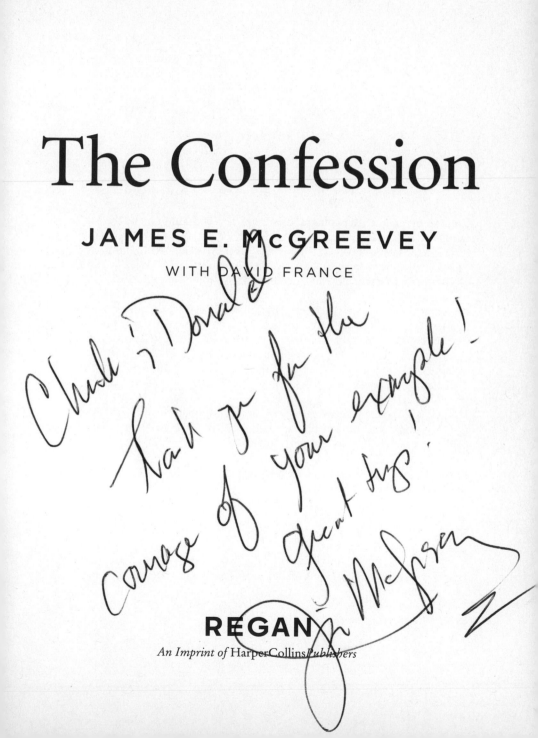

REGAN

An Imprint of HarperCollinsPublishers

THE CONFESSION. Copyright © 2006 by James E. McGreevey. All rights reserved. Printed in the United States of America. No part of this book may be used or reproduced in any manner whatsoever without written permission except in the case of brief quotations embodied in critical articles and reviews. For information, address HarperCollins Publishers, 10 East 53rd Street, New York, NY 10022.

HarperCollins books may be purchased for educational, business, or sales promotional use. For information please write: Special Markets Department, HarperCollins Publishers, 10 East 53rd Street, New York, NY 10022.

For editorial inquiries, please contact Regan, 10100 Santa Monica Blvd., 10th floor, Los Angeles, CA 90067.

FIRST EDITION

Designed by Kris Tobiassen

Library of Congress Cataloging-in-Publication Data has been applied for.

ISBN 10: 0-06-089862-3
ISBN 13: 978-0-06-089862-5

06   07   08   09   10   WBC/RRD   10   9   8   7   6   5   4   3   2

FOR MOM AND DAD,
AND MY DAUGHTERS, MORAG AND JACQUELINE,
WHO TAUGHT ME UNCONDITIONAL LOVE

When the mind is less amenable to instruction and
cannot be cured by milder means,
why should it not be helped by having a dose of
poverty and disgrace and general ruin—dealing
with evil by evil?

— SENECA, "ON THE SHORTNESS OF LIFE"

CONTENTS

I.

How These Things Happen

1.

ONE LATE-SUMMER SUNDAY NIGHT IN 2002, WELL BEFORE MY political career collapsed, I was helping my wife, Dina, tuck our daughter into bed. Well, not helping, exactly. Even as I stood in the bedroom doorway watching my family, my ear was glued to a cell phone. Through the phone came the voice of a former employee named Golan Cipel. In a spectacular lapse of judgment, I had put Golan on my payroll while at the same time initiating a secret sexual relationship with him.

A few weeks earlier, both arrangements had ended badly, after press questions about his qualifications reached critical mass. Golan still hadn't recovered, and he had taken to calling me day and night to ask for his job back. I listened to him tirelessly—in part because I wanted to help him if I could, but mostly because I still loved him. But there was no way I could do what he wanted.

I loved Golan Cipel, a handsome and bright man a few years my junior, and I wanted him to be happy. But I was a married man, a father, and the governor of New Jersey. There was no chance he could rejoin my administration.

I had no reason to believe that Dina suspected my affair with Golan, or even the fact that I was gay. She probably already knew I didn't love her anymore, not in the way a man loves his wife. It had been a long time since we'd last been intimate. Lately, what drove us forward had been little more than the momentum of a public life.

Maybe unconsciously I wanted to bring it all to a head that night. How else can I explain why I answered Golan's phone call in her presence? The longer I stood in that doorway watching my wife and daughter and listening to my former lover on the phone, the closer my world came to imploding. Nothing I told him mollified his pain, which I believe had more to do with his stalled career in government than with our failed affair. He missed me, I felt sure, mostly because he missed having access to power.

"My life is over," he was saying. The bad press, he claimed, had ruined his reputation. "Nobody is supporting me out here."

"We'll get through this, Golan," I assured him. "This is the big leagues. You're going to get knocks."

Dina had a rule about not interrupting our daughter's time with work calls, and as I struggled to get off the phone, I watched her growing increasingly angry. But then I saw a light bulb flick on in her eyes. She tucked Jacqueline into her covers and pushed past me in a rage, just as I was hanging up.

After we were safely out of Jacqueline's earshot, she turned and glared at me.

"This whole thing is ridiculous," she said.

I knew exactly what she meant. "What thing?" I asked anyway.

She walked back toward me, in the darkened hallway, until we were close enough for her to study my face. "Are you gay?"

All my life I had dreaded that question. Others had asked it, and I can't think of a time when I lied affirmatively about my sexuality, but I lied every day by omission and obfuscation. And I allowed others to lie for me. My marriage to Dina was a major part of that lie; that much I knew consciously. As our years together ticked by, I found it harder and harder to deny the truth. Being gay is a fundamental part of my being—the core of who I've always been, and the thing I had repressed and run from all my life.

For a brief moment I thought I could stop running that day. But I didn't have the nerve to tell my wife the truth. Instead I said nothing.

I'VE NEVER BEEN MUCH FOR SELF-REVELATION. IN TWO DECADES of public life, I have always approached the limelight with extreme caution. Not that I kept my personal life off-limits; rather, the personal life I put on display was a blend of fact and fiction. Dishonesty creates not only a lack of truth but a tangle of truths. I invented overlapping narratives about who I was, and contrived backstories that played better not just in the ballot box but in my own mind. And then, to the best of my ability, I tried to be the man in those stories.

In this way I'm not at all unique. Inauthenticity is endemic in American politics today. Those who would be leaders are all too often tempted to become what we think you want us to be—not leading at all, but following our best guess at public opinion. We tailor our public positions to reflect poll results and consultants' advice, then feed that data back to you in flattering ways. Everything from the clothing we wear to the places we vacation is selected data for political gain; even the food we eat is chosen with strategic calculation. The public square has never been so clamorous with deception.

This is, in fact, the defining characteristic of American political life today, and it is a dangerous slippery slope. For too many politicians winning has become the end goal of politics, trumping both ideology and ethics. An ambitious politician quickly learns, as I did, to countenance and even sponsor fundamentally corrupt behavior while insulating himself, for as long as he can, behind a buffer of deniability. I'm not talking about criminal misconduct—the kind of thing that leads to the occasional political corruption scandal. I'm talking about the hundreds of ways that politicians—or their representatives—can push the envelope on ethics, morals, and truth in our quest for power. In my experience, ethical compromises are not just a shortcut to office; for all but the wealthy, they are all but compulsory. The political backrooms where I spent much of my career were just as benighted as my personal life, equally crowded with shadowy strangers and compromises, truths I hoped to deny. I lived not in one closet but in many.

Even this is not uncommon. In the months since I resigned my office and my public trust, I have learned how the pressures of society seem to force so many of us into deep denial and disintegrated lives. Many people have confided in me about their own struggles for authenticity, whether in their jobs, their marriages, or their spiritual lives. Like me, they felt their sense of self fracture beneath the pressures of social conformity, feeling helpless to reverse their course even as they longed for the courage to do so.

At times, I've wondered if we're a nation of individuals careening down the wrong highway.

The true story of my life—what the composer Ned Rorem called "the cinema of myself"—had no connection with the script I polished for public consumption. And it was a cinema with no audience but one. It seems ridiculous to me now, but in all those years I never once spoke the word *gay* about myself. Not in a heart-to-heart with a friend, not in a therapy session, not even in a sexual liaison, of which there were plenty. Not even to Golan. Even in private, we never gave words to our love affair; we called it "this," or simply "us." I once told him, standing in the governor's mansion, "I would leave all this for you." But neither of us ever used the word *gay*.

Oh, I knew it was my word, my reality. I have been certain almost all my life that God made me different, and at least since the age of thirteen I have been coping with this circumstance by not coping with it—by adopting artifices, changing myself rather than the world that would not embrace me. I chose the coward's route, courting girlfriends as a teenager and an adult, carrying on misguided romances for theatrical effect, marrying two women who deserved better. And in my private moments I mined every book I could find on homosexuality, not for affirmation but for tricks to use in curbing my desires. In other words, I *managed* my homosexuality. Or thought I did.

Many people my age—born late in the baby boom—long ago came to terms with being gay and have thrived despite daunting obstacles. Moreover, in the past thirty years they have transformed the culture in ways large and small. Mine is the generation that built a mighty gay rights movement. That battled AIDS. That turned the stereotype of the married, blackmailed homosexual into the mainstream characters of *Will & Grace*. And that left behind such beautiful legacies as *Becoming a Man*, Paul Monette's searing memoir of identity and community, which I only discovered after my own troubles, when he was already dead.

Yet through most of these years I lived at arm's length from myself, unable to use my self-knowledge to live an honest life. I will say in my defense that it's an awful thing to expect a child of thirteen to pit himself against everything he holds dear—from his outsized ambitions to his beloved family and the church of his salvation—for the sake of something so small as private happiness. I could not do it at thirteen, and once I had started down the path of self-denial, I saw no alternative but to stay the course. But the result was that I became the married, blackmailed homosexual that I reviled. And for too many years I did nothing to stop it.

There were moments—at nineteen and twenty-one, here and there in my thirties and forties—when the ripping misery of this life became too great, moments when I thought about "becoming gay" and all that that entails. In the end, though, sheer willpower always brought me back to the community I cherished, the bike paths of Carteret, New Jersey, where I grew up, and the precincts of Trenton, where there were no gay lawmakers, just heterosexuals and me. I lived those years in constant fear of discovery, a flutter of pure panic skating constantly on the lining of my diaphragm. I never forgot for a minute that I was what my childhood friends mocked, what I thought my parents would reject—what my loving God supposedly condemned to limitless suffering. I didn't need overt hostilities to know they were all around me. I stayed within the bounds of the culture I was born into—those borders like the invisible pet fences that train a dog to stay close to home by promising electric shocks if he ventures beyond the property line. I sat on the porch of my lonely self-denigration, sure of nothing but the perils in the yard.

THIS WAS A SICK-MAKING EXISTENCE. I SUPPOSE THAT GOES WITHout saying. Looking back, I realize how often in my life the voices of prejudice emanated not from the prejudiced outside world but from my own mind, bent against me.

During my first run for governor, in 1997, I remember sitting in the backseat of a campaign car as it pushed north along the beautiful Garden State Parkway, and glancing exhaustedly out the window to see one of those enormous green parkway signs welcoming the river of cars. In a moment of wishful fantasy, I looked up and saw, or imagined I saw, my own name—not the name of Christine Todd Whitman, the sitting governor I was running to unseat—at the bottom of the sign. Yet this was no happy hallucination:

across the daydreamed billboard, I saw, someone had spray-painted the word *HOMO*.

I shook my head to clear the image, but it didn't go away, and I broke into a cold sweat. Of course this was nothing more than a trick of the imagination, but its truth was inescapable. *I might be gaining in the polls*, I thought. *I might one day be governor, maybe even run for president. But no matter how I lived my life, I would still be a despicable thing at my core.*

If I had been handed, as a teenager, the groaning platter of secrets and half-truths that would feed me till middle age, I never would have had the courage to pretend to be heterosexual. But I can't imagine I would have pursued my heart's desires forthrightly, either, such was my self-hatred. Twice I contemplated the priesthood; more often, suicide. It was only when I stood beside my beautiful wife and loving parents one August morning at the New Jersey State House and declared, "My truth is that I am a gay American," that my stomach's alarm system finally defused and my solar plexus went still for the first time in my life.

The writer Armistead Maupin once said, "My only regret about being gay is that I repressed it for so long. I surrendered my youth to the people I feared when I could have been out there loving someone. Don't make that mistake yourself. Life's too damn short." He was right: I lost forty-seven years.

The life I've led since then has been truthful, but it hasn't all been easy. In the weeks after announcing my affair with Golan, my career and my marriage slipped away, both excruciating losses. And one cold fall afternoon in the last days of my term, I glanced out the window of the governor's sedan to see one of those big green parkway signs bearing my name. This was no hallucination: across it someone had actually painted *Fag*. I watched the sign pass by the window as if in slow motion, stunned to see my dark daydream brought to life. The thing I feared most in the world had happened to me—my once-private truth now escaped from my imagination into the real world.

And all I felt was grace.

Mine has been a long, trying, and sadly common journey, and one that's still just beginning. I have a long way to go before finding the genuine *me.* Living an authentic life is surprisingly challenging, I have found; the tricks and shortcuts of my old life protected me from a lot of difficult truths, which now I must face without flinching. As painful as that is, it is also spiritually rewarding in a way I have never known before. I'm rebuilding my relationship with God, the greatest victory to come from this defeat.

In the process, I've had to reforge bonds with all of my old friends; to my surprise and joy, they've all stayed with me for the ride. Being honest about myself has not cost me a single friendship. On the contrary, I feel closer now to everyone in my life than ever before, blessed with their love and respect in a way I never recognized.

I haven't yet fully integrated my new sense of relief with my history of fear. I am still very cautious about making decisions about my personal and professional life. Many friends and family members have advised me to stay focused on the moment rather than dwelling on the past. There is not a great appetite for my memoir among this group. My father, whose love for me has never wavered, recently mailed me a photocopy of the dictionary page containing the word *calumny,* concerned with what I might include in these pages. "Please remember the words of St. Paul," his accompanying note said, "'the greatest of these is charity.'"

But those of us who come to embrace our true identities later in life have a unique need to revisit our divided pasts in order to mend our hearts and face our lives to come. So carefully, candidly, and with great hope, I rewind the cinema of myself for one more viewing, this time without shame.

2.

PERHAPS MORE THAN ANY DAY IN HISTORY, AUGUST 6 IS ASSOCI-
ated with fireballs and light: it is the anniversary of the Hiroshima bombing,
which claimed tens of thousands of lives but may have saved even more by
ending the war, and the Feast of the Transfiguration of Christ, marking that
moment when the face of Jesus "did shine as the sun and his garments became
white as snow," transmitting the interior brightness of his divinity. To my father, a fervent Catholic who twice enlisted in the marines, these were great
omens for the birthday of his first child and only son, in 1957. He named me
James Edward McGreevey after his older brother, an amateur boxing star,
World War II hero, and Navy Cross and Bronze Star recipient who fell on the
shores of Iwo Jima when he was just nineteen—a great patriot and Dad's lifelong idol.

My two sisters and I—Caroline came a year later and Sharon in 1962—
were second-generation Americans, like just about everybody in the insular
Roman Catholic universe of our childhoods. We lived first in Jersey City, a
community of new Americans from Romania, Poland, Italy, Greece, and especially Ireland, our own ancestral home. As different as these populations
were from one another, we all had the Roman Catholic Church in common,
whether it was Our Lady of Czestochowa Church on Sussex Street or
St. Aedans on Bergen or St. Paul of the Cross on Hancock. The parish you
came from was the center of your culture and source of your pride, and the
seat of all power in your life. If you wanted a job or a raise, ran into trouble
with the authorities, had disputes at home or school, you turned to your
parish priest, who was as much in charge of your daily well-being as of your

spiritual health. He was politician, therapist, employment broker, match-maker, judge, and jury, and his authority was unchallenged within the parish.

When I was almost five we moved a few minutes away to the new working-class suburb of Carteret, still just eighteen miles from Ellis Island, where our grandparents on both sides first touched American soil. Having come this far across the Atlantic, the McGreeveys and my mother's family, the Smiths, weren't about to pull up roots again.

My father's family was in law enforcement, a longtime haven for Irish Americans. Looking at the old pictures of the Jersey City Police, I'm still awed at how strong a lock the Irish had on the force: Flahertys, Cahills, Geoghans—all unsmiling Irishmen with square jaws and boxer's noses. On Sundays it wasn't unusual to see whole precincts show up for communion en masse, pistols at their sides.

After serving in World War I, my grandfather Mike went to the monsignor at All Saints parish on Pacific Avenue for help finding work. All the monsignor had to do was tell City Hall, "I'm sending Mike McGreevey up to see you." Next thing you knew, Mike did very well on the police department test. This was the legendary power of the turned-around collar, and Mike never forgot it. Landing the job made my grandfather one of the fortunate men in his community, and his luck continued throughout his career walking a beat in the old 4th Precinct along Communipaw Avenue.

Being a cop earned you automatic security and respect. In our world, it was one of the best jobs you could have, just a notch below the priesthood. Yet the dress blues never came with much money, and Dad's family scraped by in the hardscrabble Lafayette side of the tracks in Jersey City. My dad recalls a spartan childhood of hand-me-down clothing and backyard vacations.

Ireland was never far from my grandfather's thoughts. Although he died before I turned ten, I can still hear the heavy brogue in his voice as he regaled my sisters and me with stories from Bainbridge town in the County Down or read aloud from the papers about "the Troubles in the North." He was consumed by Unionist Protestant discrimination against Catholics, including the clergy; indeed, he'd come to America in the first place in search of freedom. "You're halfway to heaven if you're an American citizen," he used to tell us.

He joined the local Sinn Fein chapter here, back before the group became a subject of controversy. Mike considered Sinn Fein a noble force for Irish independence, on a par with the American revolutionaries and other freedom fighters, and saw the struggle for freedom in the North of Ireland in religious terms, as an effort to free Catholics from Protestant repression. His faith was constant, and he wore it proudly. "It doesn't take any guts to be Catholic in the south," he'd say. To him, the Church of Rome wasn't just a religion but part of his core identity, no less absolute than race or gender, and it fostered within him a thirst for justice and equality. The streets of Protestant communities in Ireland were paved, he complained, while the streets of his own Catholic ghetto were strewn with rubble; Protestant schools were properly lit and equipped with books while Catholic schools were poor, the backward domain of the Church. Protestant men enjoyed employment opportunities, while the Patricks and Michaels of the Catholic neighborhoods were typically unemployed. Once he arrived on American shores, my grandfather's social conscience gave him a great affinity for African Americans and other downtrodden minorities.

Mike's first wife, my paternal grandmother, Margaret Hart, died long before I was born, while giving birth to my aunt Roseanne. She left behind five children, and Mike did what widowers did at the time: he sent the kids to live with his sister Catherine Cullen and her husband, Frank, a record keeper for the Railway Express, while he went looking for a new bride.

In my recollection, Catherine was the epitome of the lace-curtain Irish Catholic—prim and immaculate, empathetic and extremely resourceful. I remember hearing one story about her that's almost certainly apocryphal, but might as well be true. When her beloved dog, a tall-shouldered Irish wolfhound, died, she couldn't afford to have the local veterinarian dispose of the remains. At first she tried putting him out with the trash, but local ordinances prevented such things and the rubbish haulers left the remains behind. So Catherine put her late pet in a box, wrapped him with flowery paper and ribbons, and placed the alluring package on the backseat of her unlocked car. In certain parts of Jersey City back then, strangers could be counted on to help dispose of such things.

That same resourcefulness helped Catherine keep Mike McGreevey's children fed, until he met Mary Theresa McCrikard on a boat ride down the

Hudson. Mary raised his children as her own and gave him two more. My father, John Patrick McGreevey, known universally as Jack, loved and respected his stepmother as much as he did his late biological mother.

Dad was in high school when World War II began drawing to a close. He didn't want to let the Allies close up shop before he could get over there for a taste of battle, so on August 27, 1945, his seventeenth birthday, he went to New York City to sign up with the marines. He never considered another branch. "The Marine Corps is a department of the navy," he liked to say. "The *men's* department."

To his dismay, they rejected him as medically unfit for duty because of a deviated septum. Not to be deterred, Dad and his best buddy, Tommy McDonald, went to a small recruiting center beneath the Newark Post Office to try again three months later. He was in luck. There was only one guy there doing physicals, and this time it was a pharmacist, not a doctor. Better yet, the man reeked of liquor. Dad saw his chance and took it, talking fast and keeping his distance, giving him no chance to peer up his nose. He was cleared that day for basic training.

But he was still underage, and the recruiters needed permission from his parents, so without hesitation Dad signed his father's name. Serving his country was the most important calling in my father's life, as it remains today; I know no greater patriot—no greater American—than him. I'm sure his father was behind him all the way.

He shipped out to Japan to join the occupation forces, then to China with an artillery company known colloquially as the China Marines. From there Dad sailed to Guam, in the South Pacific, where he rose to the rank of sergeant. His posting was as a drill instructor. There never was a man better suited for this job, as you will come to understand. In all these years, Jack never talked much about what he saw on his tour. But his fraternal bond to the corps has remained constant; every November 10 he celebrates the corps' birthday.

When Harry Truman committed troops to the Korean War in 1950, Dad reenlisted and served out that conflict in California, preparing soldiers for battle. For him, going from the China Marines to the so-called Hollywood Marines was a bit of a slide, but Jack McGreevey was never one to question the wisdom of the corps, and he served his new posting with undiminished patriotism. "The only difference with boot camp for the Hollywood Marines," he jokes, "is that every night in California, I had to put chocolates on their pillows."

When he returned east, the GI Bill paved the way for him to enroll at Seton Hall University, a Catholic college in South Orange, New Jersey. After six years of night classes, he had a diploma . . . and a wife, which, he confesses, was his goal in the first place. He met my mother, Veronica Smith, in an art history class. "If you don't think I'm the type to study art, you're right," my father has said. "I went to find a lady."

He soon made a career for himself in trucking, as director of national accounts for a firm that handled Sears and other large movers. Keeping the fleets crisscrossing the country while calming nervous contractors required equal measures of charm, logistical savvy, shrewdness, and leadership ability. Fortunately, these are my father's abundant resources. Dad borrowed his personal motto from the Marine Corps: *Plan your work and work your plan.* As self-evident as it may seem, this is a profound operating principle, and much more difficult done than said. Success was never accidental, he would say; it was always the result of a vision and hard work. Dad had singular focus, and his drive was unrelenting. Every night, even after his long days at the office, Dad would sit at the kitchen table, meticulously plotting out the coming days. He never took a step without first weighing the consequences, and once he determined his precise move, he never wavered from the course or let anything stand in his way. He made his choices with perfect instincts and the swift assurance of a prizefighter. And if he ever made a mistake (hypothetically, that is—I can't think of a significant mistake he's made), his mind would plot out a seamless correction.

As comfortable as my parents eventually became, they never lost track of where they came from. They never moved from the simple clapboard house where I grew up. In his free time, Dad made it his job to keep a watchful eye on hundreds of old folks in our part of the state, driving ailing veterans to the VA for checkups or elderly ladies to the pharmacy. I always knew when he had one of these errands scheduled; his mood would brighten and a familiar jauntiness entered his step. This was the highlight of his week.

I tell you all this about my father and his family for one reason. He is not the shrinking, absent father figure whom mythology wrongly blames for "creating" homosexual children. Nor is he the overweening, underloving cartoon commonly accused of wounding the heterosexuality out of kids. There is no bigger lie about gays than the one that says that we're created by faulty parents. My father was as loving and difficult, as demanding, forthright, proud, faithful, work driven, and family focused as any man could be—an ordinary man, if you will, but by my lights unmatched. It was from him that I learned to appreciate the special privilege of being an American. I inherited his call to service and compassion for the less fortunate. And though it's taken me much of my life to figure it out, I also learned the importance of embracing one's unique identity. Dad is indivisibly Irish, Catholic, American, veteran, husband, father, and more—not one of those roles could be eliminated without destabilizing the great personal force that is Jack McGreevey.

AND MY MOTHER, RONNIE? SHE IS AS FAR AS ANYONE COULD GET from the overprotective smotherer (or the emasculator or the infantalizer) conjured up by prejudice. My mother is brilliant, utterly sensible, passionate in her beliefs, and fearless in letting you know them. She wasn't always the most effusive person; as one of her former students recently stopped me to say, she was a wonderful professor, but "Boy, was she tough!" My mom inherited, from her English-Irish parents, what we used to call an "upper lip." She keeps her head, but speaks her mind. We kids always knew where we stood with her—and still do. Sometimes her forthrightness can be bracing, but it's always infused with her profound love and deep intellect, as well as a liberal's sense of fairness.

I was sitting on her lap the day our little black-and-white burned with images of white police officers turning fire hoses on black kids in Birmingham, scattering them through the streets. I was terrified. She was furious. "It's un-American," she fumed. "They're trying to right a terrible wrong, and they're being treated like hoodlums." The forcefulness of her beliefs—almost a moral defiance—made me sure that her side would prevail.

One thing that may have made Mom so open-minded on social issues was that her father was a rarity in our community: a convert. Born into an Anglican family, Herbert Smith took up the Church of Rome in order to woo my Liverpudlian grandmother, Mary Theresa Brown (two of my three grandmothers were named Mary—it's a Catholic occupational hazard). They arrived in America around the turn of the century, and ultimately Grandpa became such a part of the Jersey City Catholic community that he was named Grand Marshal of the Holy Name Society Parade, the first time that honor was bestowed on someone not born into the Church. My mother still has a newspaper clipping bearing the headline CONVERT LEADS HOLY NAME PARADE.

In contrast to my paternal grandfather, who possessed an enormous body and even bigger voice, Herbert was lanky and elegant, and somewhat stern. He was also a bookish man, with a weakness for English history. When I was young, he used to have me sit at his knee and read through the lineage of English monarchs from Arthur to Elizabeth. I can't imagine that many Americans in my generation can still name all the Tudors, the Stuarts, the Normans, and the Anglo-Saxons. He also drilled me on foreign affairs—and even on local union matters, which were close to his heart. Grandpa was a member of the International Union of Operating Engineers, making a good living in heavy construction.

Being a union man, Grandpa was consciously on patrol for the Good Fight. His faith in collective bargaining never wavered. But there came a time after the Great Depression when he had a falling out with the union hall—none of us grandkids is clear on the details—and was effectively blacklisted. Work assignments stopped coming his way, which plunged the family into painful hardship. But Grandpa never turned his back on the IUOE. Eventually the feud drew to a close—as mysteriously as it began—and the Smiths were restored to the burgeoning middle class.

He and my grandmother settled in Jersey City's relatively comfortable Greenville section and also kept a beachside bungalow in Cliffwood Beach. It wasn't quite the Jersey Shore, whose resorts were popular among the upper crust. No celebrities went to Cliffwood Beach, with its collection of seasonal homes standing shoulder to shoulder on the sand.

Of all my relatives, Grandma Smith, from whom I get my curly hair, was by far the most powerful influence on my life. The Church was her whole world. She attended Mass daily. From her I learned to say a novena, the Stations of the Cross, and the joyful, sorrowful, and glorious mysteries of the rosary. One of my earliest memories is watching her click her thumbnail on one bead after another, to the rhythmic murmur of her prayers.

My sisters generally found other things to occupy them during our visits, but my grandmother always asked me to sit beside her and pray the rosary with her. At first I agreed reluctantly, out of a sense of obligation; I would have preferred playing soccer outside with my grandfather. But soon I came to value these times with her. My grandmother taught me more than just the orthodoxy of religion; she helped me discover and explore my spirituality and my interior life. Teaching me to say my Our Fathers and the Apostles Creed, she showed me how to still my mind and focus on my connection with the Divine. I could feel my faith expanding as I understood Mary's sacrifice in the virgin birth (which teaches us humility), Christ's condemnation (a lesson in patience), and the miracle of his resurrection (the source of all faith and hope). At the end our prayers would turn to Christ himself: "O my Jesus, forgive us our sins, save us from the fires of hell, lead all souls to Heaven, especially those who have most need of your mercy."

My grandmother's spirituality was something she thought about and talked about almost constantly, something she lived. The saints and their stories were so familiar to her that it sometimes seemed as though she existed among them, gleaning strength from the lessons of their lives. Before setting out on a journey, Grandma prayed to St. Brigid of Ireland, a high-spirited adventurer; if her hairbrush was misplaced, it was St. Anthony of Padua she'd turn to—or, more likely, ask me and my sisters to invoke.

> St. Anthony, St. Anthony
> Won't you come down?
> Something is lost and
> Can't be found.

Around her home, Grandma kept dozens and dozens of saint figurines—some no larger than her outstretched hand, others a foot or more high. They multiplied on her mantelpiece, windowsills, and shelves; she kept St. Anthony atop her dresser, and the Virgin Mary stood watch on the ledge over the sink. I thought of them as her spiritual militia—St. Dominic, the beekeeping monk, casting a defensive gaze toward the door, while St. Jude Thaddeus, patron saint of hospital workers like my mother, watched the flanks.

"Is this place looking a little *Italian?*" Grandma once mused.

"No, Grandma," I said, although no other Irish house I'd visited had so many saints.

In very unsubtle ways, Grandma let me know that she was training me for the priesthood—in particular the Jesuit priesthood, which she considered the Church's Special Forces. Where we came from, nothing matched the thrill of having a relative receive a call from God. Whereas some Catholic families seemed to put great stock in the social value of having a priest in the family, Grandma's motives were pure. For her, dedication to Christianity was an end in itself, its own and perfect good.

The Smiths produced six children, including two who did not survive. My mother was their third child, named Veronica after the saint who offered Christ a towel to dry his face on the day of his crucifixion. So I suppose it was meant to be that Ronnie, as everybody calls her, would grow up to be a nurse and professor, caring for patients at New Jersey's best hospitals while leaving her indelible mark on generations of young nursing students.

She was still in school when she married my father in 1956, and they began their family just eleven months later. But my mother never allowed her career to take a backseat. After graduating from Seton Hall, she earned her nursing degree at St. Vincent's in New York, then a masters at Columbia University and another at Seton Hall in preparation for a teaching career. In this regard she stood out from other women her age, especially Catholic women.

There is no containing my mother's ambition to be of service; it's something I have always admired in her and I feel blessed that she passed it down to me. For her, serving others was a spiritual *obligation*, an integral part of God's purpose for man on Earth. Had she been born in this generation, she would almost surely have become a physician. Many of the women of her time pursued nursing or teaching—they were the major career pathways available in those days—but my mother's commitment was its own kind of calling, one that stemmed from a deep love of medicine, a faith in the body's capacity to heal, and a certain knowledge that God's will prevails. Watching her tend to her patients, and to her students at Middlesex County College in Edison and Muhlenberg Regional Medical Center in Plainfield, I was always awed to see how deeply Mom understands the human condition.

In the McGreevey clan, she is our bedrock. Whenever any of us has come to her in confusion, she has talked us through to clarity. If we felt inadequate, she gave us tools to overcome. When sadness or illness strikes, she had an unfailing ability to usher us back to health.

As I said, she wasn't exactly indulgent, not when it came to the bumps and scrapes of childhood. Once, when I was about seven, I was playing in a park around the corner when I lost my footing and landed headfirst on a concrete bench post. My scalp split open and started streaming with blood. The wound looked much worse than it was, of course, but I ran home terrified. On my way I passed Mrs. Decelis, our next-door neighbor, who took one look at me and screamed as if she'd seen a ghost, which only frightened me more. By the time I reached our kitchen, I was sure I was close to death. Mom looked down from the dishes and sized up my condition. "Here," she said calmly, handing me a cold, wet cloth. "Put this against your head." My fear vanished instantly.

My mother's steady nerves have helped our family weather even the most heartbreaking passages. When her father, Herbert Smith, was in his late seventies, he began using a cane to steady himself as he moved around the small one-bedroom apartment he shared with my grandmother. One afternoon he left the cane leaning against a door, and my grandmother, whose vision was failing, fell over it, shattering her hip when she landed. She was rushed into surgery, but her age complicated the procedure, and my grandfather was so overcome with worry that soon he was in the same hospital as his injured wife. For five months my mother cared for them both, never leaving the hospital. But my grandfather was suffering from a broken heart, unable to forgive himself for his wife's accident, and despite my mother's efforts he succumbed a short time later.

When my grandmother was discharged, she came to live with us; twice daily my mom guided her through physical therapy, not always with Grandma's eager consent. But soon she was strong enough to move to a small apartment over my aunt and uncle's home in Rutherford, where she lived on for many years. When she died, her whole family gathered around her bed in prayer. My mother leaned into her ear and whispered, "It's okay to let go. Daddy is waiting for you to come home."

Then Grandma's mouth opened and the life in her escaped.

A few minutes later, I was startled to see my mother calmly dialing the local health department to notify them of Grandma's passing. I was still dazed, unable to do anything, even cry.

Seeing my distress, my mother comforted me in the way she knew best. "Here," she said, taking my hand and cupping it under my grandmother's chin. Together we eased her mouth closed. "Her jaw will lock soon, and we don't want it to be open when that happens. Hold it right here, like this; that will help keep Grandma's mouth closed, as it should be." To this day I'm not sure if what she told me was true or a distraction. But I did as I was told, and as a chaos of grief filled the room, I focused all my attention on my grandmother's cooling chin and her beautiful face, and in time my own heartache became manageable.

3.

"ONE LIVES BY MEMORY . . . AND NOT BY TRUTH," IGOR STRAVIN-sky wrote. In my case, I have lived by neither. My memories of my early years are curiously spotty. Specifics, like the names and faces of friends or teachers—even of close relatives—sometimes seem to float around in my mind in a useless muddle, blurry and disconnected. Dates, simple anec-dotes, the ephemera of a child's life are all upturned and broken, as if at-tacked by a vandal. It is really remarkable what I don't know or can't be certain of. Until this book was nearly finished, I had always believed that all three of my grandmothers were named Mary. My father had to remind me that his biological mother, whom I never met, was named Margaret. Long reminiscences about her life may have filled our dinner conversation, but the details have all melted away.

What color was our house? I couldn't say. What did my father tell me about his time in the service? Nothing comes to mind—really, nothing. I think back now and wonder if it was the anniversary of Nagasaki, not Hi-roshima, that coincided with my birth. I should know this; we even used it in campaign materials. "James E. McGreevey was born on the anniversary of . . ." Nothing.

In place of hard facts are sharply detailed feelings: moments of elation and pride; large doses of hope; ultimately discouragement, pain, and a soul-racking fear.

More than anything else I recall being, or trying very deliberately to be, a perfect child. Not a Goody Two-shoes, but a kid who did good, who worked hard and met every expectation. I strove to achieve in the excessive way that psychotherapists tend to regard with concern. My drive was unrelenting. I know I overreacted to the expectations my teachers and parents had for me. But while other kids might have considered them goals to strive for, to me they were marching orders. It never occurred to me to ignore them. Whether I was motivated by some sort of religious duress or the pressures of the firstborn son, I can't say. But I approached the small tests of a young boy's life with the anxiety of a rookie pitcher at the World Series. My future rode on every single move.

To put it another way, I had an almost electrifying feeling of being observed. I suppose this is not unusual for a Catholic of my generation. We were raised to believe that God kept unsparing records on every one of us, each new entry composed in permanent ink. Before God, my life and heart were an open book.

I do know that I was a good reader, from the time I was very young. Besides poring over the Elizabethan histories my grandfather shared with me, I remember as a youngster reading about Greece and Rome with my dad, as well as the wartime biographies he loved—MacArthur and Churchill, Patton and Eisenhower. The other kids made fun of me for lugging around these weighty books in grammar school, but I loved them, and cherished the time my father and I spent together reading them. Where my mother was training her children to be curious scholars, I later realized, Dad was schooling us to be leaders. He took an extraordinary interest in my progress in school and church, my interaction with adults and other children, my overall social development. For my ninth birthday, I believe it was, and every year thereafter, he addressed my card this way: "To my lad of great expectations." The words were almost unnecessary; I knew just how high those expectations were. I also felt sure they were not misplaced.

I'm sure he also encouraged my two sisters, but not in quite the same way. They grew up to be very accomplished women—Sharon's a principal and Caroline became a nurse. But he invested a different kind of attention in me; he drove me harder.

Once I was out in the world, I faced my first real-world challenge: getting Virginia Jones, my kindergarten teacher, to like me. I won her over handily. I remember feeling pride in my quick mastery of alphabet and vocabulary, and I believe I also courted her attentions with polish and politeness. But beyond that I recall little; the year has slid, as Maya Angelou once wrote of her own experience, "into the general darkness just beyond the great blinkers of childhood."

Mrs. Jones was the only African American on faculty at Pvt. Nicholas Minue Elementary School in Carteret, and in all these years she has never failed to send a holiday card, addressed in her magnificent calligraphy. Today she is in a nursing home, where I write to her regularly. When I asked her to help me remember our year together, the first thing that came to her mind was my fastidious presentation. "You were always dressed so neatly," she said. "The shirt, the tie, the trousers; your hair was combed nicely. I used to think to myself: There's a future president or something." In truth, future presidents haven't always stood out for sartorial splendor in kindergarten; Bill Clinton admits in his memoir that he avoided wearing crisp new outfits because they drew attention to his unwanted girth, and Jimmy Carter, child of the Depression, was lucky to show up in overalls, one dollar a pair. By contrast, I never appeared in school without a necktie, and seldom without a jacket.

My kindergarten class was in a public school. After that, I attended only Catholic schools, where uniforms were required. Earning the admiration of the nuns and priests at St. Joseph's Grammar School was my main objective. I was never teachers' pet—I wasn't the sort of kid who would tattle on other kids. Nor was I ever the top grade-getter. But I can say without hesitation that I was the hardest working child at St. Joe's. I was the kind of kid who loved Monday mornings, racing to school and working diligently to prove myself to the nuns and priests with quick answers and rapt attention.

By far the most difficult challenges there were our two principals, Sister Imelda and, later, Sister Eugene, a Servants of Mary nun who changed her name to Sister Patricia after Vatican II allowed such liberties; eventually we even got to see her hair. But in 1963 the sisters still dressed the same way they had in the thirteenth century, in flowing habits with floor-length robes and veil and collar wimples that pinched their faces into swollen expressions of discomfort. Sister Imelda, my principal until the fifth grade, was an omnipotent figure. She moved through the polished halls soundlessly and without sign of effort, as though propelled on muffled skates. Sister Eugene was the fearsome nun of legend. Without warning, a stealthy hand could shoot from her sleeve and pin any boy against the lockers, his feet dangling off the floor. She was nearly indiscriminate in her disciplinary zeal. The slightest provocation would call her to action. But she never once turned her attentions to me. In these eight years at St. Joe's, that was my major accomplishment.

THE CHURCH AND HER DESIGNATES WERE AN IMPORTANT FEATURE of my childhood. I am blessed to know only honorable and decent clergy, not the embittered nuns or child-abusing pastors of the sort who fill newspaper articles and fuel lawsuits these days. I believe my excellent experience is shared by all my relatives, going back many generations and continuing through the present. I do not think we were simply lucky. I believe the overwhelming majority of men and women who heed the Lord's call are exceptional human beings.

Outside of school we had little interaction with the nuns, who seemed to disappear back into the convent as soon as the last child had mounted his bicycle and left for home. Their secret lives were a cause of great fascination for us. Over the years, as Vatican II progressed, we watched with astonishment as they hemmed the black robes of their habits, lifting them to show their ankles and later their knees; then one day their transformation was complete, and they appeared uncomfortably before us in secular clothing and mannish hairdos. We never knew how this affected their spiritual lives, but it could not have been any less jarring for them than it was for us. Those stiff cornettes must have been uncomfortable to wear, but they symbolized the nuns' sacred purpose, and to me at least they were the most glamorous of fashion statements.

If our nuns were inscrutable, our priests were omnipresent. You couldn't ride your bike down Roosevelt Avenue in Carteret without spotting one of them going about his daily ministrations. Priests, especially old Father Patrick Lyons, were regular visitors to our home, occasionally at mealtime. Father Lyons was a man of great humility and, to me, the model of decency. He believed that children should be taught to pray, just as they should be taught to read, and he gave us the skills to discover our faith. "Don't pray to God only when you need something," he told me. "Tell God you love him. Talk to him the way you talk to your best friend. Share your life with God, and he'll share his grace with you in return."

When Father Lyons was nearing the end of his life, he asked my sister Sharon to pray for him so that when he died and arrived in purgatory, her prayers would form a basket that would lift him to Heaven. "And when I reach Heaven," he promised, "I will then pray for you and begin to weave a basket that will be waiting for you in purgatory."

The Dolans were among our most prominent family friends in Jersey City, and they had two priests in the family: Father Charles and Father James. When they visited we would discuss everything from the state of the world to Mrs. So-and-So's many illnesses; after dinner, if he was in the mood, Father James would linger in the living room singing "Danny Boy" and "This House" well into the evening. What a talented man he was. In Carteret there was a saying: "The three major occupations for Irishmen are the priesthood, politics, and poetry." Father James practiced them all.

In matters of the Church, I wanted to succeed. I was determined to demonstrate to Father Anthony Gaydos, our stocky parish priest, that I deserved his support and recognition. I wanted him to recognize that my performance was not just conscientious but downright godly. That was the highest measure of significance in our world: *godliness.* There was an old Irish maxim we heard a lot as children, lifted from the hymn called "St. Patrick's Breastplate": "Christ be with me, Christ within me, Christ behind me, Christ before me, Christ beside me, Christ to win me, Christ to comfort and restore me, Christ beneath me, Christ above me, Christ in quiet, Christ in danger, Christ in hearts of all that love me, Christ in mouth of friend and stranger." Everything you do, in other words, should be Christ-centered; that's how we were expected to behave, and that's what I believed, as I still do today.

I prayed every day as instructed, anxious to be the best Catholic I could be. I wanted the priests to understand my fealty to the Church, my knowledge of doctrine, and my willingness to be a soldier for Christ. Consciously and deliberately, I tailored my actions in ways I knew would meet the approval of the priests, the pastor, and the nuns—a policy that, you can imagine, didn't exactly endear me to some of my peers. I was not popular with the other kids. In church and school, they tended to leave me alone. I never doubted why. From the time I was seven, I had a sense of myself as being different. No matter how much I tried, I just didn't fit in. Even before I had any words to describe it, I remember concluding that there was something about what I *was,* not just about what I was *doing,* that set me permanently apart.

My faith, and the encouragement I received from church leaders, held me together through this realization. Yet there was a time in my early youth when I confessed to being very confused about who this God was. I recall studying the Baltimore Catechism with Sister Anthony—this is a crisp memory—and discovering that the more I studied it the more confused I became. The Baltimore Catechism, which has since been dropped, was an extremely technical and doctrinaire introduction to Catholicism, required reading for all young American Catholics since 1885. In question-and-answer format, it spelled out the teachings of the Church, from "What befell Adam and Eve because of their sin?" to "How should we keep the holy days of obligation?"

But I found it maddeningly elliptical. Consider this passage:

1. Q. Who made the world?
   A. God made the world.

2. Q. Who is God?
   A. God is the Creator of heaven and earth, and of all things.

3. Q. What is man?
   A. Man is a creature composed of body and soul, and made to the image and likeness of God.

4. Q. Is this likeness in the body or in the soul?
   A. This likeness is chiefly in the soul.

5. Q. How is the soul like to God?
   A. The soul is like God because it is a spirit that will never die, and has understanding and free will.

6. Q. Why did God make you?
   A. God made me to know Him, to love Him, and to serve Him in this world, and to be happy with Him forever in the next.

"Sister Anthony," I finally admitted, "I've read and prayed on it, but I'm having trouble figuring out who God is, how to picture him. And if I can't picture him, I can't know him—can't know who I'm praying to."

The sister was kind. "God," she said, "is love." It was the first time I had heard that straightforward description. "You can't see your mother's love, but you know it's there, don't you?" I nodded. "You know it's there because you can feel it, isn't that right?" It was. "Same thing with God. You *feel* His presence. That's your knowledge."

As a youth, I could indeed feel God all around me, in the lives of my parents and grandparents, especially my maternal grandmother. And I felt it most when I was able to be present in the moment, sitting quietly in our backyard or basking in the ordinary banter that filled our home. Later I would lose track of this sensation, and with it my relationship to God—especially once I entered politics. But at least back then, I felt a unifying purpose and mission through the Church. I found God in all things, as St. Ignatius Loyola suggested, and this gave me great strength and comfort.

THE DAY OF MY FIRST CONFESSION, I PUT ON A PAIR OF CHARCOAL gray slacks, a white short-sleeved shirt, and a green tartan clip-on tie. I felt as though I stood just this side of adulthood. It was a somber milestone. Confession is the first sacrament we got to participate in fully. We had our own lines to say, some in Latin, and for months the Sisters had schooled us in our perfect recitations.

This was a day of wild anxiety for me—for all of us, I think. We were all seven years old; it was a good bet that none of us had yet committed a mortal sin. Not going to church on Sunday was the only one that loomed over our heads, and I personally knew not one kid in the second grade who had ever missed a Sunday Mass. That left us to plumb the venial sins, our misdemeanors. I gave my conscience a strict and thoroughgoing review, but in the end all I had was a list of minor behavioral infractions and a handful of un-worthy thoughts. But frankly, I had no idea how many were genuine sins.

The Sisters had been specific in their trainings. This would be a time of transformation for us. Inside that musty enclosure, speaking anonymously to an unseen voice as though to God himself, we would have our first opportunity to become sinless again, to wipe our slates clean. But there were many rules. Be succinct, they'd said. Don't go into a lot of detail. *Don't* bother the priest with frivolous things. And don't name others who sinned with you—this is not a court of law, but a personal reckoning with God.

In addition to those protocols, I understood confession to involve a complex moral appraisal of our actions. Stealing food is surely sinful, but if I stole out of hunger my culpability was mitigated. Did I know the food wasn't mine to take? *Should* I have known it belonged to someone else? On top of this was the matter of intentionality—a kind of eye-of-the-beholder clause I had a hard time wrapping my mind around. Of course I had never stolen a thing in my life, but it didn't matter. Wading through the moral forest of my soul, I found myself hopelessly obsessed with the trees.

I consulted my parents, whose advice for the big day was simple: *be rigorous.* Needing more practical pointers, I turned to Walter Lambert, a classmate with a knack for managing tricky situations. One day, Walter had tried showing me a way to make your arm numb by rubbing it with a ruler. We sat in the back of geography class scraping rulers up and down our arms, as though we were sharpening a knife without a leather strap. It hurt like hell; numbness would have been a *gift*. But Sister Imelda caught us before the experiment bore fruit. For whatever reason, she snatched up Walter and left me behind. When he returned, the numb part was between him and his chair. He never once wondered aloud why I'd been spared. I think he knew his culpability was greater than mine, and accepted his penance with contrition.

"One time I forgot to clean my room," I told him. "Is that a sin?"

Walter shrugged. "Put it in anyway," he said. "There's no downside. If it *is* a sin, you'll be in more trouble leaving it off." Now, that was a lesson in morals.

After trading notes with Walter, I decided to confess everything on my master list. Together we rehearsed dozens of times, training for our first confessions like other kids drilled for spelling-bee finals.

When the time came, our entire second grade class was summoned to form one long line in the school's vast hallway, then snaked to the school multipurpose room. There, wheeled in only on special occasions, was the confessional booth—a blond-wood, two-doored source of foreboding mystery to us all. We studied the faces of each boy and girl when they left the tiny chamber. Some emerged giggling or pink with shame. Still others appeared triumphant, as though the experience had bestowed on them a terrific peace of mind. I was filled with awe.

Walter's turn came just before mine. He tucked himself behind the towering door with confidence, but I breathed uneasy with him in there. I knew his confession so well by now that I rolled through it in my head just as I knew he was doing with the priest. When I finished, I was surprised that the door didn't swing open. For a long time he didn't emerge. The nuns had told us that priests sometimes asked for more information. What hidden nuance could they have found in Walter's confession, I wondered? What unsuspected sin lurked among his words?

At last, he was released. When I passed him on my way in, his face gave no hint of his ordeal.

The door was heavier than I expected; the whole confessional shuddered when it closed behind me. Inside the air was tight, yet somehow it also felt charged. It took my eyes a moment to adjust to the darkness as I groped for the right place to kneel. As I made the sign of the cross, my heart pounded so loudly I worried it would drown out my words. "Bless me, Father, for I have sinned," I began. "This is my first confession. I accuse myself of the following sins. I was mean to Caroline twice. I talked back to my parents once. On seven occasions I didn't clean my room. Once I forgot my chores."

As I spoke I glanced up to the grate and was surprised to see the familiar profile of Father Gaydos, the businesslike pastor at St. Joe's. No doubt about it: that was his familiar flattop, his unmistakable square nose. I even recognized the sound of his labored breathing. And I'm sure he knew exactly who I was; he'd known me my whole life.

When he began pronouncing my absolution, though, our familiarity did nothing to undermine the power of the ritual. "*Ego te absolvo a peccatis tuis in nomine Patris et Filii et Spiritus Sancti,*" he said, and I felt cleansed. Though my penance was paltry—three Hail Marys, one Our Father, and a Glory be—the sensation of grace was intense.

SHORTLY THEREAFTER, MY FATHER CALLED ME TO HIS BEDROOM for a meeting. This was unusual. Typically Dad spoke his mind around the kitchen table. I'd never been summoned down the dark hallway on the second floor before. I was filled with anxiety and curiosity alike.

"There's something I want to talk to you about," Dad said gravely, motioning for me to sit down on the bed. He reached into a dresser drawer and removed an old manila envelope, then sat beside me.

I noticed his hands tremble slightly as he opened the clasp and removed the envelope's contents, placing a number of letters and photographs in his lap. At a glance I saw that they concerned James Edward McGreevey, my namesake.

He took a breath. "My father was going to leave the body over there originally in Iwo Jima, but then he found out that the base might be turned over to the Japanese. And he said, 'To hell with that. We'll bring the body home.'"

He handed me Uncle Jimmy's funeral Mass prayer card. "Jimmy was my hero," he said. "That's why I named you for him. I always wanted a son to carry on his name, his tradition."

I nodded.

"Before he went to the Marine Corps he was a boxer. Ever heard of the Golden Gloves? The *Hudson River Dispatch* runs it. Not everybody's into boxing, especially people like me," he allowed. "Jimmy was an aggressive guy. I was going through some papers and noticed he made corporal within six months—from private to PFC to corporal that quick. And corporal means you're on the way up. This was a guy who made a talent of climbing the ladder. He made sergeant before he got blown up."

I stared at the prayer card bearing my name. We didn't speak about

Uncle Jimmy around the house much. I knew he'd died at Iwo Jima in 1945 after volunteering on what was called a "suicide mission," clearing mines from the beach in advance of an amphibious landing in the Volcano Islands. I also knew he was buried with a chest full of ribbons, but Dad felt I was now old enough to know exactly what each one meant. He wanted me to understand the significance of my name, to know the burden and honor it invested in me.

One of the documents was a commendation that accompanied Uncle Jimmy's Bronze Star, marked with a *V* to signify combat; he had earned this by carrying his injured squad leader to safety through enemy fire in Saipan. Another letter explained the Presidential Unit Citation, for the seizure of Tinian in the Marianas Islands, "unchecked by either natural obstacles or hostile fire."

Finally he pulled out a letter to my grandfather from the Secretary of the Navy on behalf of President Roosevelt, posthumously awarding my uncle the highest honor bestowed by the corps, the Navy Cross. As Dad began reading them to me, his eyes welled with tears. I had never seen my father cry before, and at first I mistook his tears for signs of a terrible grief. Only when I listened more closely did I realize that they were tears of pride.

Placed in charge of a mine removal detail, Sergeant McGreevey landed with his men against savage enemy resistance and immediately initiated mine removal operations in an effort to clear a path through the beach area for our assault tanks. Shortly thereafter, he and his squad were taken under a smashing mortar bombardment supplemented by raking machine-gun fire from strategically placed hostile weapons covering the mine field, with resulting casualties to all but two of his men. Aided by one of the two remaining Marines, Sergeant McGreevey evacuated all casualties who could be moved, and then returned to his task of removing mines. Working desperately, he consistently disregarded the blasting Japanese bombardment and, when the surviving members of his squad were killed by the merciless enemy gunfire, staunchly continued to probe and disarm the dangerous weapons alone. Although instantly killed by a shellburst as he cleared the last of the mines from the beach, Sergeant

McGreevey had succeeded in fulfilling his vital mission despite the loss of his entire squad, and his unfailing skill, indomitable determination and valiant devotion to duty in the face of tremendous odds reflect the highest credit upon himself and the United States Naval Service. He gallantly gave his life in the service of his country.

Dad looked at me. "My mother and father come off the boat from Ireland. Nothing could have made them prouder than to lose a son this way, defending freedom for their adopted homeland. He is an American hero."

IN THE SUMMER BETWEEN THIRD AND FOURTH GRADES, I BEGAN feeling more comfortable with my peers. A handful of pals and I spent countless hours riding our bikes through the woods around our homes, building a vast city of forts and make-believe hospitals. There was a marshy pond back there, brimming with wildlife, and before long we turned our attention to the business of catching frogs. We'd take them home and watch them hop around all afternoon (or longer, though we soon discovered their shelf life was very short back in our rooms).

After a time, though, we lost interest in watching them hop—and for some inexplicable reason the boredom turned to cruelty. One hot day we brought our pet frogs down to the end of a block where we knew there was a surplus of tar left behind by the public works department. One of the boys had heard that if you put a frog in the tar, it would eventually dry up and then you could "pop" it by stepping on the dehydrated frog.

It was stupid, cruel, and immature; my stomach still turns to think about it. We all took the frogs we had caught down to the "tar pits" and tossed them at the sticky trap. I can still see it now, watching the frogs jump once or twice before their webbed feet became stuck in the tar. Maybe they didn't know fear; maybe it's true that they don't feel the gradual onslaught of pain. But I could see in their eyes, as these poor creatures baked in the hot summer sun, that they were reacting—that they wanted to get away. But the longer they stayed in one spot the deeper they sank.

Later that day we returned to the scene of the crime, and my pals set about crushing the dead animals under their heels. I don't think I joined in the stomping party, that day or thereafter. But I did spend many days that summer gathering up the poor things and flinging them to their death in the tar.

Why do I include this story? To show that at some point in a boy's childhood he may find himself in need of a wake-up call, a lesson to explain the value of life. For me this lesson came, indirectly and unexpectedly, through the Cub Scouts.

I loved everything about the Scouts—wearing the uniform, reciting the Oath, gathering merit badges. The safety badge, the family life badge, the woodworking badge: each presented a discrete challenge, a defined path for achievement, and a recognized reward. These for me were like practicums for my father's adage, *Plan your work and work your plan.* I also very consciously thought of them as credentials: *If I work hard enough*, I thought, *I can become a Webelo, then a Boy Scout, and beyond.*

One day we learned that our kindhearted Scout leader had died of a sudden heart attack. As devastated as we were, the other boys and I created a vast and entertaining narrative around his passing. As part of a wicked power grab, we speculated, the assistant Scoutmaster must have failed to give the Scoutmaster mouth-to-mouth resuscitation at a critical moment, leaving him to die so that he could take over the top post. It was a horrible story, but we relished it—until the day of the wake. Dressed in our pressed uniforms and neckerchiefs, the assembled troop went to the Synowiecki Funeral Home in Carteret to pay our respects. Two by two, we approached the open casket, knelt, and said a prayer; I'm sure we all craned our necks for a glimpse of the corpse, but most of us were too short to see.

As I knelt beside the enormous wooden box, the Scoutmaster's widow was suddenly overcome with grief. She cried out and lurched toward her husband with an awful sadness, scattering us Scouts as she folded the weight of her body around him. I had never seen such grief—a contagious sorrow that traveled through the pews—and the sound of the community's sobs brought home to me, perhaps for the first time, the truth of death and a respect for life, for Scoutmasters and frogs alike.

* * *

OF ALL THE BOYS MY AGE, I WAS AMONG THE FIRST TO COMMIT THE entire Latin Mass to memory. I knew it cold, and not just by rote; I studied the Mass the way Plato studied Socrates. I sharpened my Latin vocabulary with daily drills. I mimicked the words as they flowed from Father Anthony's mouth, singing where he sang, whispering where he whispered, practicing until I could generate a faultless replica of his own incantations as they spilled over the white marble altar. When I noticed that Father Lyons said Mass in a slightly different order than Father Anthony, I made a point of memorizing each priest's unique interpretations. Even with all the other gaps in my memory, these details I still recall.

And my efforts paid off: at the age of nine I was invited to be an altar boy, among the youngest at St. Joe's. The call came one morning in early winter, when the sun was still warm. Sister Mary Louis, a delightful Servite nun with a head cover tucked below her chin, approached me quietly. "Sister Imelda wishes to see you," she said. *This can't be good,* I thought. I went to her office directly and stood nervously in the reception area of the school's administrative pod.

She looked up from her desk over the black rim of her glasses. Another nun stood behind her, regarding me cautiously. "Report to the church," Sister Imelda said.

I wasn't expecting to be handed an altar boy's surplice that day, but when it happened I was overcome with pride. To be *selected* was a heady feeling. When I threaded myself into the floor-length robe and small white alb, I knew the promises of the Church were true: I was being summoned to serve as a kind of mini-Christ on Earth, and the realization was nearly too crushing to bear. In a dream I had not long thereafter, and again from time to time throughout my life, I saw myself facedown on the white marble rostrum, prostrate before God and the bishop towering above me, receiving the gift of the Holy Spirit. *Tu es sacerdos in aeternun, secundum ordinem Melchizedek,* a priest forever in the order of Melchizedek.

A priest forever: the idea has attracted me from time to time throughout my life. As a young man I paged through seminary brochures and daydreamed about becoming "a man chosen and set apart," as Pope John XXIII wrote, "and blessed in a very special way with heavenly gifts—a sharer in divine power." I ran my fingertips over the photographs of young students with books under their arms, the Church's future leaders kicking at the hems of their cassocks, and dreamed of a life of spirit-driven purpose.

But I am getting ahead of myself. Back then, all I knew for sure was that I would make myself the perfect altar boy, bringing pride to my clan. I literally recall hearing that word sing in my mind: *perfect*. And, having attained this remarkable high office, I wasn't the first altar boy to behave in a cocky way, though I may have set new standards for self-assurance. When the bishop of Trenton, George Ahr, came to say Mass at our church, I remember feeling obliged to welcome him myself. "Your Eminence," I said, extending my small hand, "I'm Jimmy McGreevey, a fourth-grader, an altar boy—one of the youngest—and a member of [this club and that] at St. Joe's. I extend a warm welcome on behalf of myself and the other students." The bishop was gracious, and we spoke for a number of minutes before I realized that the entire congregation had turned to look at us. I could see my grandmother mouthing to my father, "Look at Jimmy, he's talking to the bishop." Most Catholics were intimidated by such visits from high Church leaders, as my father recalls. "We all treated the bishop like he was a visitor from Heaven. You didn't care. You'd be talking to anybody and everybody."

It's no wonder my father used to call me "my little statesman." From a very young age I saw myself as a leader, and when other kids were worrying about what to do with their summer vacations, I was already setting ridiculously outsized political goals for myself. I don't remember this at all, but Jim Burns, who transferred to St. Joe's from parochial school in Jersey City when we were both second- or third-graders, says I introduced myself to him on his first day as though I were the official ambassador to newcomers, adding: "I'm going to be secretary of state one day." A few years later, I had the hubris to tell Mary DeLoretto, a gorgeous girl who palled around with me at the YMCA when we were teenagers, something similar: "One day I'm gonna marry you and be president of the United States."

And yet, even back then, I knew on some semiconscious level that I could never be president—or even have a wife, not properly. I didn't yet know that I was gay, but I had that desperate sense that I was alone and destined to remain that way. I saw myself as apart from the wider world, and I had the feeling that others out there were secretly spying on me. I saw them watching me, and I saw myself being watched by them. I wanted to exist in the simple moment like everybody else, where I felt myself closest to God and embraced by my family, but that proved impossible to sustain. Scholars have described the "growing sense of distance . . . loneliness, and despair" that often characterizes the youth and adolescence of gay men and women. I felt all that and more, and it made me afraid.

This feeling, commonly referred to as dissociation, is caused when a child pushes unwanted knowledge out of his mind. My gayness was an unsettling fact even before I learned the ugly vocabulary to describe it, even before it involved sexual impulses or the prolonged period of repression and explosion that inevitably follows.

Lon Johnston and David Jenkins, two Texas professors of social work, have studied the childhood psychic damage commonly found among gay men and women who come out in later life:

> Adolescence is often known as a time of rebellion and self-discovery. Yet [for these subjects] acts of defiance and embracing their inner feelings were often curtailed during adolescence. Most participants indicated they rarely rebelled against their parents or other authority figures. Participants described intense pressure to guard the secret of their sexual orientation, and one way to guard this secret was to always be in control of their behavior. Being in control meant rarely doing anything that could raise questions in their parent(s)' and/or friends' minds about what might be going on inside the adolescent's head. . . . During this time period, adolescents focus on two developmental tasks: 'independence from the family and the development of personal identity.' This study suggests that the development of a personal identity by gay men and lesbians during adolescence is impeded by internal conflicts regarding one's sexual orientation.

I'm no social scientist, but I can assure you that this describes me perfectly. My entire personal identity was impeded during my childhood. My difference was a fact, not a theory, and it was something I could not overcome. I didn't even know what homosexuality was; gayness has only been discussed politely for the past few decades, and when I was growing up the idea made only brief appearances, mostly in the punch lines of jokes. I never heard my mom or dad, or anyone else in our large family, utter a single negative word about gays—but then again, the subject never really came up at all, good or bad. In our world, homosexuality really didn't exist.

There were glimpses on television: Paul Lynde, Liberace, and Rip Taylor come to mind, and later Truman Capote and Renée Richards, the transgender tennis player. But for the most part these were presented as "characters," outsized personalities, never explicitly acknowledged as gay. The figures themselves were as anxious as anyone to keep the subject out of public view; Liberace even took a journalist to court for calling him a "fruit flavored, mincing, ice-covered heap of mother-love" (and he won!).

I had no idea what these people were, but I never suspected that they were in any way connected to me. To me they seemed freakish, with their noisy flamboyance and cynicism, and I turned away from them in revulsion. Being gay never drew me toward anyone, not in those years; instead it pushed me away from people, even my sisters and parents. I used to lay awake in bed at night, praying feverishly to be delivered from whatever this gripping affliction might turn out to be. It felt almost exactly like loneliness, but with a kind of hopeless anguish mixed in. And despite my nightly prayers, it proved stubbornly intractable.

I WAS ELEVEN YEARS OLD WHEN MY PARENTS SENT ME AWAY TO spend the summer before sixth grade at Boy Scout camp. This was my first chance to venture out of my all-Catholic universe, and I was both excited and a little scared. It was immediately clear that I was in over my head. The camp was filled with public schoolkids who were undisciplined and aggressively competitive; compared to my St. Joe's peers, they seemed almost feral. I hadn't realized until then how deeply the nuns had driven their fearful sense of order into our little minds.

All day I tagged along behind the other kids my age, making myself helpful and cracking jokes, but it did me little good. The nuns had always put a premium on perseverance, so I kept at it as long as I could. At some point in the afternoon, though, I finally ran out of steam. I climbed into my sleeping bag early that night, when most of the kids were still shooting the bull around the campfire outside. *Not a bad day on balance*, I thought. *Try again tomorrow.*

From my tent, though, I could still hear the guys talking. And as soon as I was out of sight, they turned to mocking me—using words I'd never heard before, at least not about myself. *Fag. Homo. He's a fag. We can tell he's a fag, he doesn't like girls. Queer. You can just tell he's a queer mother-fucker. A faggot.*

I shook, then cried, in my sleeping bag. Was I imagining things? I shook my head clear and lifted an ear into the air to take another reading, but the words were the same. Still, my disorientation was so thorough that I found myself questioning where they were coming from: were they really calling me those names, or were those voices in my own mind? Try as I might, I couldn't be sure.

As my mind raced on, I remember thinking that this could play out in one of two ways. If it was a hallucination, I would have to find a way to prevent it from ever happening again. I would have to walk through life like a blind man, touching the walls around me and sniffing the air for clues, using multiple senses to get my bearings where everyone else got by with one.

If what I'd heard was true, on the other hand—if those boys really were calling me a faggot—then I was in even deeper trouble. Why? Because from where they were sitting, they must have known I could hear them. Their raised voices told me that they were presenting me with a challenge. I could either go out and confront them—and get my ass kicked for my trouble—or stay in the tent and seal my reputation as a sissy.

Until this moment, I realize now, I had never put together the pieces of the puzzle about my own life. I can't even swear that I knew, in the summer of 1968, exactly what a "fag" was. My only goal in camp had been to fit in, to win the respect of the other boys. I reviewed everything about how I had behaved that day to see where I went wrong. What could possibly have triggered their hatred?

And then it came to me: that morning, in one of my fits of eagerness to please, I had seen another boy wrestling with his knapsack, and I'd stepped forward to help him take it off. It was an innocent gesture, the kind of thing that was encouraged at St. Joe's. Camp, apparently, was a different story.

How stupid, I thought. *Stay within the lines, Jim. Don't give them any more rope to hang you with.*

As I drifted off to sleep that night, I'd made my decision: I'd be one of the guys, be as strong and masculine as possible. And as soon as I got home from camp, I resolved, I'd find a girl and kiss her. The next morning, I threw back the screen on my pup tent, headed straight for the ringleader from the night before, and began a campaign to win him over. I was persistent. I kept him close, showed him that I could work harder, chop more wood, pursue more merit badges, and navigate the forest better than any other Scout. Through sheer willpower, I turned him from a name-calling enemy into a good friend. He never knew what hit him.

IN THE SIXTH GRADE, DURING ONE OF MY SLEEPLESS NIGHTS, I discovered masturbation. And certain uncomfortable truths came slowly into focus.

Not that I was yet attracted to boys or men, not initially. But I knew masturbation was disallowed by Church teaching, that it was a form of evil. After that first time I prayed to God to keep it from happening again, but no such luck. I prayed and relapsed, prayed and relapsed, into high school and beyond. This might be the story of any red-blooded boy, but I felt totally defeated by it. If anyone was able to master this drive, it should have been me. Yet I failed again and again.

From the start, I knew I had to make a meaningful confession about this lapse, these lapses. But I wasn't about to whisper something like this into the grille at St. Joe's, where I was so intimately connected. Even though the priests had assured us that nothing we revealed would go beyond the confessional, how could I risk it? This was the first time I ever looked at a man of the cloth with suspicion.

But confess I must, so I took my sins to St. Mark's or St. Mary's, Catholic churches around the corner from the YMCA in Rahway. I remember stealing into the confessional like a bandit, yanking the words out of my mouth like they were tied to fish hooks. The shame I felt when that unseen priest gave me penance has never been surpassed. Not even when, an evening or two later, I fell off the path to virtue once more.

Months into this biblical struggle, the battleground changed entirely: for the first time an image swam into my mind at the critical moment . . . and it wasn't Mary or Ellen or Elizabeth or Karen. Unfortunately, it was—I suppose I shouldn't say his name. He was a year behind me in school. Cute, blonde, skinny—and I had a subtle feeling that he was communicating with me on a private frequency, that we understood each other, were the same. As a young gay kid you don't realize you're searching for your own kind, but you never tire of the hunt. I was thrilled to find him, to discover that I wasn't alone in the world. And I wanted him. It's not a sexual quest, or not entirely; it's a journey home.

A few weeks later I was thrilled to learn that my interest was reciprocated. We were walking home from school, reviewing the day's highlights as we often did. When we passed his house, I was surprised when he invited me in. "My brother's got a collection of *Playboys*," he said. "Wanna see?"

I was in eighth grade, he was in seventh. One thing led to another.

If he had been a girl, I might be able to tell you how we tumbled through the afternoon, what her flesh looked like in the warm light, how she made me feel all grown up. But those details never seem innocent when you talk about two boys. I will say this: it was wonderful. I felt alive. But we didn't kiss, as much as I wanted to; what is first base for straight kids is the last gate on the farthest pasture of gay sexual exploration. A kiss is too intimate, too loaded. I wouldn't kiss a man till I was in my mid-forties, twice married, governor-elect of New Jersey, and an emotional mess.

But after this boy and I finished examining the *Playboys* and one another, I went into a total terror spiral. I couldn't get home soon enough. I ripped off my clothing and scrubbed him off my skin in a scalding shower—a ritual baptismal renewal. I prayed nonstop to be free of the damnation that flooded my soul. "I will never do this again," I promised. "This is a sin, an evil thing. Have I completely lost my self-control?"

I never gave myself a free pass, not this time or any time in the future. I think it was Voltaire who said, "Try it once, you're a philosopher; try it twice, you're a sodomite." I despaired from the start. I cast around for explanations and excuses. And, for the first time, I looked outside myself for blame. *Who is encouraging me to do this?* I wondered. *Am I being set up? By whom? Who is responsible?* I wanted to believe that all this was out of my hands, that it was something visited upon me by an outside force. I wanted to be blameless. I didn't know then—nobody did—that the cause was simple biology, the effect nothing more than a boyhood crush. The only outside force I could imagine was Satan himself.

Is Satan luring me down this road? Or is he merely awaiting me at the end? Either way, I was terrified.

THAT YOUNG MAN AND HIS FAMILY MOVED AWAY FROM CARTERET very soon thereafter. But his departure didn't erase our history, which gnawed at me. I chose not to confess what happened. Instead of taking this thing to church, I took it to the Woodbridge Township Library. These days, hundreds of books are available to help gay kids understand their journeys, studies that prove that homosexuality is hardwired and immutable and undeniably common in most corners of the animal kingdom. Back then, many local card catalogues didn't even list "homosexuality." They went from *homo sapiens* directly to *homogeneous* and *homogenized.* I had to go to "Sexuality, deviant" to learn about myself, and the collected works were few and frightening. Most entries were for medical periodicals with names like *Journal of Nervous and Mental Diseases* or scientific textbooks like *Homosexuality: Its Causes and Cure, Sexual Deviance & Sexual Deviants,* and *Sexuality and Homosexuality,* whose subtitle was: "The Definitive Explanation of Human Sexuality, Normal and Abnormal." I knew immediately where on that continuum I fell.

If you haven't experienced it, it may be hard to understand the sinking feeling most every gay boy or girl of my generation experienced upon coming across this section of the library. Perhaps it's something like what a child might feel after discovering that her fluish symptoms are really the signs of a fatal illness. All I could do in response was to slam the drawer closed, terrified of being discovered, and leave the library immediately, steeped in hopelessness.

Still, in the months that followed I would return many times to peer into that card catalogue, thumbing the cards with increasing resignation. On quiet afternoons when I was sure I wouldn't be caught, I nervously trolled the stacks and pulled out the texts, reading them with sweaty hands. They did little for my state of mind. I learned that "oral regression" and "masochistic tension" had caused my "inversion." I was certainly diseased; on this point there was professional unanimity. I was a "counterfeit-sex," a "third-sex," an "intermediate-sex" with no expectation for happiness. Here was Stanley F. Yolles, MD, the director of the National Institute of Mental Health, part of the U.S. Public Health Service, saying: "With broadening parental understanding and more scientific research, hopefully, the chances that anyone's child will become a victim of homosexuality will eventually decrease." I was a scourge, a threat to society, something to be eradicated.

I was thirteen years old when I realized this.

I don't remember crying. Rather, I set a course of self-deliverance. The literature said my desires could be contained, so that's what I set about doing. I read how psychiatrists regularly prescribed exercises involving girlie magazines in an effort to heterosexualize their gay male patients, a practice then called "aversion therapy" or "conversion therapy." I bought *Playboy*s and practiced ejaculating while staring at the pictures. I locked myself away and vowed to fight this war till I won or it killed me. Certainly I would never speak a word about what happened between me and that boy. Instead I made new plans: I would make a fresh start, enroll in a parochial high school in another town. This is how small things become secrets, how the closet door is built.

4.

I ALWAYS FELT MASCULINE, MALE, APPROPRIATE. GENDER CRISIS was never part of what I was going through. In 1980, the term *gender identity disorder* (GID) was taken up by the American Psychiatric Association to describe young boys who persistently adopt girlish behaviors (and girls who do the reverse), and even today the term is sometimes used to diagnose gay kids' discomfort in their own skin. But a more enlightened school of academics have shown that gender dysphoria is extremely common among all kids, regardless of their sexuality; they maintain—and I agree—that the category itself is wrongheaded, another way to categorize gayness as a pathology. A girl who favors baseball mitts over manicures is no more "disordered" than any boy on her Little League team.

As a child, I never had much interest in baseball or football; not until I started swimming at the YMCA did I start to develop confidence in my physicality. But I never showed any tendency to favor my female side. Some people have since told me that my slenderness, or something about the way I carry myself, suggests a certain persuasion. I reject this outright. It irritates me when people think they can pick all gay guys and lesbians out of lineups, or when I hear someone say "Aha! I thought so" after finding out that someone they know is gay. Some of the most effeminate men I know are solidly heterosexual, inside and out. It should go without saying that gay men are just as equally diverse on the gender matrix. Same goes for women. Line up handsome Christine Todd Whitman, my predecessor, alongside glamorous Representative Tammy Baldwin, the only lesbian serving openly on Capitol Hill, and you'll know what I mean.

Frankly, I don't think there's anything out of the ordinary about me physically, anything that says "effeminate" in any way. When I came out publicly, some photo editors had a field day searching for pictures of me with a limp wrist or some other stereotypical gay signifier—as though, after decades in the public eye, they'd suddenly come across a trove of shots where I looked like a Cher impersonator. Such pictures don't exist. Some people even used their home computers to create the images they wanted, grafting my head onto Carson Kressley's body and transforming me into one of the Fab Five from *Queer Eye for the Straight Guy*. Some of that stuff was pretty funny, I'll admit, but it just wasn't me. The truth is, with my thick glasses and curly hair, I was anything but stylish. From childhood on, my dad reminds me, I "bordered on *nerd*."

One thing is true—there is something noticeable about the way I walk. But this is definitely a matter of nurture, not nature. When I was an eighteen-year-old freshman at Catholic University in Washington, I misjudged the time one evening and found myself locked inside the library after hours. I tossed my books out the window and called down for help, but the campus was empty—already evacuated for Easter recess. So I called an upperclassman I knew who was staying on campus over the break. Luckily, he answered and agreed to rescue me. When he showed up, I saw him meander toward my window with the wide-open face of a child at the circus. Later he explained he'd been smoking pot in his room when I called—something I wish I'd known at the time.

"I need help," I pleaded. "Can you call campus security?"

He shrugged. "Why don't you just jump?"

"It's too high," I said. The window must have been about fifteen feet off the ground. It was the only one I could open.

He stepped back to measure the distance himself. "I'd jump," he said. I guess the window wasn't as high as he was.

Never one to shy away from a challenge, I stupidly slid myself onto the ledge, dangled from my hands as low as I could, then let go. When I hit the ground, both my ankles shattered. Today I'm able to jog daily and swim without pain, but I'm always reminded of that foolish jump by the stiff, slightly listing limp in my stride. And never again have I pushed my luck with closing time, in a library or anywhere else.

* * *

THERE WERE ONLY TWO OCCASIONS DURING THESE YEARS WHEN I remember being physically afraid. The first time was the night at Scout camp when I overheard those campers ridiculing me around the campfire. The second incident came a few years later. In every school there is a bully. At St. Joe's that title went to a kid named John, a tall, sturdy, brash, and menacing figure we all steered clear of as much as possible. John never needed a reason to turn against one of my classmates. "I'm gonna kick your ass," he would threaten, and his promises were never idle.

One afternoon in sixth grade, John's attentions turned to me. I don't remember what set him off, but it hardly mattered; it was just my turn. "I'm taking you out, McGreevey," he said, and he named the place and time, later in the week. I knew I was a goner. I spent the next few days in a blur of fright and resignation. That first night in bed, I imagined myself fighting back; the second night I knew it was futile; on the third night I prayed for my soul.

But then the hour of my reckoning came—and nothing happened. Did he forget, I wondered? Had Sister Imelda stepped in to prevent the crime? Could he possibly have forgiven me? Pitied me? Forgotten me? I'll never know. But I stayed anxious for weeks, wondering what I'd done to provoke the beating I never got. Ultimately, the whole episode only reinforced my belief that a spontaneous life was not possible for me—that from now on I would have to think through every single move I made, abbreviate myself one gesture at a time, measure every possible risk and consequence before acting.

ARMED WITH MY NEW LESSONS, I ENTERED NINTH GRADE AT ST. JOSEPH HIGH School in Metuchen—another St. Joe's for me, but this one run by the Brothers of the Sacred Heart as a top-notch preparatory school. This St. Joe's was an all-boys school, but it was no place for roughnecks like John; here the emphasis was on academics and the tradition of service, and the only strongmen wore long cassocks. Among them was Brother Michael, a fanatical and passionate instructor in world history who inspired both fear and excellence in his students. One afternoon when he was late to class, pandemonium broke out in his classroom. As I stood by and watched, the rowdier kids started throwing anything they could get their hands on—chalk, then erasers, then books. Eventually some projectile struck the door with great force, cracking the glass and sending us boys back to our seats in dread.

Thankfully, when Brother Michael arrived, he didn't notice the damage. Instead he launched right into a discussion of *The Scarlet Pimpernel*, our reading assignment. He called on Bill Thomas, one of my classmates, to report on the story of gallantry and adventure during the French Revolution. But Bill hadn't read a word of the assignment; instead he made a valiant effort to appear prepared, concocting a fantastic narrative that had little to do with the novel at hand. Rather than call his bluff, though, Brother Michael lured him down the garden path with cunning questions, until Bill was caught up in an elaborate yarn in which French aristocrats were being shuttled across the English Channel on the backs of marine mammals. We were all trying desperately to contain our laughter. Not Brother. With each audacious new twist from Bill, he paced the room more furiously—until suddenly, just as his rage was cresting, he looked down and discovered the cracked windowpane.

"Who is responsible for this?" he bellowed. "Which one of you broke my window?" Nobody in the room dared breathe. The guilty boy bravely raised a hand, though there were plenty in the room who should have shared the responsibility. I remember watching Brother's pectoral cross swing back and forth across his chest as he taught the kid a lesson, Catholic school style.

These were the last days of corporal punishment in American schools; perhaps it was already gone from most public classrooms, but at St. Joe's it was still common, especially during freshman year. There was one short and stocky Brother the older boys called "Cannonball," for reasons that were obvious to all. One day, for example, a towering freshman named Joe Mondoro accidentally dropped a piece of paper on the stairway when Cannonball was serving as stair monitor.

"Pick it up," Cannonball said sternly.

Joe bent down begrudgingly. "Yeah," he muttered.

Cannonball took offense. "Is that, 'Yes, Brother?'" he snapped.

"Yeah," Joe said.

"When I speak to you," Cannonball intoned in his fiercely controlled voice, "you will respond 'Yes, Brother,' or 'No, Brother.' Is that clear?" And with that he lifted Joe, who must have been six feet tall and twice his weight, over his head and threw him through the plasterboard wall. The damage went unrepaired all semester, a reminder of the cost of insubordination.

At St. Joe's, *obedience* was next to godliness.

I FINALLY FOUND A GIRL TO KISS. FOR THE SAKE OF THE STORY, I'll call her Carla. It was the eighth grade, shortly after my first sexual encounter with a boy. She was a year younger, just like him, and just as attractive. All the boys paid her attention, but for some reason she was interested in me. I was hanging out with a bunch of Carteret kids one afternoon, and as we walked along the side of my house I leaned in and kissed her on the lips. With everybody watching, I had kissed a girl. *There,* I thought, *that's what it feels like to be normal.*

She kissed back, just like they did on daytime television shows. What followed was an old-fashioned necking session in the creeping dusk of a tight-knit suburb, touching and kissing and performing—the kind of scene that unspools every minute all over America. The other kids seemed impressed.

Not me. Her kisses were arousing, but there was no passion. I knew I wasn't attracted to her in that way, and I found the knowledge frustrating. Over and over I kissed Carla and touched her, searching for an organic reaction that never came. What is a kiss, actually? Why is it so different when planted on a newborn's belly than on another adult's forehead as you make love? With poor Carla, it was neither of these. Kissing her was like kissing an aunt. It wasn't her fault. I liked her, and I liked the feeling of having another human being in my arms, holding and being held. But we just didn't fit together. I suppose it's the same for a straight actor who finds himself cast in a gay love scene: it might not bother him to kiss another man, but it doesn't carry the same thrill as the real thing.

My heart had refused to obey my mind, and I was inconsolable.

* * *

YOU MAY HAVE NOTICED THAT MY MEMORIES APPEAR TO BE SHARP-ening. It's true: I am growing more attuned to them. In the months since I came out, with the help of psychiatrists, priests, friends, and family, I've been sorting through the wreckage of my history and putting things back on the shelves where they belong. I have bothered my many friends and relatives relentlessly, quizzing them on matters big and small. I've grown accustomed to the baffled look on their faces when we come across some episode I don't recall: sometimes an entire embarrassing event, some-times a story they told me just yesterday. Of course, many people have a hard time remembering everything about their lives, but apparently this is especially common among those who've spent decades in the closet before coming out.

As soon as I left office, I began consulting doctors to help me regain my emotional health; though they saw signs of everything from impulse control disorder to workaholism in my psychological profile, post-traumatic stress disorder is the most plausible culprit behind my memory lapses. In my case, the trauma went on for forty-seven years, and it was induced as much by me as by anyone else. I worked hard to ensure that I was accepted as part of the traditional family of America, building a fortress of artificial truths about myself, shoring up my own fractured identity with layers of what I consid-ered typical adolescent and adult behavior. And I spent so much mental en-ergy keeping track of these things that everything else fell into a chaos in my mind.

I know now why I did certain things, or didn't do them. I know now, for example, that my intense friendships with other men, beginning in ninth grade, involved simple crushes—that's why I ached in their presence, why I always felt slightly ill thinking about them. At the time, this felt like a kind of mental defect. I sometimes truly wondered if I'd lost my bearings. Now I know I was lovesick, that's all, like Gene Kelly in *Singin' in the Rain*.

Can you imagine a straight kid going through school never recognizing the symptoms of love? How disorienting that would be?

My best friend from ninth grade on was a classmate I'll call Sean Hughes. By senior year I was spending most afternoons with him, working on the yearbook, *The Evergreen*, where I made him sports editor just to spend more time around him. He was articulate, bright, athletic, and charismatic, and I craved his company. I thought of him as a bit of a role model for me, like Gene was to Phineas in *A Separate Peace*. But I couldn't quite keep up with him. I'd study and do well in class, like him. I could articulate theorems and syllogisms. But he excelled physically, too, leaving me in the dust on the soccer field and lettering in basketball and golf besides. On top of that, I would never have that casual, relaxed way with people that Sean had. Or his selflessness, for that matter. He knew I had a special devotion to him—probably even knew it was a romantic crush—but he never showed me anything but uncomplicated friendship in return.

Because he lived a few towns away, I sometimes spent the night at Sean's, or as much time as we could together at school. As much as I enjoyed his company, it had the confusing effect of making me feel terribly lonely. That happened a lot to me as a child, and into adulthood: even in huge, crowded rooms, even among intimate and loving friends, I could sometimes experience a devastating aloneness, cold and unnerving. I first noticed this during my visits with Sean—the closer we got the lonelier I felt. Only now does this feeling make sense to me. It was the consequence of denying my heart.

In sophomore year, I accompanied Sean to a neighborhood party. I don't recall whose family was away, but the house immediately became a warren of teenage debauchery. Beer cans popped open, marijuana joints were lit. Unlike my peers, I had no taste for alcohol. To this day I don't drink more than a few sips of wine on special occasions. And I never smoked a cigarette or tried drugs of any sort. I suppose that makes me unique among my generation of politicians, but drugs just never appealed to me. This probably had as much to do with my family heritage in law enforcement as it did with not wanting to spoil my future plans. Most of my friends hadn't drawn so sharp a line in the sand, and for the most part I don't think their youthful experiments did them lasting harm.

Sean was having a blast. Everybody was. Kids were making out everywhere, from the basement to the master bathroom upstairs, or else talking and laughing in small groups. But something about this party made me realize that I had nothing in common with them. Looking around me, I saw in their faces a simple joy that I felt would forever elude me.

Without saying good-bye, I left the party to walk around the neighborhood, taking in the fresh air. And I began to cry in a way I hadn't before or since.

By now I knew a little more about homosexuality. Amazed to learn how fully it had been embraced by the ancient Greeks and Romans, I'd read *Spartacus*, with its magnificent love scene between Antonius and Crassus. I'd also read Oscar Wilde and D. H. Lawrence, and committed swaths of *Brideshead Revisited* to memory. I had heard of the gay life in Greenwich Village, just across the New York Harbor and visible from the tops of buildings in Carteret. Still, in all my reading I had never found evidence of two men falling in love *simply*, settling down, and pursuing a life together among their family and friends.

And more to the point, I knew there was not another person at that party, or in the rich landscape of Carteret, whose life was anything like mine. For all I knew, I was the only gay kid in my school, in my neighborhood, perhaps in the whole town—and the loneliness this realization gave me was insufferable. I felt totally let down by my faith. "What did I do?" I prayed to God. "I've been good. I've prayed. I've tried to live a spiritual life. I've tried to be of service to others." No relief came. "What good can come out of this?" I pleaded. "Is this all an exercise in power? Did you make me gay as a way to humble me? Where is the relief, God? How do I find the way?"

Nothing. In those moments of suffering, I'll admit, I resented God. I felt the grip of evil, and I was angry at God for that. Theologically, I felt completely lost, totally without hope.

And in that way that teenagers do, I came to the conclusion that my only reprieve would be suicide. I will not detail the intricacies of my thinking, except to say that I never found the courage even to do that. And thus my self-esteem was further pummeled.

FORTUNATELY, THERE WERE OTHER THINGS TO THINK ABOUT, POLitics chief among them. Here again, though, I was an outcast: an Irish Catholic who took the side of Richard Nixon.

This was not a popular move in 1971. Catholics were natural Democrats to begin with, and they'd never forgiven Nixon for his fierce losing campaign against John Kennedy in 1960. And once Bobby Kennedy turned against the Vietnam War, Nixon wasn't likely to get much leeway from the Catholic bloc—not in Carteret, anyway. That's not to say that my town was antiwar; far from it. We were soldiers and law enforcement officials, or had family members who were. And we were anti-Communist to the core. More than that, we were Americans—in that eager way that first- and second-generation Americans tend to be. We answered our nation's call. We closed ranks when necessary, and waved the flag as we sent our best and the brightest off to fight the Vietcong. Eight never made it back home to Carteret. Only with time, as the war dragged on and the body count grew, did we grow divided about the war.

Not in the McGreevey household, though. Dad's views held sway, and they were the views of a marine. "Don't give ground," he would say. "Our troops need our support." But one by one our neighbors became critical of U.S. involvement in Southeast Asia. I remember, as if it were yesterday, walking by the home of one our neighbors, Mrs. Kvidahl, one day in 1967 or 1968. Mrs. Kvidahl was no hippie or political radical, and there was no better Catholic I knew. That day, on the way to school, I noticed that she'd hung a poster of Bobby Kennedy in her garage. I remember turning to my friend Eddie and saying, "That's interesting. Something is happening here."

Where Mrs. Kvidahl led, others followed, and by the early 1970s slow revolution was taking hold in our sleepy blue-collar suburb. But nothing compared to the seismic explosion that took place when one of our parish priests went the way of peace. I'll never forget the Sunday morning Mass when Father Murphy, in his melodic brogue, turned fiercely on Nixon after the Cambodia incursion. "The war," he concluded, "is morally wrong."

I was sitting with my family in our regular pew, and when he said these words I snapped around to look at my father, who as a church lector was standing beside the altar—at the elbow of the priest delivering the antiwar homily. Dad's face turned to stone. His two most adored institutions, America and the Church, which had always seemed to be on the same side of any fight, were crashing into each other head on, and you could see the agony in his eyes. I don't remember specifically what Dad spent the rest of that afternoon yelling about, but I remember the volume still. I wasn't the only McGreevey groping my way through an identity crisis in those years.

In this case, Dad had no bigger defender than me. In debate class, I went out to the *right* of Nixon when he announced an end to incursions across the twentieth parallel, in October 1972. And I was heartened when Nixon dropped the ceasefire and pushed north again during the so-called Christmas Bombing, setting off twelve days of the most concentrated air strikes in world history, which led in turn to the withdrawal of American troops within weeks and the collapse of Saigon two years later. My father and I watched these events closely on television, studied each new development in the morning's papers. It was a sober but also a thrilling time; only later, once Nixon's lies were revealed, did I come to regret my precocious early stand.

My excessive conservatism during these years also put me even further out of step with my peers. Looking back, I think my rightward turn may have been an attempt to give purpose to my isolation, as if I were saying, *What you see in me that's different is really Republicanism, nothing more sinister than that.* I acted proudly out of step, wearing ties long after they were no longer required at school and getting myself elected president of every wonky club there was, from science to German to school spirit. I was chairman of the Assembly Committee, managing editor of the newspaper, and the only kid to do four years in the debate club. I turned all my attentions to accumulating accomplishments.

I also began throwing myself into church affairs with the same energy I devoted to my schoolyard political campaigns. I even began flirting with the new charismatic movement in Catholicism, which had first blossomed in Pittsburgh in 1968 and was slowly spreading to other American cities. A group meeting in Edison welcomed me in, but I never became comfortable with the singing, dancing, clapping, and speaking in tongues. The Holy Spirit, when it entered me, told me to go back to St. Joe's, get on my knees, and say my prayers, the way Catholics have been doing for two thousand years.

At St. Joe's, even Brother Michael thought I had taken my conservatism too far. "You're too extreme, Jimmy," he told me. "Life isn't black or white.

You've got to be more balanced in your viewpoints." He counseled me to be more forgiving of the hippies and "peaceniks" I disparaged. I didn't take his advice; I was still too much of an absolutist. If Rome was against communism—as Bishop Fulton J. Sheen so eloquently established on his television show, *Life Is Worth Living*—then it must also be against Hanoi. The Church had handed me down this set of inflexible, God-given values, and I wasn't about to give any leeway in return.

I KNOW I MUST BE COMING ACROSS AS AN EXTREMELY LONELY young man, but I did have many close friends—men and women alike, who remain instrumental in my life to this day. My high school years, in fact, were crowded with social obligations and opportunities. Nothing was more important to me than the time I spent at the YMCA in Rahway, an invigorating universe inside a blocky two-story brick building near the railroad tracks. The lessons I learned at the Y have stayed with me throughout my life: leadership and consensus, ecumenism and racial tolerance, and solid values, chiefly a belief in the value of social service.

I had been taking classes and swimming lessons there for years, but in the summer after freshman year the Y gave me my first job, as assistant camp counselor. The work thrilled me. The "camp" was right there at the Y, a program of day-long activities for underprivileged kids from the area, some just a few years younger than I was. We helped organize ball games, crafts, and other recreations, as well as field trips. This was a lot of responsibility for us kids, and not without potential for disaster. One afternoon we took the campers into New York to visit the legendary Bronx Zoo. Each counselor was responsible for twelve or fourteen kids. One of the kids under my supervision was named Billy Wnuck. Unfortunately, his natural curiosity drew him to the crocodile ponds—literally. When I turned my back he climbed over the fence and bent down to pet one of those enormous creatures on the head. Our cries of alarm were enough to convince Billy to scoot back to safety in time.

Visiting these kids at their homes over on Hazelwood Avenue allowed me to see stark poverty for the first time. In one kid's home, wooden boxes stood in for furniture, and layers of unhemmed fabric served as curtains.

His ill grandmother was convalescing on a mattress on the floor. It was a scene that almost made me cry. Most of the kids at the Y camping program were there on scholarship. Often they came with no food in their stomachs and ill-fitting clothes on their backs. But there was always something to wear and eat there, and even extras to take home.

It was also a racial mixing bowl, where the color of one's skin was so irrelevant as to go unremarked. I remember the first time Patty Cannon cornrowed my hair, how excited I was to show it to my sisters and to teach them the songs the children had taught me: "Hambone, Hambone, where you been?" I wore the braids all week, only taking them out in time for Sunday Mass.

At the Y, I felt I could be totally myself. I felt none of the sense of judgment that shadowed me at the church, or the burdens I felt at school. I also felt a little more "cool" at the Y, where I didn't have to wear my goofy glasses. Even my vexingly curly hair straightened out after a swim, just the way I always wanted it.

So from May to September, I hardly left the place. I worked from seven in the morning to nine at night, loving every minute of it; the harder I worked the more I enjoyed it all, and the faster I rose in the esteem of my supervisors. As the seasons clicked past, I was swim instructor, then pool manager, then aquatics director; before long I was practically running the whole camp.

Junior prom was approaching, and with my newfound confidence I invited Nancy McKeown, a gorgeous young woman with sparkling eyes. I coaxed Sean Hughes into coming along, too, setting him up on a date with a girl I knew from the Y, and they made an attractive couple. I can't say I had a fabulous time that night, and it ended awkwardly when Dad told me I couldn't continue on to the after-party. I think I was the only member of the junior class who was home by 10:30. Still, for the first time I'd begun to think of myself as having some kind of social potential. And for this I credited my time at the Y.

But my private struggles weren't going away. I had developed a close friendship with another swim instructor I'll call Brian Fitzgerald. Brian and I were a lot alike. We were both Irish, of course. And we were both perfect sons who did what we were expected to do: overachieved in school, went out of our way at work, followed all rules unfailingly, and took immaculate care of ourselves. We were the kind of kids who flossed our teeth regularly.

Brian had a great sense of humor and solid academic training and was handsome besides: blue-eyed, blond-haired, with a taut athlete's physique. Maybe because I found him so attractive, I competed with him nonstop, which he seemed to enjoy as much as I did. We both had crushes on the same girl, and we spent months vying for her attentions. Brian and I went to sleepover camp together, even double-dated a few times, and I enjoyed cautiously pushing the limits (like trying to get the girls back to our cabin), just to make him nervous. I don't believe he tried anything with the girls. I, on the other hand, sometimes kissed or touched a girl specifically to see his reaction.

In senior year, we began a nightly ritual. After clearing all the kids out of the gym and emptying the locker room, we would turn off the lights in the pool room and sprint a few laps in the dark. He was always faster. But one evening, when I came particularly close to beating him, we got tangled up in a wrestling match—which dissolved into something entirely driven by hormones. Before it was over we had somehow ripped off one another's suits and were standing in waist-deep water totally naked. Our excitement carried us even further.

And when we were through that night, and the many other times that followed, I saw that Brian wasn't spiraling into the self-hatred that had consumed me after my first experience. I took great strength from that. With Brian, I was able to express myself sexually without hating myself. This was a lovely gift he gave me.

When the lights were on again, though, my ease always vanished. Brian, on the other hand, eventually found a way to do what I could never even imagine for myself. As I later learned, he became a doctor and moved to New England, where he lived a casual, openly gay life with his life partner. My heart ached when I heard this—not that I was pining for him, but because I pitied myself for not finding the courage to make the same honest choices. Brian had given me an opportunity to choose truth, and I missed my chance.

Since coming out I have spent a lot of time thinking about roads not taken. I realized that a part of my journey now must be to close that circle with him. So recently I called him on the telephone, not knowing what to expect. It turns out that he'd watched my coming-out speech live on CSPAN.

"I could tell you were suffering," he said. "Your coming out was much more public than mine. I'm so happy for you that it's done."

II.

Becoming a Born Leader

5.

OF ALL MY FALSE IDENTITIES, THE STRATEGIES IN MY CAMPAIGN
to be accepted, being a sworn Republican is the hardest to explain. In my
later political life, I can only be described as a Kennedy Democrat, eager to
pursue equitable treatment for the least fortunate. As my friend Eric Shuffler says, during my tenure as governor, being on the cutting edge of liberalism was the only aspect of me that was totally genuine.

Perhaps I felt back then that walking the conservative line would help
keep me on the straight and narrow. That by tying myself to the rhetoric of
the status quo I wouldn't be tempted to drift the way of my heart—to go
Brian Fitzgerald's way, toward honesty and self-acceptance. But living an
outwardly gay life in Carteret was not an option. I remained keenly aware
that before Brian could do what he did, he was forced to leave home and settle elsewhere. Gay people are often forced to migrate to pursue their lives in
freedom. I knew that, but I never wanted to leave behind my beloved family,
my church, or the landscape of my childhood. It was easier to stay in a room
falsely than to be sent out because of the truth.

Still, conservatism was a bad fit from the beginning. In my generation
the Republican standard-bearers have been less than upstanding. Nixon's
involvement with Watergate was disgraceful, and though I admired Gerald
Ford for his role as a gentle conciliator, he left only a brief and shadowed
mark on our history.

By senior year of high school, I was looking beyond the lure of Republican politics to another solution: the priesthood. Despite my struggles, I
had always been extremely devout and prayerful. I felt I enjoyed a genuine

relationship with God. I also believed that a calling to the Church could solve the problem of my sexual orientation by imposing the requirement of celibacy, just as it did for straight priests; it would equalize us, while helping in my efforts to deny my heart and climb toward grace. Such a vocation might even be easier for gays than straights, I thought—after all, we were already practiced in denial. Looking around at the priests who had touched my life, I thought I recognized more than a few homosexuals—honorable men, good teachers, but there was something about their lives (a loneliness? a higher purpose?) that seemed familiar to me, seemed encouraging.

One priest in particular, a young guy from Ireland, seemed to empathize with my struggle personally. "You are called upon to dedicate your hands, your mouth, your heart, your feet—everything to Christ," he counseled me. "Surrender everything to Christ. That is your amends." I was proud when he suggested I had what it took to become a priest; for years that was something I'd prayed for. Between the lines, I also took him to mean that the pleasures of my body should be surrendered to the Church, and that he had done the same. All at once I looked at him differently. Was he what I was? It seemed as though he was telling me something about homosexuality as well—that in one stroke I could turn away from evil (my drives) and toward good (community service and God), could go from something reviled to something revered, from "less-than" to "better-than." It was a perfect solution: my rewards would come in the afterlife, as they would for any priest.

Now I had a role model, and a plan. No longer suicide, but the priesthood.

My maternal grandmother, widowed for many years by then, was the first to hear my news. She nearly broke into tears of joy. "Grandpa would have been so proud," she cried, "to serve the Church in Her holy mission in the service of Christ!" Grandma sent prayers of thanks to Teresa of Avila and St. John of the Cross, her favorite saints, for the good news. I loved making her happy this way. More than anyone else, Grandma had taught me about faith and God and love; she taught me the value of prayer, how the saints provided guidance through life, how an afternoon on your knees at church could make a day whole. The Lenten practices were particularly mysterious and enthralling for Grandma; she taught me how, through fasting, prayer, and alms-giving—through suffering—we came to know the suffering of Christ. She and Grandpa had once made a pilgrimage to Quebec City to climb the ancient stone steps of Sainte Anne de Beaupré on their knees, reciting the mysteries of the rosary, as Catholics have done for hundreds of years. When they returned, bruised and scraped, they wore a look of utter transcendence. To Grandma, suffering was a devotion, a path to a deeper and more immediate knowledge of Christ—a lesson I have learned over and over in my life.

My parents were less thrilled. Mom believed in secular education; she wanted me to go to Princeton, to have the best education in the country. Dad was more sympathetic, but he preferred to see me follow his example and go into business.

I picked Saint Louis University, a Jesuit college in Missouri, because my local parish sent their seminarians there. I never visited the campus, but the encouragement of my local Servite priests was enough for me. I signed up after a weekend of prayer and reflection—then prayed again and changed my mind. The same thing happened, over and over, for weeks; I just couldn't decide. Finally I took that as a sign that I wasn't ready to make a lifelong commitment. Instead I headed for the Catholic University of America, an overtly academic institution chartered by the bishops of the United States.

My parents were relieved. Grandma was devastated.

"You'll come down to Washington," I told her. "We'll go to Mass at the Shrine of the Immaculate Conception. There's a very ecclesiastical atmosphere there, Grandma, you'll see: the Dominicans walk around in their white cassocks, the Franciscans in coarse brown cassocks, and diocesan priests in black. There's a little cafeteria below the main altar—we'll go for brunch. You'll love it."

And she did.

YEARS LATER, WHEN I ATTENDED GEORGETOWN LAW SCHOOL, THE tug of the priesthood would return. I still saw Christ in every aspect of daily life; as strange as it sounds, my love for him was nearly passionate. In love songs, for instance, where the lyrics turned to aching hearts and undying love, I sometimes found myself picturing Christ—perhaps because I couldn't allow myself a genuine romantic fantasy.

Georgetown is a Jesuit institution; attracted by the society's tradition of academics and independence, I joined a "candidates' program" with the Maryland Province of the Society of Jesus. My spiritual director was Bill Sneck, a Jesuit priest and a psychiatrist. He was brilliant, authentic, and spiritually demanding. Through the course of the program, Bill repeatedly asked if I could surrender my will, my purpose, my control to God. Ironically, decades later the principles of the Twelve Steps would require me to make the same decision. Yet with Bill, I was unable to answer in the affirmative.

I'd been struggling with my sexual drives long enough to know that this was no simple request. I had tried many times to surrender to Christ. I prayed for an answer to this question: was it possible to surrender *entirely*? To renounce my will for good? I had to be honest with myself: I still had never confessed my high school assignations with Brian Fitzgerald, and this weighed heavily on me. I tried to remedy this failure, sometimes confessing vaguely that I'd been "sexually inappropriate with a friend." But I knew that wasn't enough. Unfortunately, the answer always came back the same way: no, my will is too strong to surrender.

"I still feel that desire to control the circumstances of my life," I told Bill. "I am trying to hear and respond to God's direction for my life. But I still have an ego, a desire for self-mastery."

Bill didn't seem surprised. "If that's the case, the priesthood would be the wrong vocation for you," he said. "The consecrated priest must serve as a vessel of Christ, not be self-focused in any way."

I was terribly disappointed. And totally relieved.

THAT FIRST YEAR AT CATHOLIC WENT BY WITHOUT INCIDENT, good or bad. I never went out for elected office on campus. Unlike back home, I never worried about joining this club or that one at Catholic. I concentrated on being a student, of politics and theory, philosophy and theology. My interest in politics was still just an armchair hobby, like my dad's. But that changed in the fall of my sophomore year, as I looked forward to my first presidential campaign as an eligible voter. Naturally I backed Gerald Ford, who'd been appointed vice president after Spiro Agnew pleaded guilty to tax fraud and re-signed from office, then became president after Nixon resigned the following year. The nation was in a dire economic recession, with fuel shortages and spi-raling inflation; Ford was serving diligently under trying circumstances.

His opponent was Jimmy Carter, a populist and liberal. In retrospect I've come to admire Carter as one of our great American political figures, a visionary advocate for peace, social reform, and economic justice for the world's poor. I've also been moved by his humility on a number of occa-sions when I've met him personally. Back then, however, he struck me as ill equipped in comparison to Ford, and too touchy-feely to lead the country. As commentator Eric Sevareid reportedly said, at a moment when the Oval Office needed a wheeler-dealer, Carter offered "wheeler-healer" instead.

Being in Washington, I decided to sneak into President Ford's election night rally, held at a Capitol Hill hotel. The ballroom was packed with sup-porters hoisting balloons and posters, throwing confetti—the kind of quin-tessentially American tableau I associated with my father's honest patriotism. Bands were playing, reporters crawling around and shouting into television cameras—it was as loud as any football championship game. On one wall hung a huge screen projecting a map of the country, with states coloring in red or blue as results were announced. Moving east to west with the time zones always seemed to give the Democrats an advantage, so I stood in the room amazed as the map turned redder and redder with each passing hour. For a kid who had never drunk or tried drugs, I had never known such excitement.

In the end, of course, Ford lost that November night in 1976. By the time he took the dais he had lost his voice, and his wife, Betty, was left to de-liver a magnanimous concession speech on his behalf. "It's been the greatest honor of my husband's life to have served his fellow Americans during two of the most difficult years in our history," she said. I was struck by the mag-nitude of the occasion, and their grace at its center.

We all went home disappointed. But the virus of politics was now in my bloodstream. It was the first time I recognized a power structure outside of church, and it appealed to me immensely. With sudden clarity, I thought *Pol-itics will be my way to do God's work. If I can't be a priest, I'll try* public *service.*

In high school I'd always loved debate club (we called it "forensics").

Thanks to a great coach, Bob Carney, I was pretty good at extemporaneous speech, at correcting the arguments of my opponents while laying out my own with precision. I loved the scuffle of a good political debate. It reminded me of my childhood, listening to Grandpa Mike's discourses with his friends on Irish politics.

Politics—the clarity of this calling was like nothing I had ever experienced. Politics didn't just bite me, it sunk its teeth deep into my flesh.

Remembering my dad's maxim—*Plan your work and work your plan*—I got serious in a hurry. Here was my plan: I would study law and perhaps public policy in graduate programs. First, though, I felt I had to get out of Catholic University. The school has produced many prominent voices in education (a dozen college presidents), corporate America (the founder of Costco), show business (from Ed McMahon to Susan Sarandon), and religion (including countless cardinals and archbishops). But there was a dearth of political leaders among Catholic alumni: the most prominent were a few ambassadors to the Vatican.

This may have been because the school doesn't brook dissent on matters of fundamental importance to the institutional Church. In my third semester there, I had the misfortune of being in a class called Contemporary Catholic Doctrine, where I tangled with Thomas Aquinas's *Summa Theologica*. The more I questioned and challenged the professor, a mannered priest whose name I luckily can't recall, the more harshly he rebuked me. In *Summa Theologica*, Aquinas—a medieval philosopher and Dominican brother—set out what he called the "proof" of the existence of God, which he found not in nature or science but in the Bible itself. His reasoning was elliptical, and to me it seemed just as cryptic as the Baltimore Catechism that had shaken my faith so many years earlier.

His argument went roughly as follows:

1. There is something moving.

2. Everything that moves is put into motion by something else.

3. But this series of antecedent movers cannot reach back infinitely.

4. Therefore, there must be a first mover (which is God).

The deeper this discussion took us, the more excited I got about the inquiry—especially once I'd encountered the philosophy of Immanuel Kant, who flatly contradicts Aquinas in *The Critique of Pure Reason*. Kant believed that all knowledge must withstand the tests of science and mathematics, and that therefore God's existence is not provable. Kant's thinking resonated with me—much to the irritation of the priest, who scolded me severely on several occasions. I took his responses at face value, as an effort to stop my intellectual exploration, and the resistance drove a serious wedge between me and my faith in the Church. Why *couldn't* I challenge these ideas and principles, I wondered? Why was independent thought held in such suspicion? For the first time in my life, I felt my education was being *limited* by the tenets of Catholicism.

Halfway through the class, I started thinking about the Ivy League. Columbia University was only a short bus ride from home, and I filed for a mid-year transfer. My acceptance came quickly, and I headed to New York over Christmas break of my sophomore year.

I never made a better move. Columbia demanded unstinting intellectual rigor and rewarded independent thinking. The core curriculum stressed the Great Books, but encouraged us to try and rip away at them. It was tough going. For a professor like Richard Brilliant, who taught art history, it wasn't enough that your essays shed new light on, say, the great artistic rivalry between Gianlorenzo Bernini and Francesco Borromini; they also had to be lyrically composed. He rejected paper after paper of mine, marking them up as if he were a professor of English composition. I was running at such a deficit that it seemed I might not pass. Finally I made a deal with him. If he would give me the chance, I would rewrite every paper he had given a failing mark until he was satisfied with it. He agreed. And I passed that class with an A—though the poor man sometimes had to read through eight or nine drafts.

Richard Pious's course on the American presidency was dazzling. I got to hear Warner Schilling, one of the world's great experts on military policy, lecture on World War II and the cold war; and Andrew Nathan, author of major works on Chinese political history, on the Cultural Revolution. General Telford Taylor, the key U.S. prosecutor at the Nuremberg

Trials, gave evening lectures on the principles and primacy of human rights, a field he is credited with pioneering. I worked so hard to keep up that I often developed splitting headaches.

The city campus also introduced me to a new kind of diversity. For the first time in my life, I was studying side by side with Jewish and Protestant students—and, more startling to me, with agnostics and atheists. Still, I drew great strength from my faith. By request I bunked at Ford Hall, a Catholic Campus Ministries house named for the priest who brought Catholicism to Thomas Merton, a Columbia alumnus and one of my great spiritual heroes.

The liberalism of academia, and the challenges of my professors and fellow students—as well as life in the teeming Big Apple—had an unexpected tug on my political leanings. I began reading Merton and Karl Marx. I devoured Kant, Burke, Nietzsche, and Freud, inhaled Weber, Mill, and Locke. With the cold war still in high gear, I read Lenin, Trotsky, and Mao, weighing their flawed but interesting ideas. I came to understand that liberal societies were arguably better equipped to manage dynamic change, respond more acutely to market shifts, and cope with culturally diverse populations, than the totalitarian models those men espoused.

Within Catholicism, I also became aware of exciting social justice movements. Dorothy Day, the reformer who'd founded the Catholic Worker house just downtown, was one inspiration; I used to ride the subway down to help the center distribute food and clothing to the poor. The energy and passion of the Liberation Theologists especially drew me in, inspired as they were by the terrible dictatorial crimes in Latin America. Week after week, I snapped up the newest copy of *National Catholic Reporter* for the intoxicating words of Archbishop Oscar Romero of El Salvador, where three thousand people were being killed every week by forces attached to the military ruler. The other Salvadoran religious leaders remained silent while Romero railed against the killings and the system that produced such suffering.

Watching Carter navigate these shoals impressed me. While Carter's Republican challenger, Ronald Reagan, was busy painting Central America as Communism's beachhead in the hemisphere, Carter and his team felt there was something else at play there, something fundamentally human—a struggle for freedom, a chance to separate right from wrong. He pulled the plug on aid to Nicaragua and its strongman leader, Anastasio Somoza, after members of his National Guard assassinated an ABC newsman, Bill Stewart, on live television after making him lie facedown in the middle of a road. Republicans in Congress took out a full-page ad in the *New York Times* warning of another Cuba, and Carter did try to mitigate the leftward swing of the rebels. But he couldn't in good conscience free up a single American dollar knowing there was a good chance it would go to bullets for killing innocent people. I was behind him a hundred percent.

A year later, Carter made a similarly brave moral decision after government troops in El Salvador gunned down four American nuns in the jungle, where they volunteered as teachers. Autopsies showed they'd been raped and mutilated. Carter's disgust was enormous. He'd already lost his reelection bid, and in his last days he yanked all foreign aid from them, too.

When Reagan took over the following month, the White House did a complete turnaround. UN Ambassador Jeane Kirkpatrick, the architect of Reagan's foreign policy, called the nuns "political activists [in support of the guerrillas]," scolding that "we ought to be a little more clear about this than we usually are." In a famous interview, she seemed to excuse their killers by casting them as anti-Communist vanguardists. Alexander Haig, the new secretary of state, even alleged, without presenting any evidence, that the nuns may have been killed after running a roadblock, though he never explained how that might have justified their rapes. The political extremism that crept into Washington with Ronald Reagan blinded people to human suffering and to truth.

But for me the last straw was Archbishop Romero's assassination in March 1980. Pro-government death squads stormed his chapel as he stood at the altar. "I do not believe in death without resurrection," he said at Mass that day, Holy Thursday, minutes before being cut down. "If they kill me, I will be resurrected in the Salvadoran people." His death staggered the entire Catholic world. But Washington stayed its course.

During these years I changed my party affiliation and began planning my political future in earnest. It seemed the logical thing to do for a working-class kid from Carteret. I was eager to play whatever small part I could to help the Democratic Party. Perhaps I'd be a mayor, maybe even governor—that was my wild dream, to one day be governor of New Jersey.

Yet I knew even then that I could not be a gay governor of New Jersey. This was the mid-1970s, the start of Anita Bryant's rise to prominence as a cheery campaigner against gay causes. I knew of no openly gay person who had ever faced voters. Now I know that there were two: Nancy Wechsler had been elected to the Ann Arbor City Council in 1972, and Elaine Noble, a lesbian activist, won a seat in the Massachusetts House of Representatives two years later. And that was it. In a nation where 511,000 public servants held elective office, from town sheriff to county supervisor to congressman and senator, only two were openly gay. By comparison, 3,979 African Americans had been voted into office by that time.

In 1977, Harvey Milk famously raised the bar with a colorful, high-profile campaign for the San Francisco Board of Supervisors, which he won by a landslide vote. His victory was celebrated by gay people around the nation. "I thank God," a schoolteacher wrote him, "I have lived long enough to see my kind emerge from the shadows and join the human race." What became of Milk? He was hunted down and assassinated within the year—by a fellow supervisor.

EARLY IN MY FIRST SEMESTER AT CATHOLIC, I MET A WOMAN I'LL call Laura. A girl from "back home" in Hillside, New Jersey, she was a graduate of Mount St. Mary Academy, the sister school to St. Joe's, so we shared a cultural foundation. Aside from that, though, she was everything I was not: wickedly funny, gregarious, a risk taker, clever when needed (or when she could get away with it), socially fluent, always cool, and expansively curious.

She was also beautiful, with bronze skin and a thick curly head of hair. Though she had a full dating schedule and a series of boyfriends, if I ever needed a date Laura was game. We used to tell people that we knew each other from high school, playfully backdating our friendship, and everybody believed us. It explained how inseparable we seemed, and how totally keen we were for one another's company. She was my best friend, and I adored her. Had I been straight, I surely would have fallen in love with her.

Since that dreadful kiss in the sixth grade, I had not given up on girls. Through high school I had accumulated a great number of heterosexual experiences, mostly with girls I met at the Y, and mostly in the same pool where Brian Fitzgerald and I had fooled around. I can't say I was interested in these girls sexually, but I liked the physical contact, craved it even. I found it easy to perform sexually back then. I seldom had to rely on the silent movies of my imagination that became my crutch in later life. And every conquest became a résumé piece, which I broadcast instantly and thoughtlessly to anyone who would listen.

Once, when I was fourteen, my cad routine backfired on me with nearly disastrous results. My close friendship with a slightly older African American girl turned sexual during one of our weekend sleepaway trips—a fact I never missed a chance to mention the rest of the summer. The romance lasted weeks, an eternity back then. Unfortunately, word reached her younger brother, a contemporary of mine and a really big kid. He was angry with me, and ashamed, I think, that his sister was dating a "younger white guy." Only by luck did I manage to talk him out of punishing me with his fists.

In college in Washington, Laura became my newest beard, and she seemed not to mind—maybe not even to notice that I was using her this way. We kept seeing each other even after I transferred to New York City. There I told people she was my girlfriend, that I was involved with this woman who lived hours away—which allowed me to maintain the impression that I was both single and demonstrably heterosexual. Laura and I remained "steadies" when I moved back to DC for law school. We even talked about getting engaged, but she was too emotionally wise to let that happen. I don't know if she ever suspected I was gay, but I can tell you this: in all that time, we never even kissed. "Politics is your first mistress," she said more than once. *First and only,* I thought. When I finally came out, she called and laughed, in that pitch-perfect way of hers, "To think I was almost your wife!"

6.

I SPENT THE YEARS 1979 TO 1981 AT GEORGETOWN LAW SCHOOL, yet I barely noticed I was in the nation's capital. Though I went every morning to the campus on Judiciary Square, I might as well have been in Kansas. In three years I rarely set foot in a museum; I never climbed the Washington Monument; I hardly ever crossed the great expanse of the National Mall in daylight hours. In that fall of 1979, Allen Ginsberg was the keynote speaker at the first gay pride march on Washington. "The burden of life is love," Ginsberg told the crowd of seventy thousand. "The weight is too heavy— must give." Yet his words never reached me; I carried my own burden in oblivious silence, deluged by torts and contract law.

Much is made of the fact that today's Supreme Court draws heavily upon Harvard Law graduates. Georgetown was a different sort of incubator—a practical laboratory in power and justice. The curriculum was challenging; the faculty included future White House counsel Charles Ruff, Watergate prosecutor Samuel Dash, and former congressman Robert Drinan, a Jesuit priest whose tenure on the Hill was famously ended after the Vatican ordered all priests to refrain from electoral politics. In such competitive circumstances, it was tough to make friends; now and then I'd run into my old study partner Terry McAuliffe, the future DNC chairman who'd followed me from Catholic to law school, but otherwise I spent most of my time alone with my books.

My interest in law always had more to do with government than with the courtroom, with social justice more than corporate relations. The summer after my first year, when other students undertook internships at white-shoe law firms, I enrolled for coursework at the London School of Economics through a program with Notre Dame Law School. I spent my classroom hours that summer studying currency policy—these were the early days of the emerging Common Market and European Union, when currency was an exciting subject—and spent what little personal currency I had on curry and rice and cheap beer. The following summer, when most future lawyers sign up for clerkships with judges, I landed a plum position with the Department of Justice, soaking up everything I could learn about federal law enforcement. (When the FBI visited my old neighborhood to conduct their standard background search, they asked my dad if I ever smoked pot. "No," he answered correctly. "I raised him like my father raised me. A little tough love never hurt anybody.")

Back at St. Joe's, I'd absorbed the notion that every citizen has an obligation to perform "social action." As a senior, twice a week I pedaled my bike over to nearby St. Francis Cathedral grammar school, where the kids came from much more challenging backgrounds than I, to teach history and help seniors in the school's office of social concerns. Now, at Georgetown, I volunteered to teach "street law," a civics-style introduction to law, human rights, and democracy for students at Gonzaga College High, a Jesuit secondary school in the heart of Washington. The city's population is 60 percent African American, and for too many generations it has existed in a disgraceful state of poverty, squalor, and hopelessness. Congress, which supervises the district's affairs, should be ashamed of itself. But at Gonzaga, I also saw the city's future in the kids there, who were quick and bright; if given half a chance, I knew that their potential might one day outstrip their economic limitations.

My parents had made sacrifices to underwrite their kids' college educations, and I picked up where they left off, compressing my undergraduate requirements into three years by taking some credits at Rutgers and Middlesex County College and spending what I had left on my first year of law school. That first year I saved money by attending Georgetown at night, when credits were cheaper; after that I squeaked by on student loans and earnings from part-time jobs at the Department of Justice and the law school library.

In the midst of all this, too, I managed to find time to pursue my new love: politics. In the summer of 1980, I raced back to Carteret to volunteer for Congressman Bernie Dwyer, my hometown representative and a Democrat. Dwyer was part of the great tradition of Irish Americans in New Jersey politics. Governors Hughes, Cahill, Byrne—I was beginning to identify with all of them, the way I once prized the examples of Fathers Lyons, Dolan, and Murphy as powerful forces of good from my own clan. I saw a lot of myself in Bernie Dwyer, I thought then: we were both Irish and Catholic, both good on technical matters, both cranked up by the ins and outs of retail politics— the door-to-door, barbecue-to-barbecue, synagogue-to-church-basement kind of campaign that really teaches you what people want from their representatives and need from their government.

But Dwyer had something I didn't have: a wife and children. Bernie Dwyer was like his voters. You could see how they mirrored one another, identified with one another, and how significant this bond was. Cultural identities and affinities were just as strong in New Jersey in the late 1970s as they were in the 1950s. When the young Irish Catholic electorate in Dwyer's congressional district pulled the lever for him, they were embracing one of their own.

It may seem wrong to call this "identity politics," a phrase that's been adopted by academics to describe the rise of challenging political movements like feminism, gay liberation, and civil rights in the years after World War II. As anyone from New Jersey will tell you, though, "identity politics" is exactly what's practiced there. Ours is the most diverse state in the country. Indians, Egyptians, Portuguese, Italians, and Polish have all staked out particular neighborhoods as their own, as my parents' generation of Irish Americans did before them. From childhood, I know, I latched onto my parents' working-class Irish-Catholic-American identity so strongly that I couldn't see myself as anything else. It was a birthright I treasured, an idea in which I found value and comfort and a sense of belonging.

And yet, deep down, I knew that this totemic American ideal excluded me. Even in these years, questions about the nature of identity consumed me. The philosopher Charles Taylor uses the term *identity* to describe the merging of our inner voice with a capacity for authenticity; our quest to establish our unique identity, he says, represents our struggle to be true to ourselves. By this definition, I had no identity whatsoever. In fact, I was going about the enterprise entirely backward. I'd already settled on a way of being: a life in politics in the tight-knit community of my inheritance. It was my *self* that was the variable.

And so I set about trying to find a self that seemed authentic.

AFTER SITTING THE BAR EXAM IN 1981, I DASHED TO HARVARD TO collect a master's degree at the famed Graduate School of Education, which has produced countless college presidents and education secretaries and commissioners. Harvard's Kennedy School of Government might have been a better fit for me, but it was a two-year program and I simply couldn't afford it, and I did have a genuine interest in early childhood education. I never felt luckier than during the time I spent at Harvard, walking those hallowed halls and studying some of the freshest thinking anywhere on education policy, from advances in pre-kindergarten curriculum to new theories of early literacy. All of today's mainstream emphasis on testing and benchmarks was being developed back then, at Harvard's "E-School."

When Laura visited, we always had a blast. We'd go to hear jazz in Cambridge clubs, haunt bars on the Boston Common, walk the trail where Paul Revere sounded his warnings. Once we even went away for the weekend to Montreal and Quebec City, to tour some of the shrines my grandparents had visited. But no magic ever kindled between us.

As graduation approached, I began thinking more seriously about where I wanted to be when I finally entered the workforce. At the top of my list was the Middlesex County Prosecutor's Office back home. For one thing, it was as close to being a cop as a guy like me could safely get. Unlike all those men in my grandfather's generation, I'd never allowed my nose to be flattened in a boxing match, and I couldn't see myself mixing it up physically with the criminal element. But I was dead curious about what went on in criminal court. And I knew even then that my future political career would benefit from a few years in the trenches of law enforcement.

I sent a letter to the Middlesex County prosecutor outlining my credentials and asking for a job fighting crime. After seven years of higher education, I'd thought I'd amassed a pretty impressive resume: Catholic University, Columbia College, Georgetown, Notre Dame Law School at the London School of Economics, and Harvard, plus stints at the Justice Department. Yet I waited, and waited, and no reply came.

This was perplexing. When I'd circulated my résumé in the private sector I was flooded with invitations for interviews, follow-up phone calls, even offers for jobs paying $42,000 a year, which sounded like a fortune to me. Yet not even a form letter came from the county office. I sent letter after letter after letter, but never got a single response.

Over the phone from Boston one day, I happened to share my frustration with my parents. That weekend my father spotted a local politician, a family friend, at Sunday Mass with his wife. Dad asked him to "help Jimmy out." Within thirty-six hours I had an appointment to see the county prosecutor, Richard Rebeck. It was my first taste of politics New Jersey style, my first glimpse of just how well-oiled, tribal, and dependent on patronage the machine was. That local politician is a scrupulously honest fellow, and his gesture was nothing more than a simple favor for a friend. Still, in retrospect, my introduction to the slippery slope of New Jersey politics—a culture where the system of favors and friendship had a life of its own—had begun.

I flew back home with a surprising case of nervous anxiety to meet with Rebeck. He was a quiet and decent man with a reputation for directness, and he ran a competent operation—a lot to say for an underfunded, meagerly staffed office that prosecuted thousands of cases a year, a large number of them violent. I don't remember what Rebeck wanted to know about me, other than the fact that I was game. He hired me on the spot, for $21,000, half what the private law firms had offered.

I flew back to Boston to gather my diploma and finally leave academe behind me.

I WAS RAISED IN A FAMILY THAT EMBRACED HARD WORK AS THE staff of life. Every morning of my childhood I watched my father's daily rituals—rising before dawn, shaving and performing his ablutions, pulling on a starched white shirt, tie, and suit, and heading off to conquer the world. My mom was equally formal about her commitments to work and school, and after my sisters and I were older, she rejoined both. In some ways, her drive was even greater than my dad's.

Too much has been made of the so-called Protestant work ethic. I never saw men and women more tireless, more dedicated to their labors, than my parents and their Irish Catholic friends. In just one generation, they took their community from poverty to the middle class while educating their children for higher rungs, in Carteret and in countless similar parishes across the country. And they did this without greed, always giving back when they could. In service to their family and their community, my dad and mom worked dawn till dusk—still do—without complaint. Catholics of their time haven't yet been given their due.

I loved emulating them. And I loved my new work in the county prosecutor's office. I loved the feeling that I was doing good for my community, solving problems and making the world a better place. I may have been a bit idealistic, but nothing I saw at the prosecutor's office undermined my faith in American justice.

Probably because of my work in early childhood education, Rebeck sent me to work in the Juvenile Division. "Kiddie Court," as we called it, takes the juice out of a lot of young lawyers. The division was run by one of the most intuitive people I've ever met, a barely reconstructed child of the sixties named Caroline Meuly. I liked her immediately; she, on the other hand, wasn't as quick to take me in. For one thing, Caroline spotted my insecurity at once, though I thought I'd hidden it pretty well. She also saw something much more private—not my sexual identity, but my ambition, especially my naked intention to use this job as a stepping stone to political office. To her, I seemed to be "slumming" in the job. She took me down a notch or two right away. "I'm gonna call you *MOPFE*," she announced with the disarming smile that was her trademark. "Stands for *Man of the People— Former Elitist.*"

I came to love her for saying that. In a line, she unmasked my many poses. I was the geeky kid from Carteret pretending to be a Harvard Ole Boy pretending to be a streetwise lawman. She caught me every time I tried to shoehorn some Harvardism into my speech, and she mocked me for it mercilessly. Along the way she used a surgeon's skill to remove any last bit of Republican shrapnel in my system, for which I am eternally grateful. Every day, she challenged me to not run away from who I was, to drop the conservative pose I'd hidden behind in my youth and follow my truer political instincts.

Caroline was a huge influence on my sense of myself. What she couldn't touch, of course, couldn't even have known about, was how far away from integration I already was. Part of me thought, *If I can convince people I'm straight, why not affluent?* She beat back the second impulse. The first went unchallenged.

Caroline was a great teacher. When I arrived in her employ, I knew I was a good speaker, a fast study, well organized, a hard worker. But that didn't make me a prosecutor—those skills I had to learn. In one of the first cases I took to trial, I presented what I thought was a water-tight argument for conviction. Just before I was about to rest, Judge Joseph Sadofski called from his bench. "Mr. McGreevey, may I remind you that now would be a good time to introduce any evidence you might have?"

With coaching, over time, I started winning my cases.

But winning isn't always the goal. Kiddie Court demanded a copious supply of compassion. Most of the cases that came across my desk involved kids charged with selling drugs. It only took me a few weeks to realize these were among the smartest kids in their neighborhoods. Without any formal education, and with precious few role models, they had figured out capitalism and the market economy, often building vast enterprises—an amazing feat given their ages. These were kids who took risks, who not only accumulated capital but reinvested it in distribution, even manufacturing. Don't misunderstand: I loathe drugs. But it seemed to me that there was a spark of real potential mixed in with the delinquency, something to encourage alongside something to punish.

Unfortunately, the system wasn't good at doing both things at once. So time after time I'd process these boys and girls, negotiating short juvenile sentences or restrictive probation for them, only to see them back in the holding cell a few months later. Bright as they were, they hadn't learned the simplest lesson: to paraphrase Einstein, you can't do today what you did yesterday and expect different results. I hated pressing for long sentences on these cases, because everybody knew this would expose them to the worst elements of their generation. But too many kids went down that road.

I can't be sure my time at Kiddie Court changed anyone's life. I've come to recognize that we can't break that cycle without doing something about the homes and communities these kids are being returned to—hopeless landscapes that prevent even the smartest young kids from seeing promise on the horizon.

After a few months, my supervisors granted my request for transfer to the criminal prosecution division on the ninth floor. *Now* things were getting fascinating. These were the dark days before specialized sex crimes divisions, so I got a number of rape cases to try. Having had a friend who had suffered the emotional trauma of sexual abuse, I did everything I could to alleviate any increased burden on the victims, meeting with them and trying to offer not just legal representation but emotional support as well. It was rewarding work. But one case challenged the way I thought about sexual assault cases.

The complainant in the case was white, the defendant black. They had been close friends through high school. After a graduation party, they had had a sexual encounter of a disputed nature in a car parked outside a local nightclub. At the time the woman had not called the encounter an assault. Only later, after her father discovered the encounter, had she filed charges.

It was a difficult proceeding. The woman was noticeably conflicted about the charge, but she appeared to be motivated by her family's anger toward the young man. Ethically, I was concerned about the State's case, and I went back to the woman to try to ascertain her true feelings. But she assured me that she wanted to prosecute.

I was duty bound to accept her at her word. The jury, however, wasn't, and they returned a verdict of not guilty. In all my time in the prosecutor's office, I saw, almost categorically, the effectiveness of the justice system. This is one of the rare cases—certainly the only one I prosecuted—where I believe that the failure of the State's case led to a just verdict.

* * *

WHEN I FIRST GOT BACK TO CENTRAL JERSEY—AFTER A FEW WEEKS back in my old bedroom in Carteret—I rented an apartment fifteen minutes away in Woodbridge, the state's fifth-largest city, and joined the Catholic Lawyers Guild, eager to get acquainted with the area's legal community. Only a few years old, the Guild was the brainchild of Bishop Theodore McCarrick, who had been brought in from New York to found the new Metuchen Diocese after it split off from the burgeoning Diocese of Trenton in 1981.

An intelligent and well-read gentleman who understood the importance of the Church's role in the modern world, McCarrick took our young diocese by storm. I loved hearing his homilies at the new cathedral, and his speeches before our Guild, pushing us to address socially progressive issues like poverty and war. No one who knew him then was surprised that he later became the cardinal leading the powerful Washington, DC, archdiocese— or that he eventually became one of the voices of reform and compassion who helped the Church through the sexual abuse scandals of 2002.

Before long, the Guild's presidency fell vacant—and I saw my first opportunity to run for office. As a Catholic group, however, the Guild was hardly a democracy. The choice of a new president would be heavily influenced by McCarrick himself. I had no idea how to lobby him—and even though he was relatively young, and Metuchen was not especially important in the national Church, it was still difficult to get him on the phone or pin him down for a meeting. So I began to make it my business to know the priests who worked for him in the chancery. It took a while, but I figured out which priest was advising the bishop on this matter; graciously, he allowed me to make a case for my leadership directly to him. My plank, if you could call it that, was my interest in the financial plight of seniors in our community, who were pinched between skyrocketing nursing costs and a Medicaid system that subsidized the most expensive care in nursing homes but refused to bankroll home health care, a cheaper alternative preferred by many. The system kept people sicker and poorer—which were hardly Catholic principles.

Ultimately, though, I developed a good relationship with McCarrick, and he looked kindly upon my bid for the leadership role. Some called this "the work of the Holy Spirit"—a little too cynically, I thought. Sure, I campaigned. But I was excited about the job, and I went on to serve aggressively for a number of years.

A very attractive, witty, and talented lawyer named Deborah Venezia was named secretary-treasurer, thanks to her own efforts at the chancery, and together we organized professional gatherings, social mixers, discussion breakfasts, and the like. We also organized a legal clinic for senior citizens, helping them with health directives, wills and estates, reverse mortgages, and any other services they needed pro bono.

And for a brief time Deborah and I dated, if halfheartedly. Our relationship came to an ignoble end one day when a mutual friend told me that Deborah had taken up with a vet. "Of what war?" I asked. Turns out he was a veterinarian. She made a wise choice: Deborah and Barry Adler, a well-loved Woodbridge vet, are married to this day.

Besides, Laura and I were still "steadies." She was living in New York City at this time, working as a page for NBC and *Saturday Night Live*, a perfect place for a woman of her urbanity and wit. From time to time, she'd sneak me into the cast parties after the broadcasts. Way in the back of the crowded snapshots from that historic time in the show's long run, I'm sure we can be seen dancing together. Those were crazy affairs, with earsplitting music and all the excesses of the early 1980s. When someone offered us a snort of cocaine, piled on the tip of a tiny spoon, we declined.

"I put people in jail for that during the week," I said, none too politely.

Laura was mortified.

7.

WITH PERMISSION FROM MY SUPERIORS IN THE PROSECUTOR'S office, I started to attend overtly political local events. These were lavish affairs, and to me they were thrilling. In those days, the most powerful gatherings were held twice yearly for local Middlesex County officials and businessmen. I decided to go to the supper after work one night that fall, figuring I could buy a ticket at the door. But when I arrived at the fancy Pines Manor catering hall in Edison, it seemed I was wrong. Everybody there had come with their tickets in hand—no doubt doled out by county chairmen as demonstrations of their affection, or else by large contractors and vendors with proposals they hoped to advance.

I wasn't about to slink back into my car, revealing that I'd misunderstood the rules. So when I saw a large unruly party push through the door with a blizzard of tickets, I crowded in behind them.

Looking around inside was eye-opening. The ballroom was packed with hundreds of people, almost all of them Democrats—in my county the Republican Party was considered an extremist group. The attendees were buzzing around like yellow jackets at a county fair, clustering at one table, then racing off to another corner of the room in a swarm of new allegiances.

At the front of the hall was a large, three-tiered dais. On the lowest level sat the party apparatchiks; on the second level the municipal party chairmen; above them, closest to heaven, sat our elected officials. Even among them a surprising hierarchy was apparent: the most powerful and sought-after officials weren't state senators or even congressmen, but local mayors.

For one thing, the mayors outnumbered everybody else—our mid-sized county was home to twenty-five mayors ruling over villages ranging in size from tiny Helmetta (population 1,961) to bustling Woodbridge (100,421). This proliferation of sovereignties made for a large-scale redundancy of services in the area. Every mayor has his or her own road crews, code inspectors, trash haulers, and the like. And their local power came from their total control over municipal contracts—from the age-old practice of patronage.

New Jersey has taken many hits as the patronage capital of the country. Patronage is the coin of the realm. I can't defend it, as I've said. But at the time I was convinced it wasn't all bad. It certainly breaks no laws, and it can have some social benefits. Even Supreme Court Justice Antonin Scalia has extolled patronage as a tool for promoting political stability and easing the integration of marginalized groups. I believed it could do that, and more. The great old mayors of New Jersey still run their domains like magnanimous despots, taking care of the citizens, keeping the trains running on time, and maintaining cool heads through careful appointments.

But when the system goes bad, it can be disastrous. Courts in the state are crowded with politicians charged with bid rigging, bribe taking, and sundry crimes against the public trust. In fact, New Jersey leads the nation for mayors in prison.

Even more powerful than mayors are the party chairmen, or "bosses," as the media has dubbed the top officials from either party in each of New Jersey's twenty-one counties. Our boss system is a throwback to an earlier time in America, when the parties doled out jobs, housing, and food to immigrants in exchange for votes. New York City's notoriously corrupt Tammany Hall in the nineteenth century and Chicago's Daley machine in the mid-twentieth were perhaps the best-known examples of this. No one in New Jersey is handing out food in exchange for votes anymore, but the bosses still hold tremendous sway over an election's outcome.

Perhaps their most obvious source of influence comes from the bosses' control of what's known as the "party line"—that is, the line of candidates appearing in the first column on the ballot during a party primary. Nominally, of course, New Jersey holds open primaries, in which each candidate appears on the ballot and has an equal chance of being selected by the voters. But the party bosses have long realized that they could heavily weight the outcome of a primary by giving their favored candidates pride of place in a column at the far left of the ballot, bestowing on them the party's imprimatur while maintaining the illusion of an "open" race. The party line almost always wins.

Another source of power stems from the state campaign finance laws. These laws allow bosses to raise and spend fourteen times the amount of money the candidates can, cementing their Svengali-like powers. For many candidates, financial support from the bosses is essential, and most of them are all too willing to cut backroom deals in exchange for it.

This practice makes bosses the most powerful players in statewide politics. They pull strings inside town halls, the State House, the governor's mansion, and Congress. The personal payoffs can be extreme. Many bosses become multimillionaires, thanks to lucrative contracts they negotiate with officials they've helped elect. Best of all, they never have to face voters themselves. Some of them choose to hold elected office, but most of the time they're ordinary citizens tapped by their countywide party machine as chairmen—typically after they've already wrestled total control over the party. Sometimes that control lasts for many generations, and being boss becomes the family business.

This was the circus of New Jersey politics, and I'd just stumbled into the center ring.

"YOU NO GOOD SON-OF-A-BITCH!"

Looking across the banquet hall, my eye fell on a red-haired woman of forty or so, poured into a dress that put her feminine assets on display. Her makeup was running, and every time she gesticulated she threatened to dislodge the rhinestone tiara that teetered atop her elaborate coiffure.

"Who's that?" I asked a man standing next to me. He told me her name, and I recognized it from the local papers. She was a powerhouse in local Democratic politics. On the receiving end of her outburst was Bernie Dwyer, who had won his congressional campaign and was heading to Washington. Tonight he was the man of the hour.

From across the room we heard Dwyer's voice: "This is not going to happen!"

"What's she upset about, do you know?" I asked my interpreter.

"She thought Dwyer made a promise to her and she came to collect. Obviously he sees it differently."

Now the woman was growling at Dwyer. Before long she was gasping for air and sobbing. With a final shriek, she ran behind the dais to hide while she gained composure. Unfortunately, the dais's wooden structure worked like a drum, amplifying her sobs even louder. "I'm going to get him," she blubbered. "He'll never be reelected!"

"What kind of promise did he make her?" I asked, thinking it must have been monumental.

"He was going to make her director of the district office," the guy said.

Director of the district office? That was the craziest thing I'd ever heard. Who on earth would throw that kind of public tantrum at a congressman for a miserable little job like that?

Yet I was the only one in the room who seemed surprised. They all knew local politics was a cutthroat business, a place for people with ambition in their veins, not altar-boy types with squishy ideas about doing good.

I WENT TO DINNER AFTER DINNER, STUDYING THE LOCALS LIKE AN anthropologist. I slowly realized that there weren't many spectators like me present, but I never felt excluded. Not that I was officially welcomed, either. To be honest, I crashed those suppers for years. And slowly but surely it paid off, as I started making sense of the dynamics there: who was up and coming and who was on the way out, who was in charge and who was irrelevant.

My big break came at another one of those circuit stops, the George J. Otlowski League Dinner in Perth Amboy. Otlowski was Perth Amboy's mayor as well as an elected member of the New Jersey General Assembly, the lower house of the state legislature. That's another thing about New Jersey: as a state with a part-time legislature, we have a high proportion of legislators who hold other jobs in the public sphere, and power tends to concentrate in a very small number of hands. It's a small state, and it's a small political class. We all know each other's business—which can be a good thing or a bad thing, depending on your perspective.

One thing it certainly creates is the potential for conflicts of interest. The state constitution also allows legislators to hold down private-sector jobs—so, for example, an assemblyman on the finance committee might also be a bank vice president. The state has very few laws regulating conflicts of interest. For the most part, lawmakers who stand to profit from a bill can still vote on it; all they have to do is write a note to the chamber secretary assuring him they are unbiased. You can see how tempting it would be for some to behave in a purely self-interested way.

Not Otlowski. As chairman of the Assembly's Health and Human Services Committee, Otlowski was known for his forward-thinking and almost activist-like approach to public health—proof that the system sometimes works.

His League Dinner was held at a banquet hall named Seven Arches, the very model of a New Jersey political venue until it burned to the ground in 1988. The walls of Seven Arches were draped in heavy red velvet, the furniture covered in plastic. Italianate statuary, complete with spilling fountains, was scattered about on white marble bases. Absolutely everybody was there.

The most prominent guest was Alan Karcher, the speaker of the assembly, who also ran his late father's law firm. From the newspapers, I'd gotten a good impression of Karcher as a liberal Democrat in tune with the average guy. That night, asked to make a few remarks, he proved as urbane and intelligent as his reputation suggested. Karcher was a kind of Renaissance man, able to drop meaningful references to linguistics, the French Revolution, classical music, and a host of other subjects in the course of a simple toast.

Afterward, I approached him with congratulations. Within a few minutes, he asked if I'd be interested in working for him. I was taken off guard: being offered a job in the Assembly Majority Office was like being handed a miracle from heaven. The Majority Office was the locus of power for the majority party, the perch from which it enacted its legislative platforms and lent support to all party lawmakers. I had no idea what caused Karcher to select me right there; perhaps a little shy about my abilities, I responded coolly. "I'd be happy to talk about it further," I told him.

A week later, I lit a candle at Our Lady of Victories, then knocked on the door of Karcher's law office on Main Street in Sayreville. The place was crowded with books, histories and biographies and classical literature mingling with the law texts. Karcher greeted me warmly, explaining that the office had belonged to his father, an assemblyman before him. As he spoke, I stole a glance around the dusty room. On the wall behind Karcher was a linear chart of some sort. I could make out only a few titles, but what I saw suggested it was a kind of master plan for his own career in politics. On the left were his political attainments to date. On the right were his future goals.

Glimpsing the personal aspirations of a powerhouse like Karcher was tantalizing to me. I was desperate to read every word. As he spoke, I struggled to make out the smaller handwriting on the chart, careful not to let him see what I was up to. I leaned forward in my chair. I put an elbow on his desk. Whenever he looked to the ceiling or out the window for emphasis, I stole another peek. When the words finally came into focus, I was amazed: Alan Karcher was planning on becoming governor of New Jersey.

At the end of our meeting, Karcher repeated his offer to me; this time I accepted, shaking his hand like a *Jeopardy* winner. Two weeks later, I cleaned out my desk at the Prosecutor's office, gave Caroline Meuly a big hug goodbye, and left to claim the job I had earned just by being in the right place at the right time. Sometimes that's how things happen in politics. I was on the bottom rung of a very tall ladder, and I had all the unbridled confidence of an upstart. I remember the first time I walked to the entrance of the State House in Trenton, the second oldest in continual use in the nation. I looked at the parking space marked "Reserved—Office of the Governor," and I allowed myself to imagine one day leaving my car in that spot. For some reason, that's the job I set my sights on. And as long as I kept my secret, I thought I had a shot.

I can't say I loved everything about the Assembly Majority Office, where my job was to provide political direction to several legislative committees, including Health and Human Services and Law and Public Safety. For one thing, almost as soon as I arrived in Trenton, I felt an immediate antagonism toward me. Karcher's office was staffed entirely by political appointees he'd inherited from his predecessor, not civil service workers; they were resistant to his ideas, which were further to the left than they were accustomed to, and reacted with stubbornness and suspicion. Being one of Karcher's men put me at a disadvantage. And the fact that I came from Woodbridge, in his legislative district, made me seem even more beholden to him.

Still, I was over the top with excitement about being in government. Every morning, as I walked into the State House I stopped and read the plaques and the inscriptions on the portraits of all the governors. And one day I was stunned to come across a portrait of a figure in a beautiful eighteenth-century gown, complete with brocaded corset and a delicately laced fan.

His name was Edward Hyde.

New Jersey's first royal governor, it turns out, was a cross-dresser. Appointed by Queen Anne during colonial times, Viscount Cornbury, as he was also known, served as governor of New York and New Jersey despite being, as we now know to say, transgendered. It's unclear how he managed to survive, but a letter from Lewis Morris, the political opponent who ultimately did in Hyde's career, suggests how he was looked upon by his contemporaries: as "a wretch who by the whole conduct of his life has evidenced he has no regard for honor or virtue."

AS A LEGISLATIVE AIDE, I FOUND MY FIRST MONTHS ON THE JOB exhilarating. I was assigned to be staff liaison to the Health and Human Services Committee, answering indirectly to Assemblyman Otlowski. I read everything I could find on public health, including briefings created by the National Conference of State Legislatures, the National Governors Association, and assorted advocacy groups.

With Otlowski's direction and Karcher's support, I helped spearhead new bills on Medicaid and nursing homes, advocacy work I had begun at the Catholic Lawyers Guild. Families who placed a loved one in a nursing home often depleted their savings before qualifying for Medicaid, but most homes considered Medicaid only partial payment; if the family couldn't make supplemental payments, the patient could be evicted even if the family hadn't a dime left in the bank. We changed that. Today, unless a nursing home is already overburdened with Medicaid beds, no patient can be discharged simply because he or she has run out of money. We were pretty far ahead of other states in this regard.

At the Majority Office I also learned a lot about not offending people with my political ambitions—mostly by making clumsy mistakes, which is how most good lessons are learned. I can't imagine what I was thinking the day I wrote the local Chamber of Commerce leadership (and probably a dozen other groups) on Assembly stationery introducing myself and offering to visit their group and describe the workings of Trenton and the legislative process. It was pure hubris, with a side of naïveté: I was just a lowly staffer looking for a little self-promotion, offering to explain state politics as if I'd invented the concept.

Somehow a copy of one of my letters got back to Dick Coffee, the executive director of the Assembly Majority Office, who saw the opportunity for a wicked practical joke. After drawing up a fake letter back to my original addressees, he made a carbon copy and sent it to me. "We are sorry you were bothered by Mr. McGreevey's letter to your groups," it said. "This was immature and inappropriate. Rest assured that with some workplace training and in-depth psychological counseling, he will learn his rightful place and once again become a productive member of our staff."

Coffee was obviously goofing with me, but the prank made me mad anyway. I was just trying to open a dialogue with the community about what the Democratic Party was up to—the more knowledge, I thought, the better our chances to stay in power. What really bothered me, though, was the implication that I needed therapy. I guess it cut a little too close to home.

OF ALL THE POLITICAL EVENTS ON THE NEW JERSEY CALENDAR, two are so important that no political aspirant would dare miss them. The first is the New Jersey State League of Municipalities conference in Atlantic City, a three-day affair that takes place every November. Nearly twenty thousand elected and appointed officials attend the festivities, making it the country's largest gathering of public officials. The agenda is packed with panels on storm-water regulations, economic development, and the like, but in my experience no one pays a bit of attention to them. It's really just a huge frat party.

I attended my first League conference in 1983, shortly after joining the Assembly Majority Office. I hitched a ride with my friend Chris Guidette, a former reporter who ran public relations for Karcher. Hard to imagine, but I'd never been to Atlantic City before. My family didn't consider it a "wholesome" place, and not without reason; even into the 1980s its reputation was less than sterling. Still, I decided to attend at the last minute, hopping in Chris's car in Trenton at about two in the morning for the long trip south. Neither of us had a hotel reservation, much less a change of clothes. We drove through the night in torrential rain, passing through the Pine Barrens, the largest tract of wilderness between Boston and Virginia—a parcel of 1.1 million acres of quiet forest in the middle of one of America's most populous states. I'd never seen the Barrens before. I remember being struck by how desolate they seemed, how out of place and still. I felt a shiver of loneliness as I stared out the window, my feet up on the dashboard, my head against the window.

The last few miles of the trip were lit by the casinos' bright lights, which rose over the highway like Vegas in the desert. We sped through the tired, depressed city and finally pulled up in front of the casinos, magnificent and inviting, in time to watch the sun rise over the Atlantic Ocean.

Inside the Conference Hall, literally thousands of political operatives were congregated outside the seminars and hospitality rooms. I knew nobody. Chris and I hung out for a while, walking through the garishly decorated hotel lobbies and checking out a couple of presentations. But soon he attached himself to some other friends, leaving me to negotiate the event alone. With no hotel room to return to, I had nothing to do but wander through the ballrooms, picking at platters of food and striking up occasional conversations. But people weren't in the mood to talk policy.

As the day progressed, it slowly dawned on me that this event was, at base, a pickup function. Many of the attendees appeared to be politically involved, as I was, or ambitious young professionals from one of the many powerful state trade associations, lobbying groups, or industries, there to help oil the gears of government in their favor. But sex and politics are inexorably intermingled in New Jersey public life, and that weekend in Atlantic City is an annual tribute to the fact. All around me, pickups were taking place in plain sight. People would be talking about this event for weeks to come—who got lucky, who came up short, and what everybody else thought about it.

This was a terrible place not to be straight. It was like being back at one of those parties in high school again, alone with my secret in a crowded room, unable to function. And so, just like I had in high school, I left the party and started walking.

As I paced the boardwalk, I fell into a deep funk. Anxiety growled in my stomach. It was evening now, and the casino lights were shining again, reflecting against the waves. I gave myself a stern talking-to. *It'll all be fine,* I told myself, *you'll find a way to navigate it all, just as you always have.* Still, I couldn't bring myself to turn around and head back to the convention.

Instead, I walked into an Irish pub on St. James Place. The bartender was a woman named Cathy Burke (we have since remained friends), and as I sat at her bar drinking pints of Guinness, I realized I'd finally found someone in Atlantic City I could have a conversation with. She must have sensed I was upset because she let me chew her ear off for hours, talking politics, poetry, and religion. She even offered to let me nap in a room upstairs, but I chose to wait out the night on a barstool. I was stockpiling my will, preparing myself to head back.

When I finally dragged myself from the stool, a brilliant sun had risen. I couldn't see a thing. The glare gave me a feeling of epiphany, and I walked back to the Convention Center sensing that I had somehow grown tougher. Now, at least, I knew the rules I was expected to follow. I knew I would have to lie for the rest of my life—and I knew I was capable of it. The knowledge gave me a terrible feeling of power.

BY EARLY 1985, TWO YEARS INTO MY JOB, I WAS BECOMING DISILLU-sioned with how difficult it was to get anything done in the legislature. Most lawmakers were under intense pressure to bring money back to their districts, and as such they paid little attention to statewide or strictly policy-centered issues. Because of this lack of interest in affairs of state, true legislative power resides in the hands of the governor, giving New Jersey by far the strongest governorship in the nation. The state's constitution, adopted in 1947, gives governors power to appoint the secretary of state, the state treasurer, and the state attorney general, as well as power over five hundred statewide offices, including each of the county prosecutors, every judge, agency head, and cabinet member. Governors have veto power over budget line items, and can issue decrees by executive order, a privilege shared by only nine other governors.

Politically, New Jersey is a swing state, one with a long centrist tradition. At this time Tom Kean, a moderate Republican, was governor, and he was poised for an easy reelection. The Democratic Party, meanwhile, was fractured and fighting itself bitterly, unable to unite behind a consensus candidate to take him on. It looked like the Assembly was going to remain stymied.

In February, I got an unexpected call from Chris Dietz, chairman of the state Parole Board, offering kind words for my work. The call came as a surprise: as staff to the Assembly Oversight Committee, we'd recently conducted a thorough review of the Parole Board recommending a series of specific improvements. The committee's judgment may have seemed partisan, coming as it did just before election time, but we had little choice in the timing or the content of our report. In truth it was an extremely balanced report, so much so that it probably disappointed some Democrats. But it did highlight some areas where improvements were desperately needed, including one proposal considered radical at the time—a recommendation that victims be allowed to testify before board hearings.

Dietz thanked me for our report, then asked if I would consider moving over to the Board as executive director. For a twenty-eight-year-old, it was an exciting opportunity: I'd be taking the helm of an important state agency, directing a budget of more than $7 million. I wanted to accept immediately. But first I went to Alan Karcher, my mentor, and asked his blessing, which he gave enthusiastically.

For the next two years, I got to lay the groundwork that allowed New Jersey to become one of the first states in the country to consider a victim's ongoing traumas when determining whether to parole a convict—a right the legislature ultimately enshrined into law. What we proved wasn't surprising—victims of crime find comfort and relief when they are included in the decision-making process. In an op-ed of mine that appeared in the *New York Times*, I wrote that the system in all other states "pampers the accused while humiliating the accuser." We found a way to do just the opposite.

I was proud of this accomplishment and excited by the national attention that came with it. *Good Morning America* invited me to debate the issue with famed criminal defense attorney Gerry Spence. It was heady stuff.

But then, just as I was going on live television, a terrifying thought occurred to me: as soon as my image was beamed across the country, it might well land on the TV screens of dozens of men who would recognize me from anonymous sexual encounters—any one of whom could surely stop my career cold if he revealed what he knew about me. I carried on, but I was quaking the whole time.

IN THE MONTHS OF INTROSPECTION AND COUNSELING I'VE HAD since leaving the public sphere, I have learned that all my life I have suffered three distinct shames. The first is something that the psychotherapist Pia Mellody calls "carried shame," an inherited burden from which everyone suffers in one form or another—like the concept of original sin, I suppose. In my case, what I was carrying was the burden of society's and the Church's disapprobation of my core self. Gay people are especially susceptible to this, Mellody says, but it's extremely common among people in general. "You are less than," she explained to me. "You grow up convinced you are not worth anything because of this core truth about yourself."

Carried shame is a bad thing in itself, but Mellody believes that in some people it can create an acute childhood trauma. The symptoms of this are many, including emotional immaturity, an inability to achieve intimacy, a dogged feeling of unworthiness, and a spiritual freefall—descriptions of my life to a tee.

My second shame concerned inauthenticity—a term that describes what happens when you're dishonest about who you really are. In theory or practice, nobody was more duplicitous than I. Through most of my adult life there was not one person who knew who I really was, and the longer I went without amending that dishonesty, the more ashamed I felt.

A third shame, for me, concerned my behavior. From the time in high school when I made up my mind to behave in public as though I were straight, I nonetheless carried on sexually with men. *Scores* of men.

After Brian Fitzgerald at the YMCA pool, the rest were exclusively furtive encounters, mostly in seedy bookstores or public parks. Admitting this now provokes that shame all over again, but I know that I must disclose it as part of my healing journey—to free myself from the compulsion that caused me to behave that way in the first place. I was promiscuous and sexually active in ways I consider immoral and ugly. And I justified this by telling myself that I had no other choice, that my sexual urges were irrepressible, but as long as I remained in the closet I couldn't enjoy an honest and beautiful love with a man—the kind of love that goes on vacations, outfits a home together, sits side by side in church; the kind of love that can lead to a broken heart, like the one that killed my grandfather. I craved love, but sex was all that was available to me.

I should add that I was plagued by this third shame even when I *wasn't* having sex, because in my heart I wanted it so badly I might as well have been guilty. When I first left home for Catholic University, for example, I attached myself to an upperclassman I'll call Liam as zealously as I'd befriended Sean Hughes in high school. Like Sean, Liam was handsome, rugged, Irish American, and straight—with a gorgeous girlfriend to boot. The fact that he had a girlfriend made a difference; otherwise, I don't think I could have expressed my affection for him as openly as I did. Not that I ever said a word about it, of course. Instead I merely followed him everywhere. In my wallet I secretly carried a picture of him, broad and angular in a cable-knit sweater. I found excuses to study in his room, in the same dorm as mine. And one early spring evening I pretended to fall asleep on his bed. Shrugging, he tucked in next to me, and we lay side by side through the night, like brothers. My arm fell over his shoulder.

I was way too far in the closet to imagine this friendship turning to sex, even if Liam hadn't been straight. It was thrilling just to have the physical proximity, a thrill that felt a lot like love. To this day I remember what the sun looked like the next morning, and can still hear the sound of the dried leaves beneath my heels as I bounded down the steps of Gibbons Hall, filled with the promises of life.

Thereafter, we slept together platonically from time to time. Naturally, this started people talking, wondering out loud whether "McGreevey is a homo." Somehow the speculation never extended to Liam; he was a skirt chaser, not the smarmy sort but a man who demonstrably loved women. Once, he told me, people started gossiping about me in his presence, and he stood up for me. "My answer was, he's not hetero, he's not homo, he's just McGreevey," he said. Being called sexless should have bothered me, I guess, but it didn't.

Of all the people in my life to that point, no one had ever accepted me more fully than Liam. But he did ask me once if I was gay. No one had ever put the question to me so bluntly. I'm ashamed to admit I couldn't say yes, but I didn't lie either. Instead I said, "That's crazy," and left it at that. Sometimes I think that if I'd been able to respond differently—if I had just said *yes*—in that moment my whole life might have pivoted in a new and healthier direction.

Instead, after I transferred to Columbia, I developed another very close friendship, this one with a student from Sayville, Long Island, named Hugh Hackett, a runner with black hair and unforgettable blue eyes. Hugh was also Irish American, physically fit, and straight. His girlfriend was always around, and I became very close to her too. This was a pattern I would repeat throughout my life—making myself the third wheel, I think, was a way for me to develop emotional intimacy with a man while my friendship with his wife or girlfriend locked out any presumption that it would ever grow physical.

Maybe it was because I was getting older—by now I was nineteen—but my sexual interests only grew more urgent after I moved to New York. Still, I never allowed myself to fantasize any sort of gay life, perhaps because of that toxic "carried shame." I knew by now that other people my age were able to come out. In fact, there was a gay students' group at Columbia at the very time I was there. But I would never have attended their meetings or dances or read any of their literature—that's how frightened I was.

New York City was also home to a burgeoning gay community, but I only once wandered down to Christopher Street, its epicenter. On that wintry evening, I looked in the window of a gay bar and was astonished at what I saw: a crowd of happy customers, all of them dressed in western wear, leather chaps, and work shirts. I longed for the life they had in there, but then I was somehow seized with the notion that the doorway to the bar was a tunnel with no egress, that if I crossed that threshold I would be abandoning everything I cherished. Rather than going in, I walked a hundred blocks back to the Columbia campus and vowed never to go down there again.

I did befriend one gay person on campus, and I was impressed by how normal he seemed. Whether or not he knew it, though, behind his back he drew pointed comments from some of his housemates. He was considered a good guy, but exotic; I once heard a mutual straight friend make derogatory remarks about him, and I'm sure he wasn't the only one. I was oversensitive about how he was treated, so much so that I was never able to see him as a role model. The model I chose was more exotic still: Mr. Spock, from *Star Trek*. After my affair with Brian Fitzgerald, I remember very earnestly watching the show and thinking, *The Vulcans have sex every seven years. In between, they supplant all physical and emotional desires with steely intellectual rigor. I can do that.* I tried containing my attraction to Hugh Hackett. Sometimes I even flirted with his girlfriend as a distraction. I remember riding the subway downtown with the two of them, her head in my lap and her feet in his. Our flirtatiousness seemed emotionally dangerous, but in the eighteen months I spent at Columbia before graduating, thankfully nothing came between us.

At Christmas break in 1978, I said good-bye to them and took a subway downtown to catch a bus for Carteret. At Forty-second Street, I got out of the subway and headed for the Port Authority bus terminal through the flesh markets of Times Square. This was before its recent Disney-backed makeover; barkers were still openly luring customers off the street for strip shows, and young girls and old ladies could sometimes be seen plying their trade in doorways. Suddenly I was seized by curiosity—and, I'm sure, need. With time to kill, I ducked into one establishment. The lighting was awful and the place smelled of Lysol. Watching the flow of customers, almost all of whom were men, I could see the place was divided between gay and straight entertainments. I followed my instincts to the gay section. There, at the end of an aisle, I spotted a guy a year or two older than I was. I followed him into a small booth in the back of the shop, where movies were playing on a small coin-op screen.

He took off most of his clothes and knelt down before me. There was nothing enjoyable about it—it was more mechanical than anything. I wasn't even attracted to him. What I felt immediately was both relief and burden— I felt both better and worse. The thing about teenage sexuality is that it is explosive and demanding; any venting of it has a lance-the-boil quality. That goes ten times for a young gay man in the closet. The fever goes away instantly, but at the same time you're plunged into a chaos, until you feel even worse off than before. That's the third shame: You can't believe you've done this thing you swore never to do, this thing that makes you so reviled. My head was swimming with all of this as I prepared to make a hasty exit. I couldn't believe I'd allowed myself to get in this position. I even displaced some of my anger onto my partner in this encounter, as though it were something he did, not something I did, that made me feel so loathsome.

I'm not sure whether the guy picked up on this, but I was surprised when he demanded money from me. I refused. Making a scene, he followed me to the street; when I rejected him again he punched me in the eye, drawing a stream of blood. I pushed him to the ground and sprinted to my bus. Riding home with a rag pressed to my forehead, I thought back to the time my mother had comforted me for a similar injury. And these words actually came to mind: *Okay, I'd better have seven years of Vulcan reprieve coming to me before having to deal with this again.*

No chance. Instead of reducing my urges, I gradually grew less inhibited about frequenting these anonymous outlets. I visited similar bookstores and shops in New York and New Jersey and continued having sex in the small booths there until I became too famous to risk discovery.

THE ONLY PLACE WHERE I HAD EVER FOUND ANY REAL PLEASURE in these encounters was in Washington, during my law school years. At the juncture of Sixth and I Street, just around the corner from the federal and local courthouses of Judiciary Square, stood an abandoned synagogue. The once-magnificent structure, with its beautiful stained-glass Star of David over a bay of once-handsome doors, was now secured with chains and padlocks. Its windows were boarded up, its steps now strewn with litter.

Between the synagogue and the building next door was a narrow alley that led to the parking lot and the long-forgotten gardens behind the temple. Every night, rain or shine, this hidden pocket of Washington filled with men just like me—some older, some even younger, but almost all of them wearing business suits and, on most of their left hands, proof that they'd made the same compromises I had. This was no gay bar with its Village People counterculture, no Times Square with its desperation and prostitution. We were the power brokers and backroom operatives and future leaders of America. We just happened to be gay.

Well, not *gay*, exactly. In the abbreviated conversation that passed as dialogue between us, no one back behind the synagogue ever described himself that way to me. Long before the African American community coined the term to describe a world of men who mostly pass as straight but sneak sex with other men, we were on the *down low*—as men of all races have been for hundreds of years.

Discovering the synagogue in 1979 was one of the most exhilarating experiences of my time in DC. Though it was less than half a mile from the Capitol and the Supreme Court, for some reason the cops never went near the place. I felt as though I'd come upon a sanctuary at last—it was a churchlike, almost spiritual, place. Moonlight squinted through the stained-glass windows into our garden, catching an inviting eye or a face stretched in ecstasy. The sound and choreography of the place were as mysterious and soothing to me as the Latin Mass, and I studied it intently. The crowd maneuvered constantly, and wordlessly, in response to the flux of new arrivals. A murmur in one quarter could touch off a moaning chorus in another.

Shortly, I learned the ways to know who to approach and whose advance to wait for, when to move quickly, which posture said *no thanks* and which said *please*.

These situations, for me, were always sinful and unhealthy. But in this one setting I felt comfortable. It was the only place I'd ever found where I wasn't unique, where I was just one of many, where my carried shame didn't follow me. With that gone, I could finally enjoy the company of other men like me, even if only in this compartmentalized manner. I looked forward to my visits there, sometimes two or three a week. These men had made the same decisions I had made, they lived the life I expected to inherit, and among them I felt safe. Every time I left there I felt more integrated, more authentic, less full of shame.

One evening, as I stood on one of the metal platforms back there, a word came to me: *liberated.* Standing there in full sight of this group of men, I'd finally found a way to show who I was. *I am finally free,* I told myself. When of course I was just in a bigger cage.

AS I GOT OLDER, MY SEXUAL EXPRESSIONS BECAME EVEN MORE baroque. I began lurking around Parkway rest stops, exchanging false names and intimacies with strangers. I met every conceivable type this way: bikers, executives, blue-collar workers, old and young, every shade of race. In every instance I recall, the men were kind to me. But there never was an emotional meaning to these encounters, even the few that were repeat engagements. Sometimes I would look around for one familiar face or another, or even suggest my schedule to someone and hope he'd return to find me. Even if he did return at the appointed time, it just didn't matter. Besides carnality, there was no meaning whatsoever to these trysts, and they always left me cold.

One night, I was finally caught. I had pulled into the stop following one of those political dinners in North Jersey. I was in a hurry for some reason. After parking, I flashed my headlights, giving the signal that I was available. No other headlamps fired back at me. I flashed mine again and again, to no avail.

Glancing at my rearview mirror, I could see a state trooper approaching. I couldn't have been more frightened. With my heart in my throat, I tried convincing him I was innocent of the scene he and I both knew was flagrant around us. You could tell he wasn't buying it. Certain that he was thinking of writing me a summons for loitering, which would have been disastrous, I made a calculated decision to show him the prosecutor's badge I'd received as a tradition upon my resignation a number of years back. I suppose I wanted to make him believe I was there on some sort of undercover operation. This was ridiculous, of course, and really stupid. It took him just a few minutes to radio my information to headquarters to learn who I was, and who I wasn't.

When he returned to my car, he handed me back my badge. "I never want to see you here again," he said angrily. Mercifully he didn't give me a summons, which would have created a record.

"Yes, sir," I replied, pulling slowly out of the parking area. I couldn't believe how close to political peril I'd been. I vowed never to do anything like this again.

But you already know how well that worked out.

III.

How One Lives in Shame

8.

HOW DO YOU LIVE WITH SUCH SHAME? HOW DO YOU ACCOMMO-
date your own disappointments, your own revulsion with who you have become? How do you get out of bed in the morning feeling as bad as I did—or
kiss your mother hello or say a prayer in church—when your self-respect
has vanished? How can you carry on such an inauthentic life?

You do it by splitting in two. You rescue at least part of yourself, the half
that stands for tradition and values and America, the part that looks like the
family you came from, the part that is *acceptably* true. And you walk away
from the other half the way you would abandon something spoiled, something disgusting. This is a metaphorical amputation, because that other half
doesn't stop existing. You just take less and less responsibility for it, until it
seems to take on a life of its own—to become something you merely ob-
serve. Something you alone can see. And when you're on the other side, in
the shrubbery or behind the synagogue, you no longer recognize your decent self. Years later I realized I'd become both Gene *and* Phineas from *A
Separate Peace*: the soul and the body, the person who tumbled from the tree
and the person who made him fall.

Dostoevsky defined man as a creature who can get used to anything.
Yes, but not without consequences. On both sides of this divide, my behavior
began to take on something of a dreamlike hue. One side effect of this dis-
connect is that I have no detailed recollection of most of those encounters.
My good friend Ray Lesniak, who has been a pillar of support for me since
my troubles became public, thinks this makes perfect sense. "Your memory is
spotty because you weren't present in the moment," he says. "Until you get

into recovery, you're not *there* in the first place—so there's nothing to remember." I quarantined those rejected histories in the other side of my brain. My truest identity was discarded there, too—the identity that involves the interplay between our hearts and our brains, the thing that makes each of us uniquely ourselves. When I made it my goal to rid myself of the desire, I was disavowing something else: my authentic self, my humanity.

But desire doesn't go away under this kind of pressure. It mutates. In my case it went from the simple passions of a young adult—for physical and romantic love and happiness—to a particularly rank, unfulfilling variety of lust. I felt it get ranker and less fulfilling with each passing year. Every step down I took, the farther I knew I would have to climb back up. I craved the normal things about love—I wanted to kiss, I ached for a hug, I dreamed of sharing a life with someone I loved, some *man* I loved. I used to make long lists of guys I had crushes on, scribbling their names like a teenager.

But I never allowed my conquests to be anything like that. As glorious and meaningful as it would have been to have a loving and sound sexual experience with another man, I knew that I'd have to undo my happiness step by step as I began to chase my dream of a public career and the kind of "acceptable" life that went with it.

So instead I settled for the detached anonymity of bookstores and rest stops—a compromise, but one that was wholly unfulfilling and morally unsatisfactory.

There was also the constant fear of contracting HIV. Although I was extremely careful, I dreaded the disease. I knew only one person who came down with it, a friend of mine and Laura's from Catholic University. He never told anybody what he had, and died, tragically, in 1987. When we learned what had killed him, I was stunned. I guess I thought AIDS would never strike so close to home. Surely, I thought, his life can't have been any wilder than mine. So a week or so later I forced myself to take the test, anonymously, in a crowded STD clinic on the west side of Manhattan. It was a degrading and terrifying experience, though fortunately the news was good.

I tried to stop. Just as I had as a teenager, I desperately resumed my efforts to shift my sexual drive toward women, reading from books by psychologists and psychiatrists who have since been discredited as quacks. I put tight controls on my sexual fantasies. I redoubled my prayers, adding new saints and rituals with each passing year. I meditated on the primary and secondary benefits of heterosexuality, as I saw them, and even put down on paper the future I could expect as a gay American (isolation, loss of family) versus my expectations as a straight American (boundless success, happiness, extended family). I stared at *Playboy* centerfolds as instructed, hoping for a breakthrough. Never mind that real women aren't airbrushed, depilated, and siliconed like those models. The prevailing theories held that such images could "correct" sexual drives that had been arrested in childhood and redirect them to the "proper" object. Today, the American Psychiatric Association concedes that "aversion therapy" and "conversion therapy" of this sort can do only damage. At the time, though, all I knew was that my behavior was getting crazier and crazier. With each new encounter, I was getting nearer and nearer to being caught—which surely would have generated headlines, especially after I became executive director of the New Jersey Parole Board.

I know how it happens that a man like Roy Cohn, the powerful lawyer and closeted aide to Senator Joseph McCarthy, builds a sex life around male prostitutes—or an entertainer like George Michael is one day dragged out of a public toilet in handcuffs. When you repress your simple expressions of love, other, less wholesome, forms emerge to take their place. I will always remember a particular line I read in a biography of Rock Hudson, who denied being gay until days before he died of AIDS in 1985. In the 1960s, at the height of his fame, Hudson was given the chance to make love with a man in Hollywood. "I'll put it this way," the man said later, "he was *hungry*." The closet starves a man, and when he gets a chance he gorges till it sickens him.

But he doesn't give up pretenses, and that's the story of my adult life. In public, I became as avid a womanizer as anybody else on the New Jersey political scene. My unconsummated "romance" with Laura ran its course; I even asked her to marry me, praying she would know I meant this to be an arrangement, and breathed a sign of relief when she declined. In her wake came a parade of other women. I went to bed with some of them, even romanced several at later League of Municipalities conferences, making sure people saw us leaving or entering hotel rooms together. I suppose a few of those women might read this book. I'd like them to know that my interest in them was genuine. I appreciated their beauty and enjoyed holding them in my arms, especially in those earlier years. But my attraction was largely artificial, my sexual performance a triumph of mind over matter.

And it never totally did the job it was supposed to do. Rumors about me multiplied no matter what I did. I couldn't quite put my finger on where they were coming from. I sometimes worried that they were generated in my mind, the way I thought I'd imagined the Cub Scouts ridiculing me. But they were often reported to me by good friends, who were sure they weren't true but who worried that such talk might derail my career. There was one particularly persistent story that I had been caught being intimate with a man in a car in a cemetery, a story with no foundation in fact. To this day, I am sure there are people who think it was true.

The more the rumors circulated, the more public and brazen I became about my heterosexual conquests. I started checking out the strip clubs in Linden and Carteret with friends. It was amazing to me how often we ran into local political operatives and Wall Street traders in such places, mostly young-men-in-a-hurry types from working-class backgrounds. A great deal of New Jersey's networking is conducted by men while folding bills into the waistbands of women dancing in their laps at clubs with names like VIP and Cheeques. For aspiring politicians like me, these were our fraternal lodges— relaxed places to see and be seen, to blow off steam, and establish lasting and productive connections.

In our milieu, it wasn't enough to appear straight; you actually had to prove your mettle in public. I felt I had no choice but to engage the services of the women at the clubs, for show. There were times—scores of times— when I would invite friends to my apartment or hotel room when I knew I'd be in bed with a woman, just so that they'd "accidentally" catch me in the act.

Joe Suliga was one of those friends. Though he was entirely heterosexual, I saw a lot of myself in Joe. He was a gregarious and strappingly handsome kid from a working-class family in Linden, with an outsized drive to make a difference in the political realm. At the age of nineteen, he became the youngest person ever elected to the Linden Board of Education. After college he served on the Linden town council. He planned to run for state senate one day; that was the job of his dreams. Joe was an idealist who believed in public service, and an unflagging optimist about human nature, the political system, and his own role in it. And he loved women as much as they loved him. We used to order beer after beer at Cheeques, watching the dancers twirl on their poles while debating everything from local policy initiatives and tax ratables to the merits of silicone breast enhancement.

On occasion, Joe and I used to go to one of the salty Jersey Shore towns that come to life in summer, searching for female companionship. We looked like total opposites on those outings. Everything about Joe screamed confidence and enthusiasm, from his Hawaiian shirts down to flip-flops; I, on the other hand, wore dark suits and a tie wherever I went. I'm not saying I wasn't successful at attracting women. I even enjoyed the hunt, despite the pressures to perform sexually. But I never forgot for a minute that I was in Joe's world, playing by his rules.

It may seem peculiar, but being able to date women that way gave me a feeling of great power. Where most people were stuck being just one thing all their lives, I thought, I'd found a way to overcome those limitations, to become whatever was necessary in the moment. I knew there was a difference between what I wanted and what I was allowed, between my heart and my actions, but it didn't stop me. I learned to study what moves worked and what didn't, practicing and perfecting my inauthenticity. Being divided this way was never comfortable, but I found a way to live with it. People actually believed I was straight, even my closest friends—even those women. Not me. I knew in every instance that the sex was a contortion of my desires.

Ironically, as I began to climb the ladder of electoral politics, it was this dividing experience that helped me thrive. Political compromises came easy to me because I'd learned how to keep a part of myself innocent of them. Politics, like dating, involved unhappy accommodations. Throughout it, I kept a steel wall around my moral and sexual instincts—protecting them, I thought, from the threats of the real world. This stand gave me a tremendous advantage in politics, if not in my soul. The more I engaged in *doing* rather than *being*, the more alienated I became from my spirituality. My relationship with God was never more remote.

In my longing for intimacy—the gift God gave man—I was marching slowly into hell.

IN 1985, PETER SHAPIRO, A COUNTY EXECUTIVE WITH LITTLE NAME recognition but outstanding bona fides as a reformer, was chosen by the Democratic Party to take on Tom Kean. Shapiro's support came from the liberal wing of the party; I favored the more moderate John F. Russo, a Notre Dame and Columbia University Law School graduate and the president of the state senate. Russo seemed to understand the state's identity politics and working-class roots, having come from a family much like my own. He was also charismatic, having pulled together a vast political machine on the strength of his personality alone. Unfortunately, he was unable to raise the money to expand his campaign. The party pulled behind the better-funded candidate, and my man was out of the race.

It almost wouldn't have mattered. Kean's popularity was soaring, thanks to a budget surplus and a nationwide economic resurgence attributed—wrongly, in my view—to incumbent politicians. He credited his supply-side policies, though objectively the mid-eighties economic boom affected Democratic and Republican states alike. But New Jersey was undeniably in good shape, as even Kean's Democratic opponents admitted. More to the point, they were forced to admit that Kean was a good man and a good governor, the kind of centrist Republican that New Jersey is known for. An early environmentalist, Kean had always believed our state had an obligation to fight poverty and support the poor—policies that were anathema in Ronald Reagan's GOP.

But perhaps most impressive were Kean's feelings about race. He often spoke in African American churches and clubs, advocating for equal opportunity for all New Jerseyans. It wasn't just talk. He appointed a record number of blacks and Latinos to high-level state offices, including judgeships, because he believed that government should reflect the demographics of its citizens. No other governor, Democrat or Republican, made bigger strides toward a color-blind New Jersey.

Shapiro was never expected to win, but his campaign turned out to be a disaster. He failed to stake out a single position against Kean. Even some Democratic leaders seemed to favor Kean—but they pressed forward anyway, out of party loyalty. That was my bind exactly. I voted for Shapiro, but I rooted for Kean.

When election night came, the results were atrocious. Many of the state's labor unions turned out for the Republican, costing us one of our bases. Even worse, more than 60 percent of African Americans crossed party lines as well. Kean's coattails carried dozens of senators and assemblymen to victory. The Democrats lost the majority in both chambers at the same time. We were trounced.

And although Kean and I got along well, my future in government looked bleak after his victory. As a Democrat, I couldn't expect to get much higher in Kean's administration than the Parole Board. Complicating matters, Kean decided not to reappoint my boss, Chris Dietz, replacing him with a former Ocean County Sheriff who shared little of Chris's progressive vision for inmate rehabilitation. I started looking for another job at once.

Two possibilities seemed open to me: private law practice or a position with Merck & Co., the pharmaceutical giant that was one of the largest employers in the area. As a child I'd been awed by Merck's huge manicured campus on Lincoln Avenue in Rahway; surrounded by a wrought-iron fence, it struck me as imposingly grand and vibrant, our own Land of Oz. For several years running, *Fortune* magazine had named Merck America's most admired corporation. For me it was an easy choice.

I was offered a plum job as a regional manager in public affairs, involved in lobbying and some regulatory oversight. I also assumed Merck wouldn't mind if I used my work there as a home base for making a run for office, although my boss, a sagacious West Pointer named Dick Trabert, called me "transparently ambitious" in my first supervisory review. When I asked my old friend Jimmy Kennedy, an aspiring politician in town, whether he thought that was an unfair characterization, he just laughed. "Jim, everybody knows you're going to run for something."

Little did I expect that my first opportunity would be the assembly seat held by my mentor and friend Alan Karcher. In the 1989 election cycle he was planning to make a play for governor, as I'd already learned from the chart behind his desk, and he told me privately that he intended to leave the assembly seat either way. He encouraged me to make a run for it.

Jim Florio, a powerful and popular former congressman who'd lost his last campaign for governor by just 1,800 votes, had already declared for the Democratic primary. Karcher was facing an uphill battle; the Democrats were already unified behind Florio, including the most powerful party bosses. I'm not entirely sure why Karcher chose to take him on.

Among the bosses, there were three who wielded significant extra-territorial influence, carrying weight over other bosses in their regions the way archbishops prevail upon neighboring bishops. With respect, we called them "the warlords." They divided the state into thirds. The South Jersey warlord was George Norcross III, from Camden, the epitome of the kind of figures who drive politics in the state. Norcross has never held elective office or expressed interest in running. But he was driven into politics after his dad, a prominent carpenters' union official with a legendary love for race-tracks, expressed interest in an appointment to the New Jersey Racing Commission. The local Republican senator turned him down, even after Norcross repeated the request on his father's behalf, because it crossed party lines. This struck Norcross as venal and petty.

Norcross ultimately got his revenge. He orchestrated the senator's quick defeat in the following election, handing the seat to a Democrat for the first time in years.

The Camden party leadership was impressed, rewarding him with the chairmanship of the county operation when he was just thirty-two. Eventually, through party accounts and his own PACs, he was able to fuel countless campaigns throughout the southern counties single-handedly. One year, nearly seventy-five candidates owed their victories to his machine.

Norcross's strategic mastery was a boon to Democrats. It also increased his own stature. He quickly became a reckoning force in the state. Though he was a college dropout, his intelligence and hard work—plus a vast net-work of loyal connections—enabled him to build a healthy insurance division for Commerce Bank, where he was a top executive.

In Central Jersey, state senator John Lynch was the most powerful überboss—arguably, the most powerful in the state. When it came to urban planning and redevelopment, Lynch was without a doubt the smartest man in the state, maybe the nation. He orchestrated the resurgence of New Brunswick, an industrial city that had sunk into such despair by the early 1970s that the headquarters for Johnson & Johnson nearly moved out. As senate leader, Lynch championed the principles of smart growth and urban revitalization. As the years went by, we all watched as Lynch developed a taste for the financial gain those around him enjoyed. After his service in the senate, Lynch built a consulting company that worked to help developers win government approval for their projects, a peculiar form of checkbook government, though perfectly legal under the state's tattered lacework of ethics regulations. He eventually became, as he once said, "the most investigated man in New Jersey."

North Jersey was controlled by my friend Ray Lesniak, the Union County boss and longtime state senator. Ray's politically connected law firm dominated state, county, and municipal contract business in regions surrounding his legislative district and helped area developers advance their interests.

If Ray, Lynch, and Norcross agreed on a statewide candidate, nobody else had a chance. Knowing the odds were against him, Karcher tried to launch a reform campaign strong enough to bypass the party machinery. He went out to the left of Florio on most issues, putting together a nonmoneyed coalition of sixties progressives, liberal unionists, African Americans, and liberal Jews, as well as tenants, a potentially powerful bloc. But it didn't work: after a modest showing in the primary, he gave up the fight and drifted out of politics.

I WANTED TO BE MORE CAREFUL. LUCKILY, I'D MADE A FRIENDSHIP with a man who would become the most important influence on my political life. Jack Fay was a former popular state senator raised in the North Jersey mill town of Elizabeth. A former Navy Seal, he'd worked in a local factory during the day while attending college and graduate school at night to become a teacher at Linden High School. Devoutly liberal and progressive, Jack believed passionately that rather than being neutral, government should instead be an advocate for the public against business interests. He was what we used to call a Dorothy Day liberal, a man who believed that social service was an obligation. In Trenton, where he served from 1968 to 1978, he was regarded as a man of unflappable principles who couldn't be bought or sold.

Unlike so many other politicians, Jack was demonstrably honest. He lived in the same small home for twenty years, leaving it virtually untouched since the death of his beloved wife, Betty, some fifteen years ago. His only indulgences were a cup of coffee and the *New York Times* in the morning, and a thick cup of soup for lunch.

There was an old story that Attorney General David T. Wilentz, best known for prosecuting the Lindbergh kidnapping case, claimed credit for launching Jack's career in the 1960s, when he was still county boss. Years later, Wilentz went to the mat with him over a vote on parochial school financing, which Jack opposed. "Irish Catholics don't vote against parochial schools," Wilentz scolded Jack—despite the fact that Wilentz was Jewish. When Jack reminded Wilentz that his son Robert, who later became chief justice of the State Supreme Court, also opposed the bill, Wilentz thundered back, "I don't care what Robert did!"

He continued, "When I found you, you had chalk all over your jacket and trousers. Now go out there and vote responsibly." To his credit, Jack never backed down.

Jack and I were introduced at an insane political meeting in a local official's basement. Among the attendees was the tiara-wearing woman I'd seen at that meeting years before, pelting our new congressman with obscenities. Here, though, she was in her element. As she marched us through an ambitious agenda, I could see why she was so powerful; she was a tireless and agile advocate for the party.

Still, though, she seemed to take the whole process a tad too personally. We were discussing candidates for a local mayoral post when someone made the mistake of calling her favored candidate "perhaps not the best choice." She lunged at the poor guy, wrapping her fingers around his neck. Jack left the room in disgust.

When I followed him out, he invited me for a cup of coffee at the Reo

Diner in Woodbridge, a tradition we kept up almost weekly until his death many years later. He was a spiritual and ethical man, one of the really good guys. Our conversations ranged from the philosophy of government to the purpose God had for our lives.

It may even have been Jack's idea that I run for Alan's old seat. However it came about, every facet of my campaign had Jack's fingerprints on it. I loved every minute of it, from strategizing to knocking on doors. I began by making lists of all the people whose rings I needed to kiss. The 19th Legislative District, which sent two assemblymen and one senator to Trenton, covered five towns in Middlesex County: Woodbridge, Sayreville, South Amboy, South River, and Perth Amboy. I needed the support of the political powerhouses there—not just the mayors, but the five local Democratic chairmen as well. Together, they could deliver the winning votes.

I started by focusing on Woodbridge, which accounted for 50 percent of the district, and its colorful mayor, a major political force named Joseph A. "JoJo" DeMarino. JoJo was a classic New Jersey figure. A former marine and Middlesex County Sheriff, he considered himself the Kojak of local politics, right down to shaving his head and keeping an autographed photo of Telly Savalas on his office wall. He made a comfortable income drawn mostly from rents he collected from a small apartment building he owned and other real estate deals he made periodically in the area.

JoJo never went to college. But he was innately bright and an effective mayor, at least by all appearances: heavy-handed when he needed to be, an old-school wheeler dealer with Da Boyz (as he called the contractors and vendors constantly lined up outside his door), and a father figure to his constituents. He personally tended to every problem on every block of his town, from trimming trees to fixing sidewalks and sweeping litter out of alleyways. He used to carry a little notepad around with him and write down his observations of every conversation he ever had. Then, when he got back to his office, he'd send a letter perfectly recapping the issues and sending his regards to each child and even the family pets.

For JoJo, being mayor was everything. "In high school they said I'd never amount to nothing," he once told me. "I said, 'I'll be back as your boss.'"

He was predisposed to backing me because I had supported him over the years. JoJo had been mayor since 1979, but in 1983 he was briefly run out of office by a well-meaning Republican named Phil Cerria. Cerria was a good guy, but unfortunately he'd acquiesced to some of the more hare-brained schemes of his staff—like sprinkling a vanilla scent over leaf piles throughout the township to alleviate persistent odors in the area. Jack Fay and I had helped JoJo arrange his comeback in 1987; I worked mostly as a volunteer campaigner, reviewing campaign literature and going door-to-door on his behalf, but I knew he was aware of the energy I had committed.

But the secret to JoJo's comeback was Jack Fay. Jack was well known and respected in Woodbridge, parts of which he had represented before a redistricting change. He even offered to make a local cable TV commercial for JoJo. When we showed up at the recording studio, Jack was seated by a beat-up desk, with an American flag in the background. The production assistant pointed a fan toward the flag, causing the flag to ripple and Jack to squint. "I'm Jack Fay and I'm here to support Joe DeMarino," he said. "Joe is a good and decent man and deserves to be our next mayor." The spot ran almost constantly till JoJo's victory on election night.

In the two years that followed, I had worked with JoJo on a number of issues, some more successful than others. At one point, Jack and I even drafted an ethics policy plank for him in his reelection campaign. But when we tried getting him to adopt it as an ordinance after he returned to office, he all but threw us out of his office, assigning us to a kindly but secondary counselor named Herb Rosen to review the matter. Herb was a PR person. That's how JoJo seemed to view ethics—as a campaign shtick for public consumption.

NOW I PAID A FORMAL CALL ON THE MAYOR, WHO RECEIVED ME in the finished basement of his home. I reminded him of my labors on his behalf and asked for his support in my assembly bid, which he delivered in a heartbeat. "You've got a lot of ambition, kid," he told me. "Stick with me. It'll get you a good distance." JoJo took credit for launching the career of Senator Bill Bradley, the former NBA star, over a meeting in the same basement. Now he was laying claim to mine.

Even with Woodbridge in the bag, though, I still lacked enough votes to win. My primary opponent was John McCormack, the mayor of Sayreville, who already laid claim to not only his hometown but South Amboy and South River, too. That left only one town up for grabs: Perth Amboy. I'd already spent a lot of time in Perth Amboy, a city of 47,000 near the New York Harbor. The town made history as the place where the first signature was affixed to the Bill of Rights and where the first African American in the United States was allowed to vote, but it had seen better days. Many area residents suffered in poverty, and parts of the region were blighted. One morning, as I stood outside the grocery store there shaking hands, I was interrupted by a commotion.

"McGreevey, get the hell out of here!" a man shouted. "Go home! Get out!"

Looking up, I found Ed Patten, a beloved retired congressman, in the passenger seat of his car. Patten was known for attending every funeral, bar mitzvah, and First Holy Communion he was invited to. His daughter, a wonderful Catholic nun named Sister Catherine, was driving.

"Why, Congressman?"

"Nobody here votes," he said, stroking his hand dismissively outside the window before speeding off. "Perth Amboy is the asshole of the world!"

Besides my own efforts, Jack Fay did his damnedest on my behalf, attempting to work his charm on the leadership there. "We need Perth Amboy or we're dead," he kept telling me. "And for some reason they're not budging. We're going to have to go see Otlowski."

That was Mayor George J. Otlowski, the same local boss whose political dinner I crashed so many years ago. Otlowski and I had become friends—or so I'd thought—and I'd volunteered on many of his pet projects over the years. Why he wasn't endorsing me was a mystery to me and Jack alike. I'd assumed he'd sign on to my campaign instantly. Now, Jack told me, he wasn't even returning calls.

"He's going on vacation," Jack said. "We're going to have to go too."

"Bother him *during his vacation?*"

It seemed like an imposition, but that's exactly what Jack had in mind. "You want to be the next assemblyman? Make your reservations."

Of all places, Otlowski was vacationing in Key West, a challenging destination for a closeted would-be politician. We flew down in early February with Otlowski and his longtime aide, Julius Rogovsky, and sped to our cheap motel—past gay nightclubs and restaurants, bookstores and gift shops, and same-sex couples exchanging kisses or strolling arm in arm to the beach. I tried my best not to notice, but I had never before seen such simple freedoms, not in public.

"George," Jack began our pitch, "we need your support. Jim's young, he's progressive, a reformer. He's the new face of the Democratic Party in the district. People love him, you told me so yourself. He can win this, George, if we put him on the party line. You know he can."

But Otlowski was noncommittal. So we made an appointment to lobby him again in the afternoon, and every afternoon until we won him over. Of course, it wasn't all work. With another Woodbridge couple, we toured the old Hemingway homestead and the Truman Summer White House. We made regular strolls down the beach.

The constant presence of gay men caused some awkwardness, but not for Jack, I was happy to learn. When we were being introduced to the local mayor, someone mentioned that he was the first openly gay mayor in the country. "Jeez," Jack said, finding the reference unnecessary, "I want to *meet* him, not *dance* with him."

Somehow I don't think Julius Rogovsky noticed we were in a gay Mecca. After dinner one evening, he got the perverse idea of trying to drag us all into an adult bookstore. We spent twenty minutes trying to talk him out of it. The windows of the place were brimming with gay S-and-M paraphernalia. But Julius considered himself worldly—evidently he had visited Scranton, Pennsylvania, looking for women during World War II—and he headed inside alone. "I've seen it all, McGreevey," he said over his shoulder. "Nothing can shock me." He reemerged a few minutes later, looking stricken. "Never seen nothin' like *that* in Scranton," he said.

After talking ourselves silly about the 19th Legislative District for nearly a week, playing our ground game carefully, Jack and I finally asked Otlowski for his endorsement. He laughed. "Go with God," he said. "We'll campaign together as Batman and Robin."

After that, the race was a breeze. I loved retail politics: meeting people, talking to them about their concerns, sharing their celebrations. Teddy Roosevelt called this being "in the arena." There wasn't an ethnic fair or house party or religious service I didn't attend. Every morning and evening, jacket slung over my shoulder, I would knock on doors introducing myself to potential voters. I remember downing shots of vodka at 10:30 in the morning in the basement of the Saints Peter and Paul Russian Orthodox Church in South River, gorging on kielbasa at the Polish parish luncheon in Sayreville, and stuffing myself with cannolis in Perth Amboy's shrinking Italian district at night. For a sheltered Irish Catholic, it wasn't always easy for me to learn new ethnic traditions. I remember one morning when George Otlowski arranged for me to attend a Sacred Heart Roman Catholic Church communion breakfast in South Amboy. I had the honor of sitting next to the old Polish pastor, a well-known curmudgeon, and I very politely cut slices of bread from a big loaf in the middle of the table and gave us each a serving. "This is the strangest looking soda bread I've ever seen," I remarked brightly.

He was aghast. "Soda bread? What soda bread? This is babka." I had much to learn.

JOE SULIGA WAS ALSO RUNNING FOR ASSEMBLY IN THE ADJOINING district. Watching him hone his own campaigning techniques was instructive for me. He believed that a successful lawmaker had to establish an intimate relationship with the voting public, and he practiced what he preached. After the July Fourth weekend, for instance, he sent handwritten thank-you notes to everyone in his district who displayed Old Glory. People who received them were totally disarmed, even Republicans. People just loved being noticed, and appreciated him for making them feel good. I was in awe of his ability to connect with his base.

I wasn't quite as solicitous as Joe, but I did develop an ability to recall hundreds of names and faces—and file them away with some memory of their lives, like the names of their children or the health of their parents or grandparents. This came easily for me, the way memorizing the Latin Mass had years ago. At the end of each day I reviewed the "walking notes" I'd jotted down following each encounter, hoping to lay down the information in my long-term memory. Then I would write quick letters complimenting the residents on their yards or gardens and asking after their pets. Before long, I couldn't set foot in one of these neighborhoods without hearing them call out hellos like we were old family friends. "Hi, Jimmy!" they said. "Say hi to your mom!"

Still, political life seemed to come more naturally to Joe. In the midst of a tight campaign, he still found time to head to the Jersey Shore for those wild weekends of his. One Saturday I passed him near Exit 11 on the Turnpike as he headed south. When I blew the horn, he made a hair-raising illegal turn to say hello.

I looked at him in his floral shirt and sandals, in his red Mustang convertible, with admiration. Clearly, he was on his way to a fun-filled night of partying. I, on the other hand, was returning from talking at a senior center, heading off in my usual suit and tie to a weekend of church basements and diner meetings.

"You know, Joe," I said, "my dream is to come back in the next life as Joe Suliga."

He just laughed. "Coming back as Jim McGreevey is my nightmare," he said, then waved and made another squealing U-turn off to Atlantic City.

MY PARENTS SEEMED TO BE HAVING AS MUCH FUN IN THE CAMpaign as I was. My dad's mission in life was advocating for veterans, and he took me to the local VFW halls around the district every chance he got. There were breakfasts and mixers by the dozens, and I loved showing up there with Dad. But the formidable force in the family was Mom, my secret weapon. She'd come into the campaign office at dawn ready to make phone calls—and work the phones till well after dinner. She was so tireless that some suspected me of using an army of stand-ins posing as my mother. I remember Dad telling me he was driving home from work late one day and saw my mother walking from porch to porch in a distant neighborhood knocking on doors with my campaign literature.

I also turned out to be a natural campaigner. My childhood awkwardness had given way to a confident demeanor. It was as if I'd overcome all the demons of my youth.

During this time I never worried what people would make of my status as a single candidate. I'd been known to date from time to time, but I was still very young, just thirty-two years old. Older women seemed to find me handsome, especially the ladies in St. Joseph's Nursing Home on Strawberry Hill in Woodbridge, and constantly offered to set me up with their daughters or granddaughters. I played along happily. By now I'd mostly given up on anonymous sexual encounters; I'd sublimated my sexual appetites and refocused all my energy into campaigning. I consciously made a bargain with myself: if I did this well and won a seat on the assembly, the good work I would be able to accomplish would far outweigh any frustration or loneliness my chastity would cause. Priests make similar deals, mostly more effective than mine turned out to be.

But putting my sex drive behind me didn't erase my history. One day, Otlowski sat me down with a sheath of papers. "Negative research on our Republican legislative opponents," said one of his aides, pushing toward me various documents—probably details on finances, speeding tickets, and the like. In that moment, I suddenly realized how vulnerable I was. If we could get these things on my opponent, what could he find on me?

That's when the news hit the papers about my stupidity flashing that old Prosecutors' Office badge to state troopers. On April 20, 1989, Michelle Sobolewski, my campaign manager, woke me in the morning to break the news. There were two stories sharing the front page that day. The first was the story of the deadly explosion aboard the USS *Iowa*, which was initially blamed on a gay sailor until an investigation proved it a freak accident. The second story was about me. "Your career and the USS *Iowa* both exploded on the front page today," Michelle said.

I went numb. But as she read me the story, I realized it wasn't the incident I was thinking of, the time I'd been caught looking for sex in the rest stop. This was a different episode, which happened one Sunday afternoon as I was racing through Highland Park to attend a museum opening. When the police pulled me over for speeding, I showed them my license and, once again, my badge. Again, I had hoped it would get me out of a jam, but the cops gave me a ticket anyway and reported my inappropriate representations back to county prosecutor Alan Rockoff, a former judge and dear friend. He had me summoned and took my badge away. "These things are given out to former assistants assuming they're going to mount them to a plaque," he said, "not to fix speeding tickets." I felt like a stupid child.

Hearing Michelle read the story, I was relieved; at least my big secret hadn't been revealed. Of course, it was my first scandal. But Michelle just laughed it off. "You were speeding," she said. "Big deal." Still, it also meant that people were out there digging around in my background. It meant I wasn't safe.

That night, I made a long list of everything I could recall about every sexual encounter I'd had. I didn't know anybody's name, of course, but I tried recalling something to anchor each tryst in history: a snippet of conversation, something about the way he looked, whether he was kind or aloof. It came to more than twenty individuals. Then I made an assessment about each entry. What are the chances that *this one* lives in the 19th Legislative District? Would *that one* be able to find me? If *he* sees my picture in the paper, would he be likely to reveal our secret? Line after line, I imagined the worst. Is this one a threat? Could that one do me in? Blackmail, I realized, begins well before there is a perpetrator; its possibility is invented by the victim.

I had only one consolation—that anyone who'd been in the places I was worried about would be just as ashamed as I was and just as unlikely to go public.

But I had other concerns. I lived in fear that a videotape would surface from some dingy adult bookstore. I knew there were cameras; you could see them posted over the cash register and at the doors—though not in the back by the booths, where the untoward things happened. I had no way of knowing how long they kept those tapes and knew no one to ask. I did ask my friend Jimmy Kennedy, the mayor of Rahway, obliquely about my brush with the state trooper at the Parkway rest stop: if a police stop didn't result in a summons, could it still make it into public records somewhere? Politely, Jimmy didn't ask me why I wanted to know.

Plan your work and work your plan. As Election Day drew near, I found myself dating young women more frequently, including some who were helping out on the campaign, and this got a buzz going in the office about my virility. One woman in particular captured my interest—a bright and competent woman who happened to be on my campaign staff. And one lonely night we crossed a line together. It was foolish and wrong of me to do, and I'm afraid she felt hurt by me when I didn't want to continue. It was the first time in my life I realized I had power and stature over another individual, and I didn't handle it very well. I regret causing her any pain. But when word leaked out about my heartlessness, I'll admit that I found a certain power in it.

On November 7, 1989, Jim Florio beat out Republican congressman Jim Courter for governor of New Jersey, becoming the first Democrat in eight years to head to the governor's mansion. My pal Joe Suliga prevailed in his campaign to become assemblyman from Linden. And by a vote of 27,099 to 24,695, James E. McGreevey, the kid from Carteret, became the newest representative of the 19th Legislative District. Joe and I were two of the youngest lawmakers in Trenton.

9.

SINCE THE ASSEMBLY ONLY PAID $35,000 A YEAR, I DECIDED TO hold onto my day job at Merck. Dick Trabert, my boss, made sure I was carrying my weight at work, and reassigned me away from any potential conflicts. For the most part, my responsibilities there consisted of reading white papers involving federal actions and assessing their potential impact on Merck clients—nothing that conflicted with my work as a legislator. Indeed, some of my own legislative initiatives were sometimes seen as anti-Big Pharma. Trabert, a staunch Republican, tactfully held his tongue, never once interfering with my work in government. (Although when I asked his daughter on a date, I saw his handiwork behind her rejection.)

In Trenton, I focused mainly on three issues, writing or sponsoring laws on the environment, Holocaust education, and women's health care. New Jersey has the third highest rate of breast cancer in the country. Without early detection, one out of every four breast cancer victims will die of the disease. But women were routinely being denied reimbursements for a simple test that could save their lives. I wrote a bill mandating insurance coverage for mammograms, the most powerful tool in early detection.

In addition, I wrote legislation establishing a permanent Holocaust Commission, the first of its kind in the nation, and began the long work that eventually required teachers to discuss the sad lessons of hatred and intolerance from that time to all grade-schoolkids. My assembly aide, Herb Gilsenberg, a former truck dispatcher from Brooklyn, took on this effort as a personal mission. In one of his memorable letters, he wrote to the entire state legislature telling them it would be a "mitzvah," Yiddish for "good deed," if they passed the Holocaust legislation. The then-speaker, Joseph Doria, an Italian Catholic from Bayonne with an education degree from Columbia, asked me in the assembly rotunda, "What's a mitzvah?" I had to tell him I had no idea.

With the leadership of Senator Dan Dalton, we also passed the Pollution Prevention Act, a landmark law that established financial incentives to reduce usage and generation of hazardous materials. As a result, New Jersey was awarded the Best Bet Award for Environmental Achievement from the National Center for Policy Alternatives, a proud accomplishment.

I also supported Governor Florio in his record-breaking $2.8 billion state tax increase. It was a bitter pill, but an essential one if we were to balance the budget, increase aid to public schools, and increase property tax relief for working New Jerseyans, who were suffering under the heaviest tax burden in the nation.

But I also worked on a bill that had indirect impact on Merck & Co. Still advocating for seniors, I championed legislation in the General Assembly that would require doctors to accept Medicare caps as payment in full. This touched off a firestorm of anger from the medical establishment, but to their credit no one at Merck ever complained. I was sure the company's CEO, Dr. Roy Vagelos, disagreed with my position. But he had such unimpeachable integrity that he drew a bright line against indirectly interfering with legislative action.

I wasn't always diplomatic. I got a reputation as a young man in a big hurry, not the most effective image. They called me "Assembly Boy," sometimes less than lovingly. But I persevered. Just as I had at Scout camp, I identified the people who were most prone to dislike me, and I made it my business to win them over.

A FEW MONTHS INTO MY TENURE, I WAS OUT FOR A DRINK ONE night with my friend Tim Dacey. He told me he was worried about me— that I was working too much and not finding a balance in my life. He was right; I wasn't spending as much time chasing girls in Atlantic City as I used to. In truth, I'd been glad to leave that charade behind—girls were part of the campaign, not part of the administration. Of course, there were moments when I wished I had a woman on my arm, like when Governor Florio invited me and a number of other lawmakers to his home on the shore for a picnic. Everyone else brought their husband or wife, boyfriend or girlfriend; I arrived with my sister. I struck a strange Nixonian image, besides—wearing a dark suit and tie when everybody else knew enough to wear polo shirts and chinos. My friend Christine Simon, a fellow former assembly staffer, took me aside. "Jim, you can't be serious. Your sister? A suit? What are you thinking?" I didn't have a clue.

But I didn't feel compelled to date women, as long as I was working hard. Long hours were a good excuse for bachelorhood; besides, they kept my mind off my plight.

I didn't tell Tim any of this, though. I told him I felt obliged to the voters, and to Merck & Co., to work every last minute of the day.

"You're killing yourself," he said. "You worked yourself to the bone on your campaign; you deserve a break. Let's take a vacation."

He was a dear friend, and I appreciated his concern, but I turned him down. "Not this year," I said.

It was no use: Tim had already conspired with my secretary at Merck to book us both on the Royal Viking Star for a week's round-trip cruise to Bermuda. He told me it wasn't refundable. At first I was aggravated, but finally I agreed to go along. It turned out to be one of the best decisions of my life.

We left on a Saturday from the New York City Passenger Ship Terminal in Manhattan. Never having been on a cruise before, I'd always assumed they were strictly for retirees; I couldn't believe how many passengers were our age, and obviously looking for romance. Leave it to Timmy to find the cruisiest cruise ship in history, I thought. I don't think we were more than a few miles outside of New York Harbor when he'd already struck up an acquaintance with a couple of beautiful women from British Columbia. One was a blonde, the other a brunette. They were in deck chairs with their feet up, reading books poolside. My first inclination was toward Heather, the lighthearted blonde. I spent the first evening talking with her while Tim hung close to her friend. But somewhere through the second day Tim and

I—and Heather and the other woman, Kari Schutz—had a slow change of heart, and there was a switch of teams. Tim paired up with the blonde; I got Kari, a librarian about my age.

For the first time in my life, I was swept away by a woman. Bright, engaging, vivacious, Kari challenged me about literature, art, music, and politics. She was elegantly dressed, with beautiful hair and deep, dark eyes. We spent all that day talking, swimming in the pool, and feasting in the many restaurants aboard. Her stories about traveling—to China, Russia, through Europe—were riveting. Oh, she made me laugh! When I told her I was an assemblyman, she thought I meant I worked on an assembly line. "Which plant?" she asked, and I fell off my deck chair laughing.

That night at dinner I took her in my arms on the deck, leaned her against the railing, and kissed her gently—fireworks. By the time we hit our first port, St. George, we were holding hands; at the next stop, Hamilton, we rented mopeds and explored the place from top to bottom, crawling through basement pubs like college kids. This was the romance I craved, with a person who totally captivated me—she just happened to be a woman.

As different as we were, we had a lot in common. Her parents were immigrants to Canada from Scotland and Norway, blue-collar like my folks, and like me she was very connected to her Church—only she was Anglican, not Roman Catholic. She was a hard worker, well educated, not at all a snob—she wouldn't have cared if my job *was* on some assembly line. We just hit it off honestly, two individuals bobbing around on a huge sea.

When I got back to Woodbridge, I called Kari every chance I got. A dozen times in the next year I flew to Vancouver to visit her. She visited me just as often—these were proper and old-fashioned courting visits, but I couldn't wait for us to become more intimate. During one of her visits we drove into New York City for a romantic dinner at the Rainbow Room, a glorious ballroom high above Rockefeller Center. We danced and ate and sipped champagne and our heads were fuzzy with love.

I reached in my pocket for a diamond ring. "Kari," I said. "I love you. You make me very happy. I am a better person with you, a person I never thought I could be. And I think I make you happy, too. I'd love to live with you for the rest of my life. Will you marry me?" Tears poured down her cheeks as I slid the ring on her finger. She hadn't expected this at all. She nodded yes, unable to speak.

We took each other in our arms and twirled around on the dance floor for hours. I knew I loved her totally. But the thought that kept running through my head was, *I've beaten it back. Now there's no limit to what I can do.*

DESPITE ALL THIS HAPPINESS, MY POLITICAL CAREER WAS IN DANger of cracking apart. Around Thanksgiving 1990, my ally and friend JoJo DeMarino, the Woodbridge mayor, told me and Jack that he was about to be indicted for bribing a Carteret official for his vote on a city contract. He broke the news at the Woodbridge Diner after our annual Thanksgiving Day Prayer Service in Avenel. I could hardly believe my ears.

A few weeks later came another blow. An effort to redraw legislative district lines in the state—in order to follow population trends—merged portions of two districts into one. That meant that Assemblyman Tom Deverin and I would have to duke it out to see who got to keep the job. This was terribly unfair. I'd known Tom forever—his family and mine were regulars at the same St. Joseph's Masses. The other district being merged was already being represented by me and George Otlowski, to whom I now owed so many favors. I couldn't imagine running against him, either. This was a terrible bind for me.

Unfortunately, the decision was made for me in early 1991. JoJo DeMarino called a meeting of the five chairs from the newly incorporated district, plus Otlowski and Deverin—everyone, that is, but me. DeMarino, as the local party boss, had decided to throw his support to Deverin, not me. He didn't even have the courtesy to tell me in person.

I remember how I found out about the meeting. I was on the platform of the Metropark Station stop waiting for the annual Chamber of Commerce train ride to Washington DC, the other yearly event involving every elected official in the state. I called Jack Fay from the platform pay phone. "Welcome to boss politics," he said. "You've just been kicked off the line." I was furious, especially at JoJo, whose career I had helped resuscitate; I considered him a mentor and a friend. Given his indictment, and the almost impossible reelection campaign that was sure to follow, I was stunned that he would turn on me.

Next I called JoJo himself and demanded an explanation. "It's unfortunate," he said, "but I couldn't get you on the phone. I tried several times."

"Bullshit," I said. "I have an answering machine at home and secretaries at Merck and at the assembly office. You screwed me."

After conferring with my inner circle, I made a decision: I would run for mayor of Woodbridge against JoJo. At least in part, I was motivated by revenge. I even settled on an unofficial theme: "The Unindicted Democratic Ticket." But I knew I could run the town well, and I knew I could win. I was familiar with his weaknesses, and I was confident I could siphon off his brain trust—especially Jack, who was as mad as I was.

On the day I told JoJo I was taking him on, we were sitting in his white Lincoln Continental. I said, "If you had come to me and said to my face, 'This is the way it's gotta be—you're the junior man, you're off the line,' I may not have liked it, I may have been angry, but I would have accepted it."

His large head turned bright red. He ticked off all the church parishes, veterans' organizations, firehouses, and power bases that he could count on to vote for him. He had all the sanitation workers, too, because he'd hired them all. He had the town locked up. All I could expect was the Woodbridge American-Irish Association.

"I'm gonna cut your balls off," he told me.

The campaign went hand to hand through the backyards of Woodbridge. DeMarino played rough, ordering his garbage collectors to pull my signs off people's lawns. We never played that kind of dirty game—and we couldn't have spared the manpower for pulling up signs if we'd tried. Instead, I worked my ass off and signed up every volunteer I could get. I even started to accumulate party support. The family of Attorney General David Wilentz threw in behind me. The Wilentzes never liked JoJo; David once called him "the only man who could lie to God."

Ray Lesniak, the county boss, signed up too. I think Ray saw potential in me, not just for the future but, as a chance to establish a Democratic beachhead in this Republican year. Without Ray, my race had no chance.

* * *

WHEN THE HISTORY OF NEW JERSEY POLITICS IS FINALLY WRIT-
ten, Raymond Lesniak will no doubt emerge as one of our most towering
figures. Apart from the obvious political cunning that won him the chairmanship in Union County when he was still quite young, Ray is an enormously appealing figure. Women find him attractive, and he's been known
to adore them back. In fact, there is something of the screen idol about
him: his wide-open face, intense blue eyes, and suave demeanor mix with
his high-flying political standing to make him unique in the state political class.

For reading, he wears wireless glasses tinted blue, which give him a
flower-power aura. But Ray is more new age than hippie. Raised Roman
Catholic in the Polish parishes of Elizabeth, he now considers himself a
born-again evangelical Christian of a variety he has improvised along the
way. He still attends Mass at a Roman Catholic church, but he reads self-help
books voraciously and is a dedicated follower of the twelve-step philosophy
on which Alcoholics Anonymous is based. Ray was never a problem drinker.
For him, the steps are a way of life, their own spiritual movement. We're all
addicted to something that's holding us back, he believes. When people ask
Ray what he's recovering from he says, "a compulsiveness to be in control of
everything."

But pity the person who thinks Ray's not still a commanding figure. He
can be ruthlessly persuasive and single-minded—and always charming—
when he sets his sights on a goal. Winning his support and friendship gave
me hope that I might actually win my run for mayor.

As we got down to the wire late that summer and early fall, DeMarino's
attentions were distracted by his criminal case. The trial was scheduled for
October, and because I was campaigning on "integrity," he was forced to explain himself.

"I was asked to help some friends out," he once cryptically told a reporter. "That's all."

We were polling neck and neck. In a curious move, DeMarino pushed
to have his trial broadcast on local cable. He truly believed that the voters
would see how innocent he was and reward him at the polls.

But it backfired. It turned out that the county prosecutor had been secretly tape-recording JoJo for years. It didn't matter whether the case was strong or weak; his coarse language alone cost him votes. The seniors in Woodbridge tuned in every morning, and the little old Hungarian and Italian ladies were scandalized. Hearing the word *damn* was enough to send them into a spell. The language on the tapes was much worse. As I went door to door, they would say to me in horror, "Can you believe what DeMarino said today?"

JoJo was found not guilty in October 1991, but by then he'd already lost the race. The following month, in a close four-way election, I became the next mayor of Woodbridge. I packed my things at Merck & Co., married Kari in a beautiful Episcopal ceremony in Vancouver, with Jimmy Kennedy as my best man, and moved to Town Hall.

One of the first things I did as mayor was hire Paul Weiner as my corporation counsel, the town's top lawyer. Paul was a partner in Ray's law firm, Weiner Lesniak, and Ray must have known he was just what I needed, a loyal and extremely competent deputy. With just the right temperament, he was able to meet with the squabbling party stalwarts in both parties and divvy up the spoils: appointments to various town departments and offices, jobs on this crew or that agency. Some of it was patronage, always has been, but done as wisely as Paul did it, doling out the jobs can build a mighty peace. The way we did it in Woodbridge had an almost parliamentary effect; we entered a power-sharing arrangement with our adversaries, reached out to voting blocks that hadn't supported us, and gave a little back to the people who supported us. And in the bargain, we made sure everybody had a stake in running the town. Good government and good politics aren't contradictory ideas, not always.

I HAVE TO SAY, JOJO DEMARINO DID ME A HUGE FAVOR. NO JOB WAS better suited to me than being mayor of Woodbridge. In the years since then I have traveled the world and seen cities and villages that took my breath away. But Woodbridge is still my favorite place. Its roots go back to the early days of American history. Settled in the autumn of 1665 and granted a charter five years later by King Charles, the city was named either for the English town where some of the settlers were born or in fond memory of a pastor the Puritans recalled from their first stop in America, in Newbury, Massachusetts—nobody knows for sure. The first permanent printing house in America was opened here in 1751, and the first truly American periodical in the Colony was published there.

The fact that gave me greatest pride, though, was that the sons of Woodbridge hosted the first antislavery conference in American history—on July 4, 1783, six years before George Washington was inaugurated first president of the United States.

In modern America, there is perhaps no place that better embodies middle-class American values. Every ethnic group, every race, every religion and culture is represented there—not in unofficially segregated communities like I remember from my childhood, but intermingled and coexisting, and equally invested in the community. We had many prefixes, but for us what mattered was our suffix: African *American*, Italian *American*, Turkish *American*, Cuban *American*, all sharing the American dream. The St. James Street fair every October was a celebration of our diversity. So was the yearly Pearl Harbor memorial service, and every baseball game come spring. In fact, baseball season is my favorite time in Woodbridge, those warm, endless nights when floodlights glow over distant diamonds and the sounds of cheers spill out over the town.

But JoJo had left the place in a wreck. As a last-minute election-year gimmick, he had rolled back area property taxes 20 percent, telling newspaper reporters that he'd built up a surplus. Wrong. The town's $60 million budget was $24.5 million short. Making matters worse, he gave a costly raise to municipal labor unions to placate them, and then underestimated state aid. To cover costs, JoJo had raided surplus accounts.

The bookkeeping was a shambles. In one desk drawer we found $400,000 in uncashed checks made out to the township, some dating back seven years. I looked at John "Mac" McCormac, my chief financial officer. "Well, the good news is, we have no place to go but up," I joked.

I spoke too soon. On the second day of our administration, two federal agents arrived with warrants to investigate the disappearance of $650,000 in health insurance funds. Next, four of the employees I inherited from JoJo were charged with taking kickbacks from contractors. Woodbridge's government was an utter disaster.

Financially, we had no room to maneuver. I didn't want to levy new taxes. The median income in Woodbridge was only $45,000; I knew people were already pinched. But the alternative was to lay off 40 percent of the workforce, which was also unacceptable. That would mean dirtier streets, deeper potholes, and a painful shortage of health department workers, police officers, librarians, and so on.

Mac suggested a clever solution. Several other Jersey towns had shifted from a calendar year for budget purposes to a fiscal year, from July 1 to June 30. A quirk in the process for doing this would allow us to float municipal bonds to cover costs for a half-year transitional period. This way we could borrow about $42 million, enough to bridge the gap and jump-start the local economy.

It was a great solution. We took "Woodbridge Works" as our new slogan, and resolved to make sure every dollar went to services. But first, to get it past the municipal council, I needed a majority of the nine members—five of them Republicans. Jack Fay, who had simply moved into the mayor's office with me, occasionally peered over his copy of the *New York Times* to offer suggestions for working over the councilmen. Mac and I followed his advice energetically, but despite our best presentations they weren't budging.

Finally, Paul Weiner figured out why.

"They want assurances," he said. "They don't like the underwriter we're using. They named two other firms they want included—firms that just happen to be big backers of some of the Republican councilmen."

This was an eye-opener for me. I had never thought of finance houses as Republicans or Democrats. I expected the selection process to be strictly price-based. It seemed like payola to me to handpick outside firms based on who their executives were supporting—and it seemed like total fiscal irresponsibility to jeopardize Woodbridge's future in the gamble.

In fact, this was my first lesson in a system known as "pay-to-play," the financial interplay between politicians and vendors that defines public life in New Jersey. The members of the Woodbridge Municipal Council, like every other municipal official in the state who's ever had to raise campaign funds, counted among their supporters' leaders in every field, even this one. And it was understood that they owed them something in return. This would be a huge payday for any outside contractor—the underwriters, consultants, bonders, and finance houses—and an opportunity for payback. It was like a huge virtual chess game.

"What if I say no?" I asked Paul. "What are they going to do, make me lay off everybody and close down the town?"

"Jim, we're not talking about contracting to shady companies. Both underwriters are respectable firms; they just happen to have some relationship to two Republican councilmen. They just play for the other team."

"None of these companies are the Little Sisters of the Poor," Jack piped up, between puffs on a cigarette.

I didn't really care which corporation was going to handle our bonding. "A pox on all their houses," I said. "I just want to know this isn't adding costs."

"They'll get a fixed percentage of the total bond issue package," Paul said. "It's the same cost no matter who we use. In fact, we can use them all and divide the fee in thirds."

In my years in politics, this was my first difficult moral crossroad. I thought of all the political biographies I'd read with my dad. What Caesar, Lincoln, and Douglas McArthur had in common was the ability to make political accommodations to reach their goals. The high art of leadership, I knew, was the ability to chart a route to the good through a moral quandary.

I thought back to college, to Kant's famous formulations on the "Concepts of Good and Evil." Kant argued that morality couldn't be reached by judging ends and means alone. Motive, he wrote, is the main measure of whether an action is moral or not. My motive was clear and lacked self-interest. This crisis was exactly the "hypothetical imperative" he parsed: *You must do* A *in order to achieve* X. Floating bonds was a legitimate goal; compromising on vendors would surely produce that goal, without committing an egregious moral harm in itself.

Finally I capitulated and let the Republicans pick their two contractors, while keeping the one we'd originally chosen as well. It was a distasteful decision, but I believed it was a moral one, and not unethical. The taxpayers of Woodbridge benefited. Without accommodation, we would have been dead in the water.

But from my personal life I had a keen understanding of the dangers of accommodation. To get where I was, I had already made one major accommodation with the truth. *Doing* A in that instance might have justified *achieving* X. But that first compromise invariably led to many others; A became a whole alphabet of lies and half-truths.

I worried very consciously that the same thing might happen with my political career, one little compromise at a time.

IMMANUEL KANT WASN'T MY ONLY LODESTAR. I MODELED MY ADministration on the principles showcased by Stephen R. Covey in his book *The 7 Habits of Highly Effective People*, a best seller at the time. I had attended several Covey seminars and found his credo, which was a lot like my Dad's old marine maxim, very useful. It emphasized concentrated work, integrity, and measurable goals. We instructed each department to come up with mission-driven goals for the year, and I met with department heads once a week to review progress toward those goals.

Given our bare-bones operation, I did a lot of the work myself. If I saw a pothole at 7:00 AM, I would have it filled by nightfall—then put in a shift on the public works hot line, making lists of new problems to fix. I would drive around behind the snowplows and make sure they did a decent job. I was maniacal about making the town spotless. Once a month I held an open Town Hall meeting, inviting people to bring their complaints and promising to find a solution. These meetings were by far my favorite part of the job. I'd personally call people who had their lawns too high. I didn't care if they thought it was overstepping. I cared about community standards in the town.

One delicate challenge came up when I started hearing complaints about the conditions in the Little India section of town. Woodbridge has one of the largest South Asian populations in the United States, and the old-world traditions persisted among some of the newer immigrants, a fact that stirred some local prejudices. We had callers who actually said, "It smells of curry over there."

I worked to be fair, exacting, and impartial. I understood the importance of shared culture among new immigrant groups, but I also felt we would let the neighborhood's people down if we didn't hold them to the same standards as the rest of the town. When there were real violations, I sent in teams to write up tickets, which initially drew charges of racism. But we also invested in the neighborhood, widening the streets and improving the public landscaping. In the end, Indian leaders were pleased to see their area improving along with the rest of Woodbridge. Come India's Independence Day, August 15, I proudly raised the Indian national flag over Town Hall.

I attended every event I was invited to and most events I wasn't. A good friend, Mike Seidel, told me recently that I attended services at his synagogue so often he thought I was Jewish. I wanted to become everything anybody in Woodbridge wanted me to be. I taught myself seven words in every language spoken in my district—not always the right ones, but nobody cared. I absolutely adored getting to know Woodbridge. I wanted to make it the best little town in America.

My goal was to make sure everybody was happy in Woodbridge as long as I was there. If anybody had a complaint, Paul would negotiate with them and, if necessary, invite them to hockey matches on Tuesdays or football games on Thursdays—and by the next morning their concerns were resolved. We were an administration working for all the people, because we had all the people working for us.

But with Paul taking care of the backroom stuff, I was able to carry out the parts of the job that really challenged me. I put together a plan to revitalize Main Street, which had gone the way of other cities in the 1980s. The strip was rundown and abandoned; most retailers had moved out to the malls, taking all foot traffic with them. With the help of the town council, we laid brick sidewalks and added new lampposts, benches, and planters through the center of town. Anchoring the effort were plans for a new town hall, a three-story high-tech building, fully wired for the Internet. In addition, we committed new financing to the town's marina and ramp in the Sewaren section of town, making it among one of the most-used launches in the area; we invested in park rehabilitation and put computers in every school in town. It all worked. Downtown became a destination again.

Our most ambitious undertaking, though, was the Woodbridge Township Community Center, considered one of biggest in the state. Going door-to-door as exhaustively as I had, I realized that we had very few venues for local families to gather for recreation, meetings, and entertainment. In this city of 100,000 people, there was not even a YMCA. So during my tenure we raised $15 million, mostly in corporate and private donations, and built a sprawling center complete with an NHL-sized ice rink, Olympic pool, roller rink, gym, wellness center, arcade, walking track, computer lab, and pro shop. The YMCA and a company called United Skates of America agreed to come and manage the facility.

The other lesson I learned from watching JoJo DeMarino, of course, was how not to get entangled in my own power. "I don't want you getting too big for your britches," my spiritual adviser, an Irish sage from Wood-bridge named Monsignor Michael Cashman, told me after I took office. "You know what's going to determine, more than anything else, how many people are at your funeral Mass? The weather."

Besides, money was never important to me. The job paid a whopping $52,000 a year, more than enough when added to Kari's salary—she went to work as a librarian at a public school in South Brunswick. We had no trouble making payments on a condominium on Gill Lane whose back windows overlooked the tracks of an active freight rail line. My staff hated the place, finding it a bit too humble, but Kari and I made a lovely home there. Once a month or more we would take a train into New York City for a movie or play—Kari believed in what she called "our traditions," the little rituals that would become the glue to our marriage. Every December we went to Rockefeller Center to see the huge Christmas tree. Every spring we went to Florida and stayed with our friend John Pedro. Summers, when we could, we headed for a weekend at the shore.

One of our first big events as the first couple of Woodbridge was hosting the town's 325th anniversary. Kari looked stunning in a black beaded gown with a red silk bodice. The voters seemed genuinely to love her, and her interest in them was profound. Right after dinner she came and whispered in my ear mischievously, "Let's dance!" I resisted. I'm not much of a dancer, but I let her drag me to the dance floor anyway, put my hand on her waist, and got my feet moving. I'd forgotten how much fun dancing could be. Kari had a way of reminding me that our successes were in our hearts, not just our heads.

"Enjoy this," she whispered. We kissed. "You have arrived."

OUR BABY GIRL WAS BORN ON OCTOBER 27, 1992. SHE WAS AS BEAU-tiful as an angel. We named her Morag, a Gaelic derivative of the name Mary, after Kari's beloved grandmother. I was thrilled to be a father, and over the moon about having a daughter.

As a surprise for me, my dear friend Joe Vitale, the Woodbridge Democratic Party chairman, planted a giant sign on the town hall lawn: IT'S A GIRL! I drove Morag and her mom past the sign on the way home from the hospital to show them. I was so proud. I had a beautiful wife and a glorious baby girl—what every man in the public eye dreams of. It couldn't get any better than that.

While Kari was still pregnant, her father had succumbed to lung cancer after a long battle, likely the product of decades working in the Vancouver mines. Our doctors told her not to fly, so Kari couldn't attend the funeral. I know this was extremely difficult for her and her family. I would have been devastated if I'd been kept from a loved one's funeral. But for Kari, the funeral was less important than paying respects to the living, which she'd done unfailingly while her dad was still alive.

We were lucky that Kari's mother, a sturdy Scots émigré named Agnes, found the strength to come to visit her new granddaughter, despite her grief. It was heartwarming for me to see the three generations of women bonding together, celebrating life in the aftermath of a terrible death. Morag was a bright light keeping her mother and grandmother looking forward—as she still is today.

Morag gave me endless pleasure. I loved when she climbed into bed with us, cuddling and practicing her words and songs. She was a quick study, like her mother. One of my favorite things was taking her to work and letting her crawl around the mayor's office—Kennedy-like, I suppose—as I pushed through my day's phone calls.

But I sensed that something about motherhood was pulling Kari a little further out of my political world. She never was the kind of woman who could have a dozen meaningless conversations at one political function, then race off to another. When she engaged somebody in conversation, she always had things to say and found things to learn. When the subject of Second Ward chairman Gus Maciolek's prize-caliber tomatoes came up one day, I remember her telling me how he grew them: he put potassium in the soil. How did she know? I asked. "Well, he explained it to me," she said.

Kari was totally genuine; superficial encounters irked her. She liked people too much to let them glance off her meaninglessly. Naturally, she tired quickly of the political circuit. After a while it became impossible to drag her around to the events. "How can you deal with some of these people?" she asked more than once. "They don't care about you, they don't care about us. They don't care about anything." She loved the county committee members and our real friends, especially Jack Fay and his second wife, Carol, and our best friends Jimmy and Lori Kennedy. (The Kennedys were also our doppelgängers in politics, Jimmy as mayor of nearby Rahway and Lori as member of the school board.)

In small ways, I could see Kari's disappointment in me growing almost from the start. I used to think of her as a canary in the mines of Woodbridge, responding oversensitively but always justifiably to the poisons around us. But the truth was, as much as she hated interacting on the political plane, I loved it. I never missed a ribbon-cutting, chicken dinner, or funeral. Once, when the mother of a local freeholder was being laid to rest in a Byzantine rites service at a neighborhood church, I was heartened at the sight of Congressman Ed Patten, who showed up dramatically late and took the pew in front of Kari and me.

"Hey, Jimmy," he said too loudly, "wake me up when it's time for communion." Whereupon he actually stretched out for a nap and slumbered away.

I woke him up, as requested, and he accompanied Kari and me to the altar and back. His nap seemed to restore his piss and vinegar. During the recessional hymn that followed, as the priest moved toward us escorting the casket, Patten turned to me and Kari again.

"You see that priest?" he nearly shouted over the music.

"Yes, Congressman?"

"He won't give Mrs. Jacowski Holy Communion, but he's at the rectory sleeping with the housekeeper every night."

Kari went crimson with mortification. Patten had a knack for telling the unvarnished truth, but sometimes his timing was a little challenging. A quarter of the congregation had heard Patten, no doubt including the priest. I had no idea who the Jacowskis might be, but I knew I needed to bring the conversation to a quick end.

"Thank you, Congressman," I answered in a stage whisper, then joined Kari singing the hymn as loudly as I could.

EVERY MAJOR NEW JERSEY POLITICAL DECISION IS MADE IN DINERS, and Morag had been home from the hospital only a few days when I met Jack Fay at the old Woodbridge Diner to talk about the future. Jack had a plan for me, he intimated vaguely. I didn't know what he had in mind; as a newly elected mayor, I had plenty on my plate as it was. But I agreed to hear him out.

I invited Mac McCormac, the Woodbridge chief financial officer; Gary Taffet, a brilliant strategist and my chief of staff; Kevin McCabe, my aide-de-camp from town hall; Tim Dacey, whom I made director of public works; and Joe Vitale, the Woodbridge Democratic Party chairman, whom I consulted on all my moves. Collectively, these guys had become my Woodbridge cabinet.

Jack circled around his proposal, first laying out the local landscape. The Republican state senator from the 19th Legislative District, a Republican named Randy Corman, was up for reelection. In Jack's estimation, Corman was vulnerable. I had already beaten him once, when he ran against me for assembly in 1989. On the Democratic side, my only potential primary challenger was a school board lawyer named Carl Palmisano. I knew Carl; he was a nice guy, but he knew little about the ground game it would take to unseat an incumbent senator, especially in 1993, a terrible year for Democrats. Florio was heading toward a tough reelection bid. Voters were livid about the tax increase he'd signed (and I supported)—New Jerseyans already had the highest total tax burden in the nation, and they rightly demanded relief in other areas, which Florio hadn't found a way to give them. Worse, he'd gone on to sign a state sales tax on everyday items like toiletries, disproportionately affecting the working class, who spend a greater portion of their income on such necessities.

But Florio might have been able to survive that wound if not for the mighty backlash to his position against assault weapons. I shared his aversion to high-powered semiautomatic rifles like Uzis and AK-47s, whose only purpose could be killing people. When I was still in the assembly, we enacted the toughest and most comprehensive assault weapons ban in the country. We also banned large-capacity ammunition magazines, the first state to do so.

In response, the NRA went ballistic. They spent millions of dollars in advertising trying to block passage. I remember being in the chamber when the bill was being voted on. The NRA had sent in hundreds of protesters who were screaming and carrying on. Suddenly there was a loud crashing sound. Somebody had thrown a rock through one of the grand old stained-glass windows on the statehouse. It was almost sacrilegious, what they had done. But the protest had a boomerang effect, galvanizing votes in *favor* of the bill, and Florio was awarded the Kennedy Profiles in Courage Award for signing it into law.

But the NRA wasn't through with Florio. This was the dawn of shock jock radio, and they whipped a constellation of radio DJs into a frenzy, especially at New Jersey 101.5, a station reaching most of the state. Conflating the assault rifle ban with the tax increase, they fomented a full-scale tax revolt. This was NRA retribution, pure and simple. It was already clear to most of us that Florio wasn't going to survive this, and a relatively unknown and extraordinarily wealthy Republican challenger named Christine Todd

Whitman was poised to steal his office from him. Democrats across the state were shaking in their boots.

Even while everybody else was retreating, Jack thought I should make a bold strike for the senate seat.

In part, this was a grudge match for him. Jack himself had held that office until the party machine pushed him off the line a few years back for voting too independently. (He had since been named Ombudsman for the Institutionalized Elderly, where he was doing the work of saints on behalf of seniors in nursing homes, veterans in hospitals, and the like.) I loved the idea of it, the challenge of taking on the Republicans in my backyard. I also loved the idea of moving up to the senate, which I considered the next logical step for me. Being mayor was lots of fun, but I was way too young to stop my political ascent there.

I could even continue on as mayor, Jack said; he felt the voters would accept me as a dual office holder. We went around the table, and everyone agreed.

We were in the race.

But first I had to ask Kari's permission. It would entail enormous sacrifices for her, I knew. I would be campaigning for senate while serving the town as mayor, a job that already filled my days and nights. I would need more than her forbearance. I was going to need her to be at my side at countless events.

"I know you want this," she answered quickly. "I'll support you." But I knew she was frustrated and increasingly lonely.

RAISING FUNDS AGAIN SO SOON AFTER MY CAMPAIGN FOR MAYOR was a daunting prospect. When you're running for office in New Jersey, the first place you need to go—unless you're independently wealthy—is to successful businessmen and -women in the area who are hoping to land large government contracts. The self-interest is that bald. Much of the public work in the state is awarded on a no-bid basis, or in a process where factors other than price are considered; the lure of a quid pro quo is always in the air. We call the system "pay-to-play," but it's a form of sanctioned bribery—

a perfectly legal but fundamentally corrupt system that drives politics in the state.

I was starting to grow uncomfortable with pay-to-play, though I'd played the distasteful game pretty effectively in the past. Of course, not every proposition was as morally complex as that fiscal year bond issue we'd waded through. More typical was the case of a small towing outfit that made a donation to my mayoral campaign instead of supporting JoJo. I was touched. I knew the owner was risking a lot by throwing his support to me; if I lost, JoJo was sure to deny him the municipal towing contracts he wanted, which might even force him out of business. When I won, I rewarded him for his faith in me.

The system still worked pretty much the same way as we started passing the hat for the senate run. But the usual suspects were different: now we were taking meetings with lawyers, engineers, unions, industry groups, and real estate developers, all of whom were keen on influencing laws and regulations. I took care not to make any specific promises in exchange for their financial support. That would be a felony. Instead, I just found a way to say something encouraging: "We would be lucky to have you serving the people," for example. They knew how the game was played, and they knew I understood it too. Nothing more needed to be said.

AROUND THIS TIME, KARI AND I INVITED AGNES TO COME AND LIVE with us. We renovated a basement room for her; it was damp, but it was all we could afford.

I loved having Agnes around; she was smart, no-nonsense, and had a grand sense of humor. We took her with us everywhere we went—into New York for shopping, to the opera in Newark, to garden shows and art exhibits and even political events. Unfortunately, Agnes had even less patience for politics than Kari. Once, when she asked me about my future, I mentioned the governor's mansion. "That's not in the realm of possibilities," she scoffed. I never felt discouraged by her, though, only challenged—I'd always preferred to bring my detractors close. You never could tell what was going to come out of her mouth. When Kari and I took her along to a Christmas party at the statehouse, she somehow managed to corner Governor Florio alone in his office, excoriating him for his tax increases. "How can you sleep at night?" I heard her asking as I walked in the door.

The first winter after she came was an especially cold one. We had more snow than I ever remember—six, seven feet of snow. Month after month it piled, trapping people in their homes. I barely slept, running around the township trying to keep the roads open. On top of that, I was busy raising money for the senate run. My first run for mayor had cost me $250,000. At the state level, the stakes were higher—and so was the price tag. Jack set a fundraising goal for me of more than $600,000. It was like squeezing rocks, trying to get that much money out of my friends. But we persevered.

At the same time, all the lobbyists suddenly starting asking for meetings. They all wanted access, which was a sure sign they thought I could win. They were all very nice, all well dressed, but their expectations were high; I found myself uncomfortable among them, not yet sure how to respond to their demands.

I was lucky to have Jack Fay at my side throughout this period, smoking and sipping coffee over the *Times* in the corner of my office, freely dispensing his wisdom and moral guidance. It was like having Sir Thomas More on call at all times. He hated the lobbyists, whom he collectively called "the Unclean." Sometimes he would crank his glasses up to his brow and blurt out his leftist critiques of them in the middle of my meetings—startling my guests, who'd no doubt assumed he was my old grandfather or uncle I allowed to hang around the office. Finally, I had to start receiving the lobbyists in our conference room; I wasn't about to ask the great Jack Fay to clear out of my office, even for a few minutes.

I weighed their proposals, trying to make choices based on their ideologies, track records, and commitments to the community. Jack thought this was ridiculous.

"Why do you give a damn? So Joe Dem can build a million-dollar extension on his home? You should care? Whoever gets the contract is in it for the money. That's all."

He had a point. But back at home, Kari was pulling me in the other direction. She thought there was something lowly about the way Americans campaigned for office, and how, once in office, we focused on mundane things like providing services rather than points of policy. I remember saying to her once, "Kari, I'm not *supposed* to be grappling with the big issues of the day. I'm running a city. It's hard work." But of course she was mostly right. I wasn't stepping back and seeing the many moral compromises and ethical shortcuts I was beginning to take in the fundraising process. More and more, we were spending our best energies on the business of rewarding supporters and placating detractors—in other words, engaging in the business of patronage.

I tried to convince her that all of this was essential, that it was all part of building my career. To her it must have seemed like the only business of government was handing out jobs and contracts.

I must also admit that our love life went by the wayside, though she never complained. Looking back, I wonder if avoiding intimacy wasn't the real reason I worked so many late nights. More than once I do remember being relieved to find Kari asleep when I got home—I could slip in beside her without feeling any obligation.

Our worst fight came on the occasion of Morag's first birthday party, a month before Election Day 1993. I was like a robot by then, running for senate while trying to keep up with obligations at town hall. It was the same day as the Mayor's Soccer Trophy, a yearly banquet for the school leagues. To make the day memorable for Morag, Kari had baked almond tarts, scones, and an angel food cake with lemon filling. After greeting our guests, I told Kari I had to slip out for a few minutes for an appearance at the banquet. But I got caught up handing out all the little awards, and I didn't return for four hours. When I got back the guests were gone, and Kari was cleaning up in a blue funk.

"Woodbridge only has one mayor," I said in my defense.

"Morag only has one father," she shot back. She was right.

Her frustrations, which were all justified, turned to disgust when the Republicans started playing dirty politics. A friend of mine who worked at the post office called campaign headquarters one afternoon. "You are not going to believe what they're trying to nail you on," he told me. "They're mailing out a leaflet with a picture of your car in front of an adult bookstore in Times Square with a big headline: 'What was Jim McGreevey's car doing in front of this place?' "

I don't know how many times in my adult life my heart has frozen in place thinking I'd been caught. This may have been my longest seizure ever. Until I saw a copy of the flyer, I was convinced I'd been busted for sure. But the image was an obvious fake. They had pasted a photograph of my official township car, a silver Chevy Caprice, over a photograph of one of those sleazy emporia on West Forty-second Street advertising GIRLS! GIRLS! GIRLS! The text of the brochure revealed the germ of the story—that my car had received a parking ticket at eight o'clock one morning in the vicinity, which was absolutely true.

The true story, however, was completely innocent. That morning I'd raced into town for a meeting Senator Bradley's office had kindly arranged, to help me get an expedited passport for a trip to Woodbridge's sister city in the Dominican Republic, Paraiso. In my rush I'd pulled the car into a no-parking zone in front of a Catholic church and paid the fine for my impatience. How ironic was that—all the embarrassing places I'd been, and what got me in trouble was parking in front of a Catholic church.

That's how the game is played—smear campaigns, baseless allegations, and character assassinations. It was disgusting, and done without shame. The leaflet was produced by the Republican State Committee, the highest body in the GOP organization. They mailed it to every household in the 19th Legislative District on the Friday night before the Tuesday election. The parents of every kid in Morag's playgroup got a copy. Kari was beside herself with hurt. "Jim, why do people do this?" she asked. In Vancouver, this kind of dirty politics was unheard of. "I don't want to live like this, with people who would behave this way."

Neither did I. On Saturday morning I called a press conference with Democratic Party leaders and Rev. Jack Dunlap of the First Presbyterian Church of Avenel, who founded the sister-city project that runs a free clinic there. Several area pastors joined us, as did Senator Frank Lautenberg. I hammered my fist on the podium in anger, demanding a retraction and an apology. "This is made up of whole cloth," I said. "This is politics at its worst."

Ultimately, the Republican State Committee admitted it was a fake. Still, I knew it had made an impact—if not always the impact the GOP wanted. One of my supporters even said to me with a wink, "Well, at least we know what kind of mayor we have!" I'll admit, there was a part of me that didn't mind the rumor that I was interested in GIRLS! GIRLS! GIRLS!

After the dust had settled, I was elected state senator, just two years after becoming mayor and four years after joining the assembly—a hat trick that brought me to the attention of the statewide party leadership. At thirty-six, I was a young man with a future.

HOPING TO MAKE THINGS BETTER WITH KARI, I BOUGHT US ALL tickets for Walt Disney World for Christmas. We'd never been on a real vacation before—not even a honeymoon, because I was running for mayor at the time. We had always wanted to go to Ireland, but for now, given our meager finances, Florida would have to suffice.

We weren't even able to stay in any of the charming theme hotels on the Disney campus. Instead I booked us at a little Holiday Inn along the highway a few miles away. Everything was so expensive there that we all stayed in one room, including Agnes, and lived on Domino's Pizza—breakfast, lunch, and dinner.

No one was happy about the arrangements, but I tried to keep a cheerful demeanor, especially for Morag. I wanted this to be a magical experience—something she'd remember her whole life. But she wasn't any happier than the rest of us. It rained constantly, I remember. It was cold. She was sleeping nonstop, perhaps because she had a cold coming on.

She was fast asleep in her stroller on the afternoon of the fabled Disney Christmas Parade. When Santa's sleigh appeared, I thought, *Finally—this will cheer her up.* I started to wake her.

"Jim, please don't do that," Kari said. "She's two years old. You're doing that for yourself, not for her."

"Don't be silly," I assured her, shaking Morag awake. "Look, honey, Santa Claus is coming!"

The sight of a big red-suited man coming at her through the rain was too much for her. She screamed and screamed, and would not be comforted.

I LOVED KARI AS MUCH AS EVER. I ADMIRED HER AND RESPECTED her and my heart ached for her whenever we were apart. But I knew it wasn't right. If any marriage would work for me, this one would—but it didn't. She suspected this, I am sure, and it must have made her feel awful. It wasn't her I was rejecting. I loved her deeply as a friend and companion. I loved her company. I loved being on vacation with her. I loved watching her as a mother. I loved being with her. I simply wasn't made to mate with a woman; it went against my nature. But I wasn't about to say that to her or do any-thing to threaten our marriage, which I valued so highly.

After Agnes's first blizzardy winter in our condominium, the next year she and Kari decided to spend a few weeks with Morag in Vancouver, where the weather is much milder. Kari hadn't returned to work after the delivery and Morag wasn't in school yet, so there was nothing to keep them home. Morag loved seeing her extended family there, and I was happy to know they were comfortable and among family. In the spring and summer, they flew to Vancouver again. I managed to join them for a few days, but not as much as I would have liked.

If only I'd been paying closer attention, I would have noticed that Kari was removing more of her things from our home with each trip she took. She returned only briefly in 1995. I never complained. I missed my family terribly, but their absence freed up my time for political work, for which I was developing a true addiction. I loved all of it—helping people, feeling the power, tracking the backroom machinations. And the harder I worked, the less I thought about sex, or heard the whispers of my heart.

IT WASN'T AN IDEAL TIME TO BE RETURNING TO TRENTON AS A Democratic lawmaker. Jim Florio lost his reelection, as expected, and

Whitman moved into the governor's office, giving the Republicans control of the executive branch *and* both houses. My party was in a shambles. We lacked clear leadership and lost track of our vision. The party responded by turning to pollsters and consultants rather than returning to our core values—which to me have always included helping the poor, sick, and elderly; investing aggressively in the young; stabilizing the economy; defending the environment; advancing social justice; and advocating for middle class interests. We should never need to test these values with focus groups or surveys. But it was becoming popular for individual senators to employ their own pollsters, then argue among one another about the popularity of each new initiative.

Without bold vision, we weren't likely to get anything passed. The Republican majority locked us out of all leadership positions and kept us marginalized in committees. Our legislation rarely even made it to debates. It isn't overstating things to say we were totally irrelevant in Trenton at the time.

I did sponsor or cosponsor a number of meaningful but doomed bills, among them a Charter Schools proposal and a bill to cap municipal spending. Revisiting my earlier work on the Holocaust, I also sponsored a bill— the first in the nation—mandating that the terrible history of Nazi war crimes be taught to every child in New Jersey schools, lest that tragic chapter ever be forgotten. That bill ultimately passed, but for many years it wasn't a priority for lawmakers.

In frustration, then, we stood by as Whitman and her allies pushed through a series of Reaganesque policies designed to shrink government and create wide-open incentives for business investments. Whitman seemed to have her eye on higher office from the start. Indeed, she'd quickly made herself over to appeal to the conservative wing of her party. George Will dubbed her an American Margaret Thatcher, "without all that abrasiveness."

With great fanfare, she enacted three successive income tax cuts, totaling 30 percent. The top income earners got smaller reductions, but in dollar terms they reaped the biggest savings. Families earning more than $2 million a year—like Whitman and her husband, a Wall Street corporate buyout specialist—saved more than $13,000; for most New Jerseyans, the yearly savings was $350. I also saw the wisdom of giving taxpayers a little relief after the Florio debacle, but Whitman's deep cuts backfired on her, as local property taxes were raised even further to offset the shortfalls. The tax bills of ordinary New Jerseyans were largely unchanged.

Then she set her sights on energy deregulation, which at the time was a big war cry for Republicans. Dismantling government oversight of public utilities was one of the greatest scams of the 1990s. I never thought the idea made any sense. Power companies claimed that deregulation would provide consumers with competitive opportunities, allowing them to select a favorite electricity "vendor" from a menu of choices. Theoretically that would drive down prices, as it had when the telephone companies were deregulated.

But I knew energy was a different story. For generations, New Jersey had followed what was called a "rate-based rate of return" system, which accounted for the utilities' reinvestment in infrastructure and technology, factored in overhead and expenses, and established a fair rate of return for shareholders while assuring consumers weren't being gouged. It was a successful system, and as a result New Jersey had one of the most powerful grids in the nation. I argued for preserving the old system.

In the senate, I was a minority of one. Literally every other senator was enthusiastic about deregulation. "There is no question this will create competition," Senator Joseph Kyrillos, the Republican cosponsor, told me. "Competition creates more companies, and more companies means more jobs. Jim, it's a win-win. Lower cost to the consumer and more jobs in the community."

"That's bull," I said. "Mrs. Smith doesn't want a menu of options to choose from. Mrs. Smith wants to know her toaster oven will work whenever she needs it. And she wants a fair price. That's what she's got now." Besides, I said, "the multinational corporations will be running our utilities, Joe. Do you think that when my Little League team's playing in Woodbridge and the power browns out, somebody in Montreal is going to give a shit when I call up there?"

I couldn't get anybody to listen; the great mythos of competition was too alluring. Even the AFL-CIO fell into the chorus. Whitman's program passed with overwhelming support. Soon, our local utilities were controlled by a firm in Akron, Ohio, as I'd projected. And the alleged benefit to consumers never materialized. Prices never went down—and to this day nobody has ever seen a menu of providers to choose from.

But something else happened that nobody had anticipated. Some of our utility companies split into several businesses, separating the physical plants from the transmissions firms, then selling off the plants. As we later discovered, they had used this sleight of hand to divest themselves of some extremely polluted pieces of property—increasing their profit margins while taxpayers had to pay to clean them up.

This was one time when I wish my colleagues had relied on pollsters and consultants. One or two phone calls, and they might have realized what Mrs. Smith was thinking.

AS THE YEAR PROGRESSED, I BEGAN GETTING COURTED BY STATE Democratic Party officials urging me to consider running for governor against Whitman. It seemed quixotic. She had quickly become a towering national figure and an icon among women. Magazines like *Vogue* and *Mirabella* did big features on her; Newt Gingrich was touting her as VP material. In 1995 she was the GOP's choice to rebut Bill Clinton's State of the Union address, live on national television. She was the first Republican governor chosen for the job, and the first woman.

I wanted Kari to come back home and help me decide what to do, but the thought of another political campaign was revolting to her, and higher office terrified her. She told me she'd once overheard a radio shock jock making fun of Morag's name. "What kind of a person would ridicule a child?" she asked. Throughout the late summer of 1995, I implored her to return. I tried to convince her that we were just in a bad patch. "This is a long march," I said. "Just hang on with me—we're going to get to the Promised Land."

"Jim, it's about us. It's about how we chose to live our lives. I want to share my life with people who have the same value structure as I do. People who value decency, who value kindness, who value respect. We're not going through some dark and desolate night toward a new dawn, Jim. We're coming to a dark and desolate dawn."

That's when I noticed that she'd taken all her things out of the house, and everything Agnes and Morag needed too.

"Jim, this isn't how I want to spend my life," she finally told me a few months later. "Life's too short. I want to spend my life loving my family, living in a community that respects me."

I tried everything to get them back. I cashed in my stock from Merck and put a down payment on an elegant home in town with a lawn and slate roof; I mailed pictures with a note that said, "I finally get it." It didn't help. I flew to Vancouver to beg her, but she wouldn't let me stay in the house. As a husband and father, I knew I had failed.

Kari brought Morag back to New Jersey from time to time, but just for visits; their home was in Vancouver now. She never asked me to move to Vancouver with her, either. She knew I was too attached—desperately attached—to this life in New Jersey, this invention of mine.

IV.

What a Divided Self Can Do

10.

NEW JERSEY IS THE NATION'S MOST URBAN STATE, THE DENSEST in the country, squeezing 1,165 people into every square mile of land. No other state comes close. Even India, with 914 people per square mile, and Japan, with 835, have more elbow room. When Whitman became governor, with her promises to deregulate and cut big government, pressure intensified to put houses on every inch of soil. Not even the coastal wetlands were off-limits. We were quickly running out of open space. At the prevailing pace, urban planning experts warned that we could soon become the first fully built up state in the nation, unable to sustain even one more McMansion. Whitman had no interest in countering sprawl; it consumed farms at a remarkable pace, fifty acres every single day. Of course, not every part of the state was at risk. The estates owned by the wealthiest were immune to development pressures.

Unfortunately, pro-environment senators couldn't do anything about it. Most of us were Democrats. And being in the minority at the statehouse meant we were not able to get traction on any policy initiative. It was a terrific frustration to all of us, and to me especially—I'd been spoiled by my tenure on the assembly side, when we were still the dominant power. As a senator, I felt like I was just spinning my wheels. I supported efforts to roll back unplanned development, with no progress to show for it.

On top of our high real estate costs, we also had by far the highest property tax in the nation. For years the governor had administered a rebate program, sending homeowners a check for $500 or so each year to offset the exorbitant bill. We were stunned when Whitman cut that back—but then again, when it came to money, she just didn't get it. "Funny as it might seem, five hundred bucks is a lot of money to some people," she once told a reporter.

The governor didn't lift a finger to counter the one issue voters cited over and over in polls as the thing that made them angriest, and the first thing they wanted changed: exorbitant auto insurance rates. The literary critic Edmund Wilson once dismissed New Jersey as a "region that one traverses to get somewhere else," namely Philadelphia or New York City. That's not my experience; small towns like Carteret are filled with families who have lived and worked there for generations. Yet of course New Jersey is also a drivers' state, crisscrossed by highways and commuters. Ironically, no other state is less friendly to drivers. In 1997, it cost the average driver $1,000 a year to insure her car. In Iowa, she would pay less than half that.

Whitman must have been aware of the problem. It had been raised by voters in every election for the last twenty years. A formal inquiry had determined that the high rates were due to fraud. In most states, people committing insurance fraud were prosecuted and thrown in jail. Not New Jersey. Instead, the costs were simply absorbed by the companies and passed along to customers—more than 15 percent of the price of every policy was fraud related. Whitman didn't increase prosecutions appreciably in her four years. Meanwhile, auto insurance went up on twelve separate occasions, and profits doubled. Communism was dead everywhere except Cuba and the New Jersey auto insurance market.

I thought: *A person could make a go at unseating Whitman just by running on auto insurance alone.*

But I wasn't sure I wanted to be the one to do it. It was Paul Weiner, my law director, who first brought up the possibility in earnest, over breakfast with Ray Lesniak and Jack Fay one morning at the Reo Diner in Woodbridge. Of all the influential mayors, he pointed out, I had one of the highest approval ratings—I'd won my last reelection with 69 percent of the vote. He couldn't think of a better campaigner in the senate. "There's no guarantee you'll do well," he said. "She's still pretty popular. But you know we can line up a sufficient number of counties to take the primary, unite the party, and run against her."

Ray agreed. So did Jack, who was furious at Whitman. He let loose a diatribe about how she wasn't fighting the nursing home industry, had even eliminated the Office of Public Advocate in a cost saving move, removing the only interface most New Jerseyans had with their government. Even if she couldn't be beat, he liked the idea of taking her on.

"That's ludicrous," I said. The Democrats were still in disarray after the Florio debacle. Even if I had any name recognition, which I didn't, I doubted they'd be able to back me in any effective way. There was sure to be a bitter primary, and I didn't relish the prospects of doing battle with other Democrats only to be trounced by Whitman. She was smart and telegenic; people were already talking about her as part of a potential Republican dream ticket with Colin Powell. And however dispirited New Jerseyans may have been, they weren't blaming the governor, at least according to polls. Whitman's favorability scores were still relatively high. Besides that, no mayor had ever been elected governor before, much less one from a politically inconsequential town like Woodbridge.

Paul heard me out. "What do you think your chances of being elected are?" he asked when I finally shut up.

I flipped over the placemat and drew a decision tree, handicapping the odds at each stage, from gaining the bosses' support to raising money to getting endorsements.

"Fifteen percent," I said.

"Now what do you think your chances of being elected governor are if you don't run?" He had a point.

In Paul's view, I would come out smelling good even if I lost. Acquitting myself well in a primary battle would put me in a good position with the party leaders and improve my standing statewide. "And you'd be able to talk about issues that mean something to you. You're always complaining about the mayor's job being all about potholes."

Subconsciously I scribbled on the placemat two words: *auto insurance.*

BESIDES JACK, RAY, AND PAUL, I PUT TOGETHER A SMALL GROUP OF advisers to look into the possibility: Gary Taffet, Mac McCormac, Kevin McCabe, and Joe Vitale, the Woodbridge Democratic Chair.

State campaign finance laws prevented Whitman from raising money for reelection until January, but we knew she already had a number of $500-a-plate fundraisers in the pipeline. Besides that, she had at her disposal a vast personal fortune, much of it inherited from her father, the financier and Republican stalwart Webster Todd. My bank accounts held less than $2,000.

I'd done fundraising before, several times, but raising money for a governor's race would be a different ballgame altogether, and another step deeper into the minefields of pay-to-play. Governors have less control over contracts than mayors or legislators, but they control the budgeting process, another key area of concern for contractors. So now the potential donors I was meeting with were hoping I'd put $2 billion aside for road construction; once the money was allocated, they'd go to the local level to secure the contracts to spend that money. I also had to start courting—and being courted by—a whole new class of interested contributors: major developers, industry lobbying groups, and the lawyers and contractors in their orbit. I held sympathetic meetings with groups representing small mom-and-pop pharmacists and groups representing the big chains; gave equal reassurances to the trial lawyers and the defense bar; listened empathetically as the Cemetery Association criticized the Funeral Directors, and vice versa—without ever revealing my personal sympathies. And I accepted donations from them all. Each, in some way, had major business with the state of New Jersey. The decisions I would make as governor would affect them all. I could only console myself that I was breaking no law in accepting their financial support, and trust that I and my staff would never allow the quid pro quo transactions to cross the lines of propriety.

We knew we were going to need a lot of money. By Jack's estimate, the primary alone would cost more than $3 million. One reason is that our state has none of its own broadcast media markets: To reach New Jersey voters with television ads, you've got to buy time on the expensive stations in New York or Philadelphia, buys that reach a lot of people who'll never get to vote for you. And TV is the only efficient way to get your name known in New Jersey. The newspapers in the state—the *Newark Star-Ledger* and the Gannett chain of small dailies, for instance—don't reach the whole state. Press conferences in the southern part of the state don't even get covered up north.

We hired a consultant, some high-flier from DC. She talked a big game about cultivating funders, but when she got down to brass tacks we started to worry. "First thing you do," she said brightly, "is go through all your Rolodexes. Start with your relatives."

Everybody howled. "Uncle Peter's a cop," I said. "Uncle Herb is a crane operator in the union. What about Aunt Peggy? She gave me ten bucks for my first Holy Communion."

Meanwhile, the *Star-Ledger* was running front-page pictures of Whitman, showing up in beaded gowns at exclusive events. My dad, who hadn't yet signed on to the idea of a campaign, was concerned. "Where are you going with this? You're facing Douglas MacArthur and you've got a pea shooter."

The more I looked at Whitman's term as governor, though, the more convinced I was that we had an obligation to run against her. Her deep tax cuts had proved a major burden to the poor and working class, and a boon to the rich. Meanwhile, Whitman's government kept growing, despite her claim to being a small-government Republican. Even her own party leaders were furious when her budget grew past Florio's, and the size of the state workforce ballooned to almost 70,000 employees under her watch, with three times as many workers making over $70,000.

When a deficit began looming, Whitman responded with a reverse Robin Hood scheme, including a decision to raid the pension funds for state employees. This was absurd. New Jersey already had the lowest state pension payments in the country—1 percent of the salaries of covered employees versus a national average of 8 percent, according to one university report. Whitman argued that the booming stock market had overfunded the pension system, allowing the state to substantially reduce its contribution. The combined reductions came to about $3 billion, roughly the same amount she cut from the income tax.

In order to ensure big tax savings for the rich, Whitman was gambling with the future of our workers. Even Bob Littell, the Republican chairman of the Senate Budget and Appropriations Committee, called the governor's actions "fiscally immoral."

Even when she tried belt-tightening, her solutions were indefensible. Besides scrubbing the Office of the Public Advocate, Whitman abolished the

Higher Education Department—but the combined savings was only $6 million a year, and the move sent a terrible message of disregard to our young and old alike. She seemed to have no sympathy for the poor and working-class. She slashed the budget of our Division of Youth and Family Services, responsible for the well-being of our most vulnerable children, those in foster care. And she shaved state contributions to our public colleges system, where most underprivileged kids enroll, while simultaneously pushing up tuition fees there by 35 percent during her tenure. She was beginning to be greeted with hecklers at every commencement speech she gave.

"Maybe all we can do is aggravate her," Jack said. "But shouldn't we *at least* aggravate her?" It wasn't only troublemaking that Jack had in mind. He thought a principled Democratic campaign was the best way to bring the party back from the Florio Aftermath, as he called it.

We made an appointment with Steve DeMicco and Brad Lawrence of the political consulting firm Message & Media to explore the possibility. They agreed that Woodbridge's economic success story would play well in a campaign. But would it translate to all corners of the state? To find out, they asked the top pollster in the field, Doug Schoen, to measure my name recognition—still nonexistent—and the resonance of my positions. It turned out that the concerns I'd noticed in Woodbridge were shared across the state, especially about auto insurance.

"Whitman's seen as somewhat out of touch," Schoen reported back. "People still like her, but they aren't happy with the way New Jersey's heading. They see the social net disappearing, the budget growing out of control, and auto insurance—that's your big issue. People are pinned against a wall by their damned insurance payments."

I TALKED A LOT ABOUT THESE DEVELOPMENTS WITH KARI ON THE phone. She always listened graciously, but distractedly. I could tell she was glad to be away from it all. On the personal side, I was no longer begging her to come home to me, only to hold off divorce proceedings until I decided whether or not to run. There wasn't much to be worked out; neither of us was making significant money, and she wasn't asking for alimony, only child support, so we easily agreed to a nominal amount. Whenever I had a chance to visit Vancouver I always bought things for Morag and Kari both. I wanted to make sure they were comfortable; that was always my aim.

So I was stunned one night when I got back to the Woodbridge condo and found a process server with a thick envelope from Kari's Canadian attorney. I knew immediately what it was. My hands trembled uncontrollably as I read through the motion. It was humiliating—something I'm sure the lawyer cooked up, the way lawyers do, trying to get a better deal. I was being accused of terrible things, the worst being that I had used Morag as a prop for my own political aims. "It appears to me that he is not concerned with Morag's best interests, but in only presenting a facade of a united family . . . in order to enhance his political career." The words devastated me.

I sat down at the kitchen counter in my empty house and fell completely apart. I had been hanging onto a hope that we could still work through our differences. Now I was forced to face the truth, which was that I had destroyed my marriage and sacrificed my family. I had never failed at anything in my life, except love, and I couldn't find a way to accept this failure.

I took a breath and dialed Kari to ask why she had filed suit despite our understanding, and why it included such vitriolic language. She was as upset as I was. She said she wasn't responsible for the timing or content, and I believed her.

Either way, getting those divorce papers precipitated a kind of breakdown, I believe now. For days I lost my appetite and couldn't sleep. Jimmy Kennedy saw how this was destroying me, and he and Kevin McCabe arranged a hasty trip for the three of us to Miami, hoping a little fun would help me forget my troubles. I went along for the ride, but barhopping wasn't going to help me recover.

IN NOVEMBER 1996, IN ATLANTIC CITY, I DECLARED MY INTENTION to run for governor of New Jersey. In an interview at the Associated Press's offices in Trenton, I struck the main notes of the coming campaign. "The sad reality is that for far too many families in the state of New Jersey, both economically and environmentally, as well as in educational opportunity, families are not as secure as they were four years ago," I said. In the morning, the news was in all the papers—the games had begun. Unfortunately, a day or two later the paper carried the newest results of Whitman's popularity polls: 61 percent of voters rated her favorably.

A slew of other Democrats dipped their toes in the pool, but the most serious threats came from Rob Andrews, a thirty-nine-year-old four-term congressman from Camden, and W. Michael Murphy, Jr., a forty-eight-year-old former Morris County prosecutor. Former governor Brendan Byrne had the best line of the early days: "This is my favorite kind of primary: an Irishman from North Jersey, an Irishman from Central Jersey, and an Irishman from South Jersey."

I figured Murphy posed the least challenge to me. He'd served only four years as prosecutor, an unelected post. His biggest claim to party loyalty was the fact that his late stepfather, Richard Hughes, had been a popular governor in the 1960s.

Andrews, on the other hand, was a real political force. Handsome, articulate, and popular, he was strong among women and minorities and experienced in education policy, environmental issues, and even foreign policy, which was important because of New Jersey's close proximity to New York. He was also exceptionally accomplished for being so young—only two days older than I was, and already in Congress.

On policy grounds, Andrews and I shared many moderate Democratic positions. We were pro-choice, pro-environment, pro-death penalty, pro-welfare reform, and pro-gay civil rights. We were also all on record opposing gay marriage. Looking back, I remember feeling *proud* that I could sit in the editorial meetings of newspapers around the state and defend the sanctity of marriage "between a man and a woman" without ringing any bells of suspicion. I never even wrestled with the contradiction.

The closet is a sick, sick place.

With seven months before the primary in June, we drove headlong into the race, bouncing around the state to raise money and hammer away at the issues, especially auto insurance. Dad had a natural base in the American Legion and VFW halls; I'd been going to events with him long before I considered running for governor. I was probably one of the few nonmembers who attended these functions, but I loved every minute of them: award ceremonies, Pearl Harbor commemorations, Legislator of the Year dinners (several times as honoree). To me, they represent everything that's right about America.

That wasn't all. I went to every Carpenters Union and Operating Engineer Union local; to the electricians and the laborers; to the women's groups, Latino festivals, and almost every African American Church in New Jersey. I went to street fairs and picnics and ethnic festivals and flag raisings. The people there really charged my batteries. No matter what their backgrounds were, they all wanted the same thing. They wanted to believe in their communities. They wanted their streets clean and their children well educated. They wanted people to abide by the law, whether poor white Americans in Vineland, rich African Americans in Montclair, or working-class Latinos in Union City. I loved meeting people from one end of the state to the other, listening to what people wanted and figuring out how to provide it.

In New Jersey, though, the people you need to worry about aren't the voters; they're the twenty-one county chairmen—the bosses, who control the party line. If you don't make it onto the party line, your name is banished to the Siberia of that distant column on the right of the electoral matrix, unaffiliated and isolated. Jim Florio had already come out against the party-line system, which he said "harkens back to the days of backroom deals." He was right. But as a newcomer and underdog, I was in no position to buck the system—not if I wanted to win, which I did. I deferred to people like Ray Lesniak, who told the *Bergen Record:* "Neighbor speaking to neighbor is a lot better than somebody making decisions based on a thirty-second television ad."

And so we all went on our boss-hunting expeditions. Andrews, from South Jersey, could expect the southern county bosses to fall behind his campaign. With the backing of Ray Lesniak in Union County and John Lynch in Middlesex, I had the central part of the state locked up. Lesniak and Lynch also held sway in the north, but I knew that was where the battles would be fought.

Winning over a boss involves an old-fashioned courtship. Early on I landed the backing of Congressman Frank Pallone, from Long Branch, in the Central Jersey county of Monmouth. He gave interviews calling me the most qualified and "the nicest of the three candidates." Frank and I had been friends; we shared common ground on environmental policy, and he represented a substantial portion of my home county, so his support wasn't unexpected. But I also had John Lynch to thank. He'd promised Pallone to support his reelection bid if Pallone endorsed me aggressively, a quid pro quo. While Monmouth was not a major Democratic political force, having an incumbent congressman on my side so early in the race was a coup.

Murphy did well in the press, claiming the lion's share of newspaper endorsements. But he was doing poorly in the ground game; without one party endorsement to his credit, he made a virtue of necessity and declared himself the "anti-machine candidate."

Nine southern counties quickly lined up behind Andrews, accounting for about 41 percent of statewide votes. That got me nervous. We'd garnered ten northern counties, for about the same vote ratio, but in doing so we'd spent just about every political chit we had. The biggest thing we had going for us was that Essex County hadn't gone to Andrews yet. Essex encompasses 13 percent of the state's Democratic voters, and as the home of Newark, the state's biggest city, it was a major prize. We needed Essex. So did Andrews. Our campaigns were already doing hand-to-hand combat on the street.

"Hudson and Passaic haven't committed yet, either," Ray Lesniak told me. "They're waiting to see what Essex does." And somebody in Essex boss Tommy Giblin's camp was stirring up trouble. "They're peddling this story about you getting arrested in some homosexual thing in a cemetery."

That cemetery story—it kept popping up. "I told him it was all bullshit," Ray continued, "but he said, 'Tell McGreevey to get out of the race.' He wants to back Andrews."

Ray started formulating a new plan. First he met with Passaic and Hudson party chairmen, asking them to hold off till Essex committed. Passaic acquiesced, but Hudson boss Bob Janiszewski was another story. Over dinner at New York's Windows on the World, he surprised Ray. "I'm with Andrews," he said. "I'm ready to announce."

"At least wait until Essex announces," Ray pleaded, worried that the dominos might tumble behind Hudson County. Janiszewski wouldn't promise. As if just to needle us, he pushed up his scheduled press conference backing Andrews.

This concerned us. We made panicked calls to Passaic and Essex, begging for a meeting. But it didn't look good. "You're dying," Ray told me.

Next, he made his play for Essex. In political terms, it was breathtakingly daring.

We needed Tommy Giblin, the Essex County boss, to change his tune on my candidacy—to stop spreading old rumors and join the team. So Ray and Lynch promised Giblin that if I won the primary I'd make him state Democratic Party chair, something the party standard-bearer is empowered to do. Yet Giblin *still* didn't budge. He knew that a pledge like that was only good if I won; if Andrews came out on top, it would mean the end of Giblin's power and the demise of the Essex machine's centrality to state politics.

So Ray changed tactics. If he couldn't win over Giblin directly, he'd enlist the help of two other powerhouses in Essex politics, his close advisors Dick Codey, an influential state senator from Passaic, and Sharpe James, the powerful and colorful mayor of Newark.

Codey was a close colleague of mine from the senate. I'd backed him for senate minority leader in 1993, giving him the last vote he needed. Now I reached out to him personally, and he was immediately forthcoming. He called Giblin to ask him to reconsider endorsing me—and warned that there would be consequences if he refused. Codey even threatened to run his own line on the ballot, refusing to allow his name to appear in the boss-controlled party line column, and he promised to take all the local elected officials with him. Codey was popular enough that he knew he'd win no matter where his name was printed on Election Day. If he and the rest of the local delegation jumped ship, it would spell disaster for Giblin, leaving him to run a doomed line of unknowns.

Still, Giblin didn't buckle. Before long, he started giving quotes to the press favoring Andrews over me.

But it was with Sharpe James that Ray really worked his magic. James didn't want to buck the county machine. But Newark was in a rut, and he knew it. His city was one of the ten poorest urban centers in the nation, despite that New Jersey is one of the wealthiest states. A third of the population lives below the poverty line, and six out of ten children don't graduate from high school. He couldn't afford to make a mistake.

Meanwhile, I got to my old friend Calvin West, his chief of staff. A politically insightful bon vivant who'd broken barriers years earlier to become the first African American elected to Newark's city council, Calvin was totally committed to my campaign. He agreed to prep Sharpe for our meeting. "You take care of your side of the street," he said, "and I'll take care of mine."

We met at Sharpe's office. I made an earnest pitch, knowing I was preaching to the choir. "Andrews has broken with the Democratic Party," I said. "He was one of four Democrats who voted for Newt Gingrich's Contract with America. He voted against school lunches and after-school programs, Sharpe. Don Payne from the Black Caucus has all sorts of concerns about him. Look, you know I'm the best one for the community."

He may have known it, but he wouldn't budge. When we left there I thought I was doomed.

But Ray had one more trick up his sleeve. Sharpe had told him that he'd be more inclined to defy Giblin if others in the county joined him— particularly Stephen N. Adubato, Sr., an influential member of the Italian community in Newark. Adubato's pet project was the nonprofit North Ward Center for low-income families, which he ran and used as a power base. Ray pulled a few strings and got several local philanthropists to take a tour of Adubato's center. They ultimately wrote checks for over half a million dollars. It was a legitimate donation to a worthy cause—arranged for wholly political purposes. Adubato was impressed, and suddenly he was leaning toward me.

Once Adubato had flipped, Sharpe followed suit. The tide was turning our way.

Giblin was totally surrounded. We knew that other black elected officials would likely follow Sharpe's endorsement, as would other predominantly African American cities; now we could go back to Orange, East Orange, and Irvington with a better chance of getting on the line there. Giblin was at risk of seeming out of step with the black establishment. Better yet, Adubato would pull his strings among the Italians, with a similar ripple effect. I had the Hungarians, the Polish, and labor, and nobody doubted I controlled the Irish Catholics. I literally moved into Cryan's Beef and Ale on

First Street in South Orange, the nexus of Irish life in Essex, camping out there every night on the run up to St. Patrick's Day, buying rounds of Guinness for the guys.

And then I remembered: Joe Cryan, the vice chairman of the state Democratic Party—whose dad owned the Beef and Ale—came from the same part of Ireland as Tommy Giblin. I got Cryan's dad on the phone. "You've got to get me Giblin," I said.

I stalked Giblin like I was on safari, making sure my name was mentioned everywhere he went—bars, union halls, restaurants, churches, family gatherings.

The following week, Tommy Giblin called me for a meeting at Cryan's.

"We're going with you," he told me between bites of his sandwich. "It's going to be a tough election. But if you win it, I'd like to be part of any discussion regarding opportunities for the county."

"Sure, Tommy," I said. "Just do whatever is appropriate." I finished my Harp and shepherd's pie and got up to leave. But Giblin wasn't quite finished. His reputation was on the line, and he needed me to know that. If Andrews ended up winning, Giblin would look like a fool for having backed the wrong horse at the last minute.

"You better win this goddamn thing," he growled.

When I told Ray about the meeting, he let out a holler. "You're back from the dead, Jimmy," he said. "This thing's in your pocket now."

George Norcross, the Camden boss who'd gone with Andrews, called too.

"You're the Pete Rose of politics," he joked. "I don't know how you pulled that one off."

RAY BROUGHT IN HIS OLD FRIEND ORIN KRAMER TO BE OUR CAMpaign finance chairman. An exceptionally bright, cigar-chomping Wall Street hedge fund manager with a staccato patter, Kramer knew where the deep pockets were around the state. He'd helped the Clinton/Gore team raise money in 1992 and 1996, and was a golfing buddy of the president's. I was lucky to have him on board—but as a candidate with almost no name recognition, I still had my fundraising work cut out for me.

He and Steve DeMicco set a difficult schedule for me. Every morning for four hours I sat in our campaign offices in Woodbridge, working the phones. I pitched myself to ordinary people and corporate executives, people in high-end condos and the projects. I went across the state county by county: three days dialing Camden, four days calling Monmouth, Ocean, or Atlantic. I loved talking to so many different people, hearing their ideas about government and their hopes for a secure future. I especially loved talking to the retirees, and felt a tremendous kinship with older people in my state, in part because of what I'd learned over the years about nursing home billing policies.

I soon saw that organized labor was my most reliable funding base. The unions pulled out the stops on my behalf: President John Sweeney of the old AFL-CIO; Andy Stern of the Service Employees International Union; Gerry McEntee of the American Federation of State, County and Municipal Employees; Morty Bahr of the Communications Workers of America; Jimmy Hoffa of the Teamsters; Doug McCarron of the Carpenters; Terry O'Sullivan of the Laborers; Frank Hanley of the Operating Engineers, to which so many of my relatives belonged; and the other building trades.

I also found middle ground with Jews, liberals, and trial lawyers: the traditional party mainstays were backing my plans for the state over what Andrews was proposing. We adopted a new campaign slogan, "Real Democrat, Real Solutions," telegraphing the difference between me and the other Democrats, who favored conciliation to the point of capitulation. I was the progressive candidate of principle, and we wanted everyone to know it.

That said, even in January 1997 we still were losing the funding race hands down. I'd been begging for handouts since November, but by the end of February we had only $300,000 in the bank. Andrews had $400,000 after a few short weeks. Whitman was leaving us both in the dust. I remember pulling off the biggest fundraising dinner of my career, for a record-breaking $17,000 net. We all went to bed that night giddy. In the morning, the papers had front-page pictures of Whitman at her own record-breaking event, where she banked $1.2 million. As if to rub it in, she kept flying to other states to raise money for the New Jersey Republican Committee, nabbing $200,000 in Florida and $100,000 in Michigan.

My fortunes changed in small stages. A couple of big fundraisers in late

February netted enough to make me eligible for matching funds, the first candidate to qualify. Now my war chest had topped $1 million, quite an accomplishment for an unknown. I remembered the advice Doug Schoen gave: "The only way you're going to make it is by working hard." That's how we did it, by working harder than anybody.

LATER, WE GOT A REAL WINDFALL FROM THE CHECKBOOK OF CHARlie Kushner, a terrific fellow and one of the state's wealthiest developers. I'd first met Charlie at one of my campaign stops. His empire, Kushner Companies, owned or managed $3 billion worth of real estate in the tri-state area, including the prized Puck Building in Manhattan. An orthodox Jew, he was also an important philanthropist, especially generous with Israeli concerns. He knew about my efforts on Holocaust education, he told me; my latest bill was working through the senate on its way to Whitman's desk. Both his parents, he said, had survived the camps.

The day after we met, Charlie and I had a great meeting. I told him how important it was that New Jersey start improving educational quality in order to fill jobs in business and the service industry, and I described my ambitious plans for turning the state's schools into postmillennial high-tech facilities, with computerized libraries and high-speed Internet in every classroom. Education was very important to Charlie, it turned out. His philanthropic contributions to schools rank among the highest in the world. He was a major benefactor to Harvard and two schools in Livingston, New Jersey: the Rea Kushner Yeshiva High School and the Joseph Kushner Hebrew Academy, named for his father. He also served on the boards of the Rabbinical College of America in Morristown, Yeshiva University's Stern College for Women, in New York, and Touro College of New York, a four-year institution established to teach Jewish heritage. About Touro especially he spoke eloquently and with great passion.

His faith, so different from my own, was a source of strength and balance for him. He prayed every day using the Orthodox practice called "davening," in which he bowed ritualistically while reciting Jewish liturgical text. He observed the Sabbath strictly from Friday sundown to Saturday sundown, traveling only by foot and avoiding the phone unless an emergency demanded it. Following these rules helped remind Charlie of God's prominence, just as taking Holy Communion every week helped me remain Christ-centered. This was a great discovery for me.

We hit it off wonderfully; by the time I left his office I had contributions of $8,200 from him and his family, and promises for much more. Charlie had nothing to gain by backing my underdog campaign, and plenty to lose; I'll always be grateful that he took a chance on our team. As he told me more than once, "I'm doing this because I believe in the importance of the commonweal."

By the end of the year, Kushner, along with his company and various relatives, had backed me with $554,000, far more than any other contributor. In other circumstances, I might have had misgivings about taking that much money from one source, but Charlie never gave me cause for concern. He never tried to sway my thinking in any way, though he had hundreds of permits—maybe thousands—before the state of New Jersey. Any rational developer would have stayed out of an underdog's campaign. But his belief in me was sincere and heartfelt, sparked by my interest in Holocaust education. He backed me in memory of his parents' suffering. There was no other reason.

In this belief, I had the support of my campaign treasurer, Bob Long, whose job it was to conduct the "smell test" on all our donations. If his vetting ever revealed any reason to believe a donation had improper strings attached, or came from an unsavory source, he would simply send it back. Bob had a very good nose for this kind of work. He was commencing his studies for the Methodist ministry, a fact that gave me great spiritual comfort.

AS WE HEADED INTO THE JUNE PRIMARY, I WAS STRUGGLING TO keep up a punishing campaign schedule while still serving Woodbridge as mayor. On my dizzying predawn passes through town I still took notes on conditions that needed addressing, from shaggy lawns to unswept streets, calling in the offending addresses to the phone machines of my still-sleeping town hall staff. That anything got done in town in these months was a testament to my friend and secretary, Cathy McLaughlin, an accomplished civil servant and Republican County Committee member who'd jumped the aisle to join our team because she believed in the changes we were bringing to town. She maintained exacting standards at home while the rest of us were running all over the state, and she kept Woodbridge improving every day.

I had no idea what our real chances were in the primary. Doug Schoen, the pollster, wouldn't stick his neck out. "I can't say you'll win," he said, "but it'll be close." With Essex and Passaic in my camp, I had twelve of the twenty-one county lines, compared with nine for Andrews. If everyone voted party line, I'd get 60 percent of the vote, but it was still too close to call. We went into the last weeks scheming for ways to break out.

Looking around a map of the state, my eye settled again on Hudson County, where party boss Bob Janiszewski had never given in. It still didn't make sense to me. Hudson's population is concentrated in Jersey City, my family's old stronghold. I still had relatives on the police force, and my family had friends in almost every Catholic parish there. Hoboken, the little factory city that gave us Frank Sinatra, was also in Hudson. Surely I'd get more traction there with my message than Andrews would. So in the final days of the campaign we went racing all over the north in our Buick, returning to Kearny, Union City, Weehawken, Secaucus, Jersey City, and Hoboken time and again. The only way to win, I figured, would be to poach those votes.

Andrews seemed to be attempting the same thing in Essex and Bergen, where he campaigned hard despite losing the line. To my disappointment, the *Bergen Record* endorsed him over me. So I fought back, responding to his incursions sortie by sortie. I've never needed much sleep, but in that last week I felt invincible. At 1:30 in the morning on June 2, the day before the primary, we pulled into the parking lot of the Arena Diner in Hackensack. I jumped out of the car and moved from table to table, asking people for their votes. "The *Bergen Record* may think Congressman Andrews is best for Hackensack," I joked to them, "but do you see him here at the Arena Diner?" At one point I remember looking out the window; Kevin Noland, my driver, was asleep in the van.

We set up our election-day operation in a suite at the Sheraton in

Woodbridge to wait for results. I had prepared both a concession speech and a victory speech. The ballroom downstairs was filled with campaign staff and volunteers—people of all colors, ages, educational backgrounds, and social classes, a true cross-section of America.

One of the first people to arrive was a woman I'd met in a Newark housing project. Her name was Valerie Hines, but she told me I could call her "Peachy." I was thrilled to see her, and to read what she told the *Bergen Record* the next day. "I met him personally. I feel close to him—we really talked," she said. "I'm so scared because I want him to win so bad. I thought it was going to be over by now."

So did I.

As the night progressed, we were in a statistical dead heat, with Andrews slightly ahead. At 10:15, he had 39 percent of the vote; I had 36 percent. It seemed like I didn't have a prayer. Then, suddenly, my numbers surged. At 10:45 I took the lead and never relinquished it. I won by 39 percent to 37 percent for Andrews; Murphy's final tally was 21 percent.

What caused that last-minute surge? The good people of Hudson County, it turned out. Despite Bob Janiszewski's support for Andrews, those northern voters defied the machine and cast their votes for the hometown boy, carrying me over the top by just seven thousand votes.

Andrews began his concession speech down in Cherry Hill at about midnight. Back in Woodbridge, I waited for word that he'd finished before greeting my own staff and volunteers. But for some reason Andrews talked and talked, and by 1:00 AM I decided I couldn't keep the crowds waiting any longer. My address was short and sweet.

With victory, of course, came the consequence I'd never expected: I would actually have to take on Christine Todd Whitman in November. I took a deep breath and said a prayer.

When I finally got home that night, I called Kari, whose voice was the only one I really wanted to hear. "I'm so happy for you," she said. "This is what you wanted. You deserve it."

I hung up, proud but lonely.

11.

SO FAR IN THE CAMPAIGN, I'D KEPT MY SEPARATION FROM BE-coming public knowledge. Even though marriages fail all the time, I had a morbid fear that Kari's departure would somehow increase speculation about my sexuality. Nobody on my staff ever said a thing about her whereabouts. My parents asked every once in a while, knowing she was hardly ever home, but I couldn't even admit my failure to them. "She's gone up to Canada for so-and-so's birthday," I'd say, and drop the subject.

I knew it looked odd that my wife wasn't by my side for my primary victory speech. In her place stood Kathy Ellis, my press handler. The official biography on my Web site made no mention of the troubles. If anyone should ask, I told my spokesman Richard McGrath to say that we were separated. So far nobody had. But I knew I couldn't keep up the appearance of marriage while being unable to produce a wife.

It's easy to say, in retrospect, that this was my opportunity to come out of the closet—or at least to end my public charade. For a brief moment, I did wonder what my life might be like if I gave it all up. During one of my visits to Vancouver I spent some time exploring the gay section of town, watching with envy as male couples walked the street holding hands. One afternoon, for the first time in my life, I slipped into a gay bar there. While there, I was overcome with tremendous fear and anxiety; it reminded me of how I'd felt at those sophomore-year parties in Carteret. I didn't even last long enough to order a drink.

I clung to the closet doorjamb. Having lived inside those confines for so long, I didn't believe I could survive any other way. Life on the outside was frightening, so much so that I wasn't even able to recognize my options. Besides, I told myself, I had just become the Democratic Party's choice to take on a sitting governor. No openly gay person had ever done that. I had an obligation to my own lie.

With my marriage behind me, I returned to womanizing. My staffers and I made covert trips to go-go clubs in places where we hoped I wouldn't be recognized, though being recognized was part of my purpose. Gay rumors were still ricocheting around the state, but my staff had heard from Whitman's people that the governor personally ruled out capitalizing on them in any way, for which I was relieved. In truth, spending an hour with my staffers in one of these regular-guys places wasn't just a pose for me, it was a tonic—it did a world of good after a long day on the campaign trail.

But these weren't always discreet nights out; sometimes we even got a couple local mayors to come along, hitting the Mar-Cet Café in Paterson or the Bowling Alley Bar in Carteret. For years we used to joke about who had the dollar bills. Inevitably, news of our excursions found its way back to the office, unnerving staffers like Doug Heyl, a former Clinton/Gore southern field director we'd brought in to manage the campaign. Doug never confronted me directly, but Gary Taffet told me he laid down the law. "Y'all clean up your mess," he said. We didn't change our ways, but from that point on we tried to keep Doug in the dark.

Some of my political friends apparently suspected that my increased visibility would put a pinch in my style. One of them, David D'Amiano, a small-time party fundraiser I knew from Carteret, even set me up on dates with some young women he knew. I'd grown increasingly lonely since my separation; I craved companionship and contact, and sometimes I even took these women to bed. But now, for the first time in my life, I found myself unable to perform with women. I wasn't surprised. Sex with women had never come naturally to me. Sheer willpower used to get me through, but now it failed me. I felt sure this spelled the end of my dual existence. If I couldn't convince a woman I was straight, how could I expect the larger world to believe me?

SOME TIME INTO THE CAMPAIGN, I MET DINA MATOS. IT WAS AT A gathering of an absurdist political group called the Royal Association of

New Jersey—their members actually favor restoring the monarchy to power in Portugal. I thought they were joking until I got to the meeting at Seabra's Armory, a Perth Amboy catering hall overlooking the harbor. A mustachioed man calling himself the Duke of Braganza was walking from table to table with one of those joke "snake" cans that exploded with half a dozen cloth-covered springs when opened. I thought he was doing an imitation of Cantinflas. But this was the man they wanted back on the throne.

The one bright spot in the room was Dina, an uncommonly beautiful thirty-one-year-old blonde in a red double-breasted suit. I introduced myself as soon as I got the chance. We talked about the village in Portugal where she was born, and the large Portuguese community in Elizabeth where she grew up. She asked about my plans for education and taxes, my feelings about sprawl and protecting the environment; it turned out she was an appointed member of the Elizabeth zoning board. Given the company she was keeping, I was happily surprised at how attuned she was to the political riptides of state politics. We had a lot of common interests, and talking to her was fun.

When the event was over I walked her out to her car. She didn't mind when I took her hand. We leaned against the car, and I kissed her. I'm still not sure what made me do it. Loneliness, I suppose. Maybe she just seemed like the perfect politician's wife; it might have been that self-serving. Or it could have been the glass of Portuguese wine I drank. Whatever it was, she kissed back.

THE NEWSPAPERS WERE STARTING TO CALL ME "ROBO-CANDIDATE," in part for my nonstop campaign schedule but also because I could come off as a little mechanical, at least in the early days. Sometimes I was so nervous about getting my point across that I would read directly from policy papers, even in sit-down interviews with reporters. Then again, other reporters called me Forrest Gump; I liked to pretend it was because I bore a passing resemblance to Tom Hanks, but really I think it was because I seemed to stumble into good fortune as often as Forrest did. I loved how the *New York Times* saw me: "While many political experts in the state have suggested that Mr. McGreevey lacks the necessary polish to run a successful statewide campaign, in recent weeks he has shown that what he may lack in political refinement he is likely to make up in tenacity and charm."

Still, I was getting better at the game. I remember the first time I felt like a preacher during one of those rallies, at a gathering of supporters at a public high school in Woodbridge. "The car insurance crisis in New Jersey is not an accident waiting to happen—it is a chain collision stretching from the Parkway to the Turnpike, from Route 17 to the Black Horse Pike," I called out, to booming applause. "This is not a new problem. But it is a problem made worse by three and one half years of allowing the insurance industry to get away with outrageous profiteering!" The applause worked on me like jet fuel on a bonfire. To excite a crowd with something so pure as ideas gave me a tremendous feeling of purpose. I had a sense that New Jerseyans needed hope, and I was trying to help them find it, in whatever small way I could.

Even after my strongest rallies, though, I had a hard time believing I could come close to Whitman in the general election. Her approval numbers remained high; one mid-summer poll showed that 53 percent of the electorate was behind her. But she did have some weaknesses. More than half the voters disapproved of how she handled taxes, and most believed she failed to grasp the problem with auto insurance.

Meanwhile, Doug Schoen's polls showed that an awful lot of people in the state still didn't even know who I was. In July, 70 percent of voters said they didn't know enough about me to form an opinion one way or the other. But my message was finding its mark. That same month a third of voters said that auto insurance was their number one concern, and soon Whitman's approval ratings fell to their lowest since her second month in office. In late July, three-quarters of those polled said they disapproved of how she handled auto insurance; another 63 percent didn't like the way she handled taxes.

Our strategy was working. In August, Whitman conceded publicly that the race was "competitive." At a news conference, one reporter mentioned that I was trailing by seven points even though voters still had no idea who I was. Whitman got in a good line: "When the public gets to know him, that will be different." But McGrath, my spokesman, didn't miss a beat. "The bad news for Christie Whitman is, the people *do* know her, and they are giving her failing grades."

I missed Kari terribly in these busy days, but being all alone during the campaign freed me to work around the clock, allowing me to feed my addiction—to the crowds, to the power, to the business of campaigning. I loved the early morning strategy meetings over coffee and donuts at the office, and the late-night dashes for pizza. And I really loved spending time with the staff. We'd attracted an amazing group of idealistic young kids, some right out of school and working on their first campaigns. Their energy was infectious. I was a hard worker, but they outpaced me every day.

Among my favorites were two young Irish guys, both named Kevin. My driver, Kevin Noland, was in charge of making sure we got where we were going on time and safely (on time was always more important). Kevin was just twenty-four, but with his blond hair, blue eyes, and soft round Irish face he looked even younger. He had the same intense work ethic as many first-generation Americans, but sometimes he took his work a little too seriously. Now and then, as we careened across lanes of traffic trying to make our next appointment, I could see people doing double-takes in their cars, worried that he was somebody's kid brother out for a joy ride.

One morning, Kevin somehow managed to maneuver our van through densely packed crowds at a Hispanic festival in Elizabeth, where I was supposed to give a speech from an outdoor stage, alongside the local mayor. The streets were choked with people, but he got us to the stage with seconds to spare. When we bolted up to the platform together, he finally allowed himself to gaze over the throngs, which included a number of young Latin women in revealing tops and skin-tight dresses. I was waiting for him to hand me my prepared notes, but he was paralyzed by the sight. "You don't see anything like this at Irish festivals," he finally said as I plucked the notes from his jacket myself.

Kevin McCabe had joined me years earlier at town hall in Woodbridge, eventually rising to chief of staff at twenty-five. He was smart, loyal, and hardworking—his energy was amazing. Kevin could work diligently all day at town hall and campaign with labor and Irish groups all evening. I trusted him with my life—sometimes foolishly. Every now and then McCabe would take the wheel from Noland, especially in the southern counties, where the roads were less familiar. At my insistence, he ignored speed limits. More than once we were stopped for tearing past cows and cornfields at 100 miles an hour. But the state troopers were among our biggest supporters; they always sent us away with stern warnings and wishes of good luck, but no ticket.

People started joking about how young the crew was, but I always pointed out that I was running the Parole Board, a sizable state agency, by the time I was twenty-eight. I believed in the energy and insights of youth. At one fundraising dinner, Jim Florio turned the evening into a roast, poking fun at my staffers. "Most of his staff is not here tonight—it's past their bedtimes." I laughed along, but he wasn't through. "The staff people, of course, come to work in the morning on their Big Wheels, carrying their Spider Man lunch baskets. Then after naptime there's a Nintendo tournament."

It was all in good fun. But if it weren't for these young gals and guys I don't think I could have made a run for Whitman. And I wouldn't have enjoyed it half as much.

NATIONALLY, WE WERE STARTING TO GET SOME ATTENTION. WHITman was the only sitting governor up for reelection in 1997. If she lost to a Democrat, the race could help spur a party sweep in the 1998 midterms. But as often as we pushed the Democratic National Committee for help with media and financing, they all but ignored our pleas. I reached out to Bill Bradley, who'd quit his senate seat in 1996 after declaring that American politics was "broken," but he said there was little he could do.

Instead, he bequeathed me his beach walk. The former basketball star was famous for embarking on a three-day stroll down the Jersey Shore every year on Labor Day weekend, talking to citizens along the 120-mile stretch from Sandy Hook in the north to Atlantic City in the south. Years before, I had accompanied him for part of his tour. I was blown away by how long his legs were, and how much ground he could cover.

"The beach walk is yours if you want it," he said. "I don't need it anymore."

I was honored that he'd chosen me to inherit this political legacy. He even offered to accompany me on the first day. But I really wasn't meant for the beach. I've got a pasty Irish complexion that blends in fine on city streets and in windowless pubs, but always makes me look a little unhealthy by the water. Gamely, I put on my walking shoes, smeared on a thick layer of sun block, and headed to the shore. What a mistake. I started perspiring, the lotion oozed into my eyes, and my eyes began to burn, no matter how much I rubbed them with a handkerchief. Even before we left the parking lot, tears were washing down my cheeks. I'm sure people found it curious that the subject of auto insurance could upset me so much.

The Jersey Shore is one of the most pristine stretches of shoreline in the country, fringed by grassy dunes and crowded several times a year with one of the largest concentrations of migratory birds in the nation. We hadn't walked twenty yards onto the beach before one of my staffers noticed a lone pigeon making a slow and wobbly circle overhead. Then, mid-flight, it abruptly died. The poor thing rocketed out of the sky and landed lifelessly at our feet with a sickening thud.

"That's not a good omen," Bradley pointed out.

"This is going to be a hell of a race, isn't it?" I responded as my young staff circled around the corpse, rolling it respectfully into the tall grasses with their shoes.

The first people we came upon were from out of state—a pair from New York, and a family from Pennsylvania. They were extremely friendly. The New Jersey residents we approached thereafter were less cordial. "Christie's doing a fine job," they would say, or: "If you're running for governor, how come we've never heard of you?"

Burning eyes, dead wildlife, indifferent voters—it wasn't shaping up as a very productive day. Finally, I sat down with one last group, grabbing a French fry off a plate. I'll never forget this family: Ruth Arimente of Basking Ridge, her daughter Joanne Loya, and her teenage granddaughter, Jennifer Loya. None of them had any clue who I was. "Look," I said, "I'm not Whitman. I don't live her imperial life. I'm concerned about property taxes and auto insurance, just like you are. My position is more precarious now, more anxiety producing, than it was when she took office. Can you afford your property tax and car insurance payments? Because if you can, then you should vote for her. But if you can't, you should find a better way for New Jersey."

It worked. When a reporter asked Ruth whom she was going to support, she committed to me on the spot. "I go with people who look you in the eye," she said.

ONE OF MY FIRST HIRES DURING THIS PERIOD OF EXPANSION WAS Regena Thomas, a get-out-the-vote specialist with the firm IEM Message Management, whom I'd first met when she was helping coordinate Clinton/Gore campaign events in 1992. Her mission was to take my message to the African American community, a critical cornerstone of my campaign. Whitman had a bad history in this area. Ed Rollins, her political consultant in 1993, had bragged that he won her first election by spending $500,000 to *suppress* black voters. Regena was going to make sure that couldn't happen again. No amount of Republican money could override her message of empowerment. "The power in this election lies in the African American vote," she told the papers. "African Americans may not be powerful enough to make a governor on their own, but they've proven that they can cause one to lose."

We reached out to every group we could. Tassos Estafraides was our man for the Greek community. As a liaison to Latino voters, I brought in Lizette Delgado in South Jersey, Idida Rodriguez in North Jersey, and Tonio Burgos, a friend who had worked for Governor Mario Cuomo in New York. We worked hard to connect with Russians, Poles, Germans, and Portuguese, with staff members maintaining contact with each community. If you walked, we had an ethnic liaison for you.

Dina took on the job as our Portuguese-language coordinator. She was an able front woman—her day job was spokeswoman for the Columbus Hospital in Newark, so she knew how to shape and deliver a message. But she was also a natural politician, able to work a room quickly and effectively. She had cut her teeth as a volunteer with Clinton/Gore, and had long been

ack and Ronnie McGreevey's firstborn child

JAMES E. McGREEVEY

J. C. Marine Killed on Iwo

Sergt. James E. McGreevey, U. S. M. C., 19, of 50 Lafayette St., was killed in action at Iwo Jima on Feb. 19, it has been learned by his father, Michael McGreevey, a retired Jersey City patrolman.

The recipient of the Bronze Star for heroism at Saipan while a member of a demolition team, Sergt. McGreevey was a lifelong resident of Jersey City. He was inducted June 7, 1942, and went overseas in January, 1944.

Surviving, besides his father, are three brothers, Michael McGreevey, with the navy in England, and John and Peter McGreevey, and two sisters, the Misses Margaret and Rosanne McGreevey.

My father, Jack McGreevey—the greatest patriot I k

Left: Sgt. James E. McGreevey, my uncle and namesake, and my father's hero
Right: My mother, Ronnie. From my parents I learned the value of a life of service.

With Caroline *(left)* at St. Joseph's Convent in Carteret

The McGreevey kids: Jimmy, Sharon, and Caroline

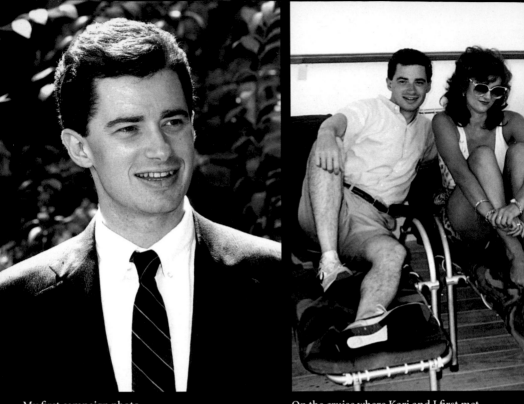

My first campaign photo

On the cruise where Kari and I first met

With mayors JoJo DeMarino of Woodbridge *(left)* and George Otlowski of Perth Amboy—two of the lions of local New Jersey politics

With three of the most important people in my life: Kari, our beautiful daughter Morag, and Jack Fay, my political mentor

With Ray Lesniak *(left with coffee cup)* and John Lynch *(right)* at a Chicago Irish pub during the 1996 Democratic convention. Lynch and Lesniak were two of the smartest and most powerful bosses in Jersey politics throughout the 1990s.

My family with Bill Clinton during the 1997 campaign. *(From left)* My sisters Sharon and Caroline, Mom, Clinton, Dad, and my aunt and uncle, Kathleen and Herb Smith.

Left: Elie Wiesel has always been an inspiration; I was honored to meet with him after sponsoring the bill establishing the state's permanent Holocaust Commission.
Right: On our 2000 trip to Paraiso, Woodbridge's sister city in the Dominican Republic, Kevin Hagan and

Christie Todd Whitman, who ran a clean campaign against me when she might have done otherwise

Dina and I on our wedding day, overlooking the White House lawn

Election night, 2001: a dream realized

Taking the oath of office, just weeks after Dina brought Jacqueline home from the hospital

Jason Kirin *(left)* and Kevin Hagan were among the young staffers who gave heart, soul, and sweat equity to the campaign, and I was honored to have them join the administration.

The State of the State Address, January 2002

A gathering of governors: Jim Florio, Tom Kean, Brendan Byrne, and Donald DiFrancesco *(right)*, who served out Christie Whitman's term after she left to join the Bush administration in 2001

The annual Marine Corps birthday celebration is always a highlight for my father, who spoke at the ceremony in November 2002.

Speaking at the Ground Zero cornerstone ceremony, July 4, 2004, with Mayor Mike Bloomberg and Governor George Pataki of New York, and Port Authority chairman Tony Coscia. I was grateful for their strong partnership after 9/11.

President Bush and I disagreed on scores of issues politically—from the environment to funding for schools and roads—but he was unfailingly gracious to me and my family.

Greeting the crowds with Jacqueline

Signing our groundbreaking Highlands Act on August 10, 2004, one of my proudest achievements. Just two days later, my life would change forever.

With Golan Cipel in 2001

"My truth is that I am a gay American": August 12, 2004

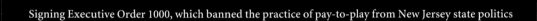

Signing Executive Order 1000, which banned the practice of pay-to-play from New Jersey state politics

Receiving an honorary doctorate from Kean University with my great friend Ray Lesniak, who helped me get through it all

With Jacqueline *(above)* and Morag, the lights of my life

With my partner, Mark O'Donnell

involved with the National Women's Political Caucus. Thanks to her efforts I was in every Portuguese-language church, diner, picnic, street fair, christening, and store opening in the state. Of course, that could only account for so many votes; more than anything, these campaign stops were an excuse for us to see each other.

Our romance was blossoming in semisecret, though my staff all knew what we were up to. Dina called my cell phone so often that Kevin Noland started calling her the Mad Dialer. I still missed Kari, but Dina shared my ambitions; I knew she was more comfortable with the idea of becoming first lady. But aside from stolen moments—after an event in Atlantic City, for instance, or during a drive to Hyde Park, FDR's stately home along the Hudson River—we rarely got to spend much time alone together. Instead we talked politics on the phone late into the night, comparing notes and sharing insights. I grew to cherish her companionship and friendship.

Things between us changed somewhat when my marriage troubles were revealed in the summer. A reporter from the *Bergen Record* had dug Kari's legal brief out of a Vancouver courthouse. I was mortified to pick up the morning paper and see my marital woes—ratcheted up by a lawyer's hyperbole—reprinted for all to read. My phone rang off the hook, and when one reporter got through, I said, "Kari's the only woman I ever wanted to marry." I was telling the truth. Yet now I felt free to start hinting about my relationship with Dina, and began bringing more attention to her at campaign stops.

Years later, Dina accused me in legal papers of courting her, and ultimately marrying her, for purely political reasons. That's not true. I treasured her companionship, and in my way I loved her. But as a gay man, I could only love her so much. She deserved more.

WHEN OUR FIRST DISAPPOINTING POLL RESULTS CAME IN, I BLEW a gasket. I suppose if I hadn't been so exhausted, I might have been more forgiving to my staff. I was demanding, almost impossible to satisfy—there wasn't a shoulder I didn't look over constantly, a decision I didn't second-guess. I knew exactly why our numbers were lagging. We weren't hitting our targets with seniors, which was inexcusable. I had the best pro-senior policies of any candidate. I adopted the AARP's planks as my own. And I'd felt a personal connection with every senior citizen I'd ever met.

We were in a car racing to a radio interview down the shore when I lashed out. Unfortunately, I took out most of my rage on poor Kevin Noland, whose only job was to get us to appointments on time. I threw my cell phone at the dashboard, inadvertently striking him on the shoulder.

"Our grassroots operation is an embarrassment!" I hollered. "By this point, we should have been in five thousand senior centers! Seniors should be lining up to volunteer! You think we can win like this?"

Just then, the phone rang. It was the radio station wondering why we were so late. Kevin had driven right past the exit.

"Turn around!" I bellowed, kicking the dashboard with the heel of my shoe.

"There's another exit coming up in a couple miles," he said meekly.

"I don't care about the exit. Turn around now!"

In due time Kevin found the station, but not before I had a chance to call up every member of my senior campaign staff for a tongue-lashing. One of them must have called Ray to tell him about my meltdown, because when I got back in the car for the trip home, he'd filled my voicemail box with messages.

"Look, I don't care how you treat your staff—that's none of my business," he said when I called him back. "It's your campaign I'm worrying about. You're trying to do too much and it shows. You've got to delegate. You need a campaign manager you can trust. Somebody who can get everything done for you. You need to be a full-time candidate. At the end of the day a lot of people can manage a campaign, but there is *only one candidate*. Let somebody else sweat the little stuff."

It was a classic woodshed conversation. I knew what he was saying, and I knew he was right: letting go of anything was antithetical to my character. I needed to let the pros run the business, and stick to what I did best—connecting with the people, like a box of soap flakes on the shelf.

But I also read a deeper admonishment into Ray's words. We were sailing into the rapids now on the fundraising side; the donors were getting bigger, their expectations more challenging. Whatever Ray was trying to tell me, I realized in that moment that I was going to have to start removing my-self from the darker business of deal making. After all, no one ever blames the box of soap flakes for the backroom arrangements that got it moved to the front of the store. Insulation, deniability, immunity—those were the re-wards of delegation. I decided, right then and there, that I needed to relin-quish control and let the cards fall as they might.

I immediately called Gary Taffet, who ran my operation in Wood-bridge, and offered him the job. I'd known Gary for years. I knew everybody in his family. I trusted Gary to make the difficult decisions without my in-put. With him in charge—and me as the product—the campaign began to sail a lot more smoothly.

WHITMAN AND I AGREED TO TWO TELEVISED DEBATES. THEY WERE a huge opportunity to improve my name recognition, and we rehearsed like madmen. As a stand-in for Whitman we recruited Marianne Espinosa Mur-phy, an articulate former state superior court judge who also happened to be the former wife of Michael Murphy, the candidate Andrews and I had bested in the primary. She was a formidable adversary, but I kept my message tightly focused: education, taxes, and auto insurance.

Jimmy Kennedy was the coach I listened to most closely. He and his wife, Lori, were always trying to quash my professorial tendencies, my wonkishness. "Go to the real Jim," Jimmy told me. "Play this thing like you were back at the monthly Woodbridge Town Hall meetings. Just bantering and sharing your perspectives with the locals. That's your strength."

It's going to take a lot more than that, I thought. Whitman's job ap-proval rating was back up to 55 percent, and polls showed her beating me by a wide margin. And then, just before the debate, Ray Lesniak came to me with a problem.

"There's a hooker in the Middlesex County Jail who's calling around saying she knows you," he said.

Myra Rosa was a heroin addict from Woodbridge who'd spent the bet-ter part of the last decade in and out of jail. Two years earlier, in 1995, she'd started peddling this story that we'd been involved. It was a pure lie. This is no whitewash: I've made it clear that I'd known many women, and men, through the years. Rosa was not one of them. We never even met. I still wonder why she targeted me for her dubious claims—or, perhaps more to the point, who put her up to it.

I told Ray the truth—that I had no idea who she was. He believed me, even though he knew as much about my personal life as anybody at the time. He had already sent one of his men to the jailhouse to talk to her, hoping to ascertain just how crazy she was: *very* crazy, it turned out. "She says you used to pick her up in a white van, for over two years, sometimes screwing her at your condo. She can even identify the cat and the blue rug."

"I haven't had a cat since I was fourteen years old, Ray. And I've never had a white van. Yes, I have a blue rug, but what American doesn't have a blue rug?" I was angry. "She says I was picking up a streetwalker in my own legislative district? I may be crazy, Ray, but I'm not *that* crazy."

Right after Ray's man interviewed her in jail, a guy from a place called Lucky 7 Bail Bonds bailed her out, representing an anonymous source. Gary, who had a million connections in Woodbridge, wracked his brain wondering who might be posting her bail. "The *Star-Ledger*?" he wondered.

That made little sense—they didn't need to spring her from jail to get her story. "Republican State Committee," I suggested, half seriously. A week or two later, John Lynch sent some of his guys around asking questions, and they drew the same conclusion.

"Well, whoever it is, we have to do something about the prostitute," Ray said. "I heard she already talked to the *Star-Ledger*. They're going to do a story."

"She needs a vacation," somebody suggested. Ray, Paul, and Gary all thought it was a good idea. Ray said he could take care of it. I don't know how they convinced her, but within the week she was riding the roller coasters at Disney World. On her way out of town she apparently "hired" a lawyer who took a sworn statement from her disavowing the McGreevey story.

OUR BIG TELEVISED DEBATE CAME LESS THAN TWO WEEKS BEFORE the general election, on October 21, 1997. It was held at Birchwood Manor in Whippany, a colonial-era village that made world history fifty years earlier when the first television broadcast signal was sent from there to New York City. Our one-hour event, which was sponsored by the Chamber of Commerce, was broadcast on channel 57 in Philadelphia and on WWOR-TV, an independent station based in Secaucus that served New Jersey and New York. I was a forty-year-old state legislator taking on a Republican powerhouse, but with my party's backing I felt confident. Looking around the room I saw many friendly faces, including Ray and all the young turks from the office. Jimmy and Lori Kennedy were there, too. As mayor and first lady of Rahway, they'd been invited to sit with my old boss, Dick Trabert, at the Merck & Co. table.

Whitman and I were joined on stage by the libertarian candidate, Murray Sabrin. I'd encouraged his campaign, assuming he might bite into Whitman's right flank. But I wasn't expecting the Chamber crowd to be in his camp or mine. I knew the business community was squarely behind Whitman, wary of my attacks on the insurance companies. Even so, I was surprised when my opening remarks were met with such ice.

The first question was better—a slow ball, about auto insurance.

Whitman put forward her newest cockamamie plan, saying she would promote a change in the regulations allowing people to buy less insurance on their car, for a savings of 25 percent. This was clearly no victory for the motorist, who would be more financially vulnerable in the long run. She basically rolled over on the issue. "If lowering auto insurance were easy, I would have done it," she said. "Tom Kean would have done it; Jim Florio would have done it, or Brendan Byrne would have done it—because that's how long we've had the problem." I had her just where I wanted her.

I got off some zingers on other matters, too, calling Whitman a "borrow-and-spend Republican" and mocking her plan to finance a tunnel to Atlantic City so that people could race to the casinos without crossing through town. This would only hurt the city's locally owned shops and gas stations, I pointed out—while protecting the out-of-state businesses that owned the casinos. I didn't exactly set the studio audience on fire with my comments, but I was surprised to see that even my best friend, Jimmy Kennedy, was sitting on his hands; he was anxious not to offend his hosts from Merck, the largest employer in his town. The only one applauding at their table was his wife, Lori.

It didn't really matter; I knew I'd turned in a solid performance. The next day's *New York Times* had three articles about my candidacy, and a new Quinnipiac University poll showed Whitman's lead narrowing to a mere eight points. The debate had done what it needed to do—introduce me to the voters. I couldn't have been more pleased.

But only a few hours after the debate, I invited a *Star-Ledger* reporter into the campaign office for what I thought would be a glowing feature on our campaign. Instead she asked about Myra Rosa, the hooker. "I swear to you, I never met this crazy woman," I told her. I could tell she didn't believe me. When she left I felt my future draining out of the room with her.

I was despondent. I called Ray Lesniak, and within hours a copy of Rosa's disavowal was faxed to newspapers around the state. Thankfully, the subject went away—until a month later, when it surfaced again during a dinner in New York with Ray, Orin Kramer, and Senator Bob Torricelli. "I think the *Ledger* is going with a weekend story on that prostitute," Orin said.

Furious, I called the *Ledger*'s city desk on my way out of the restaurant. The switchboard put me on hold for so long that I was already stuck in traffic on the New Jersey Turnpike when an editor came to the phone. The story wasn't running on the weekend, he said, and promised that I'd receive a call from John Hassell, one of the paper's top reporters.

Hassell called on Monday. "I'm sorry, Senator, but we had to ask these questions," he said. "The story is all over the place."

"John, I will take a lie-detector test. Find somebody of your choosing to administer the test and I'll take it," I told him. "I don't want you to ask me about my entire life, I haven't been an angel, but ask me whether or not I've ever met this woman."

John said he'd heard the *Philadelphia Daily News* was all over the story. It seemed too late to contain it. I reminded him that this wouldn't just destroy my career, it would harm my family. "Seems like you have a choice," he said. "Do you want us to break the story, or do you want an irresponsible paper like, oh, *The Trentonian* to splash it all over the front page?"

"That's like asking, *Do you want to be killed by a firing squad or cyanide? The results are the same. An innocent man dies.*"

At my request, John put me in touch with his editor in chief, Jim Willse, so I could make my case directly. In the end, Willse made the decent call.

WITH THE CLOCK RUNNING OUT, I WAS STILL DESPERATE FOR SUP-port from the DNC. We called and called. Georgia senator Max Cleland came and spent a day hunting for votes, which I greatly appreciated. So did Joe Biden and Joe Lieberman, good party stalwarts and lovely men. But for some reason we couldn't get a dime's worth of financial or strategic support. Finally, I took a train to Washington to put in a personal appeal. Steve Grossman, the national chairman of the Democratic Party, was polite; he gave me a cup of coffee and a couple of cookies, like I was a Cub Scout on a field trip. "I'm the guy who won the Jersey primary—maybe you heard something about it?" I said sarcastically.

"We're a little bit more worried about Washington," he said. "Washington is falling apart." The special prosecutor had locked the Clinton administration into a defensive mode on a number of fronts, all of them meaningless and politically charged. Nobody knew it yet, but the Monica Lewinsky scandal was about to explode.

Soon, Hillary Clinton came and did a women's event with me—she impressed me immensely. When she arrived she asked to see my polling numbers and demographics analyses, and she had smart things to say about the thrust of our campaign.

Eventually my pleas reached the president's office. Bill Clinton recognized that mine was a David-and-Goliath campaign, and he personally came to my aid, making two tours with me on the stump. He was wonderful and kind. He asked about my life's story, where I grew up, and how Kari and I fell in love (when I told him we'd met in Bermuda, he said that he and Hillary had conceived Chelsea there). I was amazed at how easily, in the chaos of a political campaign, he could close everything out except the person he was speaking with; it was an extraordinary talent.

I'll never forget sitting in the back of a campaign car when our conversation turned to the plight all Democrats were facing. "To get a white guy to vote for a Democrat," Clinton said, "first you have to strap him down to a gurney, give him every reason in the book, then wheel him into the voting booth yourself—and pray it works. That's how tough it is."

White men especially react negatively to a nasty campaign, he said. Neither side had gone negative yet, but there were early warnings that it could go bad. Whitman had filed an official complaint alleging that my leased campaign car was a sweetheart deal—at $335 a month for a stripped-down Mercury, nobody took the complaint seriously.

On my side, John Lynch had hammered the Whitman administration after $344,000 in state money was used to settle a sexual harassment suit against former assembly speaker Chuck Haytaian, a Republican who served as chairman of the state GOP. Whitman fired back that Lynch was "not one to talk," citing an old report that his wife had called the cops during a fight at Lynch's condo. Lynch was arrested but his wife dropped the charges and refused to testify against him.

But Clinton advised us to steer clear of such distractions. "Stick to the issues," he said. "Don't get sidetracked. Just keep hammering away on taxes and auto insurance. You have to be Luke Skywalker and you have only one chance to lob that torpedo into the Death Star, so you have to be focused and disciplined in your message." I loved him for saying that.

Everywhere we went together on those two days, he whipped Latinos and African Americans into a patriotic frenzy. They adored him and forgave his political errors. The previous year he had won New Jersey by a seventeen-point margin. I appreciated his generosity in allowing some of his glow to spill over onto me. Just being able to sit with him in the backseat of the sedan as we tooled through our stops made me feel like I had arrived, no matter how the campaign ended up.

"My God," I found myself thinking. "What if I actually win this thing?"

It was then, as I drove along with the president down the Garden State Parkway, that the illusion of a Parkway sign with my name on it bled into my thoughts. And as I watched the word *HOMO* take shape on that sign, in towering spray-painted letters, I was haunted by the idea that Clinton might see what was happening, though I was pretty sure it was all in my mind.

* * *

THE LAST WEEK OF THE CAMPAIGN WAS A BLUR OF POLLS, RALLIES, photo opportunities, and sleepless nights. We ran through nursing homes and union halls, hospitals and parks. As we trolled from town to town, a loudspeaker affixed to the roof of our campaign vehicle blasted away at our themes. In Jersey City, where I prayed at St. Patrick's, the church where I was baptized, we played a tape that went like this: "This is Jimmy McGreevey, a native son of New Jersey. He'll reduce your car insurance by ten percent. He said it. He means it. He'll do it."

One of our last visits, arranged by my dad, was with a group of homeless veterans. These guys aren't a well-known voting bloc, but I went because they represented the problems we were campaigning to fix. They were all races and ages, with credentials from Korea to Desert Storm. Many seemed to be in need of medical and mental-health services. One guy had been living under a bridge, he told me; when the local cops had run him off, he'd lost all of his possessions, including his VA documents. Their stories broke my heart. I prayed that night for victory, so that we could do something positive for these men.

Joel Benenson, a Democratic pollster from Doug Schoen's office whom we brought aboard for the final months, was starting to get excited about our chances. Whitman was holding on to her eight-point lead in the polls, but even hours before the balloting stations opened, 18 percent were still undecided. "It's a horse race," Joel told me. I stuck to my message as the clock ticked down, repeating phrases from my stump speech to anybody who would listen. I was exhausted, sleep-deprived, even a bit delirious at times. My very last reporter interview was with NJN's Michael Aaron. When the lights snapped on, he asked me how I was enjoying the weather. I was so charged up, I didn't even hear him. "New Jersey has the highest property taxes and the highest auto insurance rates in the nation, and among the lowest test scores in schools," I said as he burst out laughing.

On November 5, Election Day, we rented out suites and a large ballroom at the East Brunswick Hilton. I spent the night before with Dina, talking about what might happen if I won. Though it went unmentioned, we both knew we would marry as soon as the divorce was finalized. Still, our relationship wasn't yet public, and that night she stayed away from our hotel suite to prevent any hint of scandal. My parents and sisters joined me there, along with Ray, John Lynch, George Norcross, and former governors Florio and Byrne. Jack Fay, my mentor for nearly a decade, came to see how these things were unfolding. We turned on the television and watched the thousands of fans and volunteers who'd gathered downstairs, dancing and celebrating in the ballroom. It looked exactly like that party for Jerry Ford that I'd crashed twenty years ago.

"After this, it's the White House," Jack said to me. "You know that, don't you?"

Because of the way the polls were counted, I was in the lead all day. It wasn't until 11:37 PM that the horse-country precincts were counted, pushing their native daughter to a maddeningly narrow victory. She pulled it out with just 27,000 votes, beating a young, unknown suburban-town mayor by a mere 1 percent margin. She may have won the race, but as the editorial writers pointed out the next day, her near defeat at the hands of a political unknown had left her political career in tatters.

It was after midnight when I called Whitman to congratulate her. She was gracious in victory. "I wish you well in your political career," she said. I told her the same.

IT'S SHOCKING HOW QUICKLY YOUR POLITICAL MIGHT WILTS AND withers after a loss. In minutes, the state troopers had withdrawn. All the heavy hitters were out the door, the lights died down, and I was an ordinary citizen again. I looked over to Kevin McCabe. "Well, it's back to potholes."

That night a group of the boys headed back to my Woodbridge condo for cigars and brandy: Jimmy Kennedy, Jim Burns, Kevin McCabe, Frank Doyle, and me—the Irish Mafia, we called ourselves. Kevin had planned for us to watch a movie on TV, *Michael Collins*, about the IRA founder known as the Lion of Ireland.

On the way I ran into Dina in the parking lot. We sat a while in my car talking before heading home.

"It's been a long night," I said.

"We have to look to the future," she said. "It starts again tomorrow."

I looked over and found she was crying. We hugged. I kissed her. I felt totally loved and supported by her. I knew how much she had put into this campaign, and how exhausted she was, too.

Just then we looked up and saw a familiar reporter. Neither of us wanted the morning's papers to include a coda about the candidate and his secret girlfriend, so Dina got out of the car and strode purposefully back to the Hilton. Watching her disappear into the building, I thought to myself: *You're at a fork in the road. You could give this up and be yourself. This is your last chance.*

12.

OVER THE YEARS, I'VE THOUGHT A LOT ABOUT WHY I MADE THE choices I did after the '97 defeat. Fundamentally, I think that living in the closet made it almost impossible to do anything differently. I knew many fine gay people by now. My information technology director in Woodbridge, Michael Esolda, was engaging, integrated, and at ease with himself—and accepted in the office. The same was true for my personnel director, Jim Ringwood. I envied them. My Woodbridge hair stylist, Mark Esposito, was also gay, and I looked at his long-term relationship with longing. But by now I was caught up in something I couldn't control, a lie that had taken on a terrible momentum.

I think I decided that my ambition would give me more pleasure than integration, than true love. I fell for my own mythology.

On Christmas and again over Easter, I flew to Vancouver to be with Kari and Morag, who by now was an impressively intelligent and well-adjusted five-year-old. During one of those visits, Kari and I signed the papers finalizing our divorce. Although I was devastated, I wanted to acknowledge that we were still good friends, perhaps better now than before. I bought her a "divorce ring," and she slipped it on her finger with a smile.

Later that night, I walked along the icy Fraser River back to my hotel. It was unusually cold, and a light snow was falling. I remember rejoicing in the feeling of being unmarried and totally anonymous, as if a world of possibilities was suddenly available to me. It was freeing to be in a city where nobody knew me, unencumbered by the tethers of Carteret and Woodbridge, my church and my community. Here, I thought, I could be a truer person.

I knew what Kari believed was true, that I'd lost my spiritual course. Part of me didn't want to return to New Jersey. I had an opportunity to start all over again, to drift away like so many other fast-burning politicians had. But the thought of vanishing like that simultaneously filled me with despair. I couldn't get beyond one simple fact: I'd lost by a mere 27,000 votes. My political potential was enormous. The thought of another campaign was exhilarating, and the thought of being governor intoxicated me. On election night, a *New York Times* reporter showed me what the morning's headline would have been had I won. I couldn't get it out of my mind.

I looked up to the moon through the snowflakes, the same moon that shone over my condo back home. I thought, *Why am I able to wrestle with my authenticity here, but not there? Why do I feel so caged there?* I was forty, entering middle age, yet still incapable of being myself at home, and incapable of leaving.

I felt *compelled* to keep running for governor. Coming to this realization made me feel not suicidal, exactly, but morose. I had a deep feeling of anguish. My grandmother would have called it a "heavy Irish melancholy." It's hard to describe how it feels to surrender your soul to your ambition.

I was forfeiting any hope of personal happiness—and doing it consciously now, not out of some teenager's confusion. Standing on the river's esplanade, I recommitted myself to this split, dishonest life in order to play my hand in politics.

Among other things, I was anxious about marrying Dina. She was a good and compassionate friend. But our romantic life was troubled from the start. I know this disturbed her. It may even have raised questions in her mind about my sexual orientation. But we never discussed this aspect of our relationship. It was not a topic that held any promise of benefit for either of us, so we soldiered on as lovers without addressing it. By this stage in my life, there were no women I felt capable of romancing in traditional ways. I saw marrying her as another step along a road I couldn't get off.

Sexuality couldn't be the only thing that mattered to me, I told myself. There must be millions of Americans who sleep beside their wives every night and don't make love to them. Surely there were thousands of gay men who sleep next to their partners without making love to them, either. Why should I be different?

You may be wondering, *Did he give a thought to whether this was unfair to Dina?* Of course I did. I believed I was offering her some things she truly coveted: the stability of marriage, the prospect of a loving family, a chance to share a life of public service, political excitement in spades. Of course the list of things I was overlooking was just as long: honesty, intimacy, true romantic love. But all I could do was to try to make it work. That was all I'd ever known how to do.

About a year later, I read a story in *Esquire* about Congressman Michael Huffington, whose struggles as a gay man in politics were all too familiar. I read the story as though it were about me: "At age thirty-three, Mike Huffington made a resolution; I am straight, I will get married. I will have children. I will never sleep with another man again." The closet, he admitted, had been his key to political success; the more the door cracked open, the less potential he was seen as having. Stories about him had swirled around in Democratic and Republican circles for years, and it only got worse when his wife, Arianna, left him in 1997, after a failed Senate run. The *New Yorker* made fun of him for "washing his hands frequently," a nasty little jab at his masculinity that even George Will, no friend of gay rights, condemned as "ad hominem." Finally he came out in *Esquire,* because he had no choice; the gossip mill had turned his closet door to glass.

As I headed home from Vancouver for my second marriage, I hoped my story would play out differently: that living with Dina would help me enforce the boundaries I'd been trying to maintain for years. If I stayed single, with no structural safeguard, there was no telling what sort of volatile situation I might get into.

Instead, with Dina, I would have a partner. I should have known that would be unfair to her, and it was blind of me.

WOODBRIDGE WAS IN PRETTY GOOD SHAPE, AND DIDN'T NEED AS much remedial attention as it had in the early days. So I was free to work on exciting new projects. With the help of a sizable grant from Road Packaging Systems of Keasbey, New Jersey, we put computers in every classroom in each of the township's twenty-three schools and wired them all to the Internet. The $3 million initiative made our school system unrivaled in telecommunication and access to the information superhighway. We also brought major improvements to Ford Park, the town's tarnished jewel, and built a $200,000 state-of-the art playground using an army of more than 600 Woodbridge volunteers.

But there were occasional storm clouds over Woodbridge, including a Whitman-sponsored plan to build a $22 million facility in the township for up to three hundred dangerous sex offenders and the criminally insane. Our objections weren't simple NIMBY complaints. Woodbridge was already home to two large-scale correctional facilities. A third would be a tremendous burden—and an indefensible act of payback from Whitman. We sued and eventually blocked the project.

Our darkest moment came one night in 1999, when racist vandals attacked the First Baptist Church of Woodbridge. Windows were broken, racial slurs spray-painted on walls, garbage cans overturned in the yard. Even the tires of the choir members were slashed. In my lifetime I can't remember so vile an act of hatred so close to home. Walking through the churchyard, I was nauseated by the damage. Many of the parishioners were friends of mine; I couldn't stop thinking how frightened they must be. The parish they loved, where I myself had worshiped dozens of times, had been defiled. But Woodbridge showed what it was made of in the aftermath, rallying together as Christians, Jews, and neighbors of all faiths to prove that the hatred of a few couldn't unravel the loving fabric of our community.

In November 1999, I won reelection as mayor by a landslide, with 86 percent of the vote.

But I never stopped campaigning for governor. The papers remarked that my first press conference after losing the '97 race "sounded like a campaign speech," and they were right. I never even slowed down. My months were packed with speeches to Holocaust survivors, visits to churches and synagogues, dinners at VFW halls and labor events, gala fundraisers, and private meetings at diners with the bosses and warlords.

My first goal was to lock up the ballot lines as early as possible, to foreclose the need for a primary so that I could devote my energies to the general election. So I courted each of the county chairmen constantly, starting with Hudson County's Bob Janiszewski, who had gone against me last time.

I dropped by his home fully nineteen months ahead of schedule to tell him how much his support would mean to me.

He invited me to stay for breakfast. Stroking the head of his ferocious-looking Doberman pinscher, he asked about my plans for state government and spoke expansively about the kinds of support he could deliver to the right candidate.

I appreciated his candor. But I told him all I needed was his endorsement on the party line. I had won Hudson last time out, and I was sure I'd win it again. What I was looking for was momentum. If I had Janiszewski's backing this early, it could help me convince other bosses who opposed me four years ago.

No matter what I said, though, I couldn't get Janiszewski to commit. So I went to ask Paul Byrne, his political operative and best friend since First Holy Communion, for his blessing. Instead of answering me, he regaled me with a long story about his own fiftieth birthday party. It seemed his friends had bought him a ticket to the Dominican Republic, where they'd rented an entire whorehouse for his exclusive pleasures.

"Jimmy? I felt like a six-year-old kid in a Dunkin' Donuts," he said. "I knew I couldn't eat them all, but I sure as shit had fun thinking about it!"

A few weeks later, Bob Janiszewski called and gave me Hudson, just like that. I never found out what turned him around.

But it wasn't long before everybody in New Jersey learned that Janiszewski was a man in trouble. He pleaded guilty to taking more than $100,000 in kickbacks from vendors and went away for forty-one months. His greed, it turned out, was bigger than all of Hudson County.

I was disappointed, but not surprised. I'd been in state politics long enough to know it was a game for saints and scoundrels. But deep in his indictment papers was another startling revelation. Long before his arrest had become public, he had turned state's evidence and started taping conversations with other New Jersey politicians and contractors—even Paul Byrne, perhaps his oldest friend in the world. A surprising number of them fell into his trap. One of the cardinal rules of New Jersey politics is, there's no such thing as a private conversation. Governor Byrne once told me this, as though imparting a philosophical truth from the ages. "Somewhere along the line," he said, "you are going to be taped by someone wearing a wire." This is why so many political meetings start with a big bear hug—a New Jersey pat down among friends.

But Janiszewski outsmarted everyone. He had hidden the recorder in his dog's collar. I have no idea if he tried to catch me saying something inappropriate that morning, but nothing ever came of it.

DINA HAD ALWAYS WANTED TO SEE PARIS, BUT I COULD NEVER AF-ford that for us. So on the second week of February 2000, we compromised and headed for Montreal by car, a six-hour drive. It was going to be our first real vacation together.

Somewhere north of Albany, in the Adirondack Mountains, Dina took the wheel and I lowered the back of my seat for a nap. I was in a half-dream state, excited about seeing the sites of my grandparents' pilgrimages. I was planning to propose to Dina there; in my pocket I had a diamond ring, a simple stone in a tasteful gold setting. I was hoping she wouldn't find it too understated.

When I felt the car jerk into a spin, I snapped my eyes open. Dina had hit a patch of black ice and we were whipping around at top speed on the Adirondack Northway. An eighteen-wheeler was bearing down on us. I grabbed the steering wheel and pulled the car hard to one side, avoiding the truck but sending us crashing into the guardrail. Luckily, we came to a stop there. We could have flipped over or bounced back into traffic. Neither of us was hurt, but we were badly shaken.

We had no idea where we were. Our cell phones didn't work. Taking the wheel, I was able to get the car back onto the Northway, but the back wheels had been knocked out of alignment, and it was nearly impossible to keep the car heading forward. Loose pieces of twisted metal were dragging behind us, sending a curtain of sparks in our wake. We lurched to the next exit and found a gas station located near the bottom of the ramp. The attendant agreed to have a look at the car in the morning, and at his suggestion we called a bar in the nearest village to find a place to stay. They had one room available; we agreed to take it sight unseen.

I can't recall the name of the village, but I'll never forget it: down on the heels and shut tight for the winter. The owner sent somebody to pick us up—a patron, judging by the perfume of gin on his breath and his tendency to drive with one eye closed. He got us back to town by the grace of God. Our room was cold and had two twin beds, but we didn't mind squeezing into one of them. Being alive and warm was enough. (Even better was the sight of our old friend Congressman Bob Menendez when we turned on the TV, speaking on the floor of the House.)

The next morning, we wandered through the desolate mountain village until we found a place serving breakfast. We both ordered the blueberry pancakes, and they were the best things we'd ever tasted. The other patrons were fun and welcoming—one turned out to be distantly related to my friend Ed McKenna, the mayor of Red Bank, New Jersey.

Despite our close call, we were starting to enjoy ourselves. "Let's go shopping!" Dina called out playfully.

"Deen," I said, "we're in the middle of nowhere! Did you see a place to shop?"

One of the restaurant owners chimed in with a few stores we'd missed, tucked away on side streets. So we headed out, ready for adventure, and spent the day ducking in and out of doorways and meeting kind and fascinating people. It may have been a first for me, having a whole day ahead of me with no obligations. It had taken me a near disaster to experience something so simple.

We stayed in the village about thirty-six hours before the mechanic told us it would be another week before our car was ready. So we hopped on a train and continued on to Montreal without it. The accommodations there—at the Queen Elizabeth Hotel on Rene Levesque Boulevard—were luxurious, but hardly superior to our twin bed over the bar.

Valentine's Day fell on our second night in the French quarter. After we'd enjoyed another outstanding meal, I reached for the ring in my pocket. "We never made it to Paris," I said. "We barely even made it to Montreal. It takes a special person to handle the challenges and the difficulties of the career I've chosen. In a way, this trip is almost an allegory for our relationship. Whatever life throws at us, Deen, if we're together we'll be able to handle it.

I'm asking you to share this journey with me, to bear its ups and downs. I'd be blessed if you'll be my wife."

I slid the ring on Dina's finger, as tears rolled off her cheeks. She never looked more beautiful than she did that night.

THREE WEEKS LATER, I HEADED FOR ISRAEL, PART OF A DELEGATION of 750 elected officials, politicians, and cultural leaders organized by the United Jewish Federation of MetroWest, which covers Essex, Morris, Union, and Sussex counties. I'd been there twice before on political junkets. This trip, called Mission 2000, was billed by the agency as a chance for us to meet donors and open our eyes to Israel's significance in world affairs. Among us were Jon Corzine, at the time making his successful run for the Senate, and his Republican challenger, Jim Treffinger, the Essex County Republican executive, as well as Congressman Rodney Frelinghuysen, state Senate President Donald DiFrancesco, and mayors and party loyalists from both sides of the aisle.

Our schedule was full. We visited the Knesset, traveled to the Old City in Jerusalem, met farmers in the Negev Desert, and lunched with officials from then–prime minister Ehud Barak's office. The trip's organizers thoughtfully accommodated Roman Catholics on Ash Wednesday with a side trip to the Church of the Nativity in Bethlehem, built by Constantine the Great in the year 335. We visited the Golan Heights, over which Israel's dominion is contested; Modi'in, a large city where we helped plant cypress trees to symbolize our solidarity; and a West Bank settlement called Ofakim—"New Horizon" in Hebrew— where students performed a musical for us.

The settlements, built on land Israel won in war in 1967, were a topic of conversation and controversy among us. Over lunch one day, I had a chance to talk to Yitzhak Rabin about them. He advocated withdrawing the settlers from the Golan Heights. "It costs forty-five thousand dollars a year to protect each settler," he told me. "And for what? There's no economic return. It's not an investment. I'd rather be investing in irrigation systems and farms in the Negev, because that's an investment in Israel's future." I was surprised at how clear, straightforward, and objective his argument was—in a part of the world defined by centuries of emotion.

One afternoon, we took a bus trip to a local arts center in Rishon Lezion, a sprawling but rather featureless city just five miles outside Tel Aviv. We were greeted there by the mayor, but it was his thirty-two-year-old communications director who caught my eye. That's too casual a way to put it. My attraction to him was immediate and intense, and apparently reciprocated. From the minute I walked into the building, I felt it. Our eyes met over and over before we were introduced. "This is Golan Cipel," he said. "He is familiar with New Jersey—for a number of years he worked at the Israel embassy in Manhattan."

We shook hands for a long time. "I followed your campaign very closely," Golan said. "Twenty-seven thousand votes is a very narrow margin." He went on to describe my strengths among various constituencies, remarking how well I'd done among white men—a rarity for Democrats, as he well knew.

"You would have won with better outreach to Orthodox Jews," he added.

I was startled by his knowledge of my campaign. We talked through the length of the reception, and his insights were dead-on. At lunch I made sure to sit next to him. "Democrats take Jews for granted. It's a powerful constituency. With Orthodox, you pick up Jewish Republicans, so actually you pick up two votes instead of one. You have to develop relationships with them," he said. "You've got a good record on Israel. Your efforts on Holocaust education are strong. More people need to know that. In 1997, you got a good percentage of the overall Jewish vote. But if you'd gotten even a small number of Orthodox votes, and all of the Reform Jews, you would be governor today."

He had smart ideas about my current campaign, but I admit I was only half listening. Watching this handsome man talk—and show an interest in my political standing—totally mesmerized me. Nobody commits to memory the demographic standings of a politician halfway around the world as an academic exercise. I was flattered beyond anything I'd ever experienced before. From there our conversation moved naturally to the personal, and we talked about our lives and goals and dreams.

I assumed he was straight, but what was happening at this lunch if not flirting? I flirted back, a bit shamelessly. But he matched me compliment for compliment. I can't say I ever had a more electrifying first meeting—so dangerously carried out in a room full of politicians who could ruin us both. I fell hard.

Immediately afterward I went to the junket organizers and requested to be seated next to Golan again at dinner. Years later, one of them was quoted saying he knew exactly what was going on. "They couldn't take their eyes off one another," he said.

RIGHT OUT OF HIGH SCHOOL, GOLAN HAD SERVED FIVE YEARS with the navy of the Israeli Defense Force, part of his country's compulsory military service, and another ten years in the reserves. That explains a lot about his straight-backed comportment and his black-and-white world view. He was graduated from New York Institute of Technology, where he also earned a master's in communication. He had never married, and at least on our first meetings he didn't mention a girlfriend. He wasn't quick with such personal details. Rather, he spoke with passion about his career in politics. Besides his stint at the consular office in New York, he had clocked some time as an aide in the Knesset, at a job that seemed similar to mine at the assembly, marking up bills and researching issues. He'd landed a big job with the mayor of Rishon Lezion, a city of over 200,000; Meir Nitzan was almost like a father figure to Golan.

But the job was just a stepping stone, he admitted to me at dinner that night. Having seen and experienced so much in his young life, he had a wanderlust he wanted to quench.

Impulsively, I invited him to join my campaign. He said he was thrilled at the chance.

BY JUNE 2000, I'D RAISED $9 MILLION, MORE THAN I'D SPENT IN my first run for governor, and well on the way to my goal of $40 million for the whole campaign. I say that as though this was easy, but the opposite was true. Unless you're a Clinton or a Bush, $40 million is an obscene amount to pull out of pockets. By way of comparison, that's two-thirds the annual budget for Woodbridge, a bustling middle-class city of 100,000 tax-paying citizens. I was having to attend six and seven fundraising events every single day. Most of the time I had no idea where I was or who I was talking to. In the car between events, staff members would brief me hurriedly on the attendees, their histories and connections—just enough for me to parrot a few lines of familiarity on my way through the room before dashing on to the next event.

We decided against setting up a finance committee with a powerful chairman. Given the enormous egos in New Jersey, anyone we anointed would surely offend a powerful segment of potential funders. So instead we set up numerous finance committees, each one organized around a policy area: infrastructure, development, business, and so on. When we invited people to take part, we asked for maximum allowable contributions. "These are investments," we said, "in a very sound political calculus." We were that sure we would win.

By now, I knew that you can't take large sums of money from people without making them specific and personal promises in return. In our campaign, people weren't shy about saying what they expected for their "investments." An unusually large number wanted powerful postings—board appointments to the Sports Authority or the New Jersey Economic Development Authority, for example, which were coveted not just for their prestige but because they offered control over tremendously potent economic engines, with discretionary budgets in the tens of millions. The plum was the Port Authority of New York and New Jersey; directors there controlled a multi-billion-dollar budget and helped direct development projects that determined the geographic landscape of the East Coast. It was amazing to me how many people openly and aggressively lobbied for this job.

I tried to stay as naïve about this horse trading as possible. I allowed my staff to intimate things to donors, and I know John Lynch and the other bosses were doing the same thing. It would be a felony for any of us to promise a posting in exchange for a contribution. But we'd long since learned to walk this side of a dangerous line.

Often I'd be called in to seal a deal before a check was written. Invariably, the contributor would tell me how much it would mean for him to be appointed to the Port Authority.

"I know New Jersey would benefit from your public service, wherever you give it," I might reply. If pressed, I would add, "What is your vision for the Port Authority?"

Too often their answers said more about their quest for power than concern for our state's future. Sometimes they spoke of having achieved financial security in their lives, freeing them to pursue a new passion or challenge.

"Thank you for letting us consider you," I'd say.

For an influential executive who was about to hand over $100,000, that often wasn't enough. "Will you consider me for the Port Authority?" he was likely to push.

My standard reply was, "You'd be great in a number of positions."

"Will Port Authority be one of them?"

This is the daredevil's dance every politician faces, from the biggest campaigns to the least significant. It is why fundraising is so corrosive and why campaign finance reform is so necessary. There has to be a better way to further democracy without exposing the naked ambitions of politicians to the power-lust and greed of political donors, a volatile combination. Any politician who wants high office as urgently as I did is the weaker partner in this negotiation.

My responses were always governed by a trio of concerns, all in constant tension with one another: legal, ethical, and financial. The law was always my bottom line; what I said was always determined by what could be done legally. Remembering Governor Byrne's warnings about body wires, I consciously avoided saying anything that might be construed as an illegal quid pro quo.

But in order to get the money I needed I gave myself a lot more leeway when it came to ethics. I made a threshold decision to stay out of the weeds of fundraising, and let others cut deals on my behalf. I didn't monitor things closely enough. Part of me—the purely ambitious part of me—didn't care enough.

I was running for office for all the right reasons. I wanted to help bring about decency, justice, and compassion for working families and those who had no voice in the halls of Trenton. But I couldn't do any of that without getting elected; at least that's what I told myself. That doesn't exonerate me for my shortcuts. I was becoming too adept and too clever at making these accommodations. Increasingly, this James E. McGreevey, this political construct, was looking like a stranger to me.

I DIDN'T HAVE TO WORRY ABOUT A DIVISIVE PRIMARY THIS TIME out. The whole state Democratic machine was in my camp. For safety's sake, Ray Lesniak organized a dinner of the warlords at a loft he kept in New York's Tribeca. Senators Jon Corzine and Bob Torricelli, the state's ranking Democrats, were both there, and both pledged their support. I'd secretly worried that Torricelli wanted to run for the job himself—he'd hinted at it in past campaigns, and if our party regained power in Trenton that fall, the work of a Democratic chief executive could be very rewarding. So I was relieved to hear him say he had no ambitions for the job.

On June 28, we held our most successful fundraiser ever, at the same East Brunswick Hilton where I'd waited for results in 1997. In one night we raised $3.2 million, a statewide record and a display of my increasing strength. In a gesture of confidence and magnanimity, I had the checks written to the State Democratic Committee, not to my campaign. The Committee could give the money to the candidate of its choosing for any significant race in the state. Ray Lesniak counseled against doing this so early in the race, afraid that someone would come out of the woodwork to declare against me, using my own money to buy ammunition. But I wasn't worried. The Committee director was Tommy Giblin, the Essex County boss. I'd put him there myself after 1997, as I promised I would. New Jersey politics might have the nastiest ground rules in the country, but it still follows an old-world ethos. Rule number one is, Don't double-cross your friends.

I assumed I'd get half of that money back in grants from Giblin, with most of the rest going to get-out-the-vote efforts in the twenty-one counties. That would amount to much more money than if I had gone out to raise funds directly. State campaign finance laws at the time limited contributions for individual campaigns to $1,800 a person per election cycle, but they allowed each donor to give up to $30,000 in so-called soft money. It was worth the small risk I was taking.

Besides, my campaign was nearly on automatic pilot. I was still working the retail side tirelessly, running myself ragged with eighteen-hour days on the trail. Two-thirds of the bosses had given me the line. I was the 800-pound gorilla.

Or so we thought. One day in early July, a local reporter reached Ray by cell phone while he was on the golf course. Torricelli was declaring for governor, the reporter said. "That's impossible," Ray said. "That would make him the biggest hypocrite in the world. And Bob Torricelli's not like that."

I immediately called Giblin to ask him to freeze the money, but it was too late. Torricelli, it turns out, had been lured into the race by my $3.2 million good deed. He'd already asked for a contribution, and Giblin, with a misguided sense of fair play, promised parity. That one infusion would be enough to jump-start the senator's campaign. Giblin couldn't see the unfairness of it. Only a few did. Chuck Chiarello, the Atlantic City chairman, was one of the good guys; he called it an "outrage" that, now that the state party finally had a rainmaker, his own party leaders were using the money to run the rainmaker out of town.

I was furious; this was a huge problem. Torricelli was a very powerful senator, as attractive to voters as he was to the ladies (he was known for dating the likes of Bianca Jagger and socialite Patricia Duff). In our polling, his approval ratings were fourteen points better than mine. People knew him better than they knew me. He was a *900-pound* gorilla.

Over the next few days, my endorsements began unraveling. Nobody wanted to be on the wrong side of a pair-up involving me and Torricelli, whom we all called the Torch. I picked up the *New York Times* one morning to find Rocco Mazza, the executive director of the Democratic committee of Bergen County and an old friend of mine, singing Torch's praises. "The party senses that McGreevey would make a fantastic candidate, but the difference is that Torricelli has statewide stature and national stature, and is far superior in the gravitas department. It's the difference between filet mignon and New York strip steak."

That really hurt.

Then Bergen, which had already committed to me, suddenly announced for Torricelli. So did Camden, Morris, and Burlington counties. We had to move fast. In Hudson, Bob Janiszewski, who'd already given me his support after my tireless lobbying, switched to Torricelli. I begged him to hold off any announcement, then got Bob Menendez on the phone. I had great respect for the congressman, who represented parts of Hudson, and I knew he held a grudge against Torricelli. The last time a Senate seat was open, Menendez had gotten Torricelli's backing to run for it, but at the last minute the Torch double-crossed him and switched his allegiance to Jon Corzine. Surely he'd understand that Torricelli's mercurial politicking wasn't good for Hudson County.

Menendez agreed to back me publicly. He called up the mayors and other party leaders in Hudson and got their support as well, then called Janiszewski. "If you're with Torricelli, you're looking at a full-scale revolt," he said. Thanks to him, Hudson came back to my column.

Then I marched through the seven southern counties and got the chairmen, at least, to hold off their commitments for a few days. I was buying time; sooner or later Torricelli would have to return to Washington, and perhaps his lights would dim by then. But Torricelli was already claiming he controlled the south. In the long run, I knew he'd get the line there. George Norcross, the warlord from Camden, told me as much himself.

The only thing I could do was let Torricelli know how bloody a battle it was going to be. One day in late July, he sent out a press release announcing endorsements from five southern union locals. We went into rapid-response mode. Kevin McCabe pulled together a press conference with 150 labor heads and militants from South Jersey: locals representing most of the state's building and construction workers, along with communications workers, civil servants, firefighters, teamsters, and electricians, all squeezed into a Trenton conference room. They accused Torricelli of dividing the Democratic Party with his self-serving efforts and promised their votes for me in South Jersey.

The newspapers were already calling this a party civil war. The point we wanted Torricelli's people to hear was this: every place he gains a little, we'll gain too. When Torricelli announced that the mayor of Bayonne was with him, we convinced dozens of leaders in four South Jersey counties, including many mayors, to join me, threatening a sweep through the south. He was going to need a strong constitution to take us on—and as much energy as we had, which of course was impossible.

Instead, he began hammering away at Essex County, with its cache of votes in Newark. We already knew Giblin was vulnerable; I tried reasoning with him, to no avail. If Giblin went with Torricelli, I was sunk.

For the third time in my career, I had to turn to Ray Lesniak to save my career. Once again, he felt the key was Sharpe James.

Ray arranged a dinner for us one Friday night at the Millennium Club, a nightclub in Newark owned by Sharpe's son. The place was so dark inside, it took a while to adjust our eyes—and as soon as we had we were blinded by the pulsing laser lights. Then the sound system went on, so loud we couldn't hear a thing. Walking through the main dance hall we came upon a smaller room with cabaret tables. My friend Calvin West, Sharpe's chief of staff, was there already. So were Sharpe and Regena Thomas, the party operative. Ray and I were the only whites in the place.

Ray began by sharing a piece of news. Earlier that day, East Orange chair Catherine Willis had told us she wanted to announce for McGreevey, but she was waiting for Giblin's "permission." This irritated Regena Thomas, who played adroitly to her audience. "What? That white boy thinks he can tell people who to support?"

Ray and I got down to business, pushing Sharpe every way we knew how. We tried policy, we tried loyalty, but none of it seemed to be working. Finally, Ray asked Sharpe to step outside for a walk, just the two of them. I don't know what went on out there, but when they returned to the table, Sharpe was ready to give me his backing in the primary.

We went back to Giblin with the news. He hadn't yet declared for Torricelli, but he'd been making increasingly derisive comments to the press about my chances. He was impressed by our fortitude, he told us, but he wasn't about to go out on a limb. He commissioned his own poll that weekend, and fortunately it gave me a slight lead over Torricelli among likely Democratic voters, thirty-five to thirty-one. That was a good sign—Gilbin wanted to back a winner.

But what sealed the deal happened that Saturday, twelve days into our skirmish with the Torch. Robert Bowser, the mayor of East Orange, was holding his annual picnic, one of the major political gatherings on Essex County's calendar. When Torricelli showed up in the morning, he had no individual relationships with anybody there. When I arrived in the afternoon, my friends chanted my name.

That was the last straw. Torricelli's candidacy died in Mayor Bowser's backyard. He withdrew on Monday.

A few months after the Twelve Days War, as it came to be known, I asked Ray what he and Sharpe had talked about that night outside the Millennium Club. "I made Sharpe a commitment that he never called me on," was all he would say.

These days, Ray Lesniak is a changed man and a role model for me. He's recommitted himself to a spiritual quest and turned his back on the kind of soulless political wheeling-dealing we both practiced with such gusto back then. Among the stalwarts in my life since I quit the governorship, he has been the most demanding and the most supportive. "Welcome back to the human race," he said back then.

But during my years in politics I never saw a better fighter than Ray.

Since then, we've both walked away from the battleground, each in our own way. Ray has taken on the Twelve Steps as a way of life, their own spiritual movement. For me they serve as a way to recover from my drive to be liked at all costs, which sometimes allowed me to make decisions based on self-interest and not ethics. For instance, when Sharpe James later ran a difficult campaign against a young reformer named Cory Booker, I stood by his side as he vituperated against Booker—an African American Rhodes Scholar—for not being married. He actually called him a "faggot white boy" in a public address. Thank God I wasn't at his side that day.

Thanks to Ray, and the road we've since traveled together, I know I'd never let things like that go unanswered again.

One day recently, I asked him what he and Sharpe James had talked about that night in Newark. "That's going to have to stay between Sharpe and me," he said.

* * *

WHEN GOLAN FIRST CALLED, I WAS ECSTATIC TO HEAR FROM HIM. I half expected he'd forgotten about my job offer, but he'd already made his travel plans. We talked about the sort of work he'd be doing and how much we both looked forward to seeing each other again. Through the summer, his calls became more frequent, and I always looked forward to them. But soon they shifted from personal matters and were more about the logistics of moving halfway around the world. He was having trouble obtaining a work visa and said that I'd need to sponsor him. But my campaign office was months away from bringing in minority coordinators, so I couldn't do it that way.

As time went on, I grew disenchanted with our plan to import Golan, but I never wavered from it. I had two full-time jobs, as mayor and as candidate, but in my spare time I tried to intercede with the INS on Golan's behalf. Meanwhile, he became increasingly demanding, raising his voice with me, challenging my commitment to him joining my staff. I started putting his calls through to Sean Nolan, my administrative assistant, with instructions to say I was out of the office.

I can see in retrospect that these phone calls were premonitions of what was to come. But I wasn't heeding the warnings then. I was trying to fix his visa problem, but coming up with no solution. Ultimately, I hit a brick wall.

"It's not gonna work," I told him finally. Part of me was relieved. His calls were a huge drain on me, and besides, I wasn't looking forward to cultivating a full-on longing for something I couldn't have. But a bigger part of me was disappointed.

I also knew he was right about my campaign strategy. I'd gone back to study the polls. My results were mixed, as he'd said. I didn't have an outreach program to the diverse Jewish community. Having an Israeli aboard would help me cross into conservative enclaves. In one move, I could create a unifying strategy.

Golan was disappointed, too. "Is there anyone else who might need someone who's versatile in Hebrew?" he asked. "They could sponsor me and I could work with you."

The only person I could think of was Charlie Kushner. I'd been meeting regularly with Charlie since the last campaign, and he remained my heaviest contributor. The next time I saw him, I told him about this smart young Israeli. "There's something very attractive about Golan coordinating the Jewish vote, because it's a tough and diverse community."

I showed him the demographics charts. "I did very well with ethnic Catholics and middle-class groups. Whitman did well with the affluent—the vote divided mostly along economic lines. She did well with upscale Protestants, too. But look here. She also did relatively well with the Jewish community. I still carried it by a mile, but for a Republican she made tremendous inroads with the Reform vote, and look at her numbers with the Orthodox."

Charlie was interested. "Could he work with the Lakewood Yeshiva?" he asked. He was close with the religious leadership of Lakewood, New Jersey, home to one of the largest yeshivas in the world. "If the rabbi there says, 'I'm voting for John Smith,' everybody votes for John Smith. Not ninety percent—*everybody*. In 1997, they all went Republican."

"That's exactly what we'd use him for," I said. "Not just Lakewood Yeshiva, but the whole community: Reform, Conservative, Orthodox—all the sects. But I can't sponsor him. Can you find a job for him?"

It was a lot of work for Charlie, who had to handle all the INS filings, but he managed to bring Golan to New Jersey by early fall 2000, putting him to work part-time in one of his real estate offices. Someone on my staff found him an apartment, a few doors down from me in Woodbridge. Immediately he began directing my campaigning in Jewish strongholds around the state, doing just the kind of work he promised to carry out.

But there was a problem. My campaign staff loathed him. For one thing, he didn't think he had any hierarchical relationship to the rest of the staff. He billed himself as occupying a separate orbit altogether. He dialed my cell constantly and nagged Kevin Hagan, my political director, on nearly a daily basis to get on my calendar. Kevin complained to me directly. "The guy's an asshole. He doesn't work well with others. He doesn't understand that this is a team. You can't allow him to circumvent the process and go directly to you. It undercuts our authority. It undercuts the campaign structure. This is a very important constituency, obviously. But we're running a statewide campaign here. You're not running for mayor of Jerusalem."

I knew what he meant, but I defended Golan. "To be fair," I said, "everybody else on the campaign is American—African *American* or Irish *American*. This guy dropped in here from I don't know how many miles away, just to do campaign work for this guy he met only once in Israel. That says something to me. My God, *I* wouldn't pick up and move to Israel to work on somebody's campaign."

The truth was, Golan was good at what he was doing. He was befriending all the powerful rabbis in the state, getting to know their congregations, their families, their personal interests. He was working Jewish women's groups, schools, and athletic clubs. There wasn't a prominent Jewish leader in the state he wasn't lobbying or planning to lobby. In no time, he delivered every major Jewish organization in New Jersey.

Watching him work was as exhilarating as it was exhausting. I knew it was going to produce the deciding votes. And once or twice, climbing back into the campaign car after an endlessly long day wearing yarmulkes, I kicked off my shoes and spread out on the backseat, resting my feet across his knees. He didn't seem to mind. With my eyes closed, I could allow myself to pretend I had it all: the governorship, the family, the male lover—and the final piece of the puzzle, love. I thought he was my angel.

To quote the desert monk Hermas, he was "the wrong angel."

IT WAS A MAGNIFICENT, SUNNY DAY IN OCTOBER 2000, WHEN DINA and I got married at the Hay-Adams Hotel, across Pennsylvania Avenue from the White House. A slight breeze lifted Dina's veil as we took photos.

A Washington wedding was my idea. In my mind, it was a kind of campaign stop—in a longer campaign that might someday carry me to the Senate, perhaps, or the White House. In the elegant ballroom at the Hay-Adams, I was laying down a marker. Dina would have preferred a Catholic Church service, but my divorce made that impossible unless I filed an annulment, which I refused to do for Morag's sake. So first we had picked one of the gorgeous candlelit chapels at Georgetown, and we found an ancient

Jesuit priest who agreed to marry us in defiance of Rome. But after we had the invitations printed up, we discovered that he'd mixed things up—the chapel used for "non-orthodox weddings" was elsewhere on campus, and in pictures it looked as attractive as a frat house. So we settled on the Hay-Adams for the ritual Mass and reception, preceded by a small church wedding back in Woodbridge with Father Bob Counselman at Trinity Episcopal Church.

After our ritual affirmation of our marriage, in the presence of our dearest friends, including Ray Lesniak, Calvin West, and the Kennedys, we moved on to the reception. With gorgeous tapestries lining the walls, and cocktails being served on a sweeping veranda overlooking the White House lawns, it was as grand as a royal wedding.

Whatever the imperfections of our marriage, we were taking one step away from our ordinary lives.

WITH THE DEMOCRATIC PRIMARY BEHIND US, I WAS READY TO meet the Republican challenger. According to a Quinnipiac University poll, 48 percent of the state's registered voters were behind me.

The Republican primary, meanwhile, was something of a surprise. Whitman had been tapped by the new Bush administration to run the Environmental Protection Agency—a peculiar choice, frankly. During her tenure, law enforcement efforts against air and water polluters in New Jersey had effectively stopped; fines had dropped by 70 percent. The staff at the New Jersey Department of Environmental Protection was slashed by 738 jobs. And the state's anti-sprawl regulations were totally dismantled: more virginal open space was handed over to developers during her tenure than at any other period in New Jersey history.

Donald DiFrancesco, the congenial state senate president, filled in as acting governor for her remaining few months. But he wasn't satisfied serving as acting governor and soon threw his hat in the ring for the Republican primary. He ran a relatively decent campaign against Bret Schundler, a self-made Wall Street millionaire whom even state GOP leaders found impossibly right wing. Schundler was progun, antichoice, and out of step with New

Jersey's traditionally moderate brand of Republicanism. He ran a brutal primary campaign, tearing DiFrancesco limb from limb. It won him the nomination handily, but his performance was so unseemly that few Republican loyalists had the stomach to campaign with him.

I couldn't have asked for an easier target. All the way through August I had a sizable lead, even grabbing 14 percent of Republicans in independent polls.

If my luck was cresting, my old pal Joe Suliga's was a tidal wave. Poll after poll showed he was on his way to becoming senator from the 20th Legislative District. His Republican opponent, a former Olympic gold medalist, was twenty points in the dust. Every time I bumped into him along the campaign trail, an awesome pride showed on that large face of his. Joe was about to land the job of his dreams. So was I. And I was thrilled for both of us.

ON THE CRYSTALLINE BLUE MORNING OF SEPTEMBER 11, 2001, I GOT up early as usual and worked out at The Club at Woodbridge before beginning a long day of campaigning. After a quick meeting at headquarters at eight o'clock, we raced down to Ocean County to talk to a group of senior citizens about tax relief. Driver Joe Massimino Jr., my "body man," Jason Kirin (whose job was to stand at my side, take notes when needed, get me in and out of buildings on time, etc.), and I had already reached the banquet facility when somebody told me that a plane had gone into the World Trade Center. I pictured a little Cessna flying off course, a tragedy on a relatively small scale. But when we got word that a second airplane had hit the buildings, the horror of the attack sank in. We found a television set and watched as both towers burned. Reporters announced that people were jumping to their deaths, a thought too awful to bear. A third plane had hit the Pentagon and a fourth was headed for the White House, at least according to early reports.

Everything changed in that moment. A distant dispute had reached our shores. Anyone could see the storm clouds of a protracted war gathering on the horizon. *Whoever did this must be made to pay*, I thought. *America can not let these deaths go unanswered.*

I also knew that among the dead would be a disproportionate number of New Jerseyans, ambitious and innocent men and women who boarded the morning train or ferry in Hoboken, Weehawken, and Atlantic Highlands for finance jobs in the Towers. In the final count, nearly seven hundred from my state perished in the attacks. One town, Middletown, lost fifty sons and daughters that morning, men and women just like the kids I grew up with in Carteret, whose only involvement in global affairs was to work hard to improve their lot in life. The majority were employed by one investment firm, Cantor Fitzgerald.

The rest of the day unfolded as if in a surreal dream, muffled and terrifying. We turned the Buick around and raced back to Woodbridge, to our families and responsibilities at home. From the Parkway we could see the two columns of smoke rising over Manhattan; an easterly wind bent them toward Brooklyn. My first call was to Dina, who was shaken but fine; my parents were also okay.

As mayor, I rolled out our own disaster plan. We prepared the police to respond in case of local attacks, which seemed less likely by midmorning as the skies overhead filled with American fighter jets. According to our emergency management policies, we provided security to local corporations, oil tanks, rail lines, and chemical plants and mobilized officers along the Turnpike, Parkway, and interstate. I raced to the campaign office, in one of Woodbridge's tallest buildings, where the burning towers were visible, about ten miles away. On the way, I stopped at St. James Church for a private prayer. Monsignor Cashman, my longtime spiritual adviser, gave me Holy Communion.

We weren't able to establish communication with New York City, so the television news and the bird's-eye view from the windows became our main sources of information. We dispatched ambulances and emergency service trucks to the city, but they were turned back at the tunnels—there were no survivors yet to tend, increasing our sense of helplessness. Our firefighters got through, though, and worked at putting out the blazes. And then we heard the terrible noise of the first tower collapsing. We ran to the top floor of our campaign headquarters, which had an unobstructed view of the unimaginable horror. My mind couldn't comprehend the losses; the truth was too awful to contemplate. When the 110-story-high second tower slammed to the ground, a chorus of cries rose up over Woodbridge's rooftops, crowded with stunned observers.

GOLAN CIPEL WAS PACING BACK AND FORTH, ARMS CROSSED OVER his chest. "The Middle East war has arrived to America," he was saying, even before we had any idea who was behind the attack. "Everything has changed. It is a new paradigm."

It was unclear what would happen to the elections, but I knew we had to suspend campaigning. I called Schundler and he agreed. We were both briefed about ongoing efforts to secure the state's airspace and harbors. We heard about National Guard deployments, coordination with the Defense Department, mobilizations at Fort Dix and McGuire Air Force Base, and intelligence briefings from the FBI in Newark. Until this moment I had never realized how colossal and complex the state's security systems were, or how imperfectly coordinated they were with New York's. National defense hadn't been even a remote part of our campaign to date. There was so much to learn.

The next several days were excruciating. Scores of Woodbridge families were searching frantically for their loved ones, but no answers came. They prayed for a miracle, that a husband or wife was alive in an air pocket in the rubble pile or wandering through the city in a daze. They photocopied "missing" posters, with heartbreaking photographs and descriptions of the clothing they wore that morning, and went to Manhattan to tape them to every building, streetlamp, and fencepost. I helped organize first responders at Liberty State Park, where the state police had set up an emergency management headquarters in view of the smoldering embers, then volunteered to help fill ferries with water and food to ship to the rescue workers.

On the second day, Jason Kirin, Kevin Hagan, and I hitched a ferry ride with Jersey City firemen to lower Manhattan. The scene was indescribably grisly: fire trucks twisted and flattened by falling debris, the grimy firefighters with specially trained dogs lowering listening devices into crevices, hoping against hope. At one point the rescue workers thought they'd heard a noise and frantically dug through the debris. For several hours we helped out, standing on a bucket brigade and moving an endless stream of stones and mortar from left to right, hoping in vain that someone's life had been spared. That night, we held a prayer vigil in Woodbridge. More than a thousand people came.

On the morning of the third day, I ran into Cynthia, a woman I knew from a local Baptist church where I occasionally attended services—we held our annual Martin Luther King Jr. services there. Cynthia's daughter was among the missing, and she was heading into the city in search of information, a dire and heartbreaking mission. She was all alone and desperate for information about her daughter, but she found a tremendous strength in her faith. "I know my girl's lost in the city," she said firmly. "I know she'll be okay, but I have to find her first. I have to find my baby."

"I'm coming with you," I said, taking her by the hand. We arrived at the family relief center Mayor Rudy Giuliani had set up at the Chelsea Piers on the Hudson River. Inside was a scene of chaotic despair. Ministers, rabbis, and priests had written their affiliations on masking tape across their chests for easy identification, so the bereft could find them quickly in their darkest hours. Muted televisions replayed footage of exhausted rescue workers, empty-handed and crying. I watched a young woman tearily handing over toothbrushes and razor blades for eventual DNA typing.

Having seen Cynthia get through that day, I am sure she's the bravest person I have ever met. Steadily, and with hope, she filled out the paperwork she believed would lead to her daughter's rescue. From her purse she pulled a photograph—I recognized the woman, just a few years younger than I was—and affixed it to her form. We prayed together over her family Bible that the girl was still alive. Alas, she was not.

I ATTENDED DOZENS OF FUNERALS IN THE WEEKS THAT FOLLOWED. Many of our Port Authority workers perished in the attack. James Lynch, a Port Authority cop from Woodbridge, was among the first confirmed dead. I had known him and his family well. At his wake I learned he was off duty that day, but when he saw the towers burning he raced to help his fellow officers—an American hero. These were working-class guys who loved their families, their communities, and most of all their country. In one day we lost Christopher Amoroso, a former football star at North Bergen High School; Kenneth Tietjin, who, after saving people from Tower One, grabbed a pack, waved to his partner, and went into Tower Two; Thomas Gorman, a Port Authority emergency services unit cop who'd taken his wife boating on the Jersey coastline to celebrate her birthday just days before; Richard Rodriquez, whose Puerto Rican heritage didn't keep him from playing in the Emerald Society Pipes and Drums wearing a tartan kilt; and Fred Morrone, superintendent of the 1,300-member Port Authority police force and a daily communicant at a Catholic church near his home in Lakewood. I didn't know Fred well, but throughout all the ceremonies his wife, Linda, was a towering figure of strength.

For New Jerseyans, as our grief expanded, the terror didn't recede. On September 18, a nationwide anthrax scare began after five letters containing the deadly bacterial spores were dropped at the post office in Trenton, destined for reporters at ABC, CBS, NBC, the *New York Post*, and the *National Enquirer*. Two more anthrax letters were postmarked in Trenton, addressed to Senators Tom Daschle and Patrick Leahy, causing a shutdown of the Senate as well as post office branches across New Jersey. The toxin was also found in curbside mailboxes in Princeton. In all, twenty-two people were infected and five died; five years later, the case remains a mystery.

The scare gave our local Woodbridge police force cause for alarm, and we met frequently to try to plan for the arrival of terrorism in the township. How would we coordinate response to an airliner attack? Quarantining after an anthrax contamination? God forbid, a nuclear event?

With all this going on, Dina was enduring troubles of her own. By this point we were expecting a child, but it was turning out to be a difficult pregnancy. She went into preterm labor on November 2, twelve weeks premature. She was ordered into bed for the duration and moved into inpatient care, first to Robert Wood Johnson University Hospital, then to Saint Peter's University Hospital under the specialized care of Dr. William Scorza. On many days, it looked like we were going to lose the fight. Scorza began administering steroids, hoping to promote lung development in the baby in the case of an extremely premature birth. Simultaneously, he put Dina on a regimen to stop contractions and dilation.

That's when Scorza noticed that the baby's heart rate was fluctuating precipitously. Worse yet, ultrasound revealed that the umbilical cord was wrapped around the baby's neck. Throughout this, Dina's courage was tremendous. I remember her lying on her back on a gurney fighting those early contractions. If our baby were born then and lived, Scorza told us, there was some chance that she might suffer lifelong complications. It was the only time I saw Dina lose her composure, but she regained it quickly.

I don't think I ever returned to the campaign trail. On November 7, 2001, I won the election for governor of New Jersey by fourteen points. What's more, my coattails proved long. Democrats retook a majority in the assembly and now tied Republicans in the Senate, twenty-to-twenty. It was a huge victory for the party, ending almost a decade of exile. I remember thanking my supporters at the Hilton and letting the state troopers drive me over to Dina's bedside so I could give her the news myself. She was so uncomfortable and worried for our baby that it was hard to find a minute to celebrate. I sat by her side, holding her hand, as I would every night for the next month, until our precious daughter Jacqueline was born by emergency C-section on December 7, still premature but healthy.

Friends and supporters overwhelmed the hospital with flowers for Dina—so many that they filled her room and several nearby. Then some idiot phoned in an anthrax scare, which the hospital administrators took to be aimed at Dina and me. Teams of hazard specialists removed the flowers immediately. It was just a prank, but after we'd worried so much about losing Jacqueline, the scare did little to elevate our moods.

AN INTENSE AND ABSOLUTELY INEVITABLE THING HAPPENS AFTER you win a big election. The jostling for power is wild. Republicans had controlled the governor's mansion for sixteen of the past twenty years, and now we were overwhelmed by pressure to bring Democrats and their supporters in from the cold. Democratic law firms, developers, investors, suppliers, vendors, and consultants of all stripes were vying for my attention. So were arts groups, women's groups, civil rights groups—advocacy agencies that hadn't had an ear in Trenton.

And there were all my many financial contributors vying for payback. I'd worked my whole life to get to this point, banking on the calculated risks of political fundraising, not to mention the winks and nudges that stand in for promises, and suddenly it all came to a head. I felt the accumulated burden of all this acutely. Kant's formula for morality was no use to me now. I had done *A and* attained *X*—only to face a much more formidable moral quandary: how would I slake the tremendous demands of those who helped me along the way? Moral certainty had never felt more elusive.

Because so much power is in the hands of New Jersey's chief executive, most significant state employees are washed out with each new administration. We had eight to nine thousand state jobs to fill, two thousand appointments to make even before taking office. Everybody wanted a piece of the action. As the single elected statewide official, I was a huge bull's-eye to special interests.

My first concern was to take care of the people who'd given day and night to running my campaigns for the past six years, tireless warriors who shared my new vision for New Jersey. At the time, I felt it was prudent to promote people I knew and trusted. What I didn't yet realize is that the people who run a campaign aren't the best people to run a government. They come with too many strings attached. They've just spent a year or more in the trenches horse trading for enormous financial donations. As soon as they land in government, everybody they dealt with comes looking for a reward, some payoff for their "investments." If I had to do it over again, many of my initial appointments would be very different, not because the people I chose were unqualified, but because they were vulnerable to temptation.

Gary Taffet, my chief of staff on the campaign trail, seemed an obvious choice for chief of staff in Trenton. I'd relied on his judgment and cool head for fourteen years; in politics, he was my closest friend. As chief counsel I chose Paul Levinsohn, a charismatic and hard-working lawyer. I'd met Paul years ago, when he was a law school student at Duke researching a paper on centrist Democrats. Over the years I'd come to trust his instincts and advice and had hired him away from the politically connected law firm Wilentz, Goldman & Spitzer, to be my campaign's finance chair. Gary, Paul, and I worked as an Iron Triangle. Gary saw to the care and feeding of the state's political players; Paul raised the money; and I did the retail campaigning.

Unfortunately, I later learned that both men were compromised. Partly that was because of the campaign roles they served on their way to state government. They were my horse traders, doing and saying what was necessary to bring in votes and money. I don't believe either of them made overt promises to any of my donors for appointments or contracts, but I know they were lobbied aggressively, as was I, and they replied with encouragements: "I'll try," or "You'd be a perfect candidate." It hadn't occurred to me how untenable it was to bring them inside. As soon as they arrived, they were slammed by people coming to collect on the promises they thought they'd heard. The pressure on them, and indirectly on me, was tremendous.

For several key appointments, I reached for candidates with broad executive experience, regardless of party affiliation. David Samson, a respected Republican, agreed to serve as attorney general. I appointed Dr. Clifton Lacy, the brilliant chief medical officer of Robert Wood Johnson University Hospital in New Brunswick, to run the Department of Health and Senior Services and Cherry Hill mayor Susan Bass Levin to lead the Department of Community Affairs. Bradley Campbell, a former Clinton administration environmental adviser, took over our Department of Environmental Protection, and Dr. William Librera, the respected superintendent of the Allamuchy Elementary School District, brought his unparalleled leadership in early childhood education to become commissioner of the Department of Education. Al Kroll, general counsel of the state AFL-CIO, was appointed labor commissioner, with Kevin McCabe as deputy commissioner. In the words of AFL-CIO president John Sweeney, we had the strongest prolabor administration in the nation.

But for a number of significant jobs, I kept my inner circle close. Regena Thomas was my choice for secretary of state, charged with overseeing programs in arts, minority culture, volunteerism, and historic preservation. Jim Davy, who had provided exemplary service as Woodbridge business administrator for almost a decade before taking over as campaign manager, was my choice for chief of operations, responsible for making the trains run on time. (He later became commissioner of Human Services at a time when that department needed fundamental structural reform.)

My old friend Roger Chugh—a Delhi native who was my campaign liaison to the Asian community—became the assistant secretary of state, an important symbolic gesture at a time when U.S. troops were preparing to invade Afghanistan. I also made Kevin Hagan deputy chief of staff; at twenty-six, he was perhaps the youngest in the history of the state, but certainly among the most able.

The Gannett newspaper chain made a big deal about the fact that I'd hired so many campaign workers—62 percent of my hires, by their tabulation. But I defy them to study any governor before or since whose appointments didn't follow the same pattern. The difference is that my appointees were people a lot like me, intelligent and capable but from working-class backgrounds. There was always a touch of class bias behind these reactions.

Some specific appointments drew quick criticism, almost all of it unwarranted and mean-spirited. Republicans were all over my decision to appoint Charlie Kushner, who with his family and business had by now donated more than $1 million to my campaigns, to the board of the Port Authority of New York and New Jersey. (I would later tap him to be chairman.) They complained it was political payback for his financial support, but that's simply wrong.

Kushner was a hugely successful businessman, a heavyweight who was equally respected throughout New Jersey and in New York political and financial circles. His reputation was unblemished. Ernst & Young, the national accounting firm, had named Charlie Entrepreneur of the Year in the real-estate category. His philanthropic efforts rivaled those of the Rockefellers and the Carnegies, and in 2000 the National Conference for Community and Justice named him Humanitarian of the Year. He had great political standing among my Jewish voters, and international clout.

This was a crucial time for the Port Authority, which was jointly administered by New York and New Jersey. The World Trade Center, which had stood on land owned by the Port, was being rebuilt. The agency needed a developer with Kushner's experience. I also needed somebody who could work seamlessly with Michael Bloomberg, New York's new mayor, and Governor George Pataki in Albany. I had strong working relationships and growing friendships with both men. But I knew I needed a smart, tough negotiator to make sure New Jersey got its fair share of the federal Homeland Security monies being allocated for the Port. Kushner could do this ably.

To the critics who couldn't see beyond the money Kushner raised for me, I pointed to New York's choice for port commissioner: a top fundraiser for Pataki and other Republicans named Charlie Gargano. An executive with a major development company, Gargano was an adroit administrator who, when push came to shove, favored Albany's interest over Trenton's. Kushner was a necessary and able counterpoint.

At the time, I thought he was totally above reproach.

But he refused my appointment three times. Eventually he accepted because he thought it was important for America. By doing so, he voluntarily stepped out of competition for any of the development dollars that would flow as a result.

DINA AND JACQUELINE REMAINED IN THE HOSPTIAL FOR SEVERAL weeks after the delivery. Between November 7 and my inauguration on January 15, whenever I wasn't visiting them or doting on them once they came home, I worked on almost nothing besides appointments.

There were a number of people I wasn't finding quick fits for, chief among them Golan Cipel. He had performed admirably in the campaign, but in a limited role. Now he made it plain that he wanted a significant portfolio in Trenton, but there was no obvious post for him. I weighed putting him in the Port Authority or the Commerce Department, places where his facility with the press and familiarity with diplomatic protocol might come in handy.

This upset Golan, who wanted a "front-office job" working more directly with me. Several times a day he demanded meetings to discuss his future. I found his insistence both boyishly charming and unbelievably churlish. My staff saw only the churlish side. He moved himself into the transition office, bragging that he had a "personal relationship" with me that gave him unassailable insights into my likes and dislikes. He actually demanded to look at office assignment charts and even redrafted my inaugural speech, all without my authority. Finally, when I'd had enough, I went to his apartment to talk to him about diplomacy and office politics. It was a fastidious place, with a fluffy cat I was surprised to learn he'd named Jimmy.

"Gole," I said. "Why do you have to fight with everybody? You've got to learn to get along, to be part of the team."

"My only team is you," he said.

But as the transition efforts progressed, I found myself increasingly relying on his advice and candor. Here was a guy who never varnished his words when talking to me, who wasn't afraid to tell me when he felt I was dead wrong.

His main interest was fighting terrorism; he was consumed by the subject. One night he made me drive with him to the foot of the George Washington Bridge to watch the police screening large trucks there, in a method he considered inadequate. Commercial trucking was then permitted to cross the bridge only a few hours each night, when inspection stations were manned. Trucking companies accommodated this rule by dropping off trailers on the Jersey side of the bridge throughout the day, so the driver didn't have to wait; another tractor would arrive once the trailer was cleared to cross.

"That's ridiculous," he said. "Any one of those parked trucks could blow up the bridge."

He had a point. Nothing about my education so far had prepared me to think that way. But Golan had grown up under the threat of terror and spent fifteen years fighting it in one way or another. He dragged me down to Cape May and along the Delaware River to Philadelphia, to study how the Delaware River Port Authority was interacting with the Coast Guard. "There is no interoperability," he said. "Their radios aren't even on the same frequency."

Talking to him, I realized that New Jersey needed an office of counterterrorism to think about security and anticipate trouble. After 9/11, acting Governor Donald Di Francesco had relied on an interagency coordinating body called the Domestic Security Task Force, chaired by the attorney general. I planned to keep that in place, but add our own intelligence-gathering wing affiliated with the state police, headed by an experienced crime fighter who could interface with state and federal counterparts.

I took to heart Golan's advice, borrowed from a Coast Guard admiral: "Crisis by definition is an intelligence failure." He must have said that ten thousand times. He gave me books to read on security strategy and arranged for a briefing with ranking Israeli generals.

But on our private stakeouts around the state, something else was happening. A tension was growing between us that excited me. He talked about girlfriends and I talked about Dina, but there was a thick subtext to our conversations that was about the two of us.

Finding Golan a job he considered acceptable was a priority, but there were many other pressing matters demanding my time. When we had our first briefing after winning office I saw what a colossal mess the state's budget was in—even before the terror assault magnified our budget troubles a hundredfold. My economic advisers were telling me we would have a $3 billion deficit in the first year alone. I'd promised not to levy taxes, so we were already in the middle of negotiating a series of difficult budget cuts: the teachers unions wanted my head on a platter, the arts community was ready to stone me, and I hadn't even been sworn in yet.

On December 10 or 11, after I rebuffed several requests for meetings, Golan reached me on my cell phone, upset that I'd been out of touch. I invited him over to the condo for a late dinner, to assure him that he had a future in the administration. He arrived in a suit and tie, dressed impeccably as always. I don't remember what I prepared for us to eat, but it can't have been very good—the kitchen is as baffling to me as a submarine's helm. But with Dina still in the hospital with our newborn, I'd been left to my own devices. In fact, I think we ate cold cereal.

He was politely appreciative. We sat at the dining room table talking and half-watching the cable news, our shared addiction. I don't know at what point it occurred to me that something more was about to happen. But I know how it started. I stretched out on the couch and placed my legs out over his knees, as I'd done previously in the car. I then leaned forward and hugged him, and kissed his neck. His response was immediate and loving, just what I'd fantasized about since the first day we locked eyes.

It was wrong to do. I wasn't an ordinary citizen any more. There were state troopers parked outside. My wife was recovering from a difficult pregnancy and C-section in the hospital. And he was my employee. But I took Golan by the hand and led him upstairs to my bed. We undressed and he kissed me. It was the first time in my life that a kiss meant what it was supposed to mean—it sent me through the roof. I was like a man emerging from forty-four years in a cave to taste pure air for the first time, feel direct sunlight on pallid skin, warmth where there had only ever been a bone-chilling numbness. I pulled him to the bed and we made love like I'd always dreamed: a boastful, passionate, whispering, masculine kind of love.

Afterward, I lay on the bed and watched Golan on the pillow next to me as he slept. At around three o'clock in the morning I shook him out of bed for his walk home, not wanting to alert the state troopers to anything amiss. When he was gone, I realized that this might all explode on me one day, but I just didn't care. I felt invincible then.

V.

The Price
of Authenticity

13.

difficult, but not impossible. I visited Dina and Jacqueline every day in the hospital, and my heart ached to have our baby home, but until they returned I spent as much free time as I could with Golan. I loved our time together, whether talking politics over cups of tea or trying to remember whose T-shirt was whose at the end of the bed. He fiddled with my hair, which I keep slicked back tightly, still unhappy with its propensity to curl. "You should comb it like this," he said, parting it with his fingers. "It's less severe."

He had things to say about my wardrobe, too. For as long as I can remember, I'd worn a standard political uniform; in my closet were a dozen dark blue suits and a hundred white shirts, so many that I dropped them at the laundry once a month, thirty at a time. Golan even counseled me on my intonation. The New Jersey in my voice made him laugh. He was a consummate public relations man. I took his advice seriously (though not enough to change my hair). I ventured into the brown aisle next time I bought a suit, and sometimes added a faint wash of color to my shirt collection.

When Dina finally got home, things changed. Our condo became a scrum of familial activity. Her parents were always around, cooing to the baby in Portuguese. My parents and sisters stopped by a lot too, as did Jimmy and Lori Kennedy; they were all eager to get to know Jacqueline, who was a beautiful fireball even when she was only a few days old. Dina was exhausted from her birthing ordeal, but she took to motherhood instinctively. I loved watching the two of them together.

Knowing how much work I had ahead of me, the crowds at the condo paid little attention to me. I raced out to the gym at dawn and didn't return on most nights until long after dinner.

Once, after an exhausting day in the transition office, I made secret plans with Golan to see him later, at his apartment. The state troopers, now my constant companions, dropped me at the condo and parked around back. When I was sure they couldn't see me, I pulled on my running clothes and slipped out the front. Golan's apartment complex was roughly half a mile away, but difficult to get to on foot. I ran along the sidewalk for a while, then below a railroad underpass before returning to the sidewalk and ducking into his building.

He greeted me in his briefs. "Did anybody see you?" he asked, closing the door quickly. We kissed, hard.

I was totally in love with this man. He loved everything I loved. Politics never bored him. He loved strategy and demographic analyses. He loved power, philosophy, justice. He never stopped thinking about these things, and that's what gave his life purpose and joy. I didn't always agree with him, but I always learned something from him. His intelligence and his compassion were equally far-reaching. More than anything, I loved how he viewed our relationship, as a political partnership without limits. Or so I imagined; we never discussed it.

"No, nobody saw me leave the condo," I answered. "They don't even let me jog alone. Last time they saw me leave in running clothes, they sent somebody to run with me."

He led me to his bedroom, past photographs of him and his naval crew and a set of painted toy soldiers, posed in some famous battle formation. Israeli folk music played on the stereo. He undressed quickly and jumped into bed.

To get what I wanted after so many years of denial was almost too much for me. Our first few times together burned so fiercely in my mind I could hardly recall them even as we were still lying together. I'll never forget the look of trust in his eyes and the dead weight of his vulnerability in my arms. But I was like a kid on his first days of drivers' ed, too thrilled to be behind the wheel, unfamiliar again with the roadways I'd known all my life.

He was patient and understanding. In fact, I believed his journey was the same as mine, that he had also taken great risks to arrive at this place of happiness, unity, and integration. And love.

When we finished our lovemaking, our thoughts returned to the enormous task we shared, building an administration from scratch in just two months, governing in a post-9/11 world. He was conversant in foreign affairs, diplomacy, and global economics, subjects that still were far from my mind. Once, he discovered that a staffer had received a letter from the Chinese consular office in Toronto and inadvertently sent a reply to the Japanese consulate, a stupid error.

"You can't let this kind of thing happen," he said to me. "You're not the mayor of Woodbridge anymore, worrying about relations between this neighborhood and that one."

"Golan, it was just a mistake."

"You can't tolerate mistakes! The terror attacks show that. New Jersey is part of the world now in a way it never was before."

I think Golan expected me to end up in the White House. Maybe that's what he loved about me—my potential to bring him to Washington. If he was using me as the engine driving his own ambition, I didn't mind. I liked seeing myself reflected in his eyes. And in a way he was my tutor, too. He shook me out of my pedestrian New Jersey parochialism. He helped me think big.

"Gole," I said, "what do you think about the New Jersey State Department? You'd be working with foreign dignitaries, heads of state."

That wasn't what he had in mind. "But I want to work with you, not on the other side of Trenton."

"How about Commerce? You could work with global trade arrangements."

"Jimmy, please—can't I work with you?"

DRUMTHWACKET, THE GOVERNOR'S MANSION IN PRINCETON, IS one of the most fabled and elegant of America's executive residences. Built in 1835 on land originally owned by William Penn, the house is a classic example of the Greek revival style, surrounded by ornate English gardens that have been celebrated for nearly a century. Charles Smith Olden, a business-man from New Orleans, was the first owner and the man who gave it its name, which means *wooded hill* in Gaelic.

Active in community and political affairs, Olden was elected governor in 1860 on a platform supporting Abraham Lincoln's stand against seces-sion. He began the tradition of aristocratic benevolence among chief exec-utives in the state. When the treasury sank precipitously during the Civil War, he reached into his great personal fortune to keep New Jersey solvent. After his death, an industrialist and banker named Moses Taylor Pyne ex-panded the structure with seven new public rooms downstairs and a dozen private rooms upstairs. A grandchild, Agnes Pyne, sold Drumthwacket in 1941, and twenty-five years later the grounds were sold to New Jersey, to be used as an official residence. Jim Florio, who moved there in 1990, was the first modern governor to use it, and I was only the second; Christie Whit-man favored her own family estate, visiting Drumthwacket only during of-ficial receptions.

Dina was looking forward to setting up home there, much more than I was. I didn't really know anybody in Princeton, one of the state's old-money enclaves. Woodbridge and Carteret, my home for four decades, were forty minutes away. More significantly, Drumthwacket had all the "official residence" accoutrements, including guards at the door and a staff of cooks, maintenance engineers, and groundskeepers. Surely this would be the death knell to any love affair, much less the unusual one Golan and I were undertaking.

Luckily, we couldn't move in right away. Although the building had been extensively renovated in the 1980s, it smelled of mold and its decor was badly outdated; as Florio once said, the restrooms were done in "early Turnpike." Moreover, it was full of lead paint and asbestos, unsuitable for a newborn. Dina and I requested an extensive renovation, and the nonprofit foundation that runs the place agreed, embarking on a $590,000 facelift funded by contributions, including money from Charlie Kushner. To avoid spending taxpayers' money, friends and family agreed to join me for a "painting party."

At least until April we would have to stay put in our tiny Woodbridge condo, down the street from Golan.

In public I struggled to maintain a professional relationship with him, but it wasn't always possible. I remember one day walking from the transition office to the statehouse with Jason Kirin, Gary, and Paul. "Jimmy, I need to talk to you," Golan whispered in my ear. We fell behind the others, no doubt blushing. I could tell that Jason, my body man, found this strange. Afterward he even said something about it.

"Golan's pretty free with his hands," he remarked.

"Israelis are very affectionate people," I told him.

THERE WAS AN UNUSUALLY MILD BREEZE IN THE AIR ON JANUARY 15, 2002. Dina and I hadn't slept well the night before, excited about the inaugural events, though the fact that recovery efforts were still ongoing in New York gave the day an appropriately somber tone. Again, costs were covered by private donations. As a favor to me, Golan joined in the planning. It was an impressive lineup. The world famous American Boychoir came to sing the "Hallelujah Chorus," one of my favorites, followed by the Shiloh Baptist Church Choir, the Southern Regional Select Choir, and the Malcolm X Shabazz High School Marching Band.

In a hint that my future was bigger than New Jersey, several national heavyweights attended, including John Sweeney, head of the national AFL-CIO.

Dina was beautiful in a red silk suit, cradling our baby in the crook of her arm. We didn't speak much in the morning as we dressed and headed over from Woodbridge, with an official state photographer recording our every move. A state police bagpipe chorus accompanied our entrance to the War Memorial in Trenton, hand in hand. My heart almost stopped when I looked out from the dais. Two thousand people had gathered to witness the swearing-in ceremony. Leaders from every religion practiced in New Jersey sent delegates. Police, firefighters, and marching bands, battalions of veterans, hundreds of union regulars representing all the trades, and schoolchildren of every size and color marched past in formation along West State Street.

I felt their expectations on me like a heavy weight, but I was happy to do my best; this new phase of my life was a burden, but a joyful one.

Dad and Mom stood with me for the swearing in, resting my hand on two Bibles Dad held—one that had been in the family for generations, and another that I used for daily devotions. As I declared the oath of office, I looked over to my mom—I prayed to carry out my term with the pure sense of service she had taught me by example.

In his invocation, Rabbi Menachem Genack, a good friend, set a tone for the day and captured my hope for the coming four years, for the state as well as the nation. "The journey ahead will not be easy," he said. "But as the Bible tells us, 'Those who sow with tears will reap with joy.' If we all join together, united, with God's help, we will surely reap a plentiful harvest of prosperity and peace, progress and yet unimagined possibilities."

I kept my address brief, touching on education, our ballooning recession, and the need to strengthen our antiterror programs. "Today we are facing a moment unlike any other in the history of our state or nation," I said. "We have witnessed in real time an attack that shattered our domestic tranquility and threatened us all. Our neighbors died. Our buildings fell. Not since the assassination of President John F. Kennedy thirty-eight years ago have we mourned so collectively as a nation, as a people.

"But in the wake of this horrendous attack, we have revealed our better angels. Police and emergency workers waded into Ground Zero searching for survivors. Families lit candles and prayed for neighbors they had never met, nor would ever know. Firemen climbed blazing stairwells and emerged at heaven's gate.

"Out of this catastrophe, we have come together. From Ground Zero, we have found common ground. We were reminded that what we do together as a community is as important as what we do one by one, or family by family. Our shared loss became our shared resolve.

"Today, our state faces a new set of challenges—the challenge of keeping our families and streets safe from further acts of terror and violence; the challenge of living within our means in the face of a national recession; and, our most important challenge, making our schools work so that we prepare our children for their future, for their challenges. These are difficult tasks. But we already have witnessed the key to their solution. If we come together as Americans—as New Jerseyans—in the same way we came together in the wake of September eleventh, there is no challenge we cannot meet, no problem we cannot solve. We need only draw upon that spirit of community — upon that same sense of passion and resolve.

"So this is my call to action. In the days ahead, each citizen of New Jersey should demand more of me. That is your right. But you also must ask more of yourselves. That is your responsibility."

Not for a minute did I feel unprepared for this challenge. With the grace of God and the inexhaustible intelligence of my loyal staff, I was certain we could march forward from the ashes of September 11—stronger than ever, embracing our diversity, proving the resilience of our great nation.

Overcome with the joy of the moment, I pulled my wife into a gentle kiss, igniting the crowd to cheers. We had arrived. Then, looking into the audience I spotted Virginia Jones, my kindergarten teacher.

"Hey, Mrs. Jones," I called out, pushing past the state troopers guarding the stage. We embraced lovingly after so many years, as television cameras jockeyed around us.

"He's our future president," she beamed.

THE LEARNING CURVE IN TRENTON WAS STEEP. FROM MY FIRST DAY as governor, I made serious miscalculations with the press. I had expected to be able to work with them the way I always had in Woodbridge; the reporters from the *Home News Tribune* were generally apt to include our point of view in their stories, and I never felt we got a bad shake. There weren't many controversies in my ten years as mayor, but whenever one came up they gave me ample opportunity to explain my decisions. I also found, in those milder circles, that the quickest way to kill a controversy was to say nothing about it. Minor dustups got bigger only when I sunk my teeth into them defensively.

New job, new rules.

In one of my first big announcements, I nominated Newark's top cop, Joseph Santiago, for state police superintendent, a position that required Senate approval. The editorial pages liked the selection; Santiago wasn't part of the trooper culture, which was dogged by accusations of racial profiling. He was also a minority, and the first Latino to be nominated for the post. In Newark, Santiago had a tremendous professional track record for cleaning up corruption. In six years, he had cut crime in half and spearheaded the arrest and prosecution of dozens of dirty cops.

All my life I've been a fan of the state police, especially the rank-and-file men and women who go out on uniformed patrol every day. But the leadership of the force needed changing, and I was convinced Santiago was the man to do it.

However, I also knew Santiago was an imperfect character, with blemishes on his personal record. He'd been arrested in the 1980s for not paying traffic tickets. In 1993 he was convicted of a disorderly persons offense for striking a corrections officer he believed had assaulted his fiancée. In an unrelated matter, the IRS caught him running an unregistered security company off the books, leveling $30,000 in fines that Santiago sidestepped with a personal bankruptcy filing.

These incidents had been thoroughly chronicled in newspaper accounts at the time. They caused me some concern initially, but Santiago assured me he would handle this new position without bringing embarrassment to the office. He said he had attended a conference at Harvard on "managing by objectives," then laid out his plan for the state police: streamlining efficiency, working more closely with the communities, helping the force to regain a strong footing after the scandals. I thought his vision was exceptional.

"This is obviously different from being a municipal police director. It's going to require a different level of authority and diplomacy," I told him.

"I'm prepared for that," he said.

Sharpe James, his boss in Newark, wasn't thrilled that I'd stolen his top cop, but he echoed my assessment. I even sought out Bill Bratton, the respected New York City police chief, for an opinion. "Great guy," he said. "He'd do a very good job."

The troopers' unions opposed the nomination, saying they'd rather see someone promoted from within the ranks. Never one to befriend his critics, Santiago responded by shaking up the force with promotions, reassignments, and pink slips. I saw nothing wrong with that—you can't change the culture of a place without shaking it up.

When statehouse reporters got wind of his record, however, they were predictably harsh. "We all have things in life for which we have made mistakes, errors in judgments," I told a reporter for the radio station New Jersey 101.5.

I took him on as my first major battle, a decision I regretted almost immediately. The senate demanded an investigation of his past, which I stonewalled, then held hearings on his qualifications even after he already began working. But Santiago's offenses weren't all in the past, it turned out. Soon after he began work, he embroiled himself in a strange bureaucratic fiction. He created a state police class, of which he was the only student, and then graduated himself from it, though there were no teachers. Why? So that he could carry a state trooper badge and a gun, and assume the rank of colonel.

Attorney General David Samson stripped him of the rank, then had to reprimand him for using it anyway. He was also publicly scolded for appearing at a political rally for Sharpe James in violation of our ethics code.

Making matters much worse, long after I'd already gone to the mat for him, unnamed informants presented Attorney General Samson with evidence that Santiago had ties to organized crime. I felt sure the allegations—that he protected illegal gambling operations and consorted with known mobsters while on Newark's payroll—were trumped up by his enemies. But once that kind of charge is in the air, it's almost impossible to make it go away.

Intentionally or not, Bill Gormley, the Republican cochairman of the powerful state Senate Judiciary Committee, was heightening the stakes. Nearly every day, Gormley was energizing the state police and their allies by hammering away at Santiago's record, challenging him to appear before a hearing to defend himself, an invitation we rejected.

After an in-depth investigation, Samson found the allegations groundless.

All the while, I was trying to answer the scandal by not answering it. Paul Aronsohn, my spokesman, and Jo Astrid Glading, my communications director, tried to convince me to address it publicly; I should have heeded their advice. But I was sure we could weather the Santiago fiasco.

I was wrong. For some reason, in September Santiago did something I found indefensible. He circulated a memo instructing that all originals and copies of documents produced in the investigation of his past be sent to his office and destroyed. When his memo was leaked to the press, I'd had enough. I still believe the man had been the target of a character assassination campaign from inside his own ranks. But my faith in his judgment was shaken, and the price of keeping him was becoming too great.

Finally I called him to the governor's mansion and demanded his resignation. He wasn't at all contrite. In fact, he went home and called a press conference, denouncing my decision while drawing the suspicious eye of the press to his sprawling home and grounds—too grand for any salary he'd been paid in public service. He was never prosecuted for taking the files, but he was formally reprimanded, and he was out of a job.

I FINALLY SETTLED ON AN AMBIGUOUS TITLE FOR GOLAN: SPECIAL counselor to the governor. The position hadn't existed before. But his value to me couldn't be contained in other offices, like communication or trade, or any of the cabinet posts. Gary Taffet and Jim Davy both knew how much I had come to rely on Golan. They agreed to the appointment, which would make him part scheduler, part policy strategist, part *consigliere*. Davy, as chief of management and operations, acquiesced to the pay grade, about $80,000.

I was pleased at the notion that I'd found a way to meet Golan's expectations, while keeping any suspicions to a minimum.

But of course neither was the case. He pressured and cajoled my deputy chief of staff, Amy Mansue, about everything from his salary to the placement of his office. We used to meet every few days in the transition office, reviewing office assignments and other logistics. But once Golan was in the picture, he complicated the geopolitics of the place, so much so that she eventually asked for a special meeting to discuss it.

"I gave him this office," she said, pointing to a perfectly adequate room on the second floor. "He won't take it. He wants the first floor, but there's no space."

This was a ridiculous crisis. "Is he nuts? Tell him to forget it."

"I did," Amy said. "He offered a compromise." She pointed to her own office, a room at the top of the second-floor stairway with a fireplace and an adjoining bullpen for staffers. "If he wants it so badly," Amy said, "I'll move."

I argued against accommodating him like this, but Golan had worn Amy down. A good friend and a real trouper, she moved down the hall.

But that didn't stop Golan's demands. Next, Jim Davy told me that Golan was refusing the salary we set. "He wants a buck-ten," he said.

That's where I should have put my foot down. Very few people in the administration were making $110,000 or higher, and his position didn't deserve to be one of them. I owed it to the taxpayers to turn Golan down, even if we weren't in the middle of a major fiscal crisis. But I couldn't find the strength to continue this battle. I remember rolling my head in weary disgust. "Give it to him," I said.

NEW JERSEY'S CONSTITUTION HAS A BALANCED-BUDGET CLAUSE, as do most states, though not the federal government. This is a good requirement, but it put me in a terrible bind. Not only did I have to come up with a working budget for the coming fiscal year that accounted for a projected $5.3 billion tax falloff; I also had to reissue Whitman's budget for the current year, with some way to make up for her $3 billion shortfall. In a $23 billion overall budget, this was a huge deficit—the largest of any state in the country.

I was hamstrung by my campaign promise not to levy new taxes. I know the Republicans were eager to see me fail on that. The first thing I did, while still in the transition office, was to ask the legislature for a moratorium on new spending. But the Republicans who were about to relinquish their majorities in both houses ignored me. They pushed through $200 million in new programs, including $6 million in gifts to the horse-racing industry, and even more tax givebacks. On my first day in office, I was furious when my state treasurer, Mac McCormac, showed me tax revenue figures that were well below projections. Our budgetary crisis was even worse than it first looked.

"They cooked the books," I seethed. "They hid the truth and they left taxpayers to foot the bill."

So at my first cabinet meeting, I blocked as much of the new spending as I could and ordered department heads to cut their operating budgets by 5 percent across the board, making up $100 million over six months. Every cut was agonizing. Next I was forced to lay off six hundred technical workers, gut the "smart growth" office that was responsible for fighting sprawl, freeze aid to municipalities, reduce college funding, end future school construction programs, and postpone dam repairs, park improvements, and new tuition assistance grants. Even my campaign promise to eliminate tolls on the Garden State Parkway was going to have to be delayed; we simply couldn't afford to lose the revenue.

Unfortunately, these poison pills weren't solving the fundamental problems in the state. I could borrow as much as $2 billion against our portion of the national tobacco settlement. But Moody's Investors Service was condemning us for not levying a tax. Cutting out fat wasn't going to make ends meet, they argued in a report on my policies. "Given the administration's pledge not to raise taxes, we do not expect the state will be able to return to structural balance and restore its reserves to strong levels for at least several years." For the first time in a decade, they downgraded the state from an Aa1 to an Aa2 rating, which meant we'd be paying higher interest rates on state borrowing.

Very tentatively, we began looking at taxes. I still vowed to not increase property taxes or income taxes. But there were some aspects of New Jersey's tax code that didn't make sense. For instance, corporations in the state were paying less now than ten years earlier, while corporate profits doubled over the same period, to $867 billion nationally. Thanks to a series of yawning loopholes, thirty of the state's biggest companies paid just two hundred dollars a year in corporate taxes. Eliminating those loopholes added $600 million in new revenues. Some may have argued that this amounted to raising taxes, but it was nothing of the kind: we were simply ending an unjust corporate welfare program that never should have been there in the first place.

But I did raise taxes on tobacco. In survey after survey, nobody ever complained about cigarette tax hikes. I added fifty cents in taxes to each pack of cigarettes sold, for $200 million in total revenue, and cancelled a $7 million cut in cigar taxes pushed through by Republican lawmakers in the days before I took over. I hated being forced into abrogating my own campaign promise. Publicly I argued that I had income and sales taxes in mind when I made that pledge. But I still felt terrible about it. There just was no other way to balance the budget.

RAY LESNIAK CAME TO SEE ME TWICE IN MY FIRST FEW WEEKS AS governor. Both visits were awkward. In the run-up to my victory, I'd grown much closer to John Lynch than to Ray. Both men had long coattails, and both were actively committed to my victory. But I was lured in Lynch's direction in part because he required an overt display of loyalty in exchange for his efforts on my behalf, whereas Ray's support for me came more loosely, without strings. But I'd also come to the conclusion that Lynch was the more powerful of the two. His hunger for influence in state politics was growing by the year.

During his two decades in the public service, John had served first as the brilliant mayor of New Brunswick during its renaissance, then as minority leader and senate president, a position once held by his own father. But just as I was being inaugurated, he decided to leave the senate and concentrate on making money in the private sector. This didn't mean he backed away from politics; in fact, just the opposite. What gave Lynch increasing power was his political action committee, New Directions Through Responsible Leadership, which doled out nearly $1 million a year in campaign contributions across the state. Going to his yearly fundraisers at Breakers in Spring Lake was like peering into a G-8 summit: the most powerful men and women in New Jersey came out en masse.

Lynch regularly dropped by my office to give me fatherly advice on my performance. I always welcomed his ideas and observations, which were unvarnished and often stern, but I took responsibility for my own decisions, sometimes to his bitter consternation. He felt I was too stridently progressive about some things and not sufficiently assertive about others, all of which was probably true.

Ray Lesniak, meanwhile, was undergoing a personal awakening of sorts that seemed to pull him away from politics, though he remained in the Senate. First a good friend of his died; then his girlfriend dumped him, sending him into a terrific tailspin. That was his catalyst for joining the twelve-step movement—to recover from his need to control his ex-girlfriend and, by extension, everything else around him. When I went to him for advice thereafter, I got AA-style maxims about not controlling everything. The "Serenity Prayer" was his driving principle now: *God grant me the serenity to accept the things I cannot change, the courage to change the things I can, and the wisdom to know the difference.*

That seemed totally irresponsible to me. I had a massive government to run. Being in control was exactly what the voters had in mind for me.

"There are too many variables, too many constituencies, for you to be thinking that way," he said. "You're stuck in the fog of the war. Find your center. Know what you want and the rest will follow. You're the lodestar."

To be honest, I thought Ray had completely lost it. I felt frustrated, like he'd walked away from the game just when it was my turn at the plate.

At the same time, a rift was also growing between Lynch and Ray, perhaps in relationship to my shifting attentions. Though they'd long been Senate colleagues, Lynch had a way of stirring up trouble between them, regularly claiming to the press that he was my most intimate adviser. Those remarks seemed intended to remind me I owed a debt to Lynch. But they also served as warning flares to keep Ray on the defensive while our personnel decisions were being hammered out. (In John's defense, Ray had also made some offhand remarks of his own to the papers.)

I found all this intramural feuding unseemly, given the huge challenges we all faced, and I blamed Lynch, whose constitutional unhappiness was becoming a poison eating at the administration.

But I took out my frustration on Ray. I tore into him during his second visit to the governor's office, calling his comments to the press corrosive and vulgar. At the top of my lungs, I demanded an apology, and a promise that he would keep his mouth shut. It was a cruel thing for me to do. He felt totally excoriated, cut down by his former protégé. He said nothing in his defense—in fact, he started crying—but I didn't stop. The power of my high office had gone right to my head; I was destroying the warlord who'd brought me this far.

When Ray left my office that day he said, very formally, "Good afternoon, Governor."

I didn't see much of him around Trenton thereafter. Whenever we bumped into one another, he always addressed me with cool respect, always as "Governor," never again as Jimmy. It was as though we had never been friends.

I KNEW HOW DIFFICULT ALL THIS WAS ON DINA, WHO WAS STRUG-gling through early parenthood nearly alone while I was locked in my own battles. We'd barely had a moment together since before she went to the maternity hospital. To remedy this, we slipped away on February 1 for a weekend in Cape May. Her parents agreed to babysit. My staff agreed to watch the government helm. We left our babies behind—our daughter and my administration—and headed down to the shore, a little jangled but glad for the relief.

On the second night, before a late dinner, we went for a walk, as we'd always loved doing before life grew so complicated. We headed south along the boardwalk toward an abandoned World War II concrete bunker and a lookout pavilion with views onto the lighthouse at the mouth of the Chesapeake Bay. It was a cold night, but beautiful.

Something about the night made me a little silly. I took Dina by the hand and ran with her across the sand, dancing a jig in the crisp moonlight. But high tide had left a four-foot cliff in the sand beneath us, and I landed with one foot on the high side, the other caught on the edge. I had snapped my thigh bone in two.

It hurt so badly I couldn't sit up. Dina dragged me a few feet inland so a tide surge wouldn't find me, then called 911. At my request, she handed me the phone. "This is McGreevey," I said. "Governor McGreevey."

The dispatcher, Ann Casher, was incredulous at first. "McGreevey?" she asked.

"Yes, the governor." I was wincing in pain. "I think I broke my leg because I ran over a sand dune. It wasn't the smartest thing in the world, but I need an ambulance," I said. "I think I need a stretcher, too."

In a few hours I would go under anesthesia and a fifteen-inch titanium rod would be implanted in my right leg. I couldn't help hoping this wasn't a metaphor for my young administration: shattered in a silly misstep on an otherwise beautiful journey. Knowing how much pain I must have been in, the anesthesiologist—a Democrat—said, "You can tell you had a Marine Corps father."

"That's not it," I told him. "I had a nurse for a mother. My father would have been yelling at somebody."

Throughout the ordeal, Dina was tremendous. She kept her head and helped me keep mine.

TEETERING AROUND ON CRUTCHES SHOULD HAVE SLOWED ME down, but it didn't. Even handicapped I covered more ground than most of my predecessors, swiveling into meetings and press conferences from one end of the state to the other. Looking back, I realize I just kept on campaigning well past the election. That, after all, is what I knew how to do—campaigning, not running a massive multi-billion-dollar operation. Anyone looking at my schedule of events might have thought I was an underdog candidate, not an incumbent governor.

The first thing I needed to sell to voters was my coming budget, which I knew wasn't going to be popular. In mid-February, I began making appointments with reporters and editors in the state to prepare them. I was a pretty good spokesman. I knew the $24 billion spending plan so well, I could flip to a line-item in an instant.

I wanted to be the only person communicating our economic policies to the media and the public. Balancing the budget was a big leadership challenge, and I felt voters had a right to know that I'd personally rolled up my sleeves and slogged through the numbers. My decision to muzzle everybody else in the government was seconded by Paul Aronsohn, my spokesman. "You want to give the people a government that speaks with one voice," he said. Many other governors and chief executives adopt similar policies.

But in my case it backfired wildly. In fact, it began an awful relationship with the press that only grew more distrustful and hostile as time went on.

On February 14, 2002—by chance it was both Ash Wednesday and Valentine's Day, and the anniversary of my engagement to Dina—I sat with the editorial board at the *Bergen Record* at their offices in Hackensack, reviewing details of the budget. They were particularly interested in my numerous campaign promises that would make driving in New Jersey more comfortable—reducing auto insurance, speeding up toll booths with a new E-ZPass system, and modernizing the Department of Motor Vehicles. New Jersey was still issuing paper drivers' licenses, making us unacceptably vulnerable to fraud in the post-9/11 world because they were so easy to counterfeit. I had proposed allocating $6 million to digitize our licenses.

Would that plan survive the economic difficulties, I was asked?

"Absolutely," I said. "After the attacks, this became an urgent goal for New Jersey. We will not skimp on security. We actually brought on a security adviser from the Israeli Defense Forces, probably the best in the world—not probably, they do the best in the world. So we are examining bid specifications."

It was a mistake for me to bring up Golan in this context. His appointment had escaped public scrutiny, and his job description was far more diverse than I'd suggested—offering security insights was only one informal part of his job. In fact, I'd tapped a tough former prosecutor, Kathryn Flicker, to head my Office of Counter-Terrorism; she would later be followed by Sid Casperson, a career counterterrorism expert with the FBI, both of whom reported to David Samson, the attorney general. Yet here I was calling Golan Cipel my "security adviser," a glib slip of the tongue.

What was I thinking? I've asked myself that question many times.

It was hubris. I was feeling invincible. I'd won office by a landslide, and then quickly squeezed $3 billion out of one budget and $5 billion out of another. I'd done all that while managing a love affair under everybody's noses. Twice Golan and I had managed to spend whole nights together— once in Philadelphia, where we'd gone for the Army–Navy game and a Jewish event; and another time for a meeting of the American Israeli Political Action Committee in Washington DC, where we had the nerve to tell the state troopers we would share a double-occupancy room "to save taxpayers' money." We grew so concerned about the troopers listening in that we made love on the floor, fearing a squeak from the beds.

"I could stay forever in this moment," I remember telling him on one of those nights.

Given how dramatic those first few months had been for me, I suppose I felt like bragging a little to the *Bergen Record*. *Look at me,* I was saying. *I'm so smart I've got an Israeli doing security.*

Little did I know how badly that would play. The next day's papers carried insightful stories about my budget, about which I was proud, and no mention of my disclosure. But I knew the *Record*'s staff had taken notice. Our switchboard was burning with calls from them, demanding Golan's background and credentials, his immigration status, and his Israeli military records. I told my staff to give out no such information, which only inflamed the paper's curiosity. It was over a week before I even allowed his name to be released.

Having a name whetted their appetite. Requests for documents flew into the office, citing the state's Open Public Records Act. We heard indirectly that they'd called the FBI and learned that Golan, as a resident alien, was ineligible for security clearance. This hadn't occurred to me, unfortunately; I'd even given his name to the White House as an emergency contact, because more than anyone else in the administration he knew where to find me night and day.

It was a big error in judgment. I trusted Golan implicitly. What's more, he came from an ally nation. But it was nonetheless extremely unwise of me to put him anywhere near our security apparatus.

Meanwhile, *Record* reporters Clint Riley and Jeff Pillets made repeated requests to interview Golan, which I quashed. My policy was to let nobody talk on any subject. But I especially didn't want Golan sitting with reporters. I had an irrational fear that they would trick him into disclosing our secret, though I knew he guarded it as vigilantly as I did. But I was also worried about his arrogance and abrasiveness—even if the reporters missed our obvious love for one another, I was concerned that he'd say something they would twist into an embarrassment. For a moment, I forgot that Golan was an experienced public relations man, more able in that regard than I.

Golan took me to task. "This makes no sense," he said. "Let me speak to the press. Allow me to tell them who I am, what my background is, what my skills are. Allow me to rise or fall on the merits."

I didn't relent. "You'd only be putting more wood on the fire, Gole. I respect your intelligence and your political instincts, you know I do. But frankly I don't want the press deciding for us who will be speaking and who won't. Ignore this. It'll go away."

It didn't. On February 20, I allowed Pillets, the *Record* journalist, to interview me for an hour about Golan. What I should have done was tell the truth about Golan's job, that as my senior counselor he advised me on a broad range of matters, *including* security policy. "Golan is just another pair of eyes on policy," I should have said. But saying that would have required me to retract my earlier braggadocio to the *Record*, and my ego rejected that course. So instead, I defended Golan.

"The Israelis live with terror every day. Their very survival depends on being prepared," I explained. "Golan has served in the Israeli military. He is uniquely qualified to point out weaknesses." Even before we took office, I explained, he had toured the state's nuclear power plants, refineries, bridges, and seaports. Riley wanted to know why I hadn't put him through a tough security check, and I explained I didn't think it was necessary.

"I know Golan and I've worked with him closely. He's a super-bright and super-competent individual who brings a great wealth of knowledge on security. Look, he's someone who thinks with a different set of eyes, and that is very hard to find. If we've learned one thing since September 11, it's that homeland security is all about communications. We've got all these agencies out there but we've got to make them work together. It's all about coordination, it's all about intelligence. Golan knows this stuff cold."

I CAN'T SAY I WAS CONVINCED THAT AN EXCLUSIVE INTERVIEW IN the *Record* would dig us out of our hole. But I was horrified when Pillets's article appeared the next day. I read it in a cold sweat. Pillets and coauthor Riley seemed to be hinting broadly that there was a homosexual subtext to Golan's appointment. For instance, rather than calling him a naval officer in the Israeli Defense Forces, where he was indeed a lieutenant, they called him a "sailor." Somehow they found he had written a collection of poems in high school, so he was also "a poet." His background was public relations, they said, not security at all.

But the worst line was this: "Democrats close to the administration say McGreevey and Cipel have struck up a close friendship and frequently travel together." It was like I was right back in Cub Scout camp again: I wasn't sure if I was reading too much into this article's innuendo or too little.

That confusion ended when my mother called me. "Jimmy, they're saying you're both gay," she said in disbelief.

It certainly wasn't lost on anybody else. Shock jocks on the radio were talking about "Little Golan," openly implying that he was my lover. I'd been in office for just five weeks, and already my secret life was in jeopardy.

I demanded a meeting with Jeff Pillets, who was summoned to my office that afternoon. For a half hour I shouted and screamed at him, putting much more emotion on display than I should have.

"What really hurt was calling Cipel my traveling companion. He and I were together only in large groups," I bellowed. "You implied something was there that is not!"

STATE SENATOR BILL GORMLEY WAS ALL OVER THE GOLAN STORY. He demanded Judiciary Committee hearings into Golan's background and qualifications, as well as into the circumstances of his appointment. This made no sense. Golan was simply an adviser—advisers have never required senate approval in the past, and I wasn't going to allow it now.

When he heard I was stonewalling, though, Gormley upped the ante. He was about to conduct a Judiciary Committee hearing into my appointment of Charlie Kushner to the Port Authority board. He told reporters he would postpone that hearing until I sent over Golan, which I wasn't about to do.

What was in it for Gormley? Here's the way I saw it. He was sincerely concerned about the prospects of an Israeli without federal security clearance assuming a sensitive position. But Gormley also happened to be close to

John Lynch, an influential political figure—being Irish Catholic bonded them more than their polar party affiliations. And Lynch had gone ballistic when I named Charlie to the Port Authority. I was never sure why this was, but it didn't matter. I knew Charlie was the best for the job—and stood by him despite Lynch's opposition. Lynch clearly wanted to impede the appointment, and must have seen the otherwise unrelated Golan scandal as a mechanism for doing it. My guess is that he pressed Gormley, who is a master at the game, to light a fire under the Golan issue.

My staff was tied in knots. By now they hated Golan, and they urged me to cut him loose. "Gormley's not going to let this fly," Paul Levinsohn told me. "As long as you stand behind Golan, he's got ammunition."

"You're taking hits," Gary Taffet, my chief of staff, agreed. "You're starting to suffer losses."

I looked for ways to correct my original mistake. Perhaps I could hold a press conference, I mused, to point out that Golan was working in many areas besides security: interfacing with counsel generals' offices, UN missions, heads of state, and federal protocol offices. And he was doing these things well. Golan favored this approach, with a twist: he wanted to give the press conference himself.

But everybody else thought it was too late. I would come across as disingenuous—despite the fact that it was true—or worse. To be retracting my own remarks this early in the administration risked making me seem out of touch and unreliable as an extemporaneous speaker. I'd put my foot in my mouth in my first free-ranging media summit, a fact we all agreed should be downplayed.

"We need to stop the hemorrhaging," Taffet said. "If we remove Golan from any external function, then Gormley will acquiesce—he will have fulfilled whatever commitment he made to Lynch, and Kushner can move forward."

We settled on a plan that in retrospect didn't fare much better than my proposal to come clean. Taffet called Gormley and promised we would "reassign" Golan to handle myriad nonsecurity issues, with the same title and salary, if in exchange Gormley would move forward on Charlie's nomination. He agreed.

Late that Friday afternoon, two weeks after the *Record* story appeared, I approached the subject at the end of an unrelated press conference. "Mr. Golan Cipel has met with me repeatedly and he has requested to be relieved of his state-security duties due to his Israeli citizenship status, which would prohibit him from receiving security clearance," I read from a script. "Reluctantly, at this time, I have accepted his request. In his new position, his responsibilities will be varied. Simply put, there is no shortage of work in the Governor's office."

THE WHOLE ORDEAL DISGUSTED GOLAN AS MUCH AS IT ANGERED me. If only he'd been allowed to speak for himself, he complained, it all might have blown over. I can't say he was right or wrong; all I know is that my approach failed miserably. This wound was self-inflicted. I'd been excruciatingly careful my whole life never to hang myself up. That's what was so crazy. I spend my whole life in the closet and in politics, never allowing the two tracks to cross. I'd mastered both universes. I had everything under control—everything but my goddamned heart, which neutralized my political instincts, rendering them useless.

My press statement hadn't killed the story. Instead it made it more deliciously mysterious to local reporters, and just about everybody in the New Jersey political class. I suspect that some former members of my state trooper detail had spied on me and Golan when we thought we were alone. In my first weeks as governor, I'd reassigned many of Whitman's detail and brought in a fresh group; perhaps I ruffled feathers doing this, and they felt free to speak their minds about their experiences.

But it was also the case that Golan had angered certain state police brass. He'd attended many of the homeland security meetings we held on counterterrorism, and often his contributions were abrupt and demanding. There was nothing accommodating about Golan's approach to security, and his attitude made him no friends.

Either way, we completely lost control of the story. Soon the papers were reporting that former FBI chief Louis Freeh had volunteered to do the job gratis, but I'd chosen an untrained, mysterious foreigner instead. This was wrong. Indirectly, Freeh—a New Jersey native—had made overtures about becoming part-time chair of our Domestic Security Preparedness Task Force. Not possible, I said. By statute, this is the responsibility of the attorney general, who by definition is in constant contact with federal authorities, counterparts in other states in the region, and statewide law enforcement officials. Our task force was not a blue-ribbon panel. It was a working agency, one that was unfortunately responding to terror threats on a nearly daily basis following 9/11. This was not a job that could be handled by anybody on a part-time basis, even someone as knowledgeable as Freeh.

I want to also make this clear: Golan Cipel was not part of the task force. His role on homeland security was never on the front lines. He had no practical portfolio there. Rather, he acted as my ears at meetings I couldn't attend and helped me formulate policy and think about security in ways no governor in the country was prepared to do at this point in time.

These were scary times, as my former attorney general reminded me recently. Being so close to New York City, we had a huge obligation. None of us had ever done anything like this before. But we acted quickly and aggressively, well ahead of most other states. Remember, the White House didn't establish its simplistic Homeland Security Advisory System—the color-coded alerts that cranked up people's anxiety levels—until March 2002, six months after America came under attack.

In short order, we established the first round-the-clock bioterrorism rapid-response teams in the nation, created under Health Commissioner Lacy. We trained more than a thousand local law enforcement officers to be our first responders in case of a direct attack, and we helped coordinate readiness with business leaders and parks officials to protect our 110 most essential sites. And we devised and implemented a state-of-the-art intelligence system—a model nationally—that let local police departments study surveillance data the minute it was intercepted.

Nobody kept track of the raw number of terror alerts we fielded in those first few months, ranging from allegations that Newark Airport was an imminent target to supposedly credible reports that tractor trailers filled with explosives were on the New Jersey Turnpike heading for the Lincoln Tunnel. I'll bet we received hundreds of such reports, maybe more. There were countless nights when none of us slept, unsure where the next attack would come. But we knew we were doing everything we could think of, everything possible, to protect the people of the state.

IN THE WEEKS AFTER THE *RECORD* STORY, THINGS BETWEEN Golan and me never returned to normal. In April, Dina and I finally moved into Drumthwacket, creating an even larger barrier to the secret affair. Now I lived behind a remotely-powered gate in a building surrounded by state troopers and domestic staff. I was miserable. Being separated from him was destabilizing for me—besides happiness and counsel, I found a calmness in being with him, the kind of peace that can only come with honesty. We saw each other regularly during meetings at the statehouse, and sometimes stole a private moment in my office. But the public life we both desired hemmed us in and ultimately kept us apart.

At my encouragement, Golan moved from Woodbridge to Princeton to be nearby. He found a townhouse he liked in the West Windsor community but was apprehensive about taking on the expense. I inspected the property with him and offered to cosign the mortgage if he needed. Clearly I was courting discovery more actively now. The trumpets of Gomorrah would have sounded if I put my signature on that mortgage. Luckily, his application passed muster without my help.

I was glad to have him so close, but it was never like Woodbridge. In our fishbowl existence, I managed to visit him there only once. It seemed like a mistake. He hadn't yet hung any curtains on the back of the house, whose windows looked into the woods.

"This is insane," I told him. "The state troopers are sitting in the parking lot."

"You see somebody out there?"

"If they get out of their car, we're finished."

Golan was as cautious as I was. We locked ourselves in his bedroom, fearful refugees from our own lives.

We were no longer as brazen as we'd been in the past. We even started curtailing our official interactions, to quell talk among the staff. But our affair continued, in a fashion. It *was* insane. We knew that reporters were increasingly curious about what appeared like a "special relationship." The Gannett chain had sent reporters to Israel; Golan's childhood friends were asked about his history with men and women.

"They're trying to prove you're a homosexual," Jo Astrid Glading, my communications director—who happens to be gay herself—warned me.

I was sure she was wrong, that she was as paranoid about these matters as I was. But Golan couldn't stand the pressure. His calls to me became more and more frantic. For him, I think, being known as gay would have been worse than death. The idea of people digging through his personal life paralyzed him with fear. He fought me repeatedly and aggressively about our media policy—he wanted to extinguish this chatter about his job in homeland security by speaking directly to reporters and setting the record straight. He wanted to come out of one closet in order to remain in another.

Of course, I have to admit that there's a chance Golan wasn't gay. I have thought about this often. Though he claimed he'd never had sex with a man before, I didn't believe him. During our relationship, he told me about a few women he'd had sex with. I was never jealous about that, though I would have been had he told me about sex with men. Since our secret became public, he has denied having a homosexual identity. I don't believe that. But taking his protests at face value, it's just possible that our shared attraction did tempt him to cross the aisle, just as my love for Kari and later for Dina had carried me into heterosexual romance.

He never expressed any conflict or regret about our time together, only frustration over the obstacles between us.

One afternoon in May, after a lengthy meeting at Drumthwacket on a long-forgotten subject, Golan stayed behind in the large, rather uncomfortable library on the first floor as the other state officials left. Dina was upstairs with Jacqueline. I looped through the kitchen and dismissed the cook and building manager, returning to the library with two cups of tea. Behind the library was a more intimate study, a small room lined with historic books and oil paintings from the New Jersey museum collection. In the middle of the room was an oval-shaped desk that was said to have belonged to Woodrow Wilson, the thirty-fourth postrevolutionary governor of New Jersey.

Golan was frustrated. He felt that I was freezing him out of my inner circle, marginalizing his contributions. It had been weeks since we'd even seen each other.

"Of course, I want to be with you—selfishly," I told him. "But my time is fully regulated now. The scheduling process is brutal. We discuss everything: is this the right meeting to have, is this an open or closed meeting, should it be ten minutes or five? We have themed weeks, Golan. Last week was *transportation,* next week is *education.* We'll be in South Jersey all week because we need to drive the message there. The governor can't take time off. I can't run to West Windsor. I *want* to be with you. I want to spend time and go over the day's events like we used to."

I closed the blinds. We kissed. There was a feeling of doom, as if we both knew this was the end. The thought made me crazy.

"I love you, Golan," I said. "You make me so happy. I've never, you know . . ."

He looked so sad just then; I knew he understood.

"I could leave all this behind. I could leave it all. I could leave the governor's office and the career in politics. I would. I would leave it all for you if you told me we'd be together forever."

He seemed shocked. "Do you mean that?" he asked.

I did mean it. For me, Golan represented a chance to be honest and true with myself, to have an authentic life in a gay relationship. I never felt more alive and passionate and integrated and healthy than when we were together.

But looking into his eyes I could see that life ever after was not a possibility. He was not willing to walk into the sunlight with me if it meant walking out of politics. He was like me that way—desperately wanting two things that could never fit together.

"Yes," I answered.

He didn't reply.

Although we never said a word about it, we both knew this was the end of our affair.

*　*　*

I DIDN'T LIKE LIVING AT DRUMTHWACKET. THE ROOMS DOWN-stairs were like a museum. The enormous dining room table was constantly set for thirty; its centerpiece was a polished sterling silver soup tureen on loan from the USS *New Jersey*, valued at $170,000. We were supposed to wear special gloves to touch it. The enormous living room was better equipped for greeting heads of state than for reading biographies in my boxers, my traditional mode of relaxation.

Upstairs, in the private quarters, I found even less solace, given my guilt about the affair and a growing knowledge that our marriage had been wrong from the start—a contrivance on both our parts. We rarely made love at Drumthwacket. Sometimes, bumping into one another in the endless corridors up there, we didn't even make eye contact. Bedtime was traumatic. I'd never been much of a sleeper before this, but now a four-hour sleep was a rare hibernation.

I spent most of my nights sitting in the building's main catering kitchen, on a tall stool, eating the split pea soup or turkey chili Cathy Reilly, the chef, prepared specially for me.

I threw more parties at Drumthwacket than all my predecessors combined. It was the way I most enjoyed spending time there. Our parties were legendary. We threw flag-raising events for just about every minority community in the state, drawing thousands of people each night; we helped them coordinate food donations from their community restaurants. We celebrated the Dominican Republic, Ireland, China, India, and Poland. You should have seen the look on my neighbors' faces in Princeton when we hoisted Ghana's flag up the flagpole.

Some of my neighbors actually complained. One of them called Olga Nini, our gracious residence manager, in the middle of a brunch for the Pakistani community, complete with a terrific ethnic band. "Olga," he snapped, "am I going to have to wake up every Saturday morning to this kind of noise?"

And sometimes the events produced the opposite effect of what I'd hoped. When we raised the Italian flag, I decided to invite Italy's ambassador to America, hoping we might increase trade relations with the country.

A procession of Italian Americans spoke about New Jersey's commitment to textiles, fashion, and design, most of which involved collaborations with Italian companies. The ambassador seemed duly impressed.

Then my last guest took the dais. I'd met Yogi Berra a couple of times, and I was so pleased he'd agreed to attend the event as one of our more prominent first-generation Italian Americans. But for some reason he limited his remarks to one stinging sentence before returning to the hors d'oeuvres table and leaving my honored guests scratching their heads.

"I'm just glad my father made the boat," he said.

ALTHOUGH GOLAN AND I CONTINUED TALKING ON THE PHONE regularly, we saw each other very few times after that. Yet reporters continued staking us out for evidence of our affair. It was crazy. Every single day, a Gannett reporter showed up at a statehouse reception to request an interview with Golan. He would sit in the lobby, hoping to catch Golan coming or going. Document requests were nearly burying our Open Public Records officer. They wanted résumés, background checks, sign-in sheets from Drumthwacket, phone records, even the 911 transcript from my broken leg.

On two separate occasions reporters asked us directly if we were romantically involved. I was thunderstruck. The first was David Twersky, the editor of New Jersey *Jewish News*, who was friendly with Golan. Golan denied the allegation angrily. He was nearly breathless with anxiety when he called to tell me about it.

"Don't worry," I said, denying my own panic. "I'm sure he was only fishing."

But when Twersky came to talk to me about it, he seemed quite confident. "Forgive me for saying so, Governor, but it is obvious to many people that you have a relationship with Golan Cipel that is quite personal, and eventually this threatens to cost you both a great deal."

I believe he told me this out of compassion; he never wrote about it. But I didn't confirm his beliefs. I didn't deny them, either, for that matter; I just let them hang in the air. Another journalist, Sandy McClure, an unctuous reporter with the Gannett chain, was not as compassionate. She sat across from me in the governor's office asking a million questions about my administration. Then she ambushed me with this one:

"Some people say you were with Golan when you broke your leg."

"Absolutely untrue, Sandy," I said in disgust. "Dina was with me the whole time. She rode with me in the ambulance, for crying out loud."

"But she could have been flown down to Cape May in the helicopter before the ambulance was called."

Oh, my God, I thought, *this has gotten completely out of hand.* One misspoken sentence had turned my private affair into a Monica Lewinsky–style scandal, and everything I'd done since had fed a mushroom cloud of suspicion. Now they'll believe anything about us. I looked at Sandy like she was insane. "All governors are subject to unsubstantiated rumors," I told her. "You should know that by now."

"People say you have a homosexual relationship with Golan," she said.

I rolled my head on my shoulders. "Sandy, that's just absurd," I said. It wasn't quite a lie: the notion that I would have a gay affair under these conditions was nothing if not absurd.

IN THE MOVIE *IMITATION OF LIFE,* A POOR AFRICAN AMERICAN woman named Annie Johnson agrees to work as a maid for a down-on-her-luck actress named Lora Meredith in exchange for food and lodging for herself and her daughter. As the years go by and the actress finds fame and fortune, their friendship and respect deepens. But despite growing up in increasing luxury, the daughter, Sarah Jane, is humiliated by her mother's history of racial subservience. Ultimately she leaves home to pass as white, cutting off all communication with her kin. In one of the most heartbreaking representations of identity clashes, her mother tracks her down and, painfully posing as the nanny who raised her, professes her love for "Miss Sarah Jane" and promises to never trouble her again.

I was reminded of that scene in June, which is Gay Pride Month in New Jersey. The governor traditionally addresses a statewide gay festival in Asbury Park, our burgeoning gay beachside enclave. I hadn't realized this until a few days before June 2, when I found it posted on my schedule. In light of my growing scandal, I considered canceling, but I worried that would send out another bucket of chum to the sharks.

It was a beautiful Sunday morning. Following Mass, I drove to the shore to make a brief address as Whitman and Florio had before me, trying to bolster my profile as a confident, benevolent, heterosexual-but-supportive governor. To underscore my point, I brought Jacqueline along, hoping my young daughter's presence would deflect any suspicion. I don't remember what I said on the stage that day. But I remember feeling both relieved and torn that I was up there speaking and not down in the throngs—that I was passing, like Sarah Jane.

Could they tell, I wondered? Did they see through my flimsy disguise? Did they pity me for lacking the courage to be true to myself?

All summer, my phone had been ringing nonstop in my pocket. It was Golan. He called me constantly, sometimes up to ten calls a day. For the first time, he was speaking—obliquely—about our affair, which he seemed to want to rekindle.

"Where's this going?" he would ask.

"It's going nowhere, Golan. Please let me get off the phone. I have a state to run. What don't you understand about that?"

I'll be honest. I sometimes thought his desperate sadness was about losing me, about losing our love. But that was just self-flattery. I think he hated losing access to power. The further apart we grew, the more frantic were his phone calls. He called and called and called.

NOTHING FASCINATED THE PRESS AS MUCH AS GOLAN. WE couldn't get a positive news story about any of our many initiatives. Besides solving two enormous budget gaps, I'd rolled out new contracts to bring the long-overdue E-ZPass system to the state, started programs that would eliminate the auto insurance burden, and set aside $28 million to enhance the Cancer Institute of New Jersey, developing a program for addressing the state's record cancer rates—the disease kills 18,000 New Jerseyans each year.

The *New York Times* said that electing me was "like getting two governors for the price of one because his work days and schedules are so densely packed." But nobody at the *Record,* the *Star-Ledger,* the local Gannett chain, or the all-news radio stations had a decent thing to say about me.

Finally another juicy story hit the headlines, but this one—involving Gary Taffet and Paul Levinsohn—offered no relief. Until the buzz around the articles reached me, I had no idea that during the campaign the two had built a sizable company on the side, buying and controlling billboards around central Jersey. They'd built this business around a little known loophole in a town's ability to pass zoning laws restricting billboards. Apparently, state-owned land was exempt. Every small town had little slivers of state-owned land, either alongside the railroad tracks or inside state parks. Even quaint villages whose planning boards barred billboard development were powerless to close this loophole. Between Election Day and my inauguration, they reached twenty-two lucrative advertising deals with fourteen powerful New Jersey companies, including one controlled by Charlie Kushner.

According to published reports—on the heels of an FBI raid—my friend and benefactor John Lynch was involved as well. Even after I'd moved over to the transition office, Lynch had evidently made phone calls on the guys' behalf, helping them secure two more licenses just ten days before inauguration day, before selling the whole business as required by law (administration officials can't have private business interests). Sometime in the two weeks before joining the administration, they sold the business for a staggering $4.4 million for a dozen billboards—a perfectly legal transaction, but an astronomical sum that made the deal look like it involved political favors. I have no idea whether Lynch netted anything from the deal. I only know that the whole thing looked atrocious.

It all unraveled in mid-2002, when Randee Davidson took over as mayor of Washington Township, in South Jersey, after her predecessor began serving a jail sentence for spending township money on a Manhattan apartment, vacation rentals, and a new Chevy Blazer. A *Philadelphia Inquirer* reporter asked her about the new billboard in town, next to the New Jersey Transit bus terminal. Given the political turmoil she inherited, it's not surprising that Davidson hadn't noticed it—even though it stood 160 feet high, the tallest in South Jersey, in a town that had long prohibited the giant signs.

Unable to learn who had built it, or under what authority, she called in the FBI. An investigation led to my senior staff members. Two days after we won the primary, the guys had gone to Washington Township zoning authorities and showed them a letter from New Jersey Transit giving them permission to erect the sign. How'd they get this letter? As the press later reported, John Lynch had called the executive director of the New Jersey Transit office on their behalf.

When I learned about these deals, I was crestfallen. I considered Gary one of my best friends in the world. His mother had served on my campaign staff. I'd entrusted my political career to him and to Paul, who was like a brother to me. A federal investigation ultimately found they'd done nothing illegal. But the public felt that they'd sullied the high office of governor by engaging in this scheme, and the backlash seriously undermined my administration.

Confronting them was one of the hardest things I've ever had to do. I had them out of the office by the end of the year. As for John Lynch? I never talked to him about this deal. But he immediately became the principal target of the federal probe, in an investigation that continued for years.

SANDY MCCLURE'S ARTICLE ABOUT GOLAN APPEARED ON AUGUST 4, 2002. The product of a "four-month investigation," it contained no new information, but its tone was staggeringly cruel. She stopped short of calling us homosexuals. But she implied not only that Golan's résumé and work experience were inflated, but that they were inflated by me.

Quoting from his résumé, she took issue with a statement deep in his description of his job at the Israeli consulate in New York, where he worked for five years, declaring that he was "responsible for portfolios on terrorism." She located the former consul from that time, who said that Golan "was not involved in anything related to terrorism." I believe the consul was wrong. As part of his efforts in the communications office, he helped devise ways to sell Israel's antiterror policies in the press, no small responsibility.

Furthermore, as I pointed out to McClure, this task was listed among many others while he was there. Although she quoted me on this point, she made me sound like I was splitting hairs, which perhaps I was. But I'd chosen Golan as my senior counsel because he was smart, tested in communication policy, experienced in international trade and business protocols, and focused on security issues. And because he never pulled his punches with me.

I released his résumé, his job description, and a sample of the kinds of things he'd been taking care of for the administration. "His job," I told her, "is to advise the governor as to critical information that may be of value in numerous circumstances, including meeting with chief executive officers of major corporations, setting forth policy areas of concern relating to the business community and economic development and responding on a case-by-case basis to information requests."

Obviously McClure didn't hear me—or preferred to continue the whisper campaign about our affair. She wrote the following:

"Who is he? What does he do? Why has he been given special treatment? And why has he been kept from public scrutiny of his credentials?" Answers to these questions, she said, were impossible to ascertain. The implication, once again, was that I'd put an unqualified man on staff because he and I were having an affair. That was only partly true. I never should have hired him. But objectively, his work history as a military officer, Knesset aide, and communications director made him qualified for the multifaceted job I gave him.

I felt pretty sure I wasn't going to be able to survive the attention that followed this newest salvo. Looking back, I think there was a part of me that wanted to get caught. Maybe that's too strong. But all my life I'd thought about what would happen if I was caught red-handed, if my secret was emblazoned on billboards for the world to see. I always imagined the fear would go away. But reading that article, interlaced with innuendo, didn't free me.

Many elected officials have had affairs while in office, often with employees. Some of them held a somber press conference about it and moved on with their lives. Even Bill Clinton lived to fight another day. I never considered such a route. Putting aside the fact that I'd made a huge error in judgment in hiring Golan and giving him a high salary and portfolio, I

knew I couldn't face the voters with what I'd done and ask for their continued support. I had never once told a soul I was gay. I simply couldn't imagine surviving it.

I surely lacked the courage to leave Dina and live on at Drumthwacket
as an openly gay man. And I knew I didn't have the fortitude to stand before
the voters and ask for a second term without my wife—any wife—at my
side.

For their part, no one on my staff ever came to me as a friend and said,
"Jim, is there anything to all of this?" We treated it all as a scandal to be ex-
tinguished. But I don't blame them. I set the tone in the administration, and
my fear was too deeply ingrained for me to handle it any other way.

SENATOR GORMLEY MADE PLANS FOR A SENATE INVESTIGATION,
threatening to force Golan to testify. My own attorney general began a
probe into the circumstances of Golan's hiring and the groundless suggestion that he never did a lick of work. Over and over, we had described his
duties: organizing international trade missions, helping to arrange a major
security conference at Princeton, and developing a model for the state's New
Jersey–Israel Commission; in addition, he advised me on intellectual property issues and federal and state regulatory policy.

But the press made all this sound murky and nefarious. They sent in requests for his daily schedules, his INS applications, even his e-mail. Not
wanting to set precedent, I personally rejected these requests as imperiling
the governor's rights to counsel and Golan's own right to privacy. I had
nothing to fear from revealing them. Like me, he was extremely circumspect
in what he wrote down. Even his birthday cards to me were addressed formally. He gave me two gifts during this time, a handsome Brooks Brothers
tie I still have and a beautiful oil painting of Old Jerusalem, which, because
he signed his name so prominently in the corner, I'd reluctantly disposed of
so visitors wouldn't get the wrong idea.

Each new volley of requests under the state's Open Public Records Act
made my staff more apoplectic. Finally, under mounting pressure, I called
Golan to a meeting at my statehouse office to ask him to leave.

I hadn't seen him in several weeks. The last time, during a weekend meeting in Drumthwacket, things were tense between us. He was too upset about his constant bad press to show me any affection. Almost every day brought a new article poking fun at the "sailor" and "poet" who "served the governor in a variety of positions."

He blamed me for it. I didn't care who was to blame.

I knew it would end when he left the administration. And frankly, his work was slipping—understandably, given the circumstances. My old friend Bob Sommer talked to me about offering Golan a job in the East Rutherford office of the MWW Group, one of the largest public relations firms in the country. The person who handled Israeli clients for the firm had quit; Golan was an ideal replacement.

I dreaded the moment. Politics meant the world to him. He'd come halfway around the world to see how far his political talents would take him in America—the way an actor goes to Hollywood or a scientist goes to NASA—and I was cutting it all short. I apologized in a million different ways.

"Gole," I said, "it's about the government, it isn't about individuals. You did nothing wrong. But you can't stay. It isn't tenable."

"You said you'd give it all up for me," he threw back at me. I suppose I had that coming. But he misconstrued what I was saying back then.

"Golan, I said I'd give it all up if you were *with* me. I'm not going to give up a career or job when you're not even with me. You've missed the point. If we're together as two individuals in love, that makes sense. But I'm not surrendering government for the sake of *your* job."

He left without promising to resign. The next time we met, for breakfast, he brought a lawyer. At the time, I couldn't imagine why. I just reiterated the situation: he'd done nothing wrong, but a political backdraft was forcing him out of the administration. Still, he did not resign.

Frustrated, I asked Charlie Kushner to talk to him. I met Kushner's public relations man, Howard Rubenstein, a long-standing friend of Israel, and even asked him to call Golan and recommend stepping down.

Finally Golan agreed. On April 14, I released news to the press.

Just as Golan had predicted, though, it only intensified the fires. A reporter cornered me and demanded to know exactly what kind of work Golan was walking away from: "What's the nature of the job he quit?"

"Mr. Cipel provided valuable input, critical thinking, and was of assistance," I said. In the next day's paper, that was translated as: *The Governor continued to stonewall reporters on Cipel's exact duties.* I couldn't win.

NOR COULD I FREE MYSELF FROM GOLAN'S INCREASING BITTERness. Almost from the minute he resigned, he began demanding his job back. He felt tricked into quitting, he said, even though he'd done nothing wrong. He found me on my cell phone at all hours, interrupting everything from daybreak trips to the gym to late-night dinners with Drumthwacket staffers. It was after one of these calls that Dina put Jacqueline to bed, then confronted me. She had every reason to demand to know if I was gay—it was being openly inferred in newspapers and radio broadcasts. These ceaseless phone conversations with Golan must have seemed like conclusive proof.

But the more I think about it, the more I'm not even sure if she actually said, "Are you gay?" Maybe she only said it with an angry flash of her eyes. Maybe I only *suspected* that she suspected. Whenever I felt I'd been exposed, whether by the state trooper who busted me at the rest area or the newspaper reporters who pieced it together, a feverlike terror would cloud my perspective and shuffle my memory. I know for certain that the reporters posed those questions to me. They repeatedly revealed this in the aftermath of my resignation, confirming my blurry memories.

With Dina, though, I can't disentangle what she actually said from what I worried she knew, and in the ugliness that has followed us I haven't seen fit to ask.

Frankly, our marriage had taken on the feeling of a business partnership almost from the day we moved into Drumthwacket. She kept her own schedule, throwing herself into official duties and responsibilities with increasing zeal. She genuinely loved serving on the board of the state's March of Dimes, for which she had a tremendous connection because of Jacqueline's complicated birth. She spoke frequently on health care issues and organized Easter egg rolls and Feasts of the Three Magi for area kids. She never tired of being first lady.

She also lavished attention and love on our baby girl, who was quickly becoming an unusually outgoing and demonstrative child. We both did. In the rare times when the three of us were alone together, Jacqueline was joyously and exclusively our focal point, an irresistible excuse for us to avoid talking about our personal troubles.

If our mounting troubles made Dina sad or angry, I rarely saw any sign of it. She was always intensely private, and in her disappointments she turned only to her family. With each passing month, her relatives spent more and more time on the second floor of Drumthwacket, crowding around the formal dining room table and confiding in one another in Portuguese. If I walked through the room, their banter ceased until I left again. Their silence told me all I needed to know.

14.

YOU DON'T GET A SECOND CHANCE TO MAKE A FIRST IMPRESSION. It's one of the most painful lessons I've learned in my life. The first impression I made for most New Jerseyans was one of scandal. Besides the billboard scandal, the police superintendent's alleged mafia ties, and Golan's mysterious tenure, there was an unfortunate stream of other defining missteps. It turned out that my commerce secretary—the Reverend William Watley of the St. James AME Church in Newark—had stuck with his chief of staff (who happened also to be a trusted member of his church) despite allegations that she'd hired five members of her own family in vague and unspecified positions, an embarrassing revelation that compelled both of them to resign. His well-meaning efforts to do the right thing produced nothing but bad press.

Meanwhile, Roger Chugh, the Woodbridge businessman who coordinated Asian Indian minority voters in my campaign and joined the administration as assistant secretary of state, was running a strange personal website that read like a lonely-hearts ad and misrepresented his position in the administration. He later drew more disturbing allegations: members of his own community said that he'd strong-armed them into making political donations for my campaign, something I can't believe is true.

As the political writers kept pointing out, I appeared to be the newest machine politician off the assembly line, yet another creature of patronage, "pay-to-play" favoritism, obfuscation, secrecy, and machine politics who'd declared a hypocritical show war against "business as usual." For obvious reasons, I tended to forgive myriad character failings rather than pass judgment on them. But it really was remarkable how many people in my administration turned out to have totally crazy meltdowns. Surely that makes me a bad judge of character, at the least.

But I realize now that I wasn't managing my staff effectively. Having spent too long isolated from "the weeds" of a campaign, I never fully made the transition to acting as a hands-on chief executive. Too often I left the engine of Trenton to manage itself. As some of my appointees slipped into unreasonable behavior, I didn't even notice. I was almost never in the office; instead I haunted the VFW halls and church pulpits I'd visited over the years, continuing on the hustings of retail politics.

There were a number of reasons for this. I felt I had to take my two consecutive budget cuts directly to the voters, not only for their support but to help make legislators feel safe supporting them. Besides, I felt much more comfortable discussing my policy initiatives with "real people." They reminded me every moment why I was a politician—to help the people of New Jersey through a difficult passage.

Yet it's also true that campaigning gave me the emotional assurance I craved, which I wouldn't find in the halls of the statehouse. Being permanently on the stump helped remind me that people liked me—that I was likable, despite my differences. Maybe I continually sought proof that I'd buried my differences deeply enough to be liked. There is no question that I needed the kind of affirmation that only campaign-style appearances provided.

In retrospect, I can see that by this point I was fractured and compartmentalized to the point of debilitation. Did I let things in government slide? Absolutely, without question. And too many of my trusted advisers slid into scandal as a result.

By the end of my first year in office, I had a dismal approval rating to show for it—just 37 percent, down from 51 percent in March, sixty days into the administration. By the following July I'd slipped even further, to 35 percent. It seemed there was nothing I could do to mitigate the harsh press. As Governor Byrne once said, "If Jim McGreevey walked on water the newspapers would say McGreevey can't swim."

On St. Patrick's Day 2003, I had something of an epiphany. I had to attend a number of functions that day, including the traditional parade down New York's Fifth Avenue as a guest of Governor George Pataki. That was a lot of fun. Not only was it a huge honor to be at the front of America's longest-running annual parade (it began in 1762), but at one point we saw my cousin Kim McGreevey, a sergeant on the Suffolk County police force, marching past in full uniform. She ran over and we kissed—celebrating the fact that our family tradition on the force continued to this day was one of my greatest thrills as governor.

But that same day I also attended the Irish parade in Bayonne, New Jersey. I had looked forward to it as a chance to stand with my own community as their governor. It was not the homecoming I had hoped. Nobody heckled me. But nobody cheered me, either, and there were a lot of folks there who challenged me sharply on the first year of my administration. This shook me terribly. I saw disappointment in the eyes of my own community, and it shamed me.

For me, it was a wake-up call.

Up to this point, I had put the blame for past performances on the in-experienced staff I'd entrusted with the administration. It was wrong to blame them alone. But after their departure, I brought in a topflight team led by Jamie Fox, my new chief of staff, and the difference was like night and day. After our year of turmoil, Jamie was just the master strategist we needed, a total pro. He came with years of experience, most notably as Tor-ricelli's chief of staff. When I first became governor, I appointed him Commissioner of Transportation, where he proved he was a great manager. When I brought him over to the statehouse, I realized just how awkwardly we'd been approaching the business of government. Jamie ran my office—and the State of New Jersey—like a field general. His instincts were always dead-on. He was also openly gay, a fact that increased my admiration for him.

But until this morning at the Bayonne parade, I had not taken any personal responsibility for the scandals and our failures to get traction on a meaningful agenda. I focused on the parts, not the whole—I saw myself as innocent of the scandals, and untouched by them.

I knew the bad press frustrated my father endlessly. Almost every day he mailed me long, handwritten letters offering his commonsense advice and ethical insights. In the fog of my war, I didn't pay them close attention. Mom was less concerned about the press than about my spiritual well-being. One day she handed me a stack of letters my grandmother had written me. I don't know where she found them, but reading them again was a powerful salve. "Pray to Grandma," Mom said, "she will guide you."

My approach to the bad press was to keep campaigning. Shaking hands and meeting people, hearing their thoughts about government, had always brought my numbers up in the past. So I kept in constant motion, I was almost never in the office.

The first thing I realized there in Bayonne was the mistake of this policy. I'd entered politics to enact an aggressive legislative agenda. That's what the voters were waiting for—not more face time with the governor. On a few matters, I'd made some significant progress, especially education. The problem was, with the din of scandal engulfing the statehouse, our victories were barely getting noticed in the press.

AT HARVARD, I HAD STUDIED THE SO-CALLED BEST PRACTICES methods, designed to determine what worked and what didn't in public education. All the studies proved that prekindergarten education and literacy meant the difference between success or failure for disadvantaged kids. If these kids couldn't read, they couldn't compete. In terms of facility with language and socialization, studies showed kids needed to be in academic settings as early as possible.

When I came into office, despite a court ruling mandating access to preschool for all three- and four-year-olds in the state's poorest districts, only about half were enrolled. Whitman's administration had dragged its feet on implementation and cut corners on quality. In 2002, the few affected students were more often than not being taught by day care "aides" who lacked proper training or expertise. I immediately allocated an extra $140 million to pre-K expansion, though I was having to slash spending elsewhere, and hired an early-childhood education expert, Dr. Ellen Frede, to oversee preschools in the state.

I also made sure that preschool teachers were getting the training they needed to teach our vulnerable kids effectively. I began offering professional development courses, inaugurated the state's first-ever New Jersey Teacher Academy, and set new minimum standards: all aides were to be on their way toward earning bachelor degrees, and all teachers were to have subject-matter proficiency in their fields. If you wanted to teach the wonders of science, you needed a science degree to prove you understood it yourself. New Jersey was one of the first states to require such standards.

What's more, there were no literacy standards for children up through third grade. How can you know how a child is doing if you don't even know what the benchmarks are? In February 2002, I signed an executive order setting third-grade literacy standards, the first in the state. I knew that a child who can't read by third grade is likely never to catch up.

In my second year, I announced a $10 million budget for reading coaches, sending early-literacy experts into the at-risk schools and helping fifty thousand students be better readers. My education counselor, Lucille Davy, and I launched the Governor's Book Club, which distributed books to kindergarteners through third-graders. I wanted to infuse literacy into kids' lives.

Our efforts paid off. By the time I left office, about 80 percent of eligible students were enrolled in preschool—100 percent in some districts. And literacy rates continue to improve. New Jersey's third-grade reading scores are now among the highest in the nation.

ANOTHER POLICY INITIATIVE I UNDERTOOK, UNDER NO SMALL amount of duress, was gay domestic partnership. Early in 2004, I signed into law a measure making New Jersey only the third state in the country to convey a bundle of rights upon same-sex couples. It was in the middle of my own long struggle with the issue. I publicly opposed gay marriage, something I'm not proud of. A gay rights group representing seven couples sued for the right to marry, and my attorney general fought back hard, getting the suit thrown out of court. I criticized the suit as detrimental to New Jersey, and even opposed the first proposal for establishing civil unions, calling it too broad and expensive.

The bill I signed was more modest. It came to me from the legislature, sponsored by Dick Codey and Assemblywoman Loretta Weinberg, making it the first domestic partnership measure implemented by lawmakers voluntarily, not ordered by the courts. Under it, unmarried gays (and straights over age sixty-two) living in committed and mutually caring relationships are empowered to make medical decisions for each other, and health insurers in the state are required to offer them the same coverage given to spouses. The law did not give other rights enjoyed by married couples, such as the right to share property acquired during marriage or the right to seek alimony or financial support when the partnership ends. Nor did it allow them to share in a partner's family entitlements in public benefits programs.

Still, it looked for a time as though even this modest bill wouldn't find enough votes for passage in the legislature. Jamie Fox made it his mission to lobby lawmakers one by one. Perhaps his biggest challenge was Senator Ron Rice from Newark, the leader of the Senate's Black Caucus, who had blocked us on other socially progressive undertakings. "Ron, I need this one," Jamie said. "This one's personal." Ron gave it to him. Not only did he vote yes, but so did just about every member of the caucus. Even Sharpe James, who besides being Newark's mayor also represented the 29th District in the Senate, surrendered to Jamie's offensive—by abstaining.

Despite being limited in scope, the bill was welcomed by most gay New Jerseyans when I signed the bill in a small ceremony at my office. Many times in my career my signature has been greeted with cheers, but never like the ovation that filled the room this day.

THE POLICY AREA WHERE WE MADE THE MOST PROFOUND IMPACT was also where we got the most push back. Environmentally, we collected more fines and more compensation from polluters in our first year than the prior administration had collected in eight, using laws already on the books. This irritated industry leaders. I joined a bipartisan coalition of states to take the U.S. Environmental Protection Agency to court to stop Midwestern power plants from polluting New Jersey's air. Naturally, this involved taking on Christie Todd Whitman, the EPA's director. As I said in my State of the State address, "If the federal government will not provide the leadership to protect the air we breathe, reduce pollution, and protect New Jersey's coast-line, then we will." In a first, we shut down a power plant in Pennsylvania because its emissions polluted our air downstream.

But it was when we finally took on sprawl that things got really inter-esting. Environmental regulations already on the books prohibited new con-struction within three hundred feet of rivers. I proposed expanding those regulations to include tributaries, streams, and creeks, all of which are equally instrumental to the state's supply of drinking water. In the stroke of an executive order, I expanded the protected footprint to include 300,000 more acres of land.

Developers went crazy. I halted scores of planned projects. Conven-tional wisdom said it was suicide to take on the single richest source of cam-paign financing in the state. As a result of their financial clout, developers were able to pull strings at every level of government—they literally owned many of the local politicians, including many bosses—and in the ancillary businesses (banking, law, insurance, unions) that make up the state's service economy.

The political establishment joined the outcry—none more than John Lynch, whose consulting firm, Executive Continental, specialized in helping developers with state contracts. Lynch and I hadn't been getting along since I'd arrived in Trenton. Now he turned on me with passion.

From the beginning, Lynch had put a great deal of pressure on me to appoint his people to ranking positions, particularly in law enforcement. He wanted his best friend and personal attorney, Jack Arsenault, in as attorney general, the prize law enforcement post, with a staff of 9,300. But Arsenault had represented the state troopers in the politically divisive racial profiling case, making him objectionable to African Americans. I had many other candidates in mind, especially Barry Albin, a highly regarded attorney from Woodbridge who eventually became a state supreme court justice. Lynch made it clear he would punish me if I went against him. So in a show of compromise, I appointed David Samson, a Republican with an immaculate record in political and legal circles. Though Samson was friendly with Lynch, the boss felt I had betrayed him nonetheless.

That may be one reason that Lynch never tired in his campaign against Charlie Kushner, whose appointment to the Port Authority was confirmed by the Senate and who I was pushing for Port Authority chair. With Lynch's agitation, Bill Gormley kept investigating Charlie until he found what he alleged were irregularities in Charlie's political contributions. Evidently, one of Charlie's trusts for a few months included a regional bank, NorCrown. A long-forgotten 1911 law prohibits bank owners from supporting candidates. Charlie argued that he was a "beneficiary" of the trust, not an "owner" under the law. But the cloud of suspicion never cleared.

FOR ME, THE ENDLESS ATTACKS ON CHARLIE KUSHNER WERE NOTHing but a political power play. I believed at the time that his integrity, decency, and commitment to public service were beyond reproach. I'd practically had to plead with him to take this job. The only reason he'd accepted was out of a sense of civic obligation following the terror attacks. Maybe Gormley had lingering resentment for me pushing Santiago through for the state police, which backfired on Santiago as badly as it did on me. He called Charlie before a committee meeting investigating his campaign contributions. Charlie refused to testify, and instead eventually resigned in February 2003, after just more than a year on the job.

Gormley is a friend of mine. But he is a master at his game in state politics. He made an art of creating crises in order to secure whatever goal he had in mind, or to accrue a debt he could call in later. This had nothing to do with his feelings about me—or even about Charlie, for that matter. It was just business.

I was reluctant to accept Charlie's resignation, but many party leaders around the state advised me to move on. "He's just a big headache you don't need right now," one of them told me. Even if I'd pleaded with him to remain, I knew Charlie had had enough of government. So I thanked him for his public service, praised his tenure in the press, and consoled him privately for the pummeling he'd endured with grace.

It struck me as particularly ironic that I was considered beholden to the warlords, when our relationship was defined by these high-level skirmishes.

A few months later, on the day I stood with the St. Patrick's Day parade line in Bayonne, I saw clearly for the first time how my relationships with

Lynch and the other bosses had been a political compromise that I'd accepted in order to advance my career. Some things I'd done, or allowed to be done in my name, were morally repugnant to me, but I did them anyway and somehow found a way to tolerate my own turpitude. I did this by "forgetting" or never allowing myself to know. I had my people strike backroom deals I kept myself in the dark about or forced from my mind if I learned too much. Obviously this is one root of my memory problems.

To feed my ambition and towering ego, I had overridden my own morality, deformed my own character. I'd become something I hated. The Holocaust survivor Viktor E. Frankl, writing in another context, called this "the mortification of normal reactions—a kind of emotional death." For Frankl, the cause was the cruelty of endless imprisonment in the camps. I had no jailer but myself.

From that day on, I made a vow to pursue my agenda no matter what the bosses and warlords had to say about it, knowing that they'd do what it took to stop me. This decision was late in coming. I wish I'd made it from the first day of my administration. But I worried that I'd never be able to raise money for reelection without Lynch, by far the most powerful warlord in the state.

Given the way things were going, however, reelection didn't seem likely. If I had any chance, it would be as my own man, not as Lynch's apologist.

But before declaring my independence, I first called Senator Corzine and Congressman Menendez to secure their support in case this erupted into a full-scale war. They backed me unconditionally. However, aides to both men leaked news of those phone calls to the *Star-Ledger*, which ran a story about my "epiphany."

Lynch's response was swift. He began seeking another Democrat to put against me in the next primary. I heard this in political gossip, but I know it was true. His elegant wife Deborah, a notable fundraiser for political and community causes, told me so herself. She and I had always had a separate friendship with one another. She showed me proof of his efforts to force a costly primary, to undo my legislative agenda, and to thwart any lasting change in the state's political climate.

"John's trying to hurt you," she confided.

I tried to play it both ways. I called Lynch. "John, the *Star-Ledger* got it all wrong," I told him. Then I canceled a contract for legal work with Jack Arsenault, knowing Lynch would take this personally.

A full-scale war was under way. The bosses were calling angrily, alleging that four or five developers were building a fund, with $1 million each, to knock me out in the next primary. This only reinforced my resolve. I ramped up the rhetoric—the only part of this campaign I think I took a bit too far. "There is *no greater threat to our way of life* than unrestrained, uncontrolled development," I said. "No longer should communities be forced to stand helplessly by while inappropriate and unwanted development occurs." I sounded like a Bolshevik. But I wanted to make the fight a public one, to engage the electorate. People had been against sprawl for years and years; if I could pull this off, I wouldn't need the warlords.

I'll never know if I could have survived. I never got to take a victory lap. But it's clear that the bosses never forgave me. Years later, after my resignation, Lynch told reporters he would punch me in the nose if he ever saw me again. "He ruined my life," Lynch said, calling my administration the "worst thirty-four months of my life." When I did bump into him at Benito's, there were no fisticuffs. I extended my hand to him genially, and he gave it a perfunctory squeeze. If Benito's were a Wild West saloon instead of the favorite Italian eatery among New Jersey pols, the flame in his eyes would have cleared the place of every living thing.

THE TACTIC WAS WORKING. I WAS TAKING THE INITIATIVE BACK from the scandalmongers and spearheading an important conversation in the state, one that could change the landscape in perpetuity. Not until months later, in March 2004, did I find out that even as we were gaining ground, the U.S. attorney's office was trying to pin corruption on me personally, as part of an eighteen-month-long undercover sting operation.

It began on December 20, 2002. That day, I swung by a holiday reception, one of my first as governor. Everybody knew I was going to be there; it was on my schedule. At some point in the evening, I bumped into David D'Amiano, the guy who was holding a cell phone to his chest.

"Governor," he called out. "Can I buttonhole you? I've got this Middlesex County farmer on the phone who's trying to save his farm. The county freeholders are trying to condemn it for development." Mark Halper, a Piscataway farmer, was desperate, he said. The freeholders, as the state's county legislatures are called, were offering $3 million to buy him out through eminent domain, and he considered it inadequate.

I did not know then—and would only learn from the U.S. attorney—that D'Amiano had charged Halper a fee of $40,000 to get to me. Or worse, that the cash had been given to Halper by the FBI, to whom he had reported the shakedown. Apparently, the FBI and the Justice Department believed I was getting some of that money; they'd put a wire on Halper to undertake a sting, and D'Amiano fell for it.

I'd known D'Amiano for years. In retrospect, I suppose the temptation to trade on our long acquaintanceship was too profitable for him to ignore.

As a favor, I took D'Amiano's phone and heard Halper's long litany of complaints. "I want nothing less than a full reprieve," he concluded.

"Have you spoken to the mayor of Piscataway?"

"He won't speak to me."

Talking to the county and township people is the usual process, I explained. "I suggest you reach out to Freeholder Director Crabiel," I said. "He's a good man. If anybody can help, he can." I then invited him to report back to D'Amiano, not to me.

Two months later, I bumped into D'Amiano again at the East Brunswick Hilton, after a meeting of the Democratic state committee. "That farmer is here somewhere," D'Amiano said. "You should hear what's going on with his case, it's like something out of Machiavelli. Nobody will talk to him, they just want to take his land in this Machiavellian move. He's trying to do a Machiavellian move in return."

He introduced me to Halper, a stocky man dressed all in black. He was angry. "The council passed a condemnation resolution," he said. "I tried to speak to Crabiel, but he won't come to the table."

Halper had then appealed to the Middlesex County attorney, without satisfaction. The only way he had figured to thwart the seizure of his land was to sell it to the state under the farmland preservation program, but he was displeased with the offer they made, too. "The Middlesex leadership is totally corrupt," he said. "They refuse to give me fair market value."

True or not, he didn't seem to be advocating well on his own behalf. "You've got to read Machiavelli on how to negotiate on this," I told him. Then I called over Amy Mansue, my deputy chief of staff, and presented Halper's grievance to her. "There seems to be culpability on all sides, people are thinking with egos rather than about the bottom-line purpose of preservation," I said—not the most elegant sentence, but according to the transcript that's exactly what I said.

Then I told a bad joke in mangled Yiddish and added it would be a "mitzvah" if we could look into the price offered by the state.

Michael DeCotiis, who replaced Paul Levinsohn as my general counsel, later determined that there was nothing we could do to increase the offer. Halper's farm was, as he said, "a shitty piece of land" littered with refuse, a place where nothing had grown for generations. It earned the lowest ranking on the state's list of desirable lands; we had no interest in offering more money.

But for me the issue didn't die there, as it should have. It turned out that Halper had asked D'Amiano for a sign that I was working on his behalf, something to justify all the money Halper had given him. D'Amiano promised that I would use the word "Machiavelli" as a code that the fix was in.

I learned about all of this when lawyers working for Christopher Christie, the U.S. attorney in the state, sent in a subpoena for information relating to our farm ranking. Under Christie, the Newark U.S. attorney's office was developing a strong reputation for prosecuting official corruption. But in this case the paperwork makes it clear they were investigating me. Jamie Fox found me a Washington lawyer, Bill Lawler of Vinson & Elkins, to see how serious the trouble was. I showed him the state records in which we had ranked Halper's farm 151 out of a possible 151, as low as any farm could be ranked.

"I don't get it," I told him. "This must be some sort of misunderstanding. Let me talk to them."

"It's too big a risk, Governor," Bill Lawler said. "The problem with these guys is, even if you tell them the truth, if they decide not to believe you they can stick you with a 1001 false statements charge."

He was referring to 18 US Code Section 1001, the law that makes it a crime to lie to federal law enforcement officers. It's the section under which Martha Stewart was convicted—they couldn't find that she committed insider trading, the crime they were investigating, but they proved she misled them in an interview. According to Bill, such cases are a common outcome of freely cooperating with federal prosecutors.

I didn't care. I knew I had nothing to hide, well, not exactly *nothing*. "There is one problem," I admitted to Bill. "D'Amiano used to set me up with women. Do I have to talk about that?"

Bill felt we could contain that fact, so I had him call and make an appointment.

We all gathered around the library in Drumthwacket one morning and listened to the tapes. I remember the surprised look on Bill's face when all was said and done.

"These are unremarkable," he said. "There's nothing bad there."

One of the assistant U.S. attorneys asked me point blank. "Were you prompted to say anything to Halper? Did you use a code word?"

I had no idea what he was talking about. In no uncertain terms I said no. The whole thing seemed absurd. I didn't know until a few weeks later that they were focusing in on the word "Machiavelli." I honestly thought I'd said it of my own volition. It's a word I've used before and since, many, many times—after all, this is New Jersey, as close to Machiavelli's cutthroat Venetian principality as any place on earth. But it turns out that Halper had been promised I would say it. I can only assume that D'Amiano's repeated use of the word while introducing the farmer (which I've struggled to recreate here as accurately as I can) planted it on my tongue.

Thankfully, the assistant U.S. attorneys accepted my explanation—but not before going public with a damning series of allegations, in which I was referred to coyly as "state official number one." Debates about why I'd said "Machiavelli" jammed the radio waves. For his part, D'Amiano—who repeatedly declared I had nothing to do with his illicit schemes—was indicted and ultimately surrendered to serve a jail term. In a way, that made him the lucky one. Having been publicly branded a corrupt politician, I never had the chance to defend myself, to dismantle the state's shoddy allegations. As long as I stayed in government, they would stick to me like glue.

"It's one thing to have everybody know you had an affair with a man," my father recently told me. "Worse than that is this allegation that Mc-Greevey defrauded people, that McGreevey was corrupt. That really hurts."

To imply that money or greed would ever motivate me to break the law is an insulting misunderstanding of who I am. Money was never important to me; it still isn't. Senator Gormley once said that I could "live on grass alone," and that isn't far from the truth. Other than the old Woodbridge condo, I've never owned a home, and after leaving office I bought my first car in decades—a Buick Century. My meager savings came from my governor's salary, $157,000 a year. Every previous governor in the fifteen years before me had brought personal wealth to the office, allowing them to give back all or most of their salaries; with child support payments and the vast wardrobes required for a chief executive and his family, I could afford to give back only 10 percent without having to borrow money. A simple perusal of my bank accounts would have borne this out. At the time, I had $7,000 to my name.

WHY WOULD THE U.S. ATTORNEY'S OFFICE GO PUBLIC WITH ALLEGA-tions when conclusive evidence already existed that I was innocent? Pure politics, though I hate to say it. Before George Bush appointed Chris Christie, a civil litigator with no experience as a criminal prosecutor, he had personally raised over $100,000 for Bush's campaign. Just days before the appointment, Christie's brother began ladling out donations to Bush and Republican causes that eventually topped $400,000 before his own indictment for illegal trading practices—earning him one of those George Bush nicknames: "Big Boy."

What's more, Chris Christie was openly contemplating a run against me. In fact, he'd been meeting with Torricelli and David Norcross, the high-ranking former chairman of the Republican Party. He was visiting senior citizens clubs, Chambers of Commerce—the fairways of electoral politics. I didn't need proof of Christie's ambitions, but I wasn't surprised when he seized the opportunity of a funeral for Glenn Cunningham, the mayor of Jersey City, to make a campaignlike speech.

I once talked to BJ Thornberry, former head of the Democratic Governors Association, about Christie's campaign against me. She believed his conduct fit a pattern of Bush-appointed prosecutors who seemed especially eager to pursue investigations of Democratic governors. At least in my own case, I felt I was innocent until investigated.

A subsequent study by the *Georgetown Journal of Legal Ethics*, looking at Christie's professionalism and that of his counterparts in Maryland and elsewhere, found exactly what I'd suspected. "His investigations into those surrounding McGreevey have raised questions about Christie's intentions and his integrity," the study concluded. "The role of the prosecutor . . . is to seek justice, not merely raise inferences about an individual's guilt. Christie's decision, thus far, not to prosecute McGreevey simply furthers suspicions that Christie lacks a case against him and that his motives are political."

AS IF IN TOTAL PARALLEL TO MY OWN LIFE, MY OLD PAL JOE Suliga's political career took its own worst blow in late September 2003. Late one night he was arrested at the Trump Marina Hotel and Casino in Atlantic City, touching off an awful spectacle that played out in headlines and television news stories for days. It seemed that Joe had never tired of the hard partying he and I used to get away with a decade earlier. That night, at the slots, it all caught up to him.

Apparently, he took an interest in an attractive young patron. But he'd had way too much to drink, and didn't notice when she rebuffed him. He made her a lurid proposal, which she swore to in a police statement; his vulgar words were duplicated on websites across New Jersey within a few hours.

Understandably, the woman called casino security, who attempted to escort Joe outside; he responded by starting a fight that was unfortunately captured on the hidden video cameras. Joe threw the first punches. The guards were forced to knock him to the ground and drag him off the casino floor by his feet. Joe was charged with assaulting the officers and with public intoxication, in addition to the sexual harassment allegation.

In his defense, friends of Joe's told the papers there was a swingers' convention at the casino that night and he'd mistaken the patron for a swinger. But that didn't matter. Now it was open season on Joe, and stories began surfacing about his longtime drinking and womanizing problems. A fellow senator told reporters that the state's budget would have been passed sooner if the lawmakers hadn't been distracted trying to sober Joe up. Then an old harassment allegation and police report surfaced, eerily like the current one. It was clear that Joe's life had spun out of control.

To his credit, he held a press conference to admit to his drinking troubles and announce he would not seek reelection. My heart broke for Joe. I know being a senator meant the world to him. Leaving politics behind— and doing so in scandal—must have broken his spirit altogether.

I also suppose it destroyed Ray Lesniak's spirits. Ray was as much a mentor and rabbi to Joe as he was to me. But Ray wasn't the type to let a friend sink into despair. I heard through the grapevine that he took Joe under his wing, even helped find a rehabilitation facility to dry him out.

THROUGHOUT THIS PERIOD, GOLAN KEPT CALLING AND CALLING. He'd grown increasingly frantic over time, always obsessed with the same themes: he should have spoken to reporters, I should have denied he was responsible for homeland security, he never should have been forced out of his job. We had this conversation literally a hundred times or more. Every time his name appeared in the papers or on radio, where the Golan Cipel caper was an unending source of fascination, it drove him to despair.

I came to the conclusion that he loved his infamy as much as he hated it. He admitted clipping the articles, creating a voluminous record of the scorn that was being heaped on him.

It made me sad to see what had become of him. But he wasn't doing anything to help himself, either. The job at MWW Group of East Rutherford hadn't panned out for him; he rarely showed up for work and lasted only a few weeks before Sommer encouraged him to look elsewhere.

Fearing he would be deported, Golan was apoplectic. Eventually State Street Partners, the lobbying firm where Jimmy Kennedy was a partner, extended him an offer. They gave him a hefty salary, $150,000 plus commissions. But Golan was still pulling his old tricks, handpicking the office he wanted—turned out it belonged to Jimmy, who gracefully moved his things to another space. He filled it with his Trenton memorabilia and two small Israeli flags. This time, though, he went into the office every day, entertaining a stream of rabbis and other power brokers. But he never signed a client—at least not for State Street Partners. Jimmy wondered if he was doing a side business from his office.

Eventually, Jimmy's partners terminated Golan for nonperformance. Part of me hoped that would be the end of it. Without a sponsor, he would lose his work permit and be forced to return to Israel. Jimmy even gave Golan airfare out of his own pocket.

During his last visit to Drumthwacket, I encouraged him to consider going back home for good. I felt I'd done right by Golan at every stage in our relationship, but now I was exhausted. But he said he wasn't finished in Jersey yet. He had lined up a job working on business deals with Israel and Russia for Shelley Zeiger, a Trenton-based developer and Jewish philanthropist. What he really wanted, though, was to return to government, something anybody with sense would have considered impossible.

"Golan, do you forget?" I asked.

"You destroyed my life," he shot back, his eyes filling with tears. "I made this enormous sacrifice, coming all the way here. You should never have listened to the people who said 'Get rid of Golan.' I never wanted to quit, Jimmy."

"It was the only option," I reminded him.

"For what? What good did it do? I read these clips every day. I read everything that's written about me. It's absurd what they say." When he left State Street Partners, the papers ran front-page stories. Golan obsessed over the coverage; he knew how many inches each paper had given the story. It was true, they made him seem silly, frivolous, and mysteriously ill-suited for any position. His reputation was in tatters. But he was doing nothing to rebuild it.

"Golan," I said, "I think you have a perverse attraction to being beat up by the press. They're saying the same things about me, but I'm not focusing on it. I'm looking forward. I'm moving a thousand miles in the opposite direction."

Ironically, my years in the closet had insulated me from any emotional damage the papers could cause. I was able to look at my presentation in the press as though it had nothing to do with me, as though it were pure fiction—because I alone knew for sure who I was. I'd made my divided self into protective armor. I never stumbled; my imposter sometimes did. I wouldn't wish this sort of immunity on anyone. It muted all sensation of one's self in the world. If the press was good, I could take little pleasure in it, either.

But Golan had been less scarred by the closet, and he felt his grief viscerally. "Bring me back to the state house, Jimmy. Please."

"Frankly, I pushed the system as far as I could, Golan, to make it accommodate you. If you're not going to work with it, the game's up. That doesn't affect my personal relationship with you. I still care about you, I still have warm feelings. I still *look* at you, sometimes, Golan. . . . That's what you don't understand."

He was disgusted. "You destroyed my life," he reiterated.

I was terribly weary of the fight. It had been two years since our last kiss, and more than a year since he left the public sector, yet he seemed incapable of handling either loss.

HAVING DRIVEN THE WARLORDS AROUND THE BEND, I FELT CURIously free to come up with creative solutions to the state's troubles. Local property taxes, for instance, were an unending vexation. Since I'd taken office two years earlier, they'd risen by 13 percent. An average tax bill in New Jersey was $5,259—a crippling figure for people living on normal incomes. This was caused mostly by our system of "home rule," in which every tiny township is responsible for everything from schools to police to sanitation—a system that produces grotesque duplications and inefficiencies, as well as a steady stream of business for companies controlled by the bosses.

At a rare joint session of the legislature in April, I presented an innovative three-part plan to fix it. I'd push for a constitutional convention in which voters could rethink "home rule," impose spending caps at the state and local level, and—at least temporarily—increase income taxes on the wealthiest residents in order to allow property tax relief for the poor and working class.

The millionaire's tax, as we came to call it, was the cornerstone of my $26.3 billion budget, targeting not millionaires, exactly, but residents who earned more than $500,000 a year. They made up exactly 1 percent of the population, and the change would raise their rate from 6.37 percent to 8.97 percent, pulling in about $800 million toward the state budget. Bush's federal tax cuts had just delivered a windfall to these same people. On average, they had received $19,000 in federal cuts. My tax would force them to pay an extra $850 in income taxes to the state. They could afford it.

As a direct consequence, about a million and a half homeowners would see increases in their property tax rebate checks. Taxpayers who earned less than $125,000 would get checks for $800, more than triple what they'd gotten the year before. Households with incomes between $125,000 and $200,000 would receive checks for $500. And—most important—about 450,000 senior citizens would see a 55 percent increases in their rebates, from $775 to $1,200.

No one in the party wanted the millionaire's tax. Dick Codey, by now the Senate president, didn't want it. He knew, as everyone else in the party did, that Florio's tax plan had set the Democrats back for a decade. Most of my top advisers were lukewarm about the idea. I remember the look on my staffers' faces when I pulled them aside one day in Drumthwacket and said: "You know, we're doing this."

"Okay," said Eric Shuffler, an energetic young lawyer I'd hired away from Torricelli to be my new counselor. He laughed nervously. "But how?"

We decided to sell the plan directly to voters. We went county to county, visiting two or three senior centers every day, sitting in people's living rooms, church basements, and VFW halls. Being from a working-class background myself, I knew they dreaded opening their property tax bills each quarter. I talked to them as someone who understood.

The road show worked. Polls showed that the people of New Jersey were so enthusiastic for the idea that Republicans didn't dare fight it. When the bill came to a vote, with Codey's and Assembly Majority Leader Joe Robert's advocacy, we won more Republican support than anyone thought possible. When the bill became law, it marked the first time anyone had raised taxes in New Jersey in fourteen years, and incongruously touched off a statewide celebration. Seniors holding balloons filled the streets outside the Trenton War Memorial and cheered as I signed the legislation.

Later that day, we held a cocktail party back at Drumthwacket to mark the occasion. A few of the bosses showed up sheepishly, but not John Lynch or George Norcross. I gave a conciliatory toast to them for their support. "I can assure you," I said to polite applause, "that I'm the only one in this room who won't be paying more taxes next year."

I HADN'T SPOKEN TO JOHN LYNCH IN NEARLY A YEAR. HIS PUBLIC criticism of my administration didn't abate. He complained that I worried too much about being liked and not enough about leading the state—a strange inversion of the facts. It was true that I took longer than I should have to convert from a 24-hour campaign machine into a 24-hour executive. But I felt my momentum was solid now, that this first term was finally shaping up as I had hoped.

I'd pushed through many initiatives that made me extremely proud. One of the most provocative had to do with stem-cell research, a hot-button issue at the White House but pure common sense to those of us who believe in the wisdom of Albert Einstein's observation that "scientists were rated as great heretics by the church, but they were truly religious men because of their faith in the orderliness of the universe." I set aside $6.5 million in the new budget to create the first state-financed stem-cell institute, part of an eventual $50 million public-private commitment to new biotechnologies. I lobbied the legislature hard and won their support, narrowly.

My own Church went into overdrive. Priests criticized me from the pulpit, conflating my support for stem-cell research with my defense of a woman's right to choose. They threw me in with the presidential bid of Senator John Kerry, who was under pressure to not take Holy Communion because he disagreed with the Church on abortion. For the bishops in New Jersey, it was one straw too many. Bishop Joseph Galante said he would refuse me communion if I entered a church in Camden, and Newark's archbishop John Myers published similar warnings in the biweekly *Catholic Advocate*.

Out of respect for them, I announced I would no longer seek communion in public Masses. But I knew I was doing the right thing. I made the stem-cell announcement at the Robert Wood Johnson Hospital in New Brunswick, surrounded by young men and women with spinal injuries, and their families. "This isn't an abstract academic debate," I said. "People are suffering today, and what we offer them is hope."

Getting the institute funded and passed was the crown of my first term. With a reelection campaign around the corner, I hoped it would help frame my priorities in the eyes of the voters.

But first I knew I would need to defang Lynch. I made an appointment to visit him at his home and bury the hatchet. This was a gesture of decency on my part. Lynch was by now the target of a handful of separate probes. I knew from my state trooper detail that he was under constant surveillance. Cruisers were stationed around the corner from his house. I assumed my arrival would be noted in some report. It was an unsuitable environment for a sitting governor to enter, but I went out of respect for his enormous influence in New Jersey, and for our long friendship. Jamie Fox and Michael De-Cotiis joined me.

Lynch's wife, Deborah, greeted us at the door, as cordial and amiable as ever. Deborah was a wonderful and loving woman. I had missed seeing her. She and I exchanged good books we'd recently read, as was our old tradition, as if no time had passed. I was surprised to see pictures of me and Lynch still hung on the family's walls.

John greeted us all warmly. And for a few hours that night—and a time or two thereafter—we worked at rekindling our friendship over pasta and desserts. It was not to be. His bitterness was extreme, but I could barely understand what it was about. He hammered at me about the "Machiavelli" fiasco, without understanding what really happened there, and said that he somehow felt personally tainted by it. He philosophized about leadership and responsible government, returning to his critical themes.

I sensed that despite his many intellectual gifts, his adoring family, and the abundant personal wealth he had amassed, John Lynch had appraised his life and found only dissatisfaction. There was nothing I could do to calm him.

IT WAS NOT QUITE SEVEN IN THE MORNING, A DAY OR TWO BEFORE Easter in 2004, when I had one of my last phone conversations with Golan. I was on the treadmill at the gym at Princeton, as I was every morning. On the treadmills next to mine were Shawn Brennan, an aide, and Sgt. Tim Whille, a state trooper assigned to my detail. When Golan's name popped up on the phone, I decided to answer it. For many months I had sent most of his calls to voice mail, on the strict instructions of Jamie Fox, my chief of staff. Jamie is a keen judge of character. I'd asked him to have breakfast with Golan once, long after Golan had left government. "He's a lunatic, a hanger-on," he reported back, not knowing our history. "Got an ego the size of Manhattan. I'm telling you, stay away from him."

But just that morning back at Drumthwacket, as I was showering, I'd wondered why I hadn't heard from him in so long. I wanted to know he was okay.

So I answered the phone.

Golan's mood hadn't improved. He wanted me to know again how I'd destroyed his life, and the rest. I listened again, wearily offering my counsel as usual. Then he surprised me.

"I told my parents," he said.

I knew exactly what he meant. He'd told his parents about our affair. This stunned me, which I'm sure was the effect he desired. He never even addressed our relationship with me, except obliquely—and never, ever on the phone. If he sat his parents down and confessed to being gay, and if he was suddenly willing to admit this on the phone, that meant he was moving in a whole new direction. What he was telling me, I felt sure, was that he was no longer going to keep the secret. It seemed like a crazy move, borne of desperation.

"Good," I said.

"I never would actually do anything inappropriate," he said. "I've never asked for anything inappropriate. I've never asked you to do anything improper."

He never talked like this. My mind raced. It occurred to me that he was probably taping the call, but I couldn't imagine why.

"What on earth are you talking about?"

"I just wanted to be clear about that. That's why I told my parents."

Perhaps he was trying to create a record of our affair which he could trade me for his job back. That would be blackmail, pure and simple. The idea made me angry.

"Gole, I value your advice and opinion, your work, and I tried to the best of my ability to find something that was both productive for you and benefited the state, and that failed. Life moves on. I want you to live a productive, vibrant life, as I do for all my friends. I've done my best to work with you, but that's all any of us can rationally expect. I don't owe you anything. I don't owe you an income. I'm prepared to work with you, but I don't owe you a position in the statehouse."

He demanded to see me, hoping to continue the conversation—or the tape recording.

"I'm leaving for Vancouver to see my daughter for Easter," I told him. "I'll call when I get back."

I suppose I had no intention of calling. He picked up on this right away.

"If I don't hear from you," he said, "I'm going to have to take action."

I didn't ask what he meant by that. I said, "Do what you have to do."

WHILE I WAS AWAY, I CONTEMPLATED NEVER CALLING GOLAN back, but that seemed unfair. I told Jamie Fox and Jimmy Kennedy that he'd threatened me, without giving specifics. Both felt a clean break was in order. One afternoon I walked along the Fraser River for two hours in Vancouver trying to decide how to handle this. I stopped downtown at the Christ Church Cathedral and prayed for a peaceful resolution. But I realized it was too late. Nothing I did now would assuage Golan. He was incapable of processing what happened to him. Fate had already determined our futures.

I invited him to visit Drumthwacket a few weeks later, on a bright Saturday morning in April. All around the mansion, daffodils had unfolded from the lawns in pure celebrations of spring. A family of ducks had nested in the small pond beside the terraced garden. No one else was at home.

When he arrived I was surprised at how unpolished he appeared: Jeans, sneakers, a windbreaker. He was shaking slightly, whether from the morning's chill or from his teeming rage—or perhaps from trepidation over what he was setting in motion, his own moral meltdown.

I listened as he vented again, petulantly and with rancor. "People are asking me questions about our relationship," he said. "People in Israel asked me. People are still interested. What do I tell them, Jim? I have to take certain steps."

I was careful about my reply. "You can answer them any way you want. God bless you, Golan, whatever happens, happens."

We walked through the house together, drinking tea. His anger did not abate, but instead returned to a plea for his old job.

"Golan, this isn't real," I interrupted. I swept the air with my hand: "You think Drumthwacket is real? It's not real. This house isn't mine. These state troopers, this helicopter—I'm just passing through, Golan. This is democracy. The privilege we have is to serve for a brief period of time. That's it, and then it goes. For you, it has gone. I'm telling you as a friend, you have to move on."

"I don't consider you a friend anymore," he said. "Friends don't do this to friends."

"Golan, I'm the only one who is still standing with you! I'm the only one who will sit with you. I'm the only one who still cares about you. Just out of curiosity, if I'm not your friend, who is?"

When he left, I tried to hug him good-bye—I'll admit, I would have patted him down for a recording device, given the chance. But he pulled away, coolly offering his hand instead. A very bad sign, I thought.

VI.

A Philosophy of Memory

15.

pearance with a mounting dread. Meanwhile, my staff was convinced we were staging a comeback, even if our numbers hadn't yet turned around. That summer, my approval rating crossed the 40 percent mark, higher than at any time in the last two years.

"We're starting to get traction," Eric Shuffler, my senior counselor, said enthusiastically. "We have a year and a half to go before the election—it's time to start campaigning on your victories. Not just the environmental stuff or balanced budget. You're the first governor to invest in stem-cell research, you passed the toughest antibullying legislation in the nation, fixed the Department of Motor Vehicles and E-ZPass. You opened experimental clinical trials for cancer research in a state with the third highest breast cancer rate, Governor. Think about it. This will be the first campaign in a generation where auto insurance isn't even an issue. You fixed it."

My most ambitious initiative, one I hoped would be the legacy of my term, was yet to come. I wanted to find a way not only to battle sprawl but to change the development dynamics in New Jersey once and for all. Billions of dollars in private investment were being lavished on new malls and residential developments, consuming more and more of our farmland. Lured by the comfortable new neighborhoods often priced below market, an endless stream of New Jersey families were leaving established communities in our historically vibrant cities, small towns, and older suburbs to put down new roots there.

Local leaders where the development was taking place thought this was good for their towns, because of the increased tax base. But that's a myth. They're not simply adding new taxpayers to the rolls. Rates are driven up as well. It's the only way to cover costs of the new expansions.

Why is that? Because for every farm tract taken over by developers, taxpayers must finance new roads, build new water treatment facilities, and outfit police forces, schools, and hospitals to serve the migrating middle class. Only the revenue associated with new developments ever gets our attention—not the costs. Engineers, contractors, and builders were making ample profits, it was true. But they weren't reinvesting those profits in the infrastructure their developments required. That was left to the new homeowners, who thought they were getting spanking new homes at bargain-basement prices.

The sad part is that the costly new infrastructure they get stuck with financing is all redundant to the systems they left behind. Across the state, perfectly comfortable cities and towns were being abandoned or underutilized. I saw this in parts of Woodbridge. Newark and Paterson hadn't seen any appreciable investment in decades. Camden was the worst. Though it's just minutes away from Philadelphia, downtown Camden looked like a war-torn Middle Eastern city, collapsed and forgotten, a desolate wasteland. Life in those circumstances is a Hobbesian nightmare. In 2003 and 2004, Camden had the highest murder and violent crime rates in the nation.

In order to attack sprawl, I knew we needed to defend our cities. I wanted to make it much more advantageous and profitable for developers to rebuild our cities, and much more cumbersome for them to bulldoze farms and forests. My environmental commissioner, Bradley Campbell, and I devised something we called the Building Intelligent Growth Map, depicting every road, stream, and river in the state. We then colored the map according to where we felt development should be encouraged or discouraged.

Though we surely never intended to throw a blanket of protection over our entire wish list, unfortunately our map came to define our campaign in the minds of our opponents. Ultimately we had to remove it from our website in the face of an overwhelming backlash—a backlash that made all our sprawl efforts that much more difficult.

Our plan was to make Camden a demonstration of our program. For starters, we invested $175 million in the city, focusing on the local college campus and improvements at the hospital. We undertook several environmental cleanup projects, beautified the parks, and modernized the sewer and water systems. Tax breaks were extended to new and growing businesses, and we streamlined the application process for building there. It was beginning to show returns. Similar reinvestments were taking place in towns across the state.

The biggest single tract of land colored as off-limits was the Highlands region in northwestern New Jersey. In addition to harboring thirty endangered or threatened species and providing outdoor recreation to millions of visitors each year, the 800,000 acres of the Highlands produced drinking water for 4 million people statewide. The population there was growing 50 percent faster than in the rest of the state. Between 1995 and 2000, twenty-five thousand acres were lost to sprawl. If development continued on that pace, the water would soon be contaminated. It was time to act. Countless governors before me had tried to freeze development there, to no avail. We were determined to succeed.

Jamie Fox and Eric Shuffler, who were as personally committed to this initiative as I was, helped devise the winning approach. In late 2003 we formed a committee to study how best to protect the reservoirs and streams there. Six months later, I accepted the Committee's plan to preserve all four hundred thousand acres of the most sensitive areas, which included the Wanaque Reservoir. It was bold. We announced a series of hearings on the study with the hopes of passing a bill by Earth Day, April 22, 2004.

No undertaking since entering politics had ever been more important to me. If I could prove that "smart growth" worked, we could save the Highlands and the towns and cities both. Future kids would have the same glorious experiences I had growing up, living in functioning small towns with vibrant Main Streets and unspoiled nature just miles away. I felt this as a daunting challenge, and a rare opportunity—the thing that drew me into government in the first place, a chance to make a difference.

But I had grossly underestimated the kind of opposition we were facing. The newspapers lauded the plan as the most sweeping and important environmental program for the state since Governor Byrne preserved a million acres of the Pinelands in 1979. But unlike the Pinelands, which consisted of remote tracts of sandy scrub land, the Highlands encompassed ninety towns in seven counties, with some of the state's choicest building lots.

The developers were outraged. They warned that my plan would wreak havoc on the housing market, driving up home prices, which were already nearing an average of $500,000. We disagreed. One real estate group took out a full-page ad in the *Star-Ledger* alarming homeowners in the region into believing that they'd be prevented from building porches or pools if the bill passed—a total misrepresentation. Farmers weren't any happier. They wanted the right to sell their land to developers at market value, and worried that the state would insist that they had to go on farming it, also not true.

A series of public hearings on the bill drew crowds five hundred strong, galvanizing opponents and environmental advocates in a way never before seen in the state. Jeff Tittel, the executive director of the Sierra Club and a staunch ally or a harsh critic of mine, depending on the occasion, called the issue the "Super Bowl of Sprawl." At one hearing, state troopers were called on to keep the proceedings calm.

By early June, the Highlands protection plan had squeaked through the Assembly. But we hit a brick wall in the Senate, where a Democrat from Gloucester, Stephen Sweeney, blocked it in committee. He and the delegation from South Jersey, which honestly wouldn't be impacted by the law at all, began fomenting local opposition among developers there who were still angry at me for my earlier preservation efforts in the region. His argument was that we were pumping substantial dollars into North Jersey to protect their water supply and landscape without any direct benefits to the south.

I knew Sweeney wasn't acting alone—he was backed by George Norcross, South Jersey's most powerful party boss. George practiced a direct and blunt form of power politics; if you crossed swords with him, you knew what the issues were. George believed it was bad economic policy to remove the whole Highlands region from future development maps. We had a serious disagreement on this.

But his opposition was causing our Highlands Coalition—an uneasy amalgamation of Republicans and Democrats—to fracture. Jack Schrier, the Morris County Freeholders' Republican chairman, was taking tremendous heat from certain conservatives in his local base. So were Leonard Lance and Bob Martin, Republican senators who supported the bill. I thought briefly about overriding George and Sweeney with an executive order protecting the four hundred thousand acres of land, but decided against it. An executive order would be temporary at best and would halt any momentum we had in favor of a permanent solution.

In the first week of June, I pulled every string possible to force the bill out of committee. Sweeney gave a condition for capitulating. He wanted a parallel law making it easier for developers to build in designated "smart growth" areas of the state. Specifically he wanted to fast-track reviews of permit applications, giving the Department of Environmental Protection just forty-five days to study the impact of any filing, hold hearings, and request changes before voting. If the review wasn't yet completed by deadline, the permits would be issued automatically.

This was unacceptable. Unless we could be sure we had the necessary regulatory wherewithal to get the job done within the allotted time, development outside the Highlands would be more likely to foul the water tables.

We pushed back. In a series of meetings at the Marriott Hotel a few blocks from the statehouse, Michael DeCotiis, my chief counsel, horse traded—not with Sweeney, but with George Norcross's brother, Phil, the managing partner of a prominent law firm. Meanwhile, we looked at our permit review process to see how nimble we could make it without sacrificing oversight.

Ultimately, we reached a compromise we felt we could live with. Some members of my staff disagreed with me on this, vehemently arguing that the so-called fast track bill was too high a price to pay for the Highlands bill. Passions ran high on the subject, but I felt that as long as I was in office, I could personally oversee the overhauling of our regulatory structure with Commissioner Campbell to make sure no new development would slip through the cracks without a thorough environmental review. On June 11, without debate on the Senate floor, the Highlands Act passed, making history as the single most sweeping environmental law in a generation—by far the most significant policy initiative I had ever undertaken.

NO POLITICIAN HAD WORSE LUCK THAN I. THE HIGHLANDS VIC-tory should have enjoyed a few weeks of positive press, even national attention. Not for the McGreevey administration. Instead, another scandal exploded—the biggest yet. Regrettably, it involved my friend Charlie Kushner. And the gallons of ink that accompanied it stained me and everybody in the administration.

Even before I appointed him to the Port Authority board, Charlie was locked in ugly fights with his own brother and sister, who claimed he had mismanaged the family company. Among other things, they claimed that he had illegally diverted company funds to help political candidates, me included. I didn't think there was anything to the charge. But Charlie later charged in a lawsuit that his own former accountant, Robert Yontef, was secretly helping his siblings develop their case against him, revealing what he knew about Charlie's bookkeeping schemes.

As their lawsuits advanced, Charlie suffered an abject surrender of his senses. In an outlandish move, he paid $10,000 apiece to two prostitutes and instructed them to lure his sister's husband and the accountant to $59-a-night rooms at the Red Bull Inn in Bridgewater, which Charlie had rigged with video cameras. Apparently, he planned to use the tapes to force them into retreat. It was an outrageous move, even by New Jersey standards.

Wisely, the accountant declined the woman's entreaty. The brother-in-law wasn't so prudent. Acting anonymously, in May 2004, Charlie mailed a copy of the sex tape to his own sister for her to see her husband's transgressions. Another copy was sent to each of the couple's children.

Making this distasteful and terribly stupid matter much worse, it turned out that Charlie's brother-in-law was a cooperating witness in a federal tax investigation against Charlie, meaning Charlie had tampered with a federal witness, a felony. Yontef was also cooperating with the probe; so, in fact, was Charlie's own sister.

Under threat of arrest, he turned himself in to the FBI in July 2004, to face charges of conspiracy, tax evasion, obstruction of an investigation, and promotion of interstate prostitution. Within the year, my dear friend Charlie Kushner—the son of Holocaust survivors, a former Humanitarian of the Year, a pillar in the Orthodox Jewish community—pleaded guilty to myriad and serious crimes before surrendering for a two-year sentence.

Through the years, I had gone to the mat over and over for Charlie, as he had so often for me. Charlie was a driven accomplished businessman, but he also was among the most generous souls I ever knew. The press pilloried me for our friendship after this ordeal. But I never got angry. I knew Charlie would return from prison wiser and healthier. Mostly, I regretted that he'd obliged the demons in his head.

This I knew so much about.

BY THE SUMMER OF 2004, I CAME TO THE REALIZATION THAT MY marriage had deteriorated beyond salvation. By that point, we were hardly speaking much at all. On the second floor of Drumthwacket, a cold wind blew.

As the long July Fourth weekend approached, I heard from Dina's scheduler that she was taking Jacqueline to the governor's official beach house at Island Beach State Park, a pristine barrier island near Seaside Park. She had already invited her parents; I wasn't expected to attend, nor, I understood, would I be welcome.

Facing the prospect of that long weekend separated from my family, I was profoundly lonely. That Saturday, as a distraction, I made a five-hour trip to help a friend move down to the shore. After dropping him off, I had the state troopers take me past Congress Hall, a beautifully renovated 200-year-old hotel on the Atlantic Ocean owned by Curtis Bashaw, whom I'd asked to serve as executive director of the Casino Reinvestment Development Authority, the state agency that had used casino revenues to restore Atlantic City's grandeur and turn it into a modern family entertainment center. Curtis was charming, exceptionally bright, profoundly knowledgeable about state politics, and an important player in the ongoing effort to redevelop South Jersey.

He was also a Republican, as he quickly admitted when we'd first met a year before. But he happened to come from a profoundly spiritual and religious background—his grandfather was Rev. Carl McIntire, the firebrand fundamentalist preacher whose sermons were broadcast on more than six hundred stations at the height of his fame in the 1960s. Communism was his main foe, but McIntire also battled some Protestant churches (those he considered too liberal), the Roman Catholic Church (which he considered "fascist") and, later, homosexuality.

Yet somehow Curtis had grown up as a well-integrated, balanced, religious, gay man, who lived openly with his partner, Will, in the same town where he grew up—and attended the evangelical church that had nourished him as a youth. "I don't buy the baby-and-bathwater stuff," he once explained, with typical good humor. "You can't accept the religion of your parents without questioning it, not if it doesn't accept you. But don't abandon it, either." Curtis told me that he'd found a way to make his faith his own. "The Bible says, 'Let the words in your mouth and the meditations of your heart be acceptable to God.' That's the bottom line. Forget about living up to some standard set down by preachers. If your words, your actions, and your feelings all align, then you've pleased God. My grandfather said it all the time."

Talking to him made me realize how far away from my faith I'd drifted. I longed for the emotional alignment I felt when I was right with my Church. Without it I felt as though I were navigating in a storm, letting each challenge determine my course. My goal was no longer to do what was right, but to do what got me to my next plateau.

I don't know why it was so important for me to see Curtis that night, but I asked the Congress Hall staff where to find him, and they pointed me toward a birthday party he was hosting nearby. I decided to crash the affair. When I arrived, the scene was something out of a dream of mine: Curtis and his partner surrounded by their extended families and friends, along with dozens of members of the local establishment; couples and singles, gay and straight alike. There were no barriers here, certainly none based on sexual orientation. Curtis welcomed me to the party, and I enjoyed the evening immensely, but by the end of the evening I had just plunged further into loneliness.

As he walked me out to the car, I squeezed his arm.

"I really admire how integrated your life is," I told him.

"You know, the root of the word *integration* is the same as the word *integrity*. When the words in your mouth and the actions of your hands and the feelings of your heart are one and the same, you're a whole person, you're integrated, and there's integrity in your life."

I don't suppose he knew then about my secret. I was suddenly overcome with a need to confess it to him. I knew he would understand better than anyone. But I didn't dare. Instead I talked about my issues indirectly, confessing that I was unhappy in my marriage and suggesting that I might want to rekindle a romance with Kari; I suppose she was a metaphor in my mind for total authenticity. "It is a rare man who can not only live a decent life, but also find love and purpose," I said. "You have that in your life."

I remember adding, "You're so lucky." Of course luck had nothing to do with it, but saying what I meant—"You're so brave"— would have revealed too much about myself.

"I'm lucky?" he said. "Look at you. You're the governor of New Jersey!"

"I climbed the ladder," I said, "but it led to the wrong world."

I DON'T REMEMBER HOW I SPENT THE EARLY MORNING HOURS OF Friday, July 23, 2004—whether I went to the Princeton University gym, or down to the crew house on Carnegie Lake, where there is a glassed-in room on the second floor with a comfortable chair for reading. I'd developed a habit of spending my waking hours away from the mansion whenever possible, and filling my time there with meetings, sometimes late into the night. Afterward I must have attended an event of some kind; a gathering with a crowd always puts me in a good mood, and I remember being pumped up when I got to the office around noon.

What I do remember is the expression of my chief of staff, Jamie Fox, when I arrived. He looked like he'd just gotten news of a nuclear accident. He pressed the fingers of one hand to his upper lip, as I'd often seen him do when anxious or angry.

"We have a bit of a problem," Jamie said. "Michael DeCotiis is on his way over." Michael was our general counsel. "We'll talk about it when he gets here."

"What is it, Jamie? Just tell me."

I didn't expect him to answer. But he looked at me brokenheartedly, lowering his hand from his face. His voice fell to a whisper. "Michael got a call from a lawyer representing Golan. He's suing for sexual assault and harassment, unless you pay fifty million dollars."

It was the other shoe I'd been waiting for. Golan would go public, on fantastically trumped-up charges, or try to extort a fortune from me to keep him quiet. Either way, since he could no longer be a part of my administration, apparently he'd decided to burn it to the ground.

The weariness I'd been feeling for a year became almost too much to stand. I rolled my head on my shoulders. Jamie looked concerned.

"We'll get over it," he said. "Michael will make this go away."

I knew he was wrong. "It's all over," I said.

THAT SUNDAY, WE WERE ALL PLANNING TO GO TO BOSTON FOR the Democratic National Convention, where John Kerry would sweep the party's nomination to oppose George W. Bush. It was to be a big moment for us. I hadn't been asked to speak from the main stage, but I was scheduled to give a talk about my stem-cell research initiative before a meeting organized by the Whitehead Institute for Biomedical Research. I'd spent all week preparing for the proceedings. I'd asked my old friends Jimmy and Lori Kennedy to come along; I hadn't seen much of my old friend lately, so I was looking forward to a week in their company.

Now I sat alone in my office dreading the outcome of Golan's gambit.

Michael DeCotiis arrived early that afternoon, joining me and Jamie in my office. That morning, Michael began, he'd received a call from a New York lawyer named Allen Lowy, alleging not only that I'd fired Golan for spurning my advances, but that our sexual encounters were never consensual. Both of these were preposterous charges. From a legal perspective, Michael was surprised that Golan's lawyer hadn't laid out the specific elements of his allegation, giving dates or any corroborating evidence.

"He wants money," Michael said. "Lots of it. And he gave a very strict deadline. If we don't meet his demands by Tuesday, they're going public."

"That's blackmail, Michael. I never harassed or assaulted Golan," I said flatly. "It was consensual from start to finish." Those were the first words I ever said out loud about my homosexuality. In retrospect, the confession was probably unnecessary, at least from Jamie's perspective; I could see in his eyes that he had surmised my truth, one gay man to another.

A silence fell over the room. Finally Jamie spoke. "I always said Golan was a gold digger," he said. "I wonder if he's been fired from another job recently. If he's without income, that would explain a few things. And if he's on somebody's payroll, I wonder if his boss knows he's blackmailing the governor."

A few phone calls later, Jamie knew a bit more. Golan had recently sold his Princeton townhouse and moved to Manhattan, where he was living in an expensive rental on Columbus Circle. He was working for Dan Tishman, the fourth-generation chief of the Tishman Construction Corporation, the massive development firm that had built the World Trade Center towers in the 1970s. "Tishman must be paying him a lot of money to afford that address," Jamie said.

"The first thing you're going to need is a lawyer," Michael told me. Jamie called Bill Lawler of Vinson & Elkins, who had helped resolve the Machiavelli case and had since become a good friend.

"I'll call Lowy back and stall him," Michael said. "I'll set up some sort of meeting with him, Bill Lawler, and me early next week."

Jamie asked what we knew about Lowy. Very little, it turned out. Michael had looked up his credentials in a legal directory and discovered Lowy was an entertainment lawyer, which struck Jamie as odd. But all we could do was play the cards we were dealt.

THE FOLLOWING DAY, BILL LAWLER AGREED TO FLY IN TO MEET ME at Newark Liberty Airport to discuss the case. My old friend Nene Foxhall of Continental arranged for us to meet in a room at the Continental Admiral's Club. He asked me a million questions about my relationship, intimate questions that were embarrassing to admit. I could see he was disappointed in me.

But I was pretty sure of one thing: the fact that I was gay did nothing to diminish Bill's affection for me. I can't express exactly how much this surprised me. It was the first test of my own self-hatred, in what would become an endless series of tests, and the first time I recognized how much I'd misjudged my friends.

ON SUNDAY, AS PREVIOUSLY ARRANGED, WE WENT TO BOSTON. Dina, Jacqueline, and I shared a suite. Dina could tell I was distracted, I'm sure, but by then our relationship was so distant that the new tension in the air went entirely unmentioned. On Monday, I delivered my stem-cell address.

On the way back, Jamie and I released the state troopers and sat on a bench in Boston Common, watching a beautiful afternoon unfold. Children played, and pairs of swans circled in the lake. I realized for the first time that I was filled with fear about the future, what it would mean to my family and my parents, to all that I'd known. I was overwhelmed with the sense that I had jeopardized everything I held dear.

But Jamie was a tremendous comfort. Without his constant friendship and love, I could never have survived what was to come.

"You're strong enough to handle this," he told me. "People are either victims or survivors, and it may be painful, but you're going to be a survivor. You'll get through this."

All of a sudden, I looked at my friend Jamie differently—not just as my chief of staff, but as a gay man. I imagined the life he lived when he wasn't in the office, the adolescence he must have endured—one that was probably much like my own. The thought that Jamie had survived his own journey gave me strength.

In the afternoon, we returned to wage the war in a small catering room on the mezzanine level at the convention center reserved for the New Jersey delegation. Huddled around the telephone, Jamie and I strategized with Bill Lawler and Michael DeCotiis, who had met Lowy at the Manhattan offices of Vinson & Elkins. Bill said that Lowy wasn't a litigator. Based on his business card, which read "Classical Alliance," he appeared to be an agent or manager for classical musicians. He arrived at the meeting without a briefcase or notepad, Bill reported, carrying nothing but a book, *Michelangelo and the Pope's Ceiling.*

"Lowy started out saying, 'If the case were to go to trial, I have no doubt we'd be able to collect damages in excess of fifty million dollars,' " Bill said. "So I said, 'Well, what did the governor do? I understand they had a consensual relationship for a period of time while Golan was a state employee, that he left state employment for reasons having nothing to do with the governor, that Golan resigned and moved on, and really hasn't had a significant amount of contact with the governor up until recently.' "

Lowy interrupted, Bill recalled, saying, "My client has been damaged, and he needs to be compensated."

"So I said to him, 'What are your claims?' I'd already researched a number of claims he theoretically might have made, but he didn't make any. He actually said he wouldn't tell me. He said, 'Your client knows what he did.' It was the strangest meeting I ever attended. I think their entire plan from start to finish is: call up governor, demand money, get money. Eventually he said, 'Write up the papers however you want, I don't care. I'll release you from anything. In exchange for fifty million.' "

That wasn't happening—if for no other reason than that I had only a few thousand dollars in the bank, and no assets to speak of.

Monday ended on a faint note of hope; Lowy had agreed to a follow-up meeting on Thursday. The more we could engage him, the better our chances of disarming him would be.

Before dawn the next morning, I walked around the convention grounds with Jim Kennedy. We circled the same fountain a number of times before I found the courage to tell him what Golan was threatening to do. "I had a consensual sexual relationship with him," I said. "Now he's suing."

God bless Jim. My oldest friend jumped right past all the difficult questions and found just the right thing to say. "What do you need from me?"

"Your prayers and support," I said.

ON THURSDAY, BILL LAWLER AND MICHAEL DECOTIIS MET AGAIN with Lowy. As before, he carried no notepad or briefcase, only his subway reading—this time, *Madame Bovary*. He seemed to play his part with a steely determination, never raising his voice or appearing unsteady or anxious, despite his apparent lack of experience.

According to Bill, he began the conversation by reiterating my innocence of these crazy charges, and added: "What are your client's goals? Whatever they are, I think I can demonstrate to you that filing a lawsuit for some unspecified claim against the governor of New Jersey is not the way to achieve them."

For the sake of argument, Bill had come up with many different decision trees regarding Golan's self-interest. If Golan needed money, a lawsuit was not the way to get it because the state is judgment-proof; no matter what I had done, the state was not on the hook for it. On the other hand, I was judgment-proof, too, because I had no money. Even if Golan were to win a court battle, which he wouldn't, he'd walk away with nothing.

If Golan's goal was to vindicate his reputation, filing a lawsuit wouldn't serve that end, either. By the summer of 2004, only a small number of people remembered who Golan was, whether or not he saw himself as an important public figure. "He may think, as he strides down the street, that everyone's whispering, 'Look, there's Golan.' But it's not the case," Bill told Lowy. "At best, if he files suit he'll be seen as a greedy, grasping, spurned lover. At worst, a blackmailer. Either reputation is worse than the one he's got now. What I'm saying is, What motivates Golan? What does he care about? Let's talk about that."

Lowy replied by hinting that Golan had claimed I sexually assaulted him in the back of a van on the way to Washington, DC, before an audience of three state troopers, a ridiculous lie. "And he tried to get rid of Golan. He had all sorts of people offer him jobs. Even the mayor of Tel Aviv offered him a job."

Finally we had something to respond to. "Mr. Lowy, even if that's true, how is it a bad thing to recommend someone for a job?" Bill answered.

"The governor is running for reelection, and this is life-and-death for him," Lowy said. "The governor needs to pay my client for the damages he has suffered. He has treated my client terribly and tried to get rid of the evidence—the evidence being Golan. And although we think we will get fifty million dollars, we'll take five."

Bill told me this with a laugh. "As your lawyer, I think I'm doing a great job," he told me. "Because already I've carved $45 million off the top."

Bill told Lowy he needed to see any evidence to determine if $5 million was a reasonable price to keep this quiet.

"You name it," Lowy said. "Photos, sexually explicit notes, eyewitnesses—I have evidence."

That can't be true, I thought. Nobody could have taken photos of us, we made sure of that. And we were always careful never to write down anything incriminating. I even signed all my birthday cards to him "Love, Jim and Dina."

Nor was it likely that we'd been seen by anybody. Bill called up the troopers who were in the van the one day Golan and I drove to DC. Nothing happened in that van. But this was in the early days of my administration, before I'd switched out Whitman's drivers; none of these three men were my fans, and I worried they might be collaborating with Golan in some way. One of them told Bill, "If I could say something bad about Jim McGreevey, I'd be happy to." But when presented with an open-ended question—"Do you recall anything out of the ordinary happening during that trip?"—none of them mentioned anything like a sexual assault.

"Let's see it," Bill said. "Produce your evidence."

Lowy shook his head no, closed his book, stood and walked out of the meeting.

Bill repeated all of this for me and Jamie, huddled around the speaker-phone in our makeshift war room. "He's totally cocky," he reported. "The scenario he's describing is inherently incredible: he's got evidence he won't show about an assault that nobody remembers, and he thinks it's worth five million bucks."

I know Jamie's reaction was to strategize, to map out a new counter-offensive. I just wanted to die. The shame and humiliation I felt talking about this with Bill and Jamie was paralyzing. For forty-seven years I had managed to avoid discussing my sexuality with anyone. Now my top advisers were wading unemotionally through the mess of my life, picking through my secrets for something they could use to our advantage. In my shock, I wasn't thinking clearly.

Jamie interrupted Bill. "Where does Lowy live?"

Bill dug out an address. We all reacted in stunned silence. It was the same Columbus Circle building as Golan's, apartment 44C compared to Golan's 24B.

"Listen to me," Jamie said. "They met in the elevator. That's gotta be what happened."

AFTER LEAVING THE LOWY MEETING, WHICH AGAIN TOOK PLACE in Bill Lawler's New York offices, Bill had paid a visit to Dan Tishman, whose headquarters also happened to be in that Columbus Circle building. I'd authorized him to talk to Tishman about Golan. Ostensibly we wanted to know what Tishman knew, if anything, about his employee's circumstances—if he was experiencing emotional or financial trouble, for instance.

But our main goal was to see if we could create a back channel to Golan. Any insight Tishman could offer us would be valuable.

Of course, we knew paying such a visit could have other consequences. Tishman, who does considerable business in New Jersey, wouldn't be thrilled to know that one of his employees was threatening the governor. We hoped he'd reprimand Golan in the sternest way possible. Without a job, he would be forced to leave the country. Of course we didn't say anything of the kind to Tishman, merely asked that he look into the matter.

I think that all Bill told Tishman was that Golan was making a false claim about an "inappropriate relationship" between the two of us. "We just want to see if his head is screwed on right," Bill said. "Maybe he's being used in some way." (For months thereafter, some engaged in wild speculation about this, naming Israel or the Mossad as possible culprits. But that never made sense to me—destabilizing the government of New Jersey hardly seemed like something that would be high on any foreign power's priority list.)

Tishman had the reaction we were hoping for. "I'll call him up and tell him I want to talk to him," he told Bill.

A day or two later, after leaving many messages, Tishman reported that Golan had finally returned his call, but refused to take a meeting. This caused me great concern. In the Jewish community, Tishman and his family are enormously influential. *Golan is walking away from everything*, I thought. *This isn't good.*

* * *

AROUND THIS TIME, I ALSO CALLED RABBI YOSEF CARLEBACH, who runs the Chabad House at Rutgers. A Lubavitcher Jew, Carlebach was an old friend of mine who also knew Golan. I told him about my affair, knowing that his Orthodox sect wasn't particularly known for liberalism on the subject. But he saw immediately the danger of Golan's actions and understood my need to talk to him. He agreed to act as an intermediary.

That night, at about eight, the rabbi drove to Golan's apartment building in New York. A doorman said Golan wasn't in. Carlebach returned at 9:30, but was told Golan hadn't returned. "I'll sit," Carlebach said. "I know he's in town. I'll wait."

On a bench in the lobby, he opened a copy of *Letters from the Rebbe*, the collected writings of Menachem Schneerson, who members of the Lubavitch faith believe was the Messiah. Ninety minutes passed. According to Rabbi Carlebach, a man dressed in black approached him and grabbed his elbow. "We know who sent you," he said. "We know who you are."

This unnerved the rabbi. "The more you talk, the more concerned I am about Golan Cipel's welfare," he said.

"And for *your* physical well-being, I suggest you leave the building," the man said.

With that, the man brusquely escorted the rabbi to the sidewalk. Before heading back to New Jersey, Rabbi Carlebach wrote a note to Golan, saying in Hebrew, "We need to talk." He slid this into his book, which he handed to the doorman. "Here is fifty dollars," he said. "Please see that Mr. Cipel gets this book. It is very important."

Unfortunately, Golan didn't respond to the rabbi's entreaty.

IN A DAZE, JAMIE, JIMMY, MICHAEL, AND I RETURNED FROM Boston to New Jersey that Saturday. I remember counseling them to keep a strong game face. I said something like, "We can't show weakness or vulnerability."

But there was little to feel good about. We'd made almost no progress. With every passing day I felt my grip on Trenton growing more tenuous.

So after dropping Dina and Jacqueline off at Drumthwacket, I did what

I'd often done when my career seemed doomed: I called my old friend Ray Lesniak. Many months had passed since Ray and I last spoke. I hoped he wasn't holding a grudge. For a fourth time, I needed his help in salvaging my career.

I reached him at the Metedeconk National Golf Club, down on the shore, and he didn't hesitate one second before agreeing to see me at his beach house at Curtis Point. I got there in just over two hours. If he hadn't already figured it out, he could tell from my face my visit was urgent.

"Salena," he said to his girlfriend. "The dog needs a walk, sweetheart."

We stood in awkward silence as Salena gathered the leash, slipped on shoes, and headed out the front door with the dog. When she'd gone from view, I told him about Golan, our affair, and his extortionate demands.

He looked at me serenely. I hadn't realized until now what an impact his new spiritual mien had had on his life. He was a changed man from the political boss who marched me through Essex County backrooms years ago. Sitting across his dining room table from me, his blue eyes radiated only friendship and concern.

"What are the facts?" he asked. I told him everything. He had a good lawyer's mind. "It's fact-sensitive, not clear-cut," he said. "But I think we can legitimately get rid of this for a lot less than five million, and a confidentiality agreement. This kind of stuff happens." He laid out a plan for a legal defense fund into which we could easily raise enough to settle this dispute. "It's not perfect, but you can justify it," he said.

I was lucky to have him back in my camp.

BILL LAWLER, MEANWHILE, HAD LEFT TOWN TO REPRESENT A client in rural Marion, Indiana—the birthplace of James Dean—but he agreed to a telephone conference with Lowy in mid-afternoon on Tuesday, August 3. It didn't go any better than their previous conversations. Lowy, in his steady voice, wouldn't take no for an answer. He wasn't dissuaded by my own lack of money, either, demanding that I reach out to my legendary fundraising network to meet Golan's demands.

Immediately after hanging up, Bill called me.

"I told him, 'The only settlement we could ever do is a legal settlement. I can't settle an extortion.'" He paused. "I might be influenced by the fact that I'm standing at a pay phone in the rain beneath an eight-foot billboard of James Dean, but I'm coming to the conclusion that this can't be resolved in a rational way," he told me.

I told Bill about Ray's plan to set up a defense fund. He said it was perfectly legal and common, but he disagreed with the notion. "Not to be disrespectful to Ray," he said, "but paying this guy off is a stupid idea. You pay an extortion demand and it's going to come back at you, one way or another. Also, how are you going to raise money? People who have supported you politically and personally and have that kind of money are smart, successful people, and when you go to smart, successful people and say, by the way, 'I'd like to borrow two hundred thousand bucks to pay off a blackmailer,' they're going to look at you like, 'What? Are you out of your mind?'"

I knew he was right. As I kept reminding everybody, most of all myself: I had never committed any sexual assault or harassment—this was only a love affair I never should have allowed myself, in a world that wouldn't understand it, with a man who was betraying me. But we pushed forward on both tracks anyway, just in case.

BILL LAWLER AND MICHAEL DECOTIIS MET WITH LOWY ONE LAST time, on Monday, August 9, at the Manhattan offices of Vinson & Elkins. Bill had requested that Golan attend, but he didn't show. Unfortunately, things only got weirder. Lowy said things like, "I recognize you don't represent State Street Partners," the firm where Jimmy Kennedy had hired, then fired Golan, "but they treated my client badly as well and we want money from them, too. This can go away if you give us four million and we get a half-million from State Street."

Bill stated the obvious, that only State Street could speak for State Street, and he reiterated his own inability to discuss a settlement without first talking to Golan or reading his claims in a legal filing.

"Let me tell you what will happen if you pay us," Lowy countered. "Golan will go away, he will disappear—at least until after the next election.

He will not have a mailing address or a telephone, his credit card bills will be forwarded to me. I won't tell you where he'll be, but he won't be in Israel. *He will disappear.*"

The implication—that my team wanted Golan to "disappear"—angered Bill, a former assistant U.S. attorney who'd represented high-profile clients including the former head of the FBI hostage rescue team who was called to testify before Congress about Waco and Ruby Ridge.

"Listen, I don't want him to go away, Lowy," Bill said. "I don't need him to go away. If he has a claim that he can prove, we'll settle it, but I'm not paying for someone to go away in the sense that you're talking about. I'm not buying silence."

Later, Bill told me that he suspected Lowy might be recording him. But he asked the question outright, and Lowy said no. "It's not the kind of question I would normally ask a colleague, but nothing about this was normal."

Recording or not, he said that his client's demands were coming dangerously close to extortion. It was the only time Lowy every raised his voice. "Don't use that word," is all he said.

THAT AFTERNOON, I CALLED CURTIS BASHAW DOWN AT CAPE MAY. I needed a friend to talk to, and at this moment I felt certain that he could offer some sound judgment. I knew he had a radio interview that morning about his work on the Casino Reinvestment Development Authority. I reached him on his cell in his car.

"Are you alone? I have something I need to tell you."

"Sure," he said.

"I've had an affair, Curtis."

There was a pause. "Okay," he said.

"With a guy."

There was a longer pause.

"And he's trying to extort money from me. It's Golan Cipel. He used to work for me. I'm trying to figure out what to do."

I didn't realize until this minute that Curtis had heard the rumors about Golan. He told me a lengthy story about a New York man he used to date—another Israeli national, strangely enough; I'll call him Eitan—who happened to have called him just days before.

"Eitan is a dear, dear friend," Curtis said. "But I hadn't seen him in two years. He said he was coming down to Cape May, so I invited him to stay with us. And when he got here he goes, 'Is your governor gay?' I asked him why he'd ask such a thing. And he said, 'A friend of mine knows this guy who says he used to date McGreevey.' Well, I had no idea what he was talking about. He said, 'His name's Golan, he's a very handsome Israeli guy.' So I think this is kind of getting around."

I listened intently. It seemed impossible to me that Golan had been gossiping about our relationship, even with friends. But if he was, containing this was going to be impossible.

"The virus is spreading," I said.

"It looks like the shit's already hit the fan, Governor."

"We're trying to get through to his lawyer," I said. "But he's being totally unreasonable. And Golan has disappeared."

"Jim," Curtis said. "I think Eitan may be your back channel to Golan, your Hail Mary pass."

I don't know why I didn't see it right away. Of course he was. "Will you do me a favor? Will you call Jamie? Jamie needs to know about this," I said.

He agreed. He also agreed to call Eitan that night and come to Drumthwacket first thing in the morning to report what he'd learned.

When he arrived that Tuesday morning, Ray and I were frantically pacing the library, beneath an oil painting of George Washington. I was due to leave in a few minutes by helicopter to sign the Highlands legislation, so there was no time to spare. Jamie and Michael DeCotiis were there, too.

Immediately we dialed Eitan's number on a speakerphone. After hearing from Curtis the night before, he explained, he'd tracked his source down at the gym. He was a lawyer named Timothy Saia—the same attorney, it turned out, whom Golan had brought along to our breakfast meeting that morning when I tried convincing him to resign. It was an interesting twist, but nobody knew what to make of it.

After some quick research, we learned that Saia worked for a politically connected firm in North Jersey where Ray knew the principals. Ray volunteered to pay his old friends a visit, hopefully shaking some information out of Saia along the way.

"You've done your gay thing," Ray told Curtis, "I'll take it from here."

In no time, Ray wrangled the firm's manager to the phone—from his vacation in Nantucket—and set up a meeting to grill Saia later in the day.

But exactly what advantage this back channel was going to give us, none of us knew. If Timothy Saia was just a friend from the gym who talked too much, as I assumed, the most we could hope for was to quiet him down. I never believed he could get Golan to sit with us, not for a minute. I began to abandon hope.

My brain went white with resignation. As Michael DeCotiis and I headed toward the Highlands Reservoir in the helicopter, I consciously thought, *This is the last time I'm going to fly over New Jersey before my resignation.* I remembered the first time I'd seen these magnificent stretches, the beautifully lush horse farms, the aerial splendor of the state I'd always wanted to lead.

I knew also that my White House dreams were dead, however this crisis played out. Even if I survived in Trenton, after what I'd been through, there was no way I could withstand the glare of national press scrutiny.

Shortly after I returned to the statehouse, we reconvened in my office to hear what Ray had learned from his meeting with Timothy Saia. It was good news. Under pressure from his superiors, Saia agreed to set up a breakfast meeting the following morning with Golan, in New York City. It was a momentary ray of hope.

Of course, Golan never showed. Lowy was there instead, which led me to wonder—as I do to this day—whether Timothy Saia was some sort of double agent.

FROM THE FIRST MOMENTS OF THIS CRISIS, WE CONSIDERED GOING to federal law enforcement. There is no bigger crime than extorting and blackmailing a public official, especially if you're a foreigner, especially now in the age of terror. Bill Lawler raised it at our first meeting. But I was reluctant, for a number of reasons. The main one was Christopher Christie, the U.S. attorney who had hounded me in the Machiavelli case. I just didn't trust him.

Bill Lawler felt we could bypass the U.S. attorney's office and go directly to the FBI, but he agreed that we should do this only as a last resort. "It lets them set the strategy," he said. "So far, we're still in charge of that, at least."

I dreaded this for another reason. I knew it would stop the extortion campaign, but it would do nothing to protect my secret. Once an official complaint was made, I knew my heterosexual pretense was over. My story would land in the pantheon of messy love affairs. Whatever Golan and I had together would be made to look like something out of one of those tawdry reality-based TV shows—an entanglement so ill-fated that we needed cops to break it up.

No matter what happened, though, I knew I owed Dina an explanation, and an apology. Ray, with his tremendous spiritual footing, helped me prepare for the moment. His faith was so strong that, in this moment, it carried both of us.

That night, I headed upstairs to talk to my wife. At the last minute, I asked Ray to join me as my confessor.

There is an elegant living room in the private wing which we rarely used. We sat there on the sofa, all three of us. I took Dina's hand. "I hadn't planned this," I told her. "It was broken off years ago. But he never let go. I want you to know how sorry I am. What I did was wrong, terribly wrong. I violated the sanctity of our marriage. I had no right to do that. I beg you to forgive me."

She was silent. I didn't expect her to be surprised.

"Now Golan is threatening to sue me for sexual assault, which is a total fabrication. We're trying everything to get to him. We have talked this over a million ways, Dina. No matter what happens with his suit, one way or the other, I may have to resign as governor."

Dina turned her gaze to Ray. She was silent for a long time. On her face she wore an inscrutable mask, neither hurt nor mad nor frightened. When she finally spoke, she said with no trace of bitterness, "Where are we going to live?"

I squeezed her hand. "We can't show weakness or vulnerability," I said.

Ray answered her question. "You don't have to worry about that, Dina. Everything will work out."

ON WEDNESDAY MORNING, I HAD TROUBLE GETTING OUT OF BED. I had a morning full of meetings and obligations, but all I could do was stare at the enormous elm outside my bedroom window, counting how many times it showed the whites of its leaves. I got to the office sometime around noon. Curtis was waiting. I brought him into my suite and closed the doors. I was relieved he was there. I started talking about the things I had hoped to accomplish in a second term. Being a Republican, he disagreed with a few. He couldn't help himself.

I also relived some highlights of my term to date. We had enacted a good deal of my social and economic agenda, despite the constant din of chaos and scandal. I was particularly proud of increasing benefits for our veterans and improving standards for the National Guard. And in keeping with the promise I made to homeless vets so many years ago, we opened the Old Glory Wing at the Veterans Memorial Home at Menlo Park, a new residential wing for forty retired soldiers needing inpatient mental health services.

All this reminiscing wasn't calming my mind, though. Psychologically, I knew I wasn't fit to be at work. The world of artifice I'd created for myself was tumbling down, and the oncoming trauma was already excruciating. You don't abandon a lie after forty-seven years without consequences. Coming out wasn't as simple as removing a mask at a costume ball. The thing I was, my private truth, was nearly as occluded from me as it was from the world. I only knew my lies, like everyone else. Losing them was like losing my identity.

I had to get back to Drumthwacket.

Curtis and I left the statehouse through a back route, down a flight of stairs, through a tunnel that dropped us off right at my car, whose state troopers were always at the ready. Back at the mansion, we went to the library. Cathy Reilly, God bless her, brought us lunch.

"I can't keep doing what I'm doing," I told Curtis. What I meant was, I couldn't go on posing as straight. "I suppose I could stay with Dina. I love and respect her, I really do. But I don't want to fix it."

"Have there been other guys?" he asked.

I didn't know how to answer. I stared at him blankly.

"Well, do you think you might be gay?"

After spending a week admitting to a gay affair, this was the first time I'd been asked what it implied about my sexual orientation.

"Yes," I said without hesitation. And then I started to cry in a way I had never cried in my life. Not sobbing, not angry—free. I felt free.

Curtis hugged me. Then he pulled away.

"That's it!" he shouted. "That explains everything! Don't you see? The truth will set you free. This is the truth! Tell it to everybody. Hold a press conference and tell the truth. And suddenly the tawdry affair with your political appointee makes sense. You were a man in the closet, and now you're free. This is huge, Jim. I think the voters will understand."

Curtis's enthusiasm was like a preacher's altar call. Tears splashed down my face. I'd never told anybody this about myself before, and every word of his affirmation lifted me on a thousand wings. The transformation in my soul was shocking and instantaneous. I had told somebody I was gay, and he was right—that explained everything.

He dialed Jamie and handed me the phone, saying, "Tell him."

"I'm coming out," I told Jamie.

"I'm coming right over," he said.

By the time Ray arrived at Drumthwacket, Jamie, Curtis, and I had become a kind of support group in the governor's mansion.

"I'm coming out," I told Ray. "I'm a gay American."

He looked at the three of us, not knowing what to say. I doubt Ray had ever knowingly been alone in a room of gay men before. Ironically, the old party boss was the most flamboyant person there, in light-colored slacks and trademark blue-tinted wireless eye glasses. Then Michael DeCotiis pushed into the room. "Guess what, Michael," Ray joked, flinging his hands in the air. "I'm gay, too!"

* * *

WHEN WE RECOVERED FROM A LONG LAUGH, I SAW MY PLAN LAID out before me. I wanted to hold a press conference on Friday, to confess my infidelity and tell my truth.

That night, I knew I would have to tell my parents. I got Sharon on the phone and asked her to gather the clan at the official beach house on the pretext that I had a major announcement for them.

As I drove down to meet them, I kept Curtis on the phone—he was driving back to Cape May to see Will and gather fresh clothes. I wanted to know what words he'd used with his parents, and how Will had broken the news to his own family; I wanted the collected experiences of this tribe to inform my language. I feared my family's rejection terribly. My need for their love and acceptance was unchanged since childhood.

I knew it would crush my father that my political career was taking this unexpected blow. But frankly what I dreaded most was my mother's disappointment over my violation of my marriage vows. Nothing was more sacred to her than honor and one's promise to God.

It all went better than it might have. My father's first response was, "You make a choice, Jim—Coke or Pepsi. You were married twice, you have two wonderful daughters. Why don't you try to make that work? Why don't you make the regular choice?"

"Dad, I've known my whole life. This is who I am."

"You will always be my son," he said, taking my hand and shaking it stiffly.

Later, he took refuge in the Church's long struggle with the issue. "Holy Mother the Church hasn't figured out this homosexuality stuff after two thousand years. So I figure I'm not doing so bad."

My mother, whose love for me has proven tremendously resilient, mostly kept her thoughts to herself. But when we parted, she took me into her arms and gave me a long and tender hug, something she hadn't done in a long time. "We will always love you, no matter what you do," she said.

Back in the car, I called Curtis with a report, but his news took precedence.

"We have to push up the press conference from Friday to tomorrow," he said. "Somebody in Golan's camp leaked the news. ABC is getting a story ready, probably for tomorrow night. Jamie says we've got to keep out in front of this thing."

I WAS DEAD TIRED ON THURSDAY MORNING, SO TIRED THAT I rolled downstairs in green sweatpants and a T-shirt before taking a shower. I was surprised to find the place overrun with political operatives, some of whom I didn't even know.

Besides Jamie and Curtis, Michael and Ray, there was Joel Benenson, my pollster; Steve DeMicco, the consultant; Hank Sheinkopf, a political consultant from New York; the political ad man Jim Margolis; and some gay community liaison whose name I don't remember. The room was out of control. But frankly so was every other part of my life.

I could barely concentrate on what was being said. They shouted over one another, rendering opinions, speculating about the press and the courts, recalling precedents and old war battles. Some thought I should strike a defiant stand; the polls showed I might survive this. Conventional wisdom, on the other hand, said I was dead. Straw polls were being taken on whether I should resign. Three times the eyes of the room moved to Curtis's chair, and everyone awaited his observations. Each time I took his sleeve and moved him out of the room, around to the smaller study behind the library, so that I could hear him out in private. Frankly, it was the only way I could know what he was thinking without the din of professional politicians interposing their own ideas.

"They're trying to drive, Jim. Is that what you want?"

"Curtis, I've just done something I've avoided for my whole life. The last thing I want to do is return to the modus operandi of the past twenty-five years. Political solutions are all they know. I need to do what's right for my wife, my family, and the state of New Jersey. I need to follow my moral and ethical compass."

When we got back to the room, somebody was laying out the consensus plan, but I interrupted.

"This is what I want to say," I told them. I motioned for Curtis to take notes.

"I admit shamefully that I engaged in an adult consensual affair with another man, which violated my bonds of matrimony. It was wrong, it was foolish, it was inexcusable. And for this, I ask the forgiveness and grace of my wife. She has been extraordinary throughout this ordeal, and I am blessed by her love and strength.

"This individual now seeks to exploit me and my family and perhaps the state through financial and legal means which are unethical, wrong, and immoral. Let me be clear, no one is to blame for this situation but me. I accept total and full responsibility for the stupidity of my actions. I must now do what is right to correct the consequences.

"I will not seek reelection in November 2005. Yet I will continue with every fiber of my being to work on behalf of those issues which are of concern and hope to all our families.

"It makes little difference that as governor I am gay. In fact, having the ability to truthfully set forth my identity might enable me to be more forthright in fulfilling and discharging my constitutional obligations. But I have made a serious error, and for that I accept the consequences."

Jamie wiped tears from his eyes. So did Ray.

"That's great," Michael said. "You own the affair, you apologize. You take the high road."

But the other people in the library, the party stalwarts, had moved on to the perimeter of the room, returning cell phone calls and positioning themselves for their next assignments, which no doubt included handicapping who would take my seat in the next election. As Curtis later remarked, "the light drained out of the room immediately for them. You were dead."

THERE WERE MANY PEOPLE I HAD TO CALL BEFORE GIVING THE speech early that afternoon. I spoke to Bill Lawler first; he was supportive. "Make your announcement, see what happens." I asked what he thought the chances were that they'd go to court anyway.

"I have to be frank," he said. "I think they're going to take this to court. They're that crazy. It only costs thirty-five bucks to file."

"We'll win," I said. "But how bad do you think the fight will be?"

"You will be vindicated, but this'll tie us up for six to eighteen months, easy."

Almost as an afterthought, I gave Bill my consent to call the FBI.

Bill was pleased that I wasn't planning to quit. But I didn't admit to him how conflicted I was about that. I knew that what I did was not just foolish, but unforgivable. Hiring a lover on state payroll, no matter what his gender or qualifications, was wrong. I knew what my ethical convictions told me: if I'd been in the state Senate and some other governor had admitted this on the statehouse stairs, I would have called for his resignation.

AS JAMIE, CURTIS, AND RAY PREPARED MY SPEECH, I CALLED KARI in Vancouver. She didn't react much when I told her I was gay. I suppose I'd known all along that she saw right through to my secret. But when I told her I thought I should resign, she reacted immediately. She asked to be put on speakerphone to address the room.

"You must not resign, Jim," she said then. "Having an affair doesn't make you a bad man. Being gay doesn't make you a bad man. You are still the same man today that you were when you were elected—good, decent, moral. New Jersey is lucky to have you as governor. You must not quit."

Her pep talk was politically galvanizing and immensely important to me personally. It opened up a profoundly candid conversation between me and my core group of supporters. They all still felt I should serve out my term, but not run for reelection. Despite Kari's vote of confidence, I just wasn't as convinced that was penance enough for my transgressions.

In the middle of this I took a call from Tony Coelho, the former House Democratic whip who had directed Al Gore's presidential campaign. I knew Tony through politics, and being active in the Portuguese community, he also knew Dina. He had offered me valuable advice in the past. This time he was calling to encourage me to step down, effective immediately. I didn't know how he learned of our growing nightmare.

Then he added a personal note. "Dina will feel she is being punished by all of this. She will be stigmatized because of your homosexuality. I know the Portuguese American community, Jim. They're going to hold this against her."

Tony also offered some sound emotional advice, which I found extremely helpful. "The only way to get through this is to believe in yourself, because no one else will believe in you without that," he said. "You have to radiate confidence. Don't go into hiding. You have to hold your head up and be positive, relentlessly positive. You will have a political future. Maybe not an elective future, but under the right circumstances, if you do this right, you can re-create yourself as a positive public figure."

JAMIE, RAY, CURTIS, AND I WRESTLED WITH MY OPTIONS. AT FIRST I was the only one in the group who thought I should quit. Finally Jamie asked a question that turned many people's opinions.

"I'm sorry, but I need to ask this," he said. "Are there other men besides Golan Cipel?"

I knew he meant in government, but I wrestled with the much broader question. Having come this far out of the closet, was I even capable of finishing out my term? I wasn't sure. As Congressman Barney Frank once commented about our respective situations: "I was clinically depressed, on drugs, seeing a psychiatrist. I wasn't functional. You can be a dysfunctional member of Congress, but not a dysfunctional governor. In Congress there are four hundred and thirty-four other people. You can't put a governorship on autopilot."

I couldn't answer Jamie. I'm sure he took my silence as confirmation that there were other Golans, which there weren't. I'm sure Curtis and Ray did, too. It didn't matter to me. What mattered was they were beginning to see that I needed to quit, to take my punishment for what I'd done, to show the voters who had entrusted me with their faith that I was truly contrite—and to begin my healing out of the fishbowl of politics.

"Curtis," I said, "I need to change the last section of my speech."

I WENT UPSTAIRS TO GET DRESSED FOR THE ANNOUNCEMENT press conference. Dina, looking beautiful and dignified as always, sat on a sofa in the formal living room. I sat beside her and we prayed together. I had found the small pile of prayer cards my grandmother used to send me when I was in college. I read them aloud, the first time I'd prayed—really prayed—in years.

This was going to be the most difficult moment of my life. But I had brought it on myself. I knew it was also her most trying time, though she was utterly innocent. I prayed for her to get through it, and for time to heal her humiliation and to erase the shame.

I decided to stay in office until mid-November, ensuring an orderly transition for Dick Codey, the Senate president, who would take over as acting governor according to the constitutional order of succession. This drew yelps from Republicans, who thought it was an underhanded way to avoid the special election law, which called for general balloting if the governor steps down with more than sixty days remaining to the term. Honestly, this never occurred to me. Nobody even mentioned the special election law until much later.

The truth was simpler than that. I worried about Dina. I knew that when we left Drumthwacket, we would move to separate residences, and I felt it would be best for us to make the transition as slowly as possible, within reason.

That afternoon, minutes before walking into the press conference, Golan's legal team made one last contact with Ray. They advanced a new, peculiar demand: $2 million and a charter for New York's Touro College to open a medical school campus in the state. It was the strangest turn of events yet: I knew Golan had his own ties to Touro. For a short time he'd even worked as a consultant for the school, though that was over a year ago. But that couldn't possibly explain this bizarre demand.

The conspiracy-mongers within our ranks all tried piecing together an explanation, but none of them made sense. Charlie Kushner was a longtime Touro booster and board member—the new medical school was to be named for his mother. Could he be involved in this, my staff wondered? Did Timothy Saia or Lowy have any business with Touro? Even Torricelli was mentioned; Touro had contracted with his lobbying firm to gain state approval for the new campus. Could this be his answer to the Twelve Days' War? None of it added up, but I couldn't spare an ounce of energy to think about it; I was worried about my wife and my daughter, about where we would live and what would happen next.

I decided to ignore Golan's new demand and go ahead with my resignation as scheduled. Members of my staff were crying uncontrollably as I entered the statehouse, holding Dina by the hand. Accompanying me that day was the last thing in the world she wanted to do, but she was the picture of composure in a crisp blue suit and a broad, guarded smile. We took our place on the dais before a hundred microphones, next to my unhappy parents.

I thought I would be queasy, racing through my resignation in a blur of words. But an easy silence fell on my mind and everything seemed to stand still as I laid my notes on the lectern, as if nothing mattered in the world besides this moment.

"THROUGHOUT MY LIFE," I BEGAN, "I HAVE GRAPPLED WITH MY own identity, who I am. As a young child, I felt ambivalent about myself. Confused. By virtue of my traditions and community, I worked to ensure that I was accepted as a part of traditional family life in America. I married Kari out of love and respect, and we have a wonderful daughter. But Kari ultimately chose to move back to British Columbia.

"I then married Dina, whose participation in political life—whose joy—has been a source of strength to me. Yet from my early days in high school and even grammar school to the present day, I acknowledge some feelings, some sense that did not put me on a level with other children in the neighborhood. And because of my resolve, and also thinking I was doing the right thing, I forced an acceptable reality onto myself. A reality which is layered and layered with all the, quote, good things and all the, quote, right things of typical adolescent and adult behavior.

"Yet at the most reflective and maybe even spiritual level, there were points in my life when I began to question what an acceptable reality really meant for me. Were there realities from which I was running? Which master was I trying to serve? I do not believe that God tortures any person simply for its own sake. I believe that God enables all things to work for the greater good.

"And this, the forty-seventh year of my life, is arguably too late to have this discussion, but it is here and it is now. At some point in every person's life, one has to look deeply into the mirror of one's soul and decide one's unique truth in the world, not as we may want to see it or hope to see it, but as it is. And so my truth is that I am a gay American. And I am blessed to live in a country with the greatest tradition of civil liberties in the world, in a country that provides so much to its people.

"Yet because of the pain and suffering and anguish that I have caused to my beloved family, my parents, my wife, my friends, I would almost rather have this moment pass. For this is an intensely personal decision, and not one typically for the public domain. Yet, it cannot and should not pass.

"I am also here today because, shamefully, I engaged in an adult consensual affair with another man, which violates my bonds of matrimony. It was wrong. It was foolish. It was inexcusable. And for this, I ask the forgiveness and the grace of my wife. She has been extraordinary throughout this ordeal, and I am blessed by virtue of her love and strength.

"I realize the fact of this affair and my own sexuality, if kept secret, leaves me, and most importantly the governor's office, vulnerable to rumors, false allegations and threats of disclosure. So I am removing these threats by telling you directly about my sexuality. Let me be clear, I accept total and full responsibility for my actions. However, I'm required now to do what is right to correct the consequences of my actions and to be truthful to my loved ones, to my friends and my family and also to myself.

"It makes little difference that as governor I am gay. In fact, having the ability to truthfully set forth my identity might have enabled me to be more forthright in fulfilling and discharging my constitutional obligations.

"Given the circumstances surrounding the affair and its likely impact upon my family and my ability to govern, I have decided the right course of action is to resign. To facilitate a responsible transition, my resignation will be effective on November 15 of this year. I am very proud of the things we have accomplished during my administration, and I want to thank humbly the citizens of the state of New Jersey for the privilege to govern."

* * *

IT SEEMS ILLOGICAL TO SAY, BUT COMPARING MY INAUGURATION to my resignation, I can't tell you which moment was most jarring. But I can tell you this: in only one of them was I my true self. History books will all say that I resigned in disgrace. That misses the point entirely. Resigning was the single most important thing I have ever done. Not only was I truthful and integrated for the first time in my life, but I'd rejected a political solution to my troubles and took the more painful route: penance and atonement, the way to grace.

16.

But after liberation? There were men who found that no one waited for them. Woe to him who found that the person whose memory alone had given him courage in camp did not exist anymore! Woe to him who, when the day of his dreams finally came, found it so different from all he had longed for! Perhaps he boarded a trolley, traveled out to the home which he had seen for years in his mind, and pressed the bell, just as he had longed to in a thousand dreams, only to find out that the person who should open the door was not there, and would never be there again.

THESE DESPAIRING WORDS COME FROM VIKTOR FRANKL, IN HIS memoir *Man's Search for Meaning,* as he describes his disorientation in the days and weeks after being freed from the Nazi death camps. Years before I left office, I remember standing inside the grim barracks at Auschwitz, unable to fathom the horrors that took place there. Surely history has recorded no darker hell.

Of course, my small story cannot compare with Frankl's. But his steadfast focus on survival, on even unwitting resilience, helped me to understand my last days at Drumthwacket. I suddenly existed in a wide-awake world, unvarnished by dreams or lies, the world I'd imagined a thousand times in my mind—only to find that I couldn't recognize it, that I could find no comfort there.

If my relief at finally coming out made me momentarily ebullient, the feeling didn't last. In fact, I sank into an agonizing depression. I couldn't sleep; my usual four hours a night were reduced to two. At work, I barely functioned. I couldn't concentrate on anything beyond my own distress. I felt a need to be doing something, but I didn't know what that something was. It was encrypted in my DNA to *plan my work and work my plan,* my dad's old maxim. I'd used the phrase so much myself that I'm famous for it; it is spelled out in countless throw pillows and carved wooden plaques that friends have given me over the years.

Yet now I had no plan, I had no work. A week before the press conference I had enjoyed a relevance and influence, a power. Now I was trivial and inconsequential. It's as if God had turned on a giant fire hose and washed away any traces of my old life. A few people reached out. Bill Clinton and John Kerry called. So did George Norcross, the warlord from South Jersey. Governor Kean kindly reminded me that I'd accomplished many good things.

But mostly my phone went silent. I was no longer of use to anybody in New Jersey.

With little else imposing on my time, I spent many of these evenings in front of the television with Jacqueline on my lap, plugging videos into the VCR. Though she was only three, I felt that Jacqueline sensed our family's troubles. She let me hold her for hours on end—consciously comforting me, not the other way around. In these days, her favorite video was a Sesame Street story in which Kermit was reluctant about having to leave his pond behind, but found in his travels that he had retained the pond in his memory. When the tape finished playing, Jacqueline would rewind it and start it again. We must have watched Kermit's apt allegory fifteen times, and each time I grew more convinced that Jacqueline was responding to its message.

Some days I didn't go into the office at all, but instead walked and jogged in circles through the stone-dust paths of the mansion's gardens, a prisoner of my self-obsession. The fall colors were brilliant that year. In the towering trees that crowded Drumthwacket's lawns I saw God's renewing powers, His beautiful sense of order and cycles, birth and rebirth. My faith was returning in small stages. Once or twice I entered a religious reverie in the gardens, convinced that my new plan was hidden somewhere in God's larger order; it would become plain to me if only I could align my heart with God's.

But peeking through the foliage were the constant reminders of my own troubles: photographers wrapped around tree limbs and balanced on fences, television trucks with their tall masts extended, microwaving images of me into living rooms in Jakarta, Melbourne, and Carteret. Much of the coverage following my resignation was respectful, but some of it claimed I'd escaped a bad situation (the mounting scandals) by drawing favorable attention to my gayness. Christie Whitman, in an appearance with Chris Matthews on *Hardball,* even charged that I was engaged in some sort of cover-up. "It's not about his sexual practice, it's about the corruption," she said. "That was a feint."

"Only in New Jersey can that be a cover-up," Matthews fired back.

The absurd implication was that I'd made up the affair, or at least magnified its gravity, as a distraction. In time, that notion actually gained some credence. In one poll, only 8 percent of respondents believed that my gay affair was the real reason I was resigning. The satirical newspaper *The Onion* picked up on the false controversy with this headline: HOMOSEXUAL TEARFULLY ADMITS TO BEING GOVERNOR OF NEW JERSEY.

I read Frankl over and over, finding words in his narrative of resilience to describe my own challenges, and to give me hope. The lessons Frankl teaches are universal. We all fight against a hopelessness, a sense of our own imprisonments. Yes, I built the gates that contained me, wreathed them with barbed wire myself. I dreaded being ripped open by bullets from the sadist in the guard tower, where I was the only gunman, a construct of my own delirium.

Mostly I'd entered a conspiracy with a world that drove gay kids into a state of dualism—part of the world but apart from it, unable to participate wholly. I hated this world. Every minute I saw what it did to me, how it twisted me against myself. How it exiled me, even when I refused to leave.

Frankl wrote, "Anything outside the barbed wire became remote—out of reach and, in a way, unreal. The events and the people outside, all the normal life there, had a ghostly aspect for the prisoner. The outside life, that is as much as he could see of it, appeared to him almost as it might have to a dead man who looked at it from another world."

In the garden on these formless days after my announcement, a "normal life" seemed further and further from reach.

* * *

WHILE I READ *MAN'S SEARCH FOR MEANING*, DINA FOUND COM-
fort in a volume called *The Betrayal Bond: Breaking Free of Exploitative Relationships.* She carried it around Drumthwacket for all the staff to see. It was
an obvious swipe, but I didn't blame her. I had it coming. Tony Coelho
called it right: I had publicly humiliated her, much more so than if my lover
had been another woman. There was little she could do to settle the score.

Dina was also very bitter about our sinking fortunes. On the door of
her office she posted a sign counting down the number of days before our
move—"before homelessness," as she'd acidly titled her countdown chart.
Every morning I saw her open the door and cross off another day.

On the second night after our lives were changed, her body gave way
under the strain. We were sitting on the sofa in the formal living room, our
demilitarized zone. We didn't have much to say to one another, but a respect—and what remained of our love—bound us together. She was crying.
Crashing waves of sobs overtook her. She was in excruciating pain. Suddenly her breathing grew labored and irregular. As she hyperventilated, her
eyes widened with panic. Then her head collapsed to one side and she
slumped over, still heaving for air. She couldn't speak to explain what was
happening to her. I feared she was having a heart attack.

"Dina, are you okay?" I called out to her. "Deen?"

The look in her eyes cycled between terror and lifelessness.

I opened her jacket. "Dina? Dina!"

I cradled her in my arms and rushed her down the long narrow hallway
to lay her in bed on the opposite end of the house. Carrying her was difficult. Each of her labored breaths was like a seizure. It rocked her in my arms,
jerking her body against my chest. Once or twice I thought I might drop her.

When I reached the bedroom, I laid her down in the covers and dialed
my dear friend Dr. Clifton Lacy, the commissioner of health. He immediately saw the problem for what it was—a panic attack, most likely brought
on by all the pressures, not a heart attack at all, thank God.

Lacy offered to drive over from Highland Park, but instead I called Dr.
Janet Neglia, a friend who is assistant director of Student Health Services at
Princeton University nearby. She rushed over with a sedative and spent

many hours with us that night, holding our fracturing family together. I will always remember her for this kindness.

With Janet's help, Dina managed to sleep through the night. Not me. I lay awake beside her, consumed with worry and guilt for bringing this trauma on her. Her suffering tore me to pieces.

UNABLE TO SLEEP, I PASSED THE NIGHT TRYING TO IMAGINE WHAT our lives would look like once we'd put this all behind us. There would be a divorce and complicated negotiations about raising our daughter. I knew Dina would find a good position in the working world; her time as first lady had showcased her many talents, and her biggest contributions were yet to come. But I prayed that she'd also find happiness and, with luck, maybe even the strength in her heart to stop being angry. Could she forgive me, I wondered? Not easily. At least one day she might understand why I did what I did.

For my future, I forced myself to imagine a career in public service that didn't involve elected office. I doubt that it's possible to live as a totally integrated person and succeed in the backrooms of America's political system. That, more than my sexuality, would prevent a comeback. Nonetheless, I hoped to find a place in public life where I could perform a valuable service for children, where I could be uncompromised and of use.

Mostly, I allowed myself to picture a life organized in harmony with my heart—the kind of life my friend Curtis had imagined for me: "When the words in your mouth and the actions of your hands and the feelings of your heart are one and the same, you're a whole person, you're integrated, and there's integrity in your life."

I fantasized about being in love, really in love—ordinary, boring, romantic love, the kind that takes you into old age, the kind my parents still have. Frankl considered love the foundation of all meaning, the highest truth to which we can aspire. In his mind always, in the darkest of his days without hope, was the luminous image of his lover, his wife. "Then I grasped the meaning of the greatest secret that human poetry and human thought and belief have to impart: *The salvation of man is through love and in love.*"

In my love was my humanness, the meaning of life.

The thought of finding love gave me comfort, which in turn gave me strength to endure these difficult days. As Friedrich Nietzsche once said, "He who has a *why* to live for can bear with almost any *how*."

MY SISTER SHARON WAS CONCERNED ABOUT MY WELL-BEING, PAR-ticularly my inability to sleep. She checked in on me every day. Reclaiming my relationship with her was an essential part of how I survived these days. She was also among the most critical of what I'd done. "You've been through a trauma," she told me. "You need to get some help for that, you need to find a therapist. But I have to say this, you also need to realign your moral compass."

If anybody else had tried telling me that in the first days after my announcement, I would have been defensive. Some things you can only hear from a sibling whose love for you is unconditional. Of course, she was right.

I called Trinity Church, the Episcopalian parish in Princeton, and asked the lead pastor there to see me for spiritual counseling. I couldn't imagine seeing a Roman Catholic priest; not now. All the years I'd spent sitting in those pews, listening to the Church's pointlessly cruel war against gays and lesbians, had helped drive me into self-denial and self-loathing. For a long time I didn't even see the hypocrisy of my actions. Coming out of my closet changed that.

Not everybody fractures the way I did. The damage takes many forms. In its relentless rigidity on sexual matters, the Church hierarchy had established unrealistic norms and standards I could not live up to, much as I tried. While I deeply loved the Church and its traditions, I realized that the Church had checkmated me into a posture of dishonesty from the time I was in eighth grade. It may be that I never once gave a fully honest confession. Ironically, all I wanted to be was faithful, but for a gay person, the Church made that impossible.

Father Leslie Smith was a godsend. He began my very slow process toward establishing an honest—and for once really meaningful—relationship with God.

Lori Kennedy showered both me and Dina with the kind of support we needed through this time. But my heart and soul needed more active intervention. Luckily, I found Dr. Richard Leedes at the Princeton Counseling Center, whose demeanor and guidance were deeply soothing. Also helpful to me was a book Jamie gave me, *Stranger Among Friends*, written by Clinton insider David Mixner. The book moved me so much that I had my secretary locate a phone number for the author—on a tour of Holland—so that I could call to thank him. I was stunned at how closely his emotional experiences as a young gay kid in New Jersey, where he grew up in poverty, mirrored my own in the working class.

But none of this was working to settle my mind or return my sleep cycles to normal. Being an overachiever, I vowed to try harder. I was going to recover from this tumult in my life with hard work and diligence.

"You're not doing it right," Ray Lesniak told me one day. Alone among my friends from politics, Ray called me constantly. We prayed together, on the phone and in person. He saw right through any façade I tried hiding behind.

On the day of my announcement, Ray gave me a book called *The Twelve Steps: A Spiritual Journey (A Working Guide for Healing)*. I had always thought of the steps as being for alcoholics or addicts. Ray, who had always enjoyed his red wines in moderation and never went in for drugs, opened my eyes. "It's a route to the Divine," he explained. "We're all in recovery from something. For me, it's about being the adult child of a dysfunctional family. I'm addicted to many things—mostly control. I've got this need to be in control of everything and everybody. You have the same addiction. Being governor only made it worse."

I had to admit he was right. I knew that what I was going through was some sort of withdrawal. The book offered me great hope: "With God's power, the twelve-step program can be a tool to relieve our suffering, fill our emptiness, and help us extend God's presence in our lives. This releases energy, love, and joy that are new to us," it promised. "If we work the steps faithfully, we notice improvements in ourselves, our awareness, our sensitivity, our ability to love and be free."

In two hours I tore through the book, answering the questions posed on each page, and contemplating the steps as they related to my life. I came to some painful and lasting realizations about myself. It is true that

I suffer from an addiction, though I barely drink and have never touched drugs in my life. My addiction is not to control or power, unlike Ray's. I'm not addicted to sex, as one might reasonably surmise from my story so far.

Rather, my addiction is to being central in the world, to being accepted and adored in the way that celebrities are adored—by strangers, in abundance. That is what I loved about campaigning—so much that I was almost never at home, sacrificing my marriage and family. I was pathologically attached to "having a public." Too often, it was more important to me than anything else. My ego demanded recognition.

My ego—that was the dopamine receptor for my addiction, the thing that needed feeding.

People with this need are often drawn to politics—just as they are to religious ministry, to medicine, or to Hollywood. Reading through Ray's book, I came to understand how my affliction had motivated me to make my pacts with the warlords, how it made me believe that I could get away with hiring Golan. And I saw how it ruined my home life, how it ultimately brought me no more permanent happiness than heroin use satisfies a junkie.

When I was finished reading the book, I called Ray immediately.

"I did the steps," I said. "They were incredibly powerful. I learned new things about myself, Ray. I see my world in a whole new light."

"Don't be ridiculous," he said. "The steps are a lifelong journey. You've only begun."

IN TOTAL SECRECY, DURING THE LAST DAYS OF MY ADMINISTRA-tion, I began drafting an executive order that I knew was going to detonate like an atom bomb in the world of New Jersey politics. For years, good government types had lobbied against our "pay-to-play" system. I never liked it, either. But I always excused it away as our statewide version of "special interest money." State government doesn't deal with a lot of ideological issues, like abortion rights or foreign policy, which motivates interest groups to donate.

So instead we reach out to companies and individuals who want to make an "investment" in their government—something they hope will pay out for them. On the state and local level, the people who donate to campaigns are exclusively self-interested. They demand something in return. Usually, they get it.

No one benefited from "pay-to-play" more than I did. Under my rule, the party had raised tens of millions from developers and lawyers who then were awarded handsome state contracts in return. The system, though perfectly legal—and, I should point out, practiced in Washington and in many other states, not just New Jersey—was morally corrupt and indefensible.

Over the summer, before I knew I would be quitting, I had made a big deal about signing a minor ethics reform bill that was remarkable for its gaping loopholes, as everyone privately acknowledged. It barred the state from awarding contracts to anyone who donated directly to the governor's campaign. But it was silent on money given to the state or county party organizations, which is in fact where most political donations are directed.

So the reforms actually made county bosses even stronger. They became filters for special-interest donations, soliciting large sums of money from government contractors on behalf of candidates, then attaching their own conditions while turning the money over to their campaigns. In actuality, it did nothing to limit my ability to raise and spend millions for my re-election—and reward my supporters with lucrative contracts. As critics complained, it was just the status quo dressed in reform clothing.

They were totally correct. I knew it then, and I didn't let it bother me. There was no way a politician with a future in New Jersey would strike a more meaningful blow to the system. But now, I realized, things had changed. To borrow George Wallace's phrase, I was "the lamest lame duck there could be." My future in state politics had ended with my resignation.

And there was something more: through the drama of the past few weeks, I'd come to realize that I could no longer make compromises with my own value structure. I'd taken a million ethical shortcuts to climb the ladder, all the time thinking that that was the only way to amass enough power to serve the collective good. But in the end I'd done a great deal of damage. Besides the harm my dishonesty had done to me personally, I'd brought shame to my family and heartache to my supporters throughout the state. I'd cast the government and my party into bedlam.

There are many aspects of my legacy that were positive and lasting. Leaving the pay-to-play system intact through phony reform measures was not one of them.

I was not going to let this huge opportunity pass. Maybe I saw this as my penance. Or maybe it was just the right thing to do. I was going to end our statewide reliance on pay-to-play for good.

As I worked on my executive order, I decided not to let anybody on my staff know what I was up to. I didn't want anyone implicated in my traitorous act. Jamie Fox and Eric Shuffler had long political careers ahead of them. If the warlords thought they were complicit, they would hound them out of government. Nor did I want anyone outside the administration to know what I was contemplating—I didn't want anyone trying to talk me out of it.

A few days before making the announcement, I did tell Dick Codey, who was preparing to be acting governor. I wanted to know that he would continue my executive order in his term, and he agreed. Luckily, he had no plans to run for the seat in his own right, making him a lame duck as well. In fact, with his support the legislature later passed the executive order into law, and he signed it.

My order was simple and effective. It prohibited donors from receiving significant state contracts if they had given any money to a winning gubernatorial candidate, the ruling state party, or the ruling county party boss within eighteen months of the contract's disbursement.

I signed it on the morning of September 22. An hour beforehand, I handed Cathy, my secretary, a draft of my signing speech, written in longhand.

"Type it up," I said. "I'm delivering it in an hour."

Somehow word leaked out to the county bosses. I spent that hour fielding their furious calls. "You'll be ruined. You'll never get another job," they said. "You're going after people's livelihood and their power."

"That's why I have to do it," I replied.

Though nobody knew exactly what I was about to announce, the state-house was packed. I was even more nervous than I'd been while announcing my resignation on live TV. It was one thing to disappoint the warlords and bosses who had aided my career, but quite another to take down the sources of their power with me.

But I was doing the right thing. It had been a long time since I'd felt that way.

"For better or worse," I said, "recent events have been a catalyst, providing me with a personal and political freedom that has enabled me to confront challenges I have avoided in the past. Today, the relationship between political fundraising and government operations has become corrosive and cancerous. Legitimate lines of behavior are blurred, ethical ambiguities are the norm, and the need to sustain an all consuming fundraising effort has become almost as important as the function of government itself.

"Like an addiction, the fundraising culture takes hold of its participants and makes them weak and unable to resist, as if the need to sustain it becomes an end in itself. The requirement to amass staggering amounts of money has created a climate which has inevitably jeopardized the moral integrity of government's basic obligations.

"Today, finally, I am seeking to put an end to politics as usual in Trenton. God knows I wish that the circumstances were different, but they aren't. In a few minutes I will be signing Executive Order number 1,000, which will provide the most sweeping campaign finance reform this state has ever seen. And I know in my heart of hearts that this is the right thing to do. Thank you."

IT WAS THE MOST HONEST POLITICAL SPEECH I'D EVER GIVEN. Not that apologizing for my marital infidelities wasn't honest, but this speech came without being prompted by threats. I had free choice. My motive was purely ethical. That's the way I'd always wanted to function in life, and now, at the end of my political career, I was as integrated on a policy level as I'd become on a personal level. It was my proudest moment.

For once, the press cheered me on. "In many ways, his statement to the press yesterday was as important as the executive order he signed," read an editorial in the *Bergen Record*. "His remarks were nothing short of an indictment of New Jersey's political system—coming from a man who made a career out of exploiting that system. But anybody who has heard or read his statement knows that it has the unmistakable ring of truth."

There's a lot more to be done before New Jersey politics is reformed. But that executive order dramatically changed the balance of power. It broke the dam.

ON NOVEMBER 15, 2004, I LEFT DRUMTHWACKET AND THE STATE-house for good. Dina moved in with her parents while remodeling a comfortable new home nearby. My sister Sharon helped me pick out furniture for a two-bedroom apartment in Rahway, which I filled with family pictures to help ease Jacqueline's shock as she shuttled between our places. My mom gave me plates and saucers, sheets and towels, and the wife of my new landlord lent me some hand-me-downs—I felt like I was twenty again, setting up my first home. It was a strange sensation sleeping there alone on my first night. The ruckus that had surrounded my whole adult life had gone completely silent.

That Saturday night, Jacqueline came to stay with me for the first time. I hadn't realized until I sat alone with her in the new place how totally disorienting this transition had been for me. Jacqueline must have been disoriented by my manner, and she cried and cried. There wasn't a thing in the house to cook for dinner, and frankly I would have had no idea how to prepare her a meal. Instead, I took her to a fluorescent-bathed McDonald's on an isolated stretch of Route 1, where I prayed we wouldn't be seen.

The place was empty except for a few high school kids, who recognized me and waved. I called out greetings but stayed focused on my daughter as we ordered chicken finger strips for two and moved to a table in the far corner.

But Jacqueline enjoyed neither the meal nor the surroundings. She let out a few screams of frustration, which I tried to muffle, and started demanding to be returned to her mother.

Why shouldn't she? I thought. Look what I've done to myself, to my family, to everything I'd held dear.

I drove Jacqueline back to the apartment and read to her in her new Strawberry Shortcake bed until she fell asleep. After church the next afternoon, I took her to see my parents, whom she adored. Taking Jacqueline in her lap, my mother immediately saw through our happy façade.

"How's it going?" she asked with concern.

I tried to muster a lie. But instead I said, "I'm worn down to nothing, Mom."

"What did you two do over the weekend?"

I told her about our lonely dinner at McDonald's, and a slightly better breakfast that morning at a bodega near my apartment before heading to church. I saw the pain mounting in her eyes as I talked.

"It's good you're going to church," she said finally. "Turn your prayers over to God."

I told her I was trying to do just that.

"You've got to distinguish between God's will for you, and your own will for yourself," she reminded me. "Seek God's will. Do God's will. That's how you will find comfort."

Then she folded her arms around me and held me in the way I wasn't able to hold my own child: she made me feel safe; she banished all care and made the future seem bearable. "I love you, Jim," she said.

SHORTLY, I BEGAN MY NEW LIFE AT THE LAW FIRM WEINER LESniak, where Ray kindly found a home for me. Unfortunately, the arrangement didn't last long; it would still be months before I realized how unready I was to take on new responsibilities.

My work involved legal advocacy on behalf of an ambitious new entertainment and retail development project called Xanadu, to be constructed alongside the Continental Airlines Arena at the Meadowlands, home to the New Jersey Nets, Devils, and Giants.

I'd been an early advocate of Xanadu, a $1.3 billion, five millionsquare-foot project that would transform the sports complex into a major destination, similar to the Mall of America in Minnesota. As governor, I'd signed the contract giving the Xanadu development rights to Mills Corp., a Lesniak client.

Perhaps it was poor judgment for me to be working for Mills Corp. so soon after leaving government, on a project I set in motion. But I'd also signed legislation directly or indirectly favoring most corporate clients of most law firms in the state.

Nothing about my work involved representing Mills or Xanadu before state agencies. The task was to form a partnership with the local YMCA and Bergen Community College to develop a state of the art workforce training site. There was no ethical conflict in my labors.

Under state law, former state employees—but not governors—are barred from working for companies they aided in government for a period of a year. The press thought I should have voluntarily obeyed the same standard.

As the media began hammering away at my Xanadu work, I threw myself more into my efforts compulsively, causing Ray to grow increasingly concerned about me personally.

"You haven't given up your addiction, Jim. Don't you see it? You're in the office twelve, thirteen, fourteen hours every day. You're working like a crazy man without knowing where you're going. You're still on the gerbil wheel, not the recovery path."

THE SUN HADN'T RISEN YET WHEN RAY CALLED ME EARLY ON THE morning of February 19, 2005. He was crying. "It's Joe Suliga," he said.

My first thought was that Joe had done something stupid again; I knew how much Ray cared about him. "Is he drinking again?" I asked.

"Jim," he said, "he's dead."

I had trouble taking it in. Joe and I had come up, and come down, together. Now he was dead at forty-seven.

"He was over at that strip joint in Linden," Ray said. "He shouldn't have been there, Jim. He was in the passenger side of the car, backing out of the parking lot. They were hit by a drunken driver. Jim, he was killed instantly."

My heart broke wide open. Joe had tried so hard to pull his life together. After his arrest in Atlantic City, he left the Senate. He followed Ray's admonishments about sobriety as best he could, but his struggles continued. Still, his life had been coming back around. He was working in Linden's government again, as chief financial officer, rebuilding his confidence and momentum in small steps, just as I was trying to do. He left behind his heartbroken wife of ten years, who had stayed at his side through thick and thin.

Ray took it all personally. "He was never in recovery," Ray said. "I told him he had to go to meetings, he had to change his life. He said he didn't have a drinking problem."

"He lived a life and a half," I said to Ray. "He lived harder than anybody I know."

"Being destructive isn't living large," Ray fired back in anger. "He lived half a life, when he had such great promise."

That night, I had a terrifying dream. I was alone in a large, dark room which was empty but for an open coffin at one end. I forced myself to look inside and found the body it contained was my own. Something grotesque and hideous had deformed the corpse—not a sudden accident like Joe's, but a force inside me that bubbled its poisons out through the skin, a stinking, acidic, molten substance that ate holes in my heart and twisted my face beyond recognition.

WE PAID OUR RESPECTS TO JOE THAT WEDNESDAY AT ST. ELIZAbeth's Roman Catholic Church in Linden. Throughout my own trauma I had held myself together, almost stoically. But from the first chords of the hymn, "Be Not Afraid," I broke down and wept. Sitting alone in an out-of-the-way pew, I cried till my collar was soaked. My sadness wasn't for Joe. I believed he had made it to heaven, finally free from his many years of struggle. My heart bled for his wife and family, who had the frightful job of bidding him farewell, and for myself. I cried for the life we both had attained, then squandered, as if it were my funeral as well.

The next day at work, Ray handed me a printout from a website for a trauma and addiction recovery clinic in rural Arizona called The

Meadows—a place frequented by the likes of actor Matthew Perry and singer Whitney Houston.

"I'm no psychiatrist. But I think you need to get away from New Jersey for a little while," he said. "I asked a friend, and he said this was a good facility."

God bless Ray; he understood this intuitively. I felt his selfless love for me in a way I'd never experienced it before. He knew I was in deep emotional despair. He'd also deduced that I didn't want to spend the rest of my years at a corporate law firm, making myself and others rich. I'd raced from the statehouse to Ray's firm without noticing how depressed and anxious I'd become. Joe's death made it clear to both of us.

I called the Meadows that afternoon and signed up for a one-week intensive program designed for people who survived a recent trauma. A few days later I sat at a Denny's outside Wickenburg, Arizona, down the street from the clinic. I didn't know it yet, but the Meadows would save my life. As I bit into my chicken salad, I thought: this Denny's is about as far from Drumthwacket as anyone has ever fallen.

MY "SURVIVORS" THERAPY GROUP MET FOR THE FIRST TIME IN the morning. There were six of us. We sat in chairs arranged in a semicircle. Our group leader was Roxy, a no-nonsense and demanding therapist with a disturbing presentation: her spiky hair was a half-dozen different colors, none of them natural.

We'd been instructed to buy stuffed animals from the Meadows gift shop to symbolize our "inner child." I didn't want to appear closed to the therapeutic value of the program, but I thought this was the stupidest thing I'd ever heard. Reluctantly I picked up a Kermit; it reminded me of Jacqueline.

Roxy gave us our first exercise. On large sheets of paper, we were to begin an epistolary relationship with our "inner child." Holding the pen in our left hand, we were to write to our adult selves using the voice of ourselves at about seven years old.

"Talk about things you're scared of," Roxy said. "Talk about things you need."

"Dear Mr. McGreevey," I began. I felt foolish, but I pressed on.

As I wrote in crooked cursive, I was surprised by how the exercise seemed to tap into something. I wrote about the fears—the terrors—my homosexuality had caused me. I'd never admitted this before. I wrote about how I blamed God for making me different, and about all the suffering that caused. My child told my adult about why he'd been an overachiever: to overcome the flawed character in his soul, to hide. "I am ashamed," my left hand wrote. "I live in a state of shame."

Layer by layer, the exercise peeled back my artifice. When I moved the pen to my right hand to compose a response, a powerful self-pity overcame me. I cried uncontrollably. Tears splashed on the page. I began to fall apart.

"You are a good little boy, Jimmy. Being gay doesn't change that," I wrote back—words I'd always craved to hear. "Don't overcompensate. The world won't hate you forever."

I went on like this for an hour. Long after the others had finished their exercise, I couldn't cut off the dialogue with my child. I kept switching hands with the pen, chatting across the chasm of my life to the adolescent I wished I could have protected.

The discarded terminology for what was happening to me used to be "nervous breakdown." At the Meadows, it was taken as evidence that the method was working, a "therapeutic response" to treatment.

Later exercises included drawing a timeline across a large piece of paper, left to right. On the top of the line, we listed our professional achievements, our "credentials"; below the line we recounted our personal histories. I was a classic case of divided self. My public narrative was crowded with achievements. Below the line I wrote just twenty-three words: "Dating Laura," "Married Kari," "Morag born," that sort of thing.

I'd lived my life entirely for public consumption behind a wall of words, while my personal life was nearly nonexistent. I started thinking of myself as a robot, a puppet. No longer Spock, but Lieutenant Commander Data, a machine incapable of genuine feelings—a creation whose sole purpose was to please others.

Roxy could tell I was still trying to please others, even in the group. "You keep trying to help other people through their issues," she told me. "Stay in the *I*. Look at *you*. Come up with your *own* solutions, Jim—not what your parents wanted you to be, or the Church wanted you to be, or your wife. Who do *you* want to be? Who *are you?*"

For me to answer that, she went on, I'd first have to learn to accommodate my own past. "Who did you injure?" she asked me one day. In front of the other group members, I named everyone from Dina to the citizens of New Jersey. She hit me with more questions, rapid-fire, not stopping to contemplate my answers. *Who is your God? Who do you resent? Who is your master? Who are YOU?* I answered the best I knew how, frustrating her each time.

"Don't play mini-governor," she snapped. "You have a chance here to self-actualize. Don't let that slip by. You have a rare chance to realign your world with your own values. You'll need to know what those values are in order to become an integrated self. You're not answering honestly, you're answering like a politician. Who do you resent, Jim? Start with Golan."

"I don't resent Golan," I told her, truthfully.

"It's latent," she said in frustration. "He betrayed you. He extorted you. Of course you resent him."

"It's a blessing, Roxy. What Golan did forced me to confront this deep-seated fear."

In my overachieving way, I thought I could get over my traumas in one week at the Meadows. I was wrong. When the workshop was over, I still couldn't answer Roxy's questions. My anxiety levels were through the roof. I was crying at every provocation, and sleeping less than ever.

At Roxy's insistence, I signed myself into the center's psychiatric wing, a level-one hospital. For more than a month I was "patient number 05271" at the Meadows. As a traumatic event, coming out and losing your job pales in comparison to what some of my fellow patients had suffered. One had returned from Afghanistan; what he did and saw there was atrocious. Another, a marine named Danny who became my best friend in the program, had served as a viper in the Corps before losing his father to suicide, a trauma that he couldn't work through on his own. In group, I was initially ashamed to discuss my sexuality, especially in front of Danny, a family man whose military bearing was so familiar to me. But he literally told me, "Cut the shit, say who you are." He never judged me.

I underwent daily intensive group therapy and private sessions with psychiatrists, who diagnosed me with severe adjustment disorder. They treated me for what they called "Dependent Personality Traits, without full disorder," which in their argot meant that I operated out of my intellect, and was not in touch with my emotions. They called this an "adapted ego state."

"Patient has a tendency to detach from feelings, advice-give, intellectualize and hold himself to unrealistic standards of perfection," my charts say. "Upon observation he had depressed mood complicated by anxiety, exacerbated by unsettled trauma and adjustment difficulties adversely affecting his ability to function on a daily basis. He has an inability to abstain from compulsive work, impulse control difficulties, and moderation issues."

Some of my treatment was silly, and some was extremely difficult. All of it worked.

THE TREATMENT PHILOSOPHY AT THE MEADOWS IS BASED ON THE twelve-step movement as reinterpreted by Pia Mellody, a drug-addiction expert and a colleague of John Bradshaw, the therapist famous for his work reclaiming and championing your wounded "inner child." Pia believes that trauma scars people in fundamental ways. The cure, she believes, is essentially spiritual—through a deep connection with the Higher Power.

Her model of recovery involves returning to childhood to reexperience your original traumas with the eyes of an adult. Throughout our lives, Mellody believes, we adapt certain unhealthy behaviors and patterns in response to our faulty childhoods. Our attachment to these behaviors and patterns eventually take on addictive forms. Drinking, or being sexually compulsive, or even developing an overattachment to ego like mine, are all ways to mask our childhood injuries.

Her answer is to tear down everything—our adult constructs (which she calls our "adapted self") and our childhood injuries (our "wounded child")— and then to rebuild our lives around a spiritual core that allows us to be imperfect. "Human beings are not created as perfect figures. Many of us get the message that we're defective or fear when we're imperfect. We can acknowledge the concept that we are imperfect, and that is the way we are supposed to be. It's what I call perfectly imperfect," she has written. True healing, she says, allows us to eliminate our adapted self, and rediscover our authentic self.

"That is what I mean by recovery," she told me. "It is really about becoming more authentic instead of adapted or living in reaction to others. You learn to actually discover who you really are, you're recovering yourself or your soul."

This resonated with me profoundly. Pia Mellody's model isn't just a method of treatment; it's a way of living. It encourages a lifestyle of honesty, rigorous self-examination, and spirituality—all the things I'd learned to live without.

I was impressed when I finally got a chance to meet her. She is an unprepossessing woman, excruciatingly honest, and charmingly self-effacing. In my life I have never met a person more in touch with her emotional gauges. She told me she had seen my resignation press conference on television. "I was thinking, What a jam for your wife, and your kids, and you," she said. "But there was a part of your energy that day that was very right. You stood up for the consequences, you dealt with the crap and the bullshit. I sensed your relief, and your shame."

Pia's brilliance is in the way she teaches others to recognize shame and disarm it. In group sessions, I was made to present the most unspeakable aspects of my sexual history. I discussed sexual conduct I barely allowed myself to remember—the embarrassing stories that fill this book. I drew wall-sized maps and trees of my moral failures, in politics and love, for all to see. Prying the lid off my shame was terrifying and hideous. But it freed me from my past.

In Pia's model, my shame emanated from my wounded childhood. If I walked away from the shame without resolving it, I was basically abandoning my child, which is the real me.

I had lived my whole life in self-hatred. In therapy, my goal was self-love.

"HOW MUCH JOY CAN YOU HANDLE?"
This was the most complicated question that Kingsley Gallup, my therapist, asked me to contemplate. Of all the lessons I learned at the Meadows,

confronting the issue of joy got closer than anything else to my problem. I'd made a conscious decision in eighth grade that my joy was dispensable—that in order to be accepted by others, I couldn't follow an ordinary heart's course through life.

After years of denial, my ability to know joy was gnarled and mutated. How else could I explain my attachment to Golan? A man almost nobody liked, a man I thought I'd loved, who in the end was nothing but disaster. There never was a promise of *joy* in that relationship, only a temporary reprieve from my misery.

In place of joy, I'd substituted pride. I had all the answers; I was my own master. I moved swiftly through a career in order to avoid the murmurs of my heart.

Finally, I answered, "Joy in abundance."

For the first time in my life I believed I had a right to my heart and all the knowledge there. I came to believe that God wants us all to be happy, to relish our lives in the moment. God wants us to love and reach for joy. That is why he gave us the capacity to love in the first place, setting humans apart from the rest of His creation.

I remembered the words of Sister Anthony: "God is love." Of course! It took me four decades to come back around to that knowledge, though I'd had it all along.

"What does God want from you?" This was the last question Kingsley posed.

Before my time at the Meadows, I might have had a single answer: God wants me to be straight. Reconnecting with the Higher Power in Arizona allowed me to see God as compassionate and gentle, accepting and supportive. This healed me spiritually. I started praying every day while in treatment, something I hadn't done since childhood. My faith was nourishing again, not punitive or fearful.

I wrote out a long list of things I believe God wants from me. Passion, struggle, compassion, courage, convictions, charity, decency, gentleness, and integrity.

Joy, most of all.

* * *

AT THE END OF THE MONTH, IN OUR LAST EXERCISE AND RITUAL, the other patients and I were asked to throw unwanted things on a big bonfire. I brought notepaper and other documents that bore my name under the governor's seal. I was immensely proud of being elected governor and of many things we accomplished during my short term. But I knew I hadn't earned the job on my own merits. Symbolically, I was rejecting the high office for which I had *planned my work and worked my plan* all of my life—a plan conceived in the dim light of the closet. It was a false me who'd won that election. The job was never rightfully mine.

I also brought along something Dina had mailed me—legal documents seeking a divorce. I didn't burn them because I was angry at her for going her own way. Nor did I mean to symbolize a desire that we'd never married. Though I wish we'd been happier together, I don't regret my years with Dina, which gave me the gift of Jacqueline—she and Morag are my two favorite people in the world.

I threw those papers onto the pyre because they represented the past. From now on, I'm heading into the future.

I CONTINUE ATTENDING TWELVE-STEP MEETINGS AND PRESS ON with my addiction recovery. I worry about how publishing this book will affect my healing journey. I know I do not come across in heroic terms. Even the parts of my legacy I'm proud of were products of my addiction, borne of the compromises I'd made. Having finally realized my errors is hardly heroic.

I do know that many people have told me that they were moved by my coming out speech. I don't flatter myself by thinking I am some sort of role model for anybody—I certainly hope I'm not. But people connected with my suffering, I think. An astonishing number of Americans live inauthentically and are unhappy living that way.

I received many letters from gay people confessing their own secret struggles with candor and shame—one from a young man I'd known for a long time who only came out after watching my own declaration. A doctor in New York said he was moved by my "courage, dignity, and strength," and that I was "truly an inspiration to many." A public school teacher in Philadelphia wrote to say that by coming out I had "reinforced the idea that homosexuals are people, too," a fact that is sadly not apparent to everyone.

I got letters written in the shaky hand of my parents' generation, from older women and men who surprised me with their equanimity. "There is no need for you to apologize for anything!" declared a woman who described herself as a lifelong Republican. A man in Hillsborough wrote requesting an autographed photograph, adding this surprisingly tender postscript: "I know that the right partner will come along."

But the most surprising letters I received were from people responding to my broader struggle to realign my life in truth. Literally hundreds of people, gay and straight, wrote to express their own hopes for authenticity. In my tortured arrival at candor, some saw a reflection of their own suffering, which gave them courage and relief. It is as the philosopher Baruch Spinoza said in *The Ethics:* "Emotion, which is suffering, ceases to be suffering as soon as we form a clear picture of it."

"I read the text of your resignation several times, and I realized that this was no ordinary man speaking," wrote another Philadelphian. "I thought of my own feelings and those of countless others who, when we were young, knew that something wasn't quite right with us and became, as you said, 'ambivalent' and 'confused.' There was no one for any of us to talk to or confide in, to show us our unique truths. Perhaps at my age I should no longer be looking for heroes. But if I'm permitted to do so, you should know that you're at the top of a very short list."

My favorite letter came by e-mail from an eighteen-year-old college student in New York State who became transfixed and empowered by what he saw as my "beautiful time of self-discovery."

"I cannot help but admit that every time I see you now, whether in a picture or commercial, I see something truly beautiful and vibrant within you. Maybe it's the potential to be exactly who you want to be. Maybe it's an honesty that emanates from you, an honesty that has proven truer than I'd imagined. I'd like to say, 'Welcome home.' The decision you made was a difficult one. But a life of greater truth, love, and beauty awaits you behind the door you've opened, in perfect love and perfect trust."

If any good comes from sharing my story, I hope I can inspire others to open their doors and reveal whatever is hidden there so that their own true beauty shines through.

MY RECOVERY MAY, AS RAY SAID, TAKE A LIFETIME. ON SOME DAYS, I can see only the work ahead. For one thing, my memory remains blurry, even after this long period of self-inspection. Perhaps my forgetfulness is self-serving; I know I violated my own moral precepts in ways I didn't want to remember. Or maybe, as some gay people have told me, repression takes its toll on memory. In any case, I think the cause is the same: shame. The compromises were too great. In order to keep going, I fractured.

I know that I must locate these memories to complete my journey. It's my central challenge these days, in fact. I'm committed to a searching and fearless rigorous moral inventory of all the things I did wrong—the fourth step. I don't know how long it will take me to finish my moral inventory; nor do I know how easily I'll be able to forgive myself once I'm done. I'm prone to self-recrimination—another problem to overcome. I just know I'll keep going to meetings until I can look in the mirror and accept my own forgiveness, even knowing how many people I've hurt or let down. That will be an amazing day.

But the work doesn't end there. I've still got to compile a list of all those whom I have harmed and make amends to them all directly. This is the most onerous part of recovery. From several people, I have already begged and received forgiveness: my parents and sisters, for example. Yet I have a ridiculously long list of people I haven't yet found a way to tell how sorry I am.

One of those people is Golan. When I got out of the Meadows, I hired a researcher in Israel to locate a phone number for him, thinking I wanted to apologize for all those things that made him feel so inadequate and angry. I wanted to apologize for hiring him onto my staff in the first place, which set into motion this long and torturous history.

I wanted to know that he was all right and to tell him I wished him no harm.

But I have not had the nerve to call him. Perhaps, as I work the steps,

I'll find that courage one day. Until then, I become more authentic and integrated one day at a time. I am reminded of the question Abba Moses, the ancient desert monk, posed: "Can a man every day make a beginning of the good life?"

To which Abba Silvanus replied, "If he be diligent, he can every day and every hour begin life anew."

There is no fear in love; but perfect love casteth out fear: because fear hath torment.

—1 JOHN 4:18

ACKNOWLEDGMENTS

I wish to express heartfelt thanks to the following for their support and critical encouragement through this process:

For invaluable editorial and research assistance: Billy Baker, Stefanie Cohen, Leela de Kretser, and Cassandra Uretz.

For reading all or parts of the manuscript: Christopher Bram, Suki Kim, Todd Shuster, Jonathan Starch, Barry Yeoman, and Ande Zellman.

For helping reconstruct the memories of my life, and giving me tools to understand their significance: Barry Albin, Curtis Bashaw, Joel Benenson, Tonio Burgos, Tony Coelho, Jim and Lucille Davy, Jamie Fox, Diane Legreide, Steve DeMicco, Kathy Ellis, David Etzion, Kevin Hagan, Dr. Bill Hait, Jeff Huber, Carla Katz, Dick Kinney, Jason Kirin, Helen Lai, Bill Lawler, Kevin McCabe, John "Mac" McCormac, Cathy McLaughlin, Patrick Murray, George Norcross III, Ted Pedersen, Eric Shuffler, Kevin Weber, and my dearest friends, Jimmy and Lori Kennedy.

For chronicling my political life so closely, and not always with rancor, I'd like to thank members of the New Jersey press corps whose work I consulted in creating this account, including John Hassell, Herb Jackson, David Kocieniewski, Josh Margolin, John P. McAlpin, Laura Mansnerus, John Sullivan, Bruno Tedeschi, and Jeff Whelan. Any errors of fact or interpretation, however, are my own.

I would not have the strength to tell these stories were it not for my brilliant psychiatrist Dr. T. Byram Karasu; the staff of the Meadows, especially Pia Mellody; and my friend, rabbi, and mentor, Senator Ray Lesniak. Through Ray I was introduced to the legacy of Bill W. and his worldwide followers, who saved my life.

For making me understand my own struggles in a larger context: Roberta Achtenberg, Richard D. Burns, Kate Clinton, David Dechman, Paul Dierkes, William Eskridge, Matt Foreman, Congressman Barney Frank, Tim Gill, Mitchell Gold, Steve Goldstein, Herb Hamsher, Mark Harrington, Fred Hochberg, Barbara Hughes, Kevin Jennings, Michel Mecure, David Mixner, Robert Remien, Joe Solmonese, Jeff Soref, Jon Stryker, Andrew Sullivan, Andrew Tobias, Urvashi Vaid, Scott Widmeyer, as well as Rev. Bill Tully and the community of St. Bartholomew's in Manhattan, and the Anglican Benedictine Community at the Holy Cross Monastery in West Park, New York, who gave me a loving place to reflect upon these pages.

And for the people who cared for my well-being through this cathartic process: The New Jersey State Police and the Port Authority of New York and New Jersey Police. Cathy Reilly and the staff of Drumthwacket, especially Olga Nini, for reminding me of the good times we shared together. Kean University president Dawood Farahi. The Continental Airlines family. Pat Leone and her staff at Pat's Café in Rahway, who gave me refuge and refills during the early crafting of this book. My brother members of the Hibernians and the Shillelaghs. And Brian Sheafer and the gang at the Rahway YMCA, who kept me sane. Mostly I owe gratitude and love to my family: my mom and dad and my sisters Caroline and Sharon; Kari Schutz McGreevey and Dina Matos McGreevey; and my greatest accomplishments, my daughters Morag and Jacqueline.

A special debt is owed the masterminds who helped put this book together, beginning with the eminent Doug Schoen, whose idea it was; my cherished friend Danny O, who made it seem possible; Ray Chambers, who when I questioned the wisdom of the project invited Deepak Chopra to pray with me; and the inestimable Bob Barnett and Jacqueline Davies for managing the business end. Governor Brendan T. Byrne, Governor Thomas H. Kean, and Tony Cicatiello for their encouragement. For her editorial wisdom, personal decency, and friendship, I owe a great debt to Judith Regan as well as her right-hand man at Regan, Calvert Morgan, whose sharp eye and keen intellect guided me every step of the way. Suzanne Wickham worked tirelessly to coordinate publicity; Donna Lee Lurker and Juliann Barbato, both of New Jersey, provided peerless production editorial support; and Cassie Jones made the whole process work.

For finding a coherent whole in the random facts, feelings, and stories of my life, and for his gift of language, my gratitude to David France, who through the process of writing this book with me has become my lasting friend.

I saved the most important acknowledgment for last: Mark O'Donnell, my partner in life, who has shown me the love I was looking for all along.

—JAMES E. McGREEVEY

INDEX